Lay Authority and Reformation in the English Church

This House I Have Built

A Study of the Legal History of Establishment in England

Is it credible then that God should dwell with men on the earth? If heaven and the heaven of heavens do not contain thee, how much less this house which I have built!

—2 Chron. 6:18

Lay Authority and Reformation in the English Church

Edward I to the Civil War

Robert E. Rodes, Jr.

The University of Notre Dame Press
Notre Dame　　　　　　　　　　London

Library of Congress Cataloging in Publication Data

Rodes, Robert E.
   Lay authority and reformation in the English church.

   Includes bibliographical references and index.
   1. Ecclesiastical law — Great Britain — History.
I. Title.
KD8605 R624   344.42'09   82-7038
ISBN 0-268-01265-2   344.2049   AACR2

Manufactured in the United States of America

Sancto
BEDAE VENERABILI
ex Voto

Contents

Introduction

Most of the first volume of this work, *Ecclesiastical Administration in Medieval England,* dealt with the law and administration of the medieval English church. In this volume, I will take up the operation of the lay power that impinged on the church's jurisdiction in the Middle Ages, and took possession of it at the Reformation. I will try to show the juridical, and some aspects of the ideological, forms under which all this took place.

The opening chapter is devoted to the medieval situation. I have tried to present schematically the different ways the royal government moved in areas which contemporary canon law or modern political theory would assign primarily to the church. It is mostly a straightforward legal account, but I have tried to show in appropriate places what the lay authorities were about, the premises on which they justified themselves, and the reasons for their success in making good their claims to act as they did.

The second chapter is a common law view of the Reformation. It covers the medieval background of the specific legislative innovations by which the religious changes were brought off, and the development of the Church of England's official account of itself as an updating, rather than a replacement, of the medieval church.

The third and fourth chapters show how church administration and lay courts respectively responded to the mandate to update the old system. The third is a schematic presentation of ecclesiastical administration at work, showing how the medieval devices were drawn on, and how they were modified. The fourth takes up the common law cases, and the recasting of the medieval lay precedents under the brilliant and sometimes tendentious antiquarianism of Coke and his colleagues.

Needless to say, the action is much affected by events offstage. One cannot deal with any aspect of the period without coming to some kind of terms with the Reformation. This is not at all easy to do. One is sometimes tempted to think of a whole population of Catholics like one's Catholic neighbor Mr. Smith being persuaded (by devout reading of vernacular Bibles), or compelled (by a venal and coercive government) to become Protestants like one's Protestant neighbor Mr. Jones. Other times, one is tempted to think that nothing much happened at all. The particular material I have to deal with lends itself especially to the latter temptation, but I hope I have not succumbed. In any event, the continuity of the legal institutions is as much a fact as any of the social and religious changes, and is as much in need of explanation. In offering a few forces of continuity to explain it, I do not mean to suggest that there were no other forces at work.

The other great offstage event is the Civil War, which is just in the offing at the point where this volume leaves off. The polarization of forces leading up to it figures a good deal more prominently in the general history of the church than it does in anything I have to tell about. The confrontation between the common law courts and the High Commission is part of my story, but nothing much else is. Laud, unlike Henry VIII, even unlike Bancroft, went about his business with no legal sophistication at all. If he had gone on long enough with his program, he would no doubt have had to clothe it in legal forms; but long before that could happen it was all swept away.

You will find this volume, if anything, more doggedly technical than the last. The common law, which is described in the first and fourth chapters, is a doggedly technical system; there is no escaping it. The third chapter provides a certain amount of relief. Ecclesiastical administration is less technical (and by the same token less effective). Also, the bishop and the archdeacon are closer to the ground where people live or fail to live as conforming Christians, while the common law judges are worried about writs and processes. I am a common lawyer and I love my trade, but perhaps it is an acquired taste.

I have only to add a few acknowledgements. Much of the research for this volume was done on the same visit to England as that for the last, and I must again express my gratitude to the Ford Foundation for the financial support, and to the Rev. E. W. Kemp (now the Bishop of Chichester) for his wise direction. Much of the writing was done on another, much later, English visit. For this I have the University of Notre Dame to thank. I have also to thank the Prior and Community of Blackfriars, Oxford, for giving me a place to work away from my charming but somewhat distracting family. Professor A. G. Dickens, Mr. F. D. Price, and the Master of Balliol (Mr. Christopher Hill) have read parts of the manuscript and made valuable suggestions. R. J. Keefe of our 1980 law school class has checked the notes. Finally, my wife has gone over all of this with a loving and critical eye, even to the intricacies of medieval patronage law. If I have not measured up to her standards of vividness and clarity, it is not her fault.

1. The King's Crown and Dignity

The Commons of England, winding up the Parliament of 1400-1 with an unaccustomed rhetorical extravagance, likened the proceedings just completed to a mass.[1] At the beginning, the archbishop of Canterbury had expounded epistle and gospel. In the middle, corresponding to the sacrifice itself, the king had given great pleasure to God by declaring his will that the faith of Holy Church be sustained, and that the laws be enforced for rich and poor alike. Now at the end, the Commons were come to say *Ite Missa Est*. And well might the whole realm join them in saying *Deo Gratias,* because things had gone so well.

It is with the notion of a Christian commonwealth that underlies this flight of fancy that the present volume deals. This notion I have called "Erastianism." I define Erastianism as a tendency to see the institutional church as only one of a variety of institutions through which a Christian society conforms itself to the will of God. This definition is narrower than the uses (mainly polemical) to which the term is customarily put, but I think it is on the whole consonant with them. It seems also to be in keeping with what Erastus (1524-83, a Swiss amateur theologian writing in Heidelberg) had in mind.

Erastianism as thus defined dominates the thinking of the medieval laity, certainly in England, probably in most of Europe. It stands in contrast to the prevailing clerical view — which I dealt with at length in the first volume of this study under the name "High Churchmanship" — that sets the institutional church over against the rest of society as a witness to the otherness and sovereignty of God.

Because most theorists were High Churchmen, medieval Erastianism is weak in theoretical formulation. Its most pervasive manifestation was a rather facile assumption of a general unity of purpose between church and state.[2] Thus, the kings subscribed Magna Carta "unto the honor of Almighty God . . . , to the advancement of Holy Church and amendment of our realm," while the prelates excommunicated "breakers of the church's liberties, and of the liberties or other customs of the realm," and the Commons looked for money to defend the realm and *its* Holy Church *(Seinte Esglise d'ycelle)* against the French. For all

1

of them, lay and ecclesiastical authority, God and man, were harmoniously committed to the peace and good order of England, the confusion of her enemies, the piety and prosperity of her people, and the salvation of their souls.

For the laity, this sense of common purpose of church and state entailed a certain utilitarian conception of the church.

> . . . a man hath thre things to governe, that is to say, Soule, Body, and worldly Goudes, the whiche ought and shulde ben principaly reweled by thre Sciences, that ben Divinite, Fisyk, and Lawe, the Soule by Divinite, the Body by Fisyk, worldly Goudes by Lawe, and these conynges shulde be used and practised principaly by the most conyng men in the same Sciences . . .[3].

Soul, body, and worldly goods are all the same kind of practical concerns to be dealt with by professionals in a practical way.

It was this utilitarian outlook that led the laity to see particular manifestations of the church as products of prudence, custom, and positive law, rather than of theological first principles.

> . . . the holy church of England was founded in the estate of prelacy by the king and his progenitors, and the earls, barons, and other nobles of his said realm, and their ancestors, to inform them and the people of the law of God, and to make hospitalities, alms, and other works of charity in the places where the churches were founded.[4]

The basic principles of the church's life, priesthood, sacraments, the papacy, might be of divine foundation, but the institutional arrangements that obtained in England were set up by kings and magnates with practical ends in view. The attitude is reflected in the rejection of the prelates' claim to tithe by divine right, and conversely, in the stern line taken against the Lollard attack on church property as such. For the English laity, the right of the church to her property and revenues was neither better nor worse than the right of anyone else to his.[5]

Here the clergy and the laity parted company. Taking as their point of departure the Gregorian High Church program of sweeping re-examination of existing arrangements in the light of first principles, the clergy did all they could to establish their rights and privileges on theological foundations independent of either custom or utility. The difference between the two approaches provided a background for many of the church-state controversies of the period. After the Becket affair, however, and the interdict in King John's time, the clergy did not pursue any of these controversies to the point of a direct confrontation of power. There were exhortations, diplomatic exchanges, and even a certain amount of passive resistance, but the ordinary course of secular administration proceeded freely on the assumption that ecclesiastical arrangements were determined not by theology but by custom, utility, and positive law.[6]

The grounds for exercising control over these arrangements were eclectic. In some cases, high policy was appealed to. There was a "law of the land" to which both church and state were subject, and no principle of ecclesiastical autonomy could stop the king from administering that law to all his subjects.[7] In other cases, the king and his ministers were concerned with more limited governmental objectives — vindicating lay interests against the clergy, or simply keeping the peace. In still other cases, and these perhaps the most numerous, the intervention of royal authority in ecclesiastical affairs rested not on the general exigencies of government but on feudal land tenure, or its ecclesiastical offshoot the right of patronage.

The churchmen, for their part, occupied an ambiguous status before the secular law. The lay courts sometimes treated the church as a foreign jurisdiction, sometimes as a branch of their own government, sometimes as a group of wealthy and influential private citizens with special organizational problems. Some acts of ecclesiastical authority were given official status; some had to be passed on by juries; some were treated as contempts of the king. The ministrations of the church were sometimes treated as public services, sometimes as feudal dues. Tenure of ecclesiastical offices and endowments was analogized to other forms of tenure, but the analogies kept coming unstuck.[8]

Note, though, that the conceptual ambiguities were technical, not ideological. Medieval English lawyers developed their concepts as they went along, and naturally they developed some inconsistencies and false starts in the process. But they had a reasonably coherent account to give concerning the place of the institutional church in their midst, and concerning their own role in ordering all things to the honor of God and the salvation of his people. It is in the light of this account that we must consider how and with what justification the secular government in fact impinged on the operation of the church.

I. Personnel and Revenues — The Rights and Privileges of the Crown

A. Prelate as Magnate.

Except for a few lands held in almoin (i.e., by praying for the donors), the bishops, abbots, and other prelates of England held their land by feudal tenure, and were subject to the duties of feudal tenants. They had to attend courts and Parliament, discharge government functions when required, and supply various sums of money, or even troops. The twofold capacity of prelate and magnate was borne with reasonable comfort in late medieval law, though it gave a bit of trouble in earlier times. It was established early, albeit not without debate, that a prelate could do homage for his temporalities with a qualification "saving his order," and that when he attended court he need not participate in a judgment of life or member. By the end of the thirteenth century, it was established that a prelate could neither use his ecclesiastical powers to further his position as a temporal magnate nor be molested by his ecclesiastical superiors for anything he did in a temporal capacity.[9]

There was some trouble finding procedures for bringing a prelate to book for his secular misdeeds. A long account of the tumultuous trial of William of St. Calais, bishop of Durham, before William II in 1089 shows well enough what the problem was. Both sides accepted that the bishop could be judged in the royal court with respect to his fief, but not with respect to his bishopric. At the same time, both sides recognized that in judging one has to judge the whole man. The outcome of the proceeding was total frustration, tempered on the king's part by the use of force.[10]

Eventually, some formula must have been found to escape this conceptual dilemma. In the fourteenth and fifteenth centuries, bishops were more or less routinely tried in Parliament for their political indiscretions and were deprived of their personal property and the temporalities of their sees. But the "person and pastorate" of the offending bishop were unaffected by such a judgment. Unless the pope could be persuaded to complete his downfall by translating him to a nominal see, it was evidently his lot to wander about in a denuded condition, living on procurations and tithes, and governing his diocese as best he could until the political climate changed.[11]

The seizure of a prelate's temporalities was not merely a measure for high political matters; it was the standard way of either bringing him into court or punishing him for any kind of contempt. The prelates objected to this practice, and attempted in the Parliament of 1351-2 to get it changed. But as it seemed there was no other way to bring them to justice (a layman would be subject to bodily attachment or to outlawry), the king would do no more for them than make it easier to save their temporalities by paying a fine.[12]

It was no doubt the status of the prelates as secular magnates that led to such controls as the king exercised over their election.[13] Contemporary rationales refer both to the king's status as founder and to the importance of the prelates in the councils of the kingdom. Before the canonical election process was formalized in the early thirteenth century, the king often played an active personal part in it, convening the electors, or even exercising some discretion over who was to participate. But after the middle of that century, his only legal rights were to issue the *congé d' élire* permitting the election to take place, and to confirm the result. He was most insistent on these rights (one chapter was heavily fined for holding an election while a messenger was on his way with the *congé d' élire,* but had not yet arrived), but I find only one instance in which he tried to use them to influence the outcome of an election. His efforts along these lines were almost entirely political and diplomatic, rather than legal. As we saw in the last volume, he was generally successful.

B. Cleric as Bureaucrat.

The king, like all magnates of the time, supported his bureaucratic establishment by bestowing benefices in his gift on clerics in his service. The king's clerics, unlike other clerics, were automatically exempted from the obligation to take orders and to reside on their benefices. Except for this privilege (which was probably more honorific than practical, as individual dispensations were freely given to those who needed them), the king's clerics were supposed to be subject to correction by their ordinaries in the same way as other clergy. As regards their personal conduct, this may well have been the case in practice also. But the royal authorities made it their business to review any act of ecclesiastical administration that came between the king's clerics and the full enjoyment of their benefices.[14] They also prevented the imposition of ecclesiastical censures on anyone in the king's service on account of anything he did in his official capacity.

The problems raised by the divided allegiance of these civil servants were less serious than one might have supposed. There were a few cases — mainly involving papal provisions, or the longstanding dispute over the tithability of wood — in which the chancellor or his clerks were complained of for letting their ecclesiastical loyalties interfere with their enforcement of the law of the land, but they were very few.[15] Apart from these cases, it was only an aberrant situation that gave trouble. A private litigant dredged up a disused canon to excommunicate a chancery clerk for putting his name to a writ of prohibition. A bishop-chancellor bestowed benefices in his gift as chancellor on the clerics of his episcopal household instead of on his chancery clerks. A cleric who kept the court rolls scrupled to write down a capital judgment, so the ensuing hanging was technically illegal. But usually, everyone knew better. A private litigant knew he had nothing but a place in the Tower to gain by excommunicating royal servants. A chancellor knew better than to trifle with his clerks. A court reporter knew enough to get a layman to write his capital judgments for him. On the whole, the work of the royal bureaucracy went off as smoothly as anyone could ask, with the king's clerics giving long and faithful service to their master, and being rewarded by him with the benefices of the church.

C. Souces of Support.

While a clerical civil servant, like his lay colleague, might have fees attached to his office, and might receive designated sums out of general or specific revenues of the crown,[16] his main compensation was in the benefices the king bestowed on him. Accordingly, the king needed a constant supply of benefices to bestow. Some of the benefices he used for the purpose were regularly in his gift — the parish churches on royal manors, or the prebends in "royal free chapels" like St. George's, Windsor, or St. Stephen's, Westminster. But a large — perhaps the largest — part of his patronage was exercised in the right of someone else. When one of the king's tenants died leaving an underage heir, the king, as guardian, could present to any benefice in the heir's gift that fell vacant during his minority. Similarly, when the temporalities of a bishopric or abbey were in the king's hands, whether because of a vacancy in the office or because of some misbehavior of the incumbent, the king could fill any vacant benefice in the gift of the bishop or abbot.[17]

Pursuant to the maxim "time does not run against the king (*nullum tempus occurrit rege)*" the king could present to any benefice vacant while the "advowson," or right to present, was in his hands, even if he had restored the estate to the owner without filling the benefice. It followed that anyone subsequently in the benefice, even a century later, was not rightfully there, as he had been introduced in violation of the king's right. Accordingly, he could be ousted in favor of the king's presentee. A statute was made in 1350 (one of several concessions to the prelates in return for a subsidy) cutting off claims to vacancies before 1326, but even that limitation was evidently not fully effective.

It must have taken a good deal of zeal on someone's part to resurrect such claims as these and prosecute them to judgment in the courts. I suspect, though I cannot document it, that the king had a staff of lawyers on retainer to do some of this work: the king's attorneys handle some of these cases in a way that reminds one of modern government tax lawyers. But in a number of cases a claim of this kind would be brought to the king's attention not by his attorneys, but by a cleric in his service who wanted the benefice for himself. The king evidently made it a practice (as did the pope) to bestow preferment in his gift on anyone with a claim to his favor who brought the preferment to his attention — it was a fairly painless way to reward his servants. Unfortunately, however, the report made by the interested cleric was not always true. On many occasions the king found it necessary to revoke a presentment on finding that he had been misinformed as to his rights.

Where the king's right to present to a benefice arose out of his custody of the temporalities of an ecclesiastical office, his claims clashed with those of the pope, who claimed the right to "provide" an incumbent of his choosing to any benefice in the gift of a churchman. This clash afforded the background to the famous Statutes of Provisors, whose operations made for one of the procedural tangles we will take up later on.

The king's sources of patronage were further extended by a right he had to make every newly appointed bishop or head of a religious house of royal foundation bestow a benefice in his own gift on one cleric nominated by the king. The designated cleric had to be given a pension (anywhere from £2 to £20) until the benefice was found for him.[18] Tender of a suitable benefice extinguished the pension whether or not the cleric accepted it, but the benefice had to be worth considerably more than the pension — mere equality would not do. Pensions of this kind were being judicially enforced by the early fourteenth century; not long afterward, a prelate had to post bond to insure his compliance before he could receive his temporalities out of the king's hands.

Lesser royal servants received a different form of ecclesiastical support through the king's right to pension them off with room and board in religious houses.[19] This right, though some fifteenth-century Year Book cases attribute it to the royal prerogative, seems originally to have been a patronal right, perhaps arising from an earlier right of the patron personally to lodge in the house with his retinue. Through the early fourteenth century, religious houses had neither a clear duty to put up royal boarders nor a clear right to refuse. A would-be pensioner might have to plod three or four times between the king and one monastery or another before he was finally placed. In the course of these maneuvers, houses seem to have received concessions to the effect that if they took in one boarder they would not be asked to take another at the same time. Such an arrangement would then be taken as a precedent unless the king expressly undertook that it should not be. In this way, the king came by the middle of the fourteenth century to have an enforceable right to one "corrody," that is, room and board for one person, in every religious house, unless the house could show that it was not founded by the king, held no land of him, and had never given a corrody at his request before, except on the express understanding that no precedent was to be created.

Similarly, the amount of the corrody — the exact quality of the sustenance provided — came to be fixed by precedent. Where the king at the end of the thirteenth century was asking that so-and-so be provided with the necessities of life, by the middle of the fourteenth he was ordering that A be provided with the same sustenance that B (or B's predecessors, if B had been remiss in demanding his full rights) had formerly had.[20]

The beneficiaries of these corrodies were generally superannuated or disabled minor servants — a king's yeoman, a man maimed in the king's service, a bailiff beaten almost to death while doing the king's business, a man with twenty years' service as a sumpter, ten in garrisons overseas.[21] Some of these brought requests into Parliament; others came to the king's attention in unspecified ways. The Duke of Bedford, arranging affairs during the minority of Henry VI, proposed to keep a book of eligible persons so that the available corrodies might be appointed to as they fell vacant.

D. Assumption of Revenues.

There were four main situations in which ecclesiastical revenues, as such, came into the king's hands to be used for his own secular purposes:

1. Custody of temporalities of vacant ecclesiastical offices — The right to custody during vacancy was a patronage right, not a royal prerogative, and some relatively important religious houses escaped its application on the ground that they were not of the king's patronage.[22] But all the bishoprics of the kingdom, except Canterbury's satellite see of Rochester, were subject to it, as were most of the great religious houses and many of the small ones. The temporalities that went into royal custody included advowsons as well as secular revenues, as we have seen. Tithes, altarage, mortuaries, and the like were of course not included, although the king sometimes had to curb the zeal of his officials in this regard. It does not appear that later kings followed William II's disreputable practice of prolonging vacancies in order to increase profits. Even so, the normal processes of election and confirmation took long enough to afford the king a substantial return.

2. Forefeitures and seizures — We have already considered the grounds on which the temporalities of an office could be taken into the king's hands. The same things were included as when custody was taken during vacancy.

3. Cells of alien religious houses — A number of French monasteries had priories or cells in England, gifts of the Anglo-Norman barons of the first century after the Conquest. These were taken into the king's hands whenever there was war with France, which was most of the time. The king took temporalities and spiritualities alike, although he made some effort to see that the latter were administered by churchmen.

4. Benefices of aliens — In the mid-fourteenth century, also as part of the war effort against France, the king took over the proceeds of all benefices he found in the hands of enemy aliens who did not reside on them.

In keeping with the general common law rule regarding guardianships and other fiduciary relations, the king was not expected to account in any way for the funds that came to him through the exercise of these rights. In fact, he used them for the general purposes of his government and household, and the compensation of those in his service. He was obliged, however, to see to the discharge of any obligations attached to any office or endowment in his hands. In the case of a religious house, for instance, he had to see to the payment of debts and the giving out of corrodies. Where he had the spiritual revenues as well as the temporal, he had also to see to the maintenance of services and the upkeep of the religious. Also, he was evidently expected to see that his custody did not interfere with the regular exercise of ecclesiastical jurisdiction.[23]

There were various procedures for exercising these different rights. In the case of vacancies, possession was taken for the king by his escheators, officials whose business it was to handle escheats and other such prerogatives, each in a designated geographical area. The escheator evidently took possession on his own initiative as soon as he heard of the vacancy,[24] and kept it until the king ordered him to put the new incumbent in seisin. The escheators were concerned only with vacancies. Temporalities seized for misconduct were taken by the sheriff or a designated custodian pursuant to a specific writ. Alien priories were given to custodians, or to farmers who paid fixed sums to the king for the right to collect the revenues. The benefices of enemy aliens were probably sequestered by the bishop and the proceeds turned over the the king[25] — a procedure like that used for collecting the judgments of the royal courts.

The religious houses mitigated somewhat the impact of royal custody during vacancies by separating the endowments of the house from those of the abbot or prior, so that only the latter came into the king's hands when the office fell vacant.[26] Even so, the periodic intrusion of strangers into the precarious financial life of a religious community was felt as a serious burden, and many communities sought to be rid of it by the payment of fixed sums. Apparently permission to do this was routinely granted on request, the amount of the payment being fixed by the Treasurer and Barons of the Exchequer on the basis of returns from past vacancies. The sum fixed upon might be an annual payment, a monthly payment during vacancy, or a lump sum for each vacancy. In any event, it entitled the community to occupy the temporalities of the vacant office (excepting in some cases advowsons or feudal dues) on the king's behalf.

Cathedral chapters sometimes made similar arrangements with the king for custody of their bishop's temporalities during vacancy of the see. These arrangements, however, were more apt to be negotiated ad hoc for a particular vacancy; even then they were not made as frequently as they were with religious houses. The king had more at stake in the bishoprics than he had in the abbeys, and his custody did not interfere with the normal functioning of the chapters as it did with that of the religious communities. When he let out his rights to a chapter, he charged a high price — £1000, for instance, for the vacancy of the see of London in 1448.[27]

Similar arrangements were made concerning the alien priories seized on account of the war.[28] Some of those were priories in name only, where two or three monks served as bailiffs or estate managers for their brethren; these the king evidently felt free to farm out to anyone he pleased, subject to a reasonable stipend for the monks. On the other hand, "conventual priories," where there were communities observing a true religious life, were almost invariably farmed to their own inmates. The rents were high, but most of the communities managed to survive until they were able to make some provision for escaping their status as aliens.

E. Subsidies

As we saw in the last volume, the king was accustomed to receive subsidies from the clergy in their Convocations, as he was from the laity in Parliament. In the early days of Henry III, both the pope and Archbishop Stephen Langton had actually encouraged such grants; later, though, things became less amicable. In 1297, Boniface VIII, with his decretal *Clericis Laicos,* attempted to forbid the making of any such grant without his express permission. Edward I retaliated by seizing the temporalities of all the clergy in the country, and restoring them one by one as their holders contributed to his needs. There were only two holdouts.[29] Oliver Sutton, bishop of Lincoln, saved both his conscience and his temporalities by leaving a sum of money lying in his house, which the sheriff seized for the king, and which the king accepted as a payment. Archbishop Winchelsea eventually got his temporalities back without paying at all — it is not clear how.

Not long after these events, the pope withdrew *Clericis Laicos,* and the king abandoned direct coercion. Thereafter, negotiations were carried on in Convocation. The king used importunity and vague threats: *"Nunc sermone blando, nunc per verba aspera quoddammodo minatoria;"*[30] the clergy responded with dilatoriness and pleas of poverty. Sometimes the king had to prorogue and recall Convocation three or four times before he got as much as he wanted. Once or twice, he made important concessions to the clergy in return for a grant. In 1380, and again in 1383, the Commons tried to increase the pressure by making their own grants conditional on a specified contribution from the clergy. But the clergy protested vigorously, and the Commons backed down.

When a sum was granted by Convocation, the bishops would appoint someone, usually a religious house, to collect it. But the collectors, once appointed, were responsible not to the bishops but to the Exchequer. They had no easy task.[31] One group of them was let off of certain sums that they dared not "for fear of death" take further measures to collect. Another was the victim of a conspiracy of local rectors to ruin him "as he has ruined us."

It is not surprising that religious houses were continually begging the king to be exempted from this onerous duty of collecting his subsidies. Beginning in the reign of Richard II, these exemptions were rather freely granted, to the great discomfiture of the bishops, who had to find suitable collectors among those not exempt. The clergy attempted on a number of occasions to include in their grants a proviso that such exemptions should not apply. A great deal of inconclusive litigation resulted.[32]

Some religious houses were also exempted from the actual payment of subsidies to the king. These exemptions were less freely given, and usually included a recital of some plausible reason — that the house was poor, and that its funds were spent in some kind of useful work.[33] But they were evidently frequent enough to reduce materially the amount realized from a given subsidy, and thus to increase the demand for further subsidies from those not exempt.

Eventually, the clergy (that is, the secular clergy, who did not benefit from exemptions, as distinguished from the religious, who did) found an ingenious way of coping with exemptions. They taxed those exempt from collecting at a higher rate than others, while those exempt from paying at all they subjected to a special subsidy for the archbishop, who turned the proceeds over to the king. These devices seem to have served their purpose fairly well until in 1488 most exemptions were abrogated by the king at the request of the Commons.[34]

Not all church property was subject to taxation for subsidies granted by Convocation. It was established that land that came into the hands of churchmen after the twentieth year of Edward I (1292), unless it was given in almoin, would pay with the laity the subsidies granted by Parliament.[35] This division gave rise to a certain number of difficulties, as where land subject to one tax was distrained to pay the other, or where one who had paid the wrong tax by mistake had to seek special exemption from paying the right one.

It should be noted that all these secular penetrations into the personnel and finances of the church rested on principles that were extremely difficult to dispute. One was that property should be held on the conditions on which it was given; the other was that the common good of a Christian kingdom concerned the church as well as the state. The first supported the feudal obligations of prelates, the custody of their temporalities during vacancy, and, presumably, the taxation of certain church lands with the holdings of the laity. The ecclesiastical authorities endeavored to prevent the impact of these secular obligations from interfering with ecclesiastical administration, and to prevent the imposition of new burdens on holdings not previously subject to them. But they did not deny in principle that such obligations could be imposed.

The second principle supported the employment of clerics in the work of secular government, the need to use their special skills and moral qualities for the common good outweighing the desirability of freeing them from worldly concerns. It also supported the imposition of taxes on church lands to maintain the king's peace and the common defense of the realm. What the church authorities claimed here was the freedom to make their own determination of the extent of their contribution to the common necessities. In this, of course, they were not entirely successful. The secular authorities maintained that matters of this kind were ultimately of temporal concern, and that any concessions to the ecclesistical authorities concerning them were attributable to the constitution of the kingdom, not to any inherent right of the church.

II. Administration — The Law of the Land

Because it was the king's business to administer the whole law, his courts and officials concerned themselves with defining the proper scope of ecclesiastical authority, keeping the churchmen (who had other ideas) within the territory assigned them, and, even inside that territory, putting down improper uses of their powers. The churchmen, as we have seen, claimed all these functions in theory for themselves. In practice, though, they submitted to the laity without much complaint. I think the laity prevailed in this incipient contest not only because they had effective procedures and physical power, but also because they had more heart for the work. It was generally picky work. There was not much in it for a man who loved philosophical, theological, or even canonical niceties; still less for a man with deep pastoral concerns. For the common lawyers, on the other hand, the scope of particular jurisdictions, and even of particular procedures within one jurisdiction, was meat and drink.

I will try to show here how they laid out the boundaries between church and state courts, how they tried to control misuse of church authority even within its proper sphere, and by what procedures they made good the rules they set up.

A. Jurisdiction of courts.

The only theological doctrines available to the courts in drawing jurisdictional boundaries were abstract to the point of triviality (the soul is ruled by Divinity, worldly goods by Law; the church deals with sin, the state with temporal wrongs, etc.). Nor did the judges and lawyers develop (as the canonists would have done) any governing general principles of their own. They simply applied to the different classes of cases that came up a combination of ad hoc judgments and rules of thumb (i.e., common law reasoning). We will have to take up the different classes one by one.

1. Property and Contract – Only land held in almoin tenure could be litigated over in the church courts. Other land was "lay fee," with which only the lay courts could deal. The Council of Clarendon (1164) set up a lay proceeding called *utrum* to determine whether a given piece of land was almoin or lay fee, so that a suit over it could be brought in the proper court. In practice, though, you could not say how land was held without saying who owned it, so the *utrum* proceeding would dispose of the case on the merits, and nothing further would remain to be tried. It fell out, therefore, that the lay courts determined all land litigation, except in the hypothetical case where both litigants admitted that the land was held in almoin.[36]

In the realm of personal actions, the lay courts used a formula: the courts Christian could not hold "pleas of debt or lay chattels" unless they were "touching matrimony or testament." The terms were all used in a rather technical way. Thus, a suit for a canonical payment like tithe or stole fees was not a "plea of debt." Nor, it seems, was a suit to recover misappropriated church funds. Similarly, a suit for a canonical payment in kind — say, for a certain beast as a mortuary — was not a "plea of lay chattels." Nor was a suit to recover property taken by sacrilege — invasion of sacred premises or violence to the clergy. The ornaments of the church and the objects used in worship were of course not "lay chattels." Nor were the sheaves of grain set aside for the parson as tithe ("severed from the nine parts") until the parson had taken possession of them and sold them. Once they were sold, though, they became "lay chattels," and a suit to recover the purchase price was a "plea of debt."[37]

The exception for pleas "touching matrimony" had to do with marriage settlements. The church courts, when they annulled a marriage, could order the return of the wife's dowry;[38] in some cases also, when they enforced or recognized a marriage, they could order an agreed-on dowry to be paid. Here, the common lawyers drew a very fine line:

> If I make a covenant to give X £10 if he will marry my daughter, he must sue in the lay court. But if I promise to give him £10 with my daughter, he may ask for it in the Court Christian.[39]

The reason for the distinction does not leap to the mind. I suppose the point is that in the first case the £10 represents a distinct promise, the marriage being quid pro quo for it, and is enforceable in an action of debt in the lay court, whereas in the second case the girl and the money are separate parts of a single promise which only the church court can enforce in full.

The second exception, that for pleas "touching testament," was more fully developed. It clearly permitted a legatee to sue in the church court for money or property left to him under a will. Whether it also permitted the executor to sue you in the church court for money you owed the deceased, or you to sue him there for money the deceased owed you was more doubtful, as we shall see.

People who wanted their contracts to be enforceable in the church courts developed a couple of devices which gave the lay courts some trouble. One was to fortify the undertaking with an oath or a "pledge of faith."[40] The latter was a promissory ceremony of pagan origin taken over by the church to bestow spiritual significance on a promise in a matter not important enough for an oath. A promise thus fortified would be enforced by the church because of the spiritual harm in not fulfilling it. The rules that prevailed in the lay courts were of course quite inconsistent with the church's taking jurisdiction in such a case; they might have permitted a penance to be imposed for the perjury or breach of faith, but certainly not the enforcement of the promise as such. Despite the rules, however, the church courts did a flourishing business enforcing debts and other contracts on this ground. Most of the cases were for small amounts, and were summarily handled. Woodcock suggests that these proceedings were popular because there was no adequate small claims procedure on the lay side, and that they were conducted with impunity because they were too petty to be worth the trouble and expense of getting the lay courts to intervene.

The other device for getting your contract into the church courts was to attach to it a promise to pay so many pounds to the papal collector for the Crusades as a penalty if you failed to perform. The papal collector would then hear a suit to make you either perform or pay the penalty. The resulting invasion of the royal jurisdiction was complained of by the Commons as early as 1306, and was made the subject of a statute in 1363.[41]

Some of the Year Book colloquies seem to envisage a general rule that, independent of other principles, the church courts could hear any property or contract case in which it could be shown that the lay courts did not afford a remedy. The framers of the Statute of Consultations (1296) evidently supposed that this was the general rule. But if there was such a rule, it was subject to many exceptions. Take for instance the case of an oath to convey land. There was no way in which this oath could be enforced in the lay courts without a sealed instrument. Yet the church courts were not allowed to enforce it because it involved lay fee.[42]

2. Tithes and Ecclesiastical Dues – In general, churchmen proceeded in their own courts to collect the tithes, mortuaries, and other payments to which they were entitled under ecclesiastical law. The lay courts accepted, and, if need be, protected their right to do so. There were some tithe cases, however, in which the presence of certain issues might lead a lay court to intervene. In a number of places, there were customs or agreements replacing the mathematical tenth by something easier to compute — all the produce of a designated part of my field instead of a tenth of the produce of the whole; so many pence to be passed one way or the other if the year's crop of lambs did not come to an even multiple of ten. There were other things — the most important was timber — which were customarily not titheable at all. The lay courts, regarding tithe as a mere customary payment in the first place, would enforce any such custom, and any such agreement if it was in writing under seal. But the church courts, regarding tithe as a mathematical tenth by divine right, would enforce a custom or agreement only if it afforded a fair substitute for the full tenth (a *modus decimandi,* as opposed to a *jus non decimandi* or *non bene decimandi*). Thus, a litigant relying on such a custom or agreement could get the lay court to stop a church proceeding against him on the ground that he would not get a proper hearing from the church.[43]

Where a suit was not over the payment of tithe, but over which of two churchmen was entitled to collect it, the case was recognized to be of ecclesiastical cognizance unless it involved a question of secular law like parish boundaries or the scope of a royal grant, or unless it affected the right of patronage in some way. The last of these exceptions threatened to swallow up the rule. Since the amount of tithe attached to a benefice affected the value of what the patron of the benefice had to bestow, the patron always had a stake in a suit on the point. Hence the lay courts sometimes treated such a suit as one over which of two patrons had the advowson of the tithes in question, and therefore as one in the exclusive jurisdiction of the lay courts.

But if the suit was over an advowson, only the patron had standing to bring it. This result was a serious one for the incumbent, whose livelihood might be affected by an amount of tithe that was too small to interest the patron. By the end of the thirteenth century, a rule of thumb was developed that balanced the conflicting interests involved: where the value of the tithes in issue amounted to less than one-fourth of the value of the benefice, the ecclesiastical court had jurisdiction.[44] If they amounted to one-fourth or more, the patron had the right to have the case heard exclusively in the lay court. But even then the case was not a simple one of lack of jurisdiction in the church courts. The ecclesiastical proceeding could not be stopped by a regular writ of prohibition; a special writ called *indicavit* was required, which only the patron could bring.

A large, perhaps the largest, part of the lay courts' involvement with tithe was caused by altercations arising out of the collection process. It was the duty of every landowner or farmer to count out every tenth sheaf at the harvest, every tenth lamb at lambing time, etc., and designate them as tithe. The parson or other churchman entitled to tithe probably had a right to look on while this was done, but he could not do it himself: if the landowner failed to set out tithes, the parson's only remedy was to coerce him through ecclesiastical proceedings.

But once the tithe was "severed from the nine parts" by the landowner, it became a spiritual chattel, and the parson could come on the land with his servants and wagons to carry it away. If he came, and there was a dispute over just what he could take with him, the matter might well come to blows. Or if two churchmen disputed the right to take tithe from that particular field, they might both come at once and a fight might ensue. The loser in any of these scuffles might bring an action of trespass *de bonis asportatis,* adding a count *quare clausum fregit* if appropriate. The lay court's handling of the case depended mainly on the status of the goods.[45]

If both parties admitted that the goods were tithe, severed from the nine parts, and it appeared that the case turned on who had a right to take those particular tithes, the court would decline jurisdiction unless the right to tithe depended on parish boundaries or some other matter of secular law. Where it was admitted that the goods were tithe, but the right to tithe was not put in issue — as where the defendant denied taking them — the lay court would try the case as it did any other. The two sets of courts had concurrent jurisdiction as they did over cases involving trees stolen from the churchyard or vessels from the church, or any other trespass to spiritual chattels.

The lay courts also tried the case where one party claimed that the goods were tithe and the other denied it. The clergy tried to put through Parliament a rule that such issues should be sent to the bishop for trial, as was done with questions of marriage or bastardy. This the government was not willing to grant. It was conceded to the clergy, however, that a general averment that goods were lay chattels would not be accepted against a churchman in such a case; the party would have to show wherein they were lay chattels before the issue could go to trial.[46] I suppose the ''wherein'' meant that some special fact had to be pleaded — that the tithe was not severed, or that the crop did not grow where the person claiming tithe said it did. This narrowing of the issue presumably helped the churchman by leaving less scope for a hostile jury.

Thenstatute setting up this rule (1377) begins ''When any person of holy church is drawn in plea . . .'' So the courts had some trouble deciding whether it was available when the defendant was a layman who took tithes as the servant of a churchman who claimed to be entitled to them. Generally, they decided that the servant should have the same rule as his master — it would be unreasonable to make the parson carry off his own grain.

Similar problems were raised, with similar results, where the parson farmed his tithes to a layman for a fixed annual payment. It was sometimes contended that this transaction made the tithes into lay chattels (as a sale after they were collected would have done), but the courts generally preferred to put the farmer in the shoes of his principal. They did, however, take jurisdiction over the farm contract itself, entertaining suits to enforce the payments due from the farmer — probably to the exclusion of the ecclesiastical courts.[47]

Before we leave the subject of ecclesiastical dues, a few more words must be said about mortuaries, a form of payment that raised much the same problems as tithes, albeit not in anything like the same volume.[48] The mortuary was a payment due a parish priest on the death of his parishioner. It was fixed by local custom in those places where it obtained, and it usually involved not a money payment but a contribution in kind such as the decdedent's best or second best animal. Unlike tithe, mortuaries had no claim to divine sanction; the church courts would not allow them to be collected without a showing of custom. It is perhaps for this reason that the lay courts would not interfere with an ecclesiastical mortuary proceeding on the mere showing that no mortuary was due. There was no reason to suppose that the defense would not be fairly entertained by the ecclesiastical court.

If a particular animal was due as a mortuary, it was not a lay chattel, so the parson's proceeding could not be stopped on the ground it was for the possession of specific goods. Where, however, it was contended that the particular animal involved in the proceeding was not the one to which the parson was entitled, the issue would be tried in the lay court.

3. Corrodies and Pensions — A corrody, as we have seen, was a quantum of support to which a given person was entitled from a hospital or religious house. A pension was a fixed annual payment in money or in kind, due from one person or body politic to another. It differed from a rent-charge in that no particular piece of land was charged with it — it was receivable "from the hand" of the person liable for it and his successors. A corrody could sometimes be quite as specific as a pension (five loaves of bread and three gallons of ale weekly, for instance).[49] The main distinction in practice was that the corrody was receivable on a day to day basis, whereas a pension was generally receivable at one or two fixed days of the year.

Perhaps it was the continuous nexus between the holder of the corrody and the burdened house that led to the common lawyers to analogize the corrody to a piece of real property. At any rate, the Statute of Westminster II (1285) permitted the holder to recover his corrody through an assize of novel disseisin, a remedy developed for possessory rights in land, but extended by that statute to a number of incorporeal rights.[50] As far as I can see, there was no serious clerical objection to this assertion of lay jurisdiction.

There was more debate over pensions.[51] These were recoverable through a writ of annuity, formed on the same pattern as those of debt and detinue, the pension being regarded as a kind of recurring debt. The lay jurisdiction was supported by the fact that the patron's rights would be affected if a benefice in his gift was subjected to a pension. I suspect also that the conceptual force of the debt analogy helped. There is some authority for saying that the lay courts would not hear a pension suit between churchmen unless a "lay contract" (sealed instrument, fine, etc.) could be shown.

The churchmen, for their part, naturally thought that they should have exclusive jurisdiction over a pension, since it came out of an ecclesiastical benefice or a religious house. They made some complaint about lay courts handling pension cases, and still more complaint about the refusal to let church courts handle them. They set forth their views in Parliament in 1376 and 1377, expressing themselves with a good deal more fire and brimstone than they generally used. But all they got from the king was a promise to have the records checked and see what had been done in the past. In fact, the document called *Circumspecte Agatis,* a compilation on ecclesiastical jurisdiction issued by Edward I in 1285, supported the churchmen's claims as fully as they could wish. But the lay judges were not enthusiastic about *Circumspecte Agatis.* It was in a pension case in 1346 that they recorded the famous statement that it was no statute because the prelates had made it themselves.

4. Patronage Rights – The king's courts, as we have seen, successfully maintained the exclusive jurisdiction to pass on claims to the "advowson" of a benefice — that is, the right of the "patron" of the benefice to present to the bishop a suitable cleric to occupy it. The exclusive jurisdiction was not confined to cases where the right to present was directly in issue. We have just considered how it applied to tithe and pension cases where the value of the benefice was in question. It was also invoked when an incumbent or would-be incumbent (especially the holder of a papal provision) sought to litigate in the church courts with the presentee of a man who had recovered the advowson in the lay courts. It was often used also to give the lay courts exclusive jurisdiction over cases involving the rights of an appropriator. The appropriator, a religious house or other body with permission to take over the revenues of a benefice, was canonically both patron and incumbent. But the lay courts would not permit such a body to use the ecclesiastical remedies of an incumbent if the secular remedies of a patron could possibly serve. For instance, if a stranger intruded into the appropriated church, the appropriator had to proceed for the recovery of the advowson rather than for the recovery of the incumbency.

The rules governing jurisdiction in advowson cases were part of a large and complex body of law in which all manner of proceedings, lay and ecclesiastical, were orchestrated in an attempt (not altogether successful) to harmonize the different interests involved in distributing the benefices of the church. It would be idle to study the jurisdictional aspects of this subject in isolation. The further ramification of the brief points just mentioned will have to be deferred until we take up the substantive law of patronage.

5. Personal Status – In certain cases, your temporal rights might depend on your personal status, while the status itself depended on ecclesiastical law. Whether you were married, whether you were a bastard (i.e., whether your parents were married), and whether you were professed in a religious order, were the common cases. As a general rule, when one of these questions was in issue in a lay court, the issue would be sent to the bishop to try.

The usual case in which a marriage was in issue was one in which a woman claimed dower (the widow's portion in her husband's lands), and the heirs denied that she was married to the deceased. These cases were uniformly sent to the bishop. I suppose that if a marriage had been in issue in a trespass action for carrying off the plaintiff's wife the same procedure would have been used. But it was not used when the question of marriage was merely procedural — went to the "abatement of the writ" rather than to the merits of the action. Thus, where a defendant claimed that a woman plaintiff had a husband and could not be heard without him, or that Mrs. X was improperly named as a plaintiff because she was really Mrs. Y,[52] the plea was either sent to a jury or refused out of hand.

The question of bastardy came up in all manner of inheritance cases. A bastard was *filius nullius,* and could be no one's heir. Nor could he have heirs of his own in any collateral line (brothers, sisters, uncles, cousins, aunts) — he had no heirs except of his own body, as the courts put it. There were important exceptions to the general principle that bastardy questions were to be sent to the bishop for trial.[53] If the alleged bastard was dead, or otherwise not a party to the proceeding, the lay court would try the question. Where the question came up in one of the possessory assizes — summary proceedings where the jury was standing by to try the issues as soon as they could be framed — the courts were reluctant to send questions to the bishop because of the delay involved. There was no uniform practice, but they tended to put questions of marriage and legitimacy to the assize if they felt that the questions turned on matters of common knowledge (e.g., whether the plaintiff's father had another wife living when he married the plaintiff's mother) that the jurors could be expected to know.

There were some cases also where the lay courts applied a different substantive law from the church courts.[54] If a marriage was annulled, the lay courts had their own rules (depending on the grounds of annulment) for whether the issue was legitimate. If a man was born before his parents were married, he was legitimate in the eyes of the church, but a bastard at common law. Conversely, in cases of adultery, the church courts would usually admit evidence that the mother's husband was not the father, whereas the lay courts in most cases adhered to an irrebuttable presumption that he was. In cases of this class, you had to plead your contention specially to keep the matter from going to the bishop. For instance, if your opponent was born before the marriage of his parents, you would have to plead that that was the case: if you pleaded simply that he was a bastard, the issue would be sent to the bishop, and you would lose. Similarly, if you were born of an adulterous union, you could not simply deny the allegation that you were a bastard; you had to plead that your mother was married to so-and-so, and you were born during the marriage.

When the bishop got a question of marriage, legitimacy, or the like from a lay court, he evidently tried it by the usual methods of canonical proof. There were no parish records of the kind that existed after the Reformation to help him. His answer, however he arrived at it, seems to have become a permanent record in the lay court, available to anyone for any purpose.[55] It was therefore possible on occasion to legitimize a suppositious child by means of a collusive suit. Legislation was sought in Parliament to curb this possibility, but nothing much came of it.

The bishop's action in response to a question from the lay court was not strictly speaking an ecclesiastical proceeding; it was a form of trial in the lay proceeding.[56] Thus, it could not be subjected to the ordinary processes of ecclesiastical appeal. Nor could it be initiated except on a request from the lay court in connection with an action pending there. If a man simply brought a suit in the court Christian to establish that he was the legitimate heir of so-and-so, a prohibition would issue out of the lay court, since the court Christian could not entertain a plea touching the inheritance of land.

6. *Decedent Estates* – As we have seen, the church, probably thanks to its interest in the souls of the faithful departed, maintained until the mid-nineteenth century a general jurisdiction over the execution of wills and the administration of decedent estates. If there was a will, it could be admitted to probate in the ecclesiastical court, and executors appointed. If there was no will, the ordinary

could administer the goods for the benefit of the decedent's soul, or could appoint an administrator to do so. Anyone interfering in this process could be subjected to ecclesiastical censures. An executor or administrator who failed to do his duty could be called to account in the original probate proceeding, or corrected in the course of a parish visitation. A person entitled to a legacy under a will could sue in the ecclesiastical court to collect it.

The lay courts did not concern themselves with these processes except to see that nobody applied them to freehold estates in land.[57] At common law, these estates were not devisable at all; in a place where they were devisable by local custom, the devisee entered in the same way as an heir, without going through probate. Oddly enough, there is no indication that the lay courts enfored the provision of Magna Carta that the ordinary should make reasonable provision for the wife and children of an intestate out of his goods, or the common law rule that a married woman could not make a will without her husband's consent. In the latter case, they would not entertain a suit by the woman's executor without a showing of the necessary consent, but they would not stop the church court from appointing him.

The only real problem in the area of decedent estates was what to do with a suit that could have been brought in the lay court by or against the decedent if he had been alive. The lay courts required an executor to answer for the decedent's debts out of the estate, and permitted him to recover property belonging to the decedent or debts owing to him. Statutes (1285 and 1357 respectively) imposed the same obligations on an administrator, and gave him the same rights. The church courts, regarding the estate and all proceedings concerning it as an indivisible whole, maintained a concurrent jurisdiction over claims of this kind. A couple of early Year Book cases talk about prohibiting such proceedings, but it does not appear that there was a clear rule on the point.

7. Correction of Morals and Redress of Private Wrongs – It was of course well understood that the correction of the personal morals of the faithful belonged to the church and not to the state.[59] Accordingly, the king's courts did not regularly deal with sexual offenses, except to the extent of denying dower to a widow who was living in adultery when her husband died. Some of the special jurisdictions moved farther in this direction than the courts at Westminster did. In those manors, for instance, where the lord had the right to a certain fee on the marriages of his tenants, he protected his right by imposing a fine of comparable amount on those who neglected the ceremony. In the case of a villein also, the manor courts attempted to make him stop committing fornication or adultery before the ecclesiastical courts got to him and put him to a penance that would interfere with the lord's right to his services or his goods.

There are also a few cases of the Star Chamber taking cognizance of cases of adultery or clandestine marriage. Some of these cases involved forcible abduction as a basis for lay jurisdiction, but not all of them did. Perhaps the remaining cases had elements of violence or influence in the background that prevented plaintiffs from seeking justice in the ecclesiastical courts.

Finally, in the City of London, and probably in other cities as well, there was a custom of jailing adulterers in secular proceedings. A Year Book case in 1485 contains a discussion of whether such a custom is reasonable, the matter being merely spiritual.[60] The judges were of the opinion (a curiously eighteenth-century opinion for fifteenth-century judges) that because adultery is a wrong to the husband and can lead to breaches of the peace it is reasonable for the lay authorities to punish it.

With these few exceptions the lay courts neither interfered nor competed with the jurisdiction of the church to deal with sexual lapses or other breaches of personal morality. Where, however, a moral fault with which the church was concerned also involved tangible damage to another person, the situation was more complicated. In cases of invasion of church premises, seizure of spiritual chattels, or personal violence to clerics, the lay courts allowed a concurrent jurisdiction — their own on account of the breach of the peace, that of the church on account of sacrilege. In theory, the lay courts claimed the exclusive right to award money damages in these cases, limiting the church courts to the imposition of penances. But in many cases the churchmen thought the payment of money was a suitable form of penance, or that a sinner ought to make restitution to those he had wronged before he could be absolved. The *Articuli Cleri* of 1315, provide by way of compromise that a church court may not impose a money penance, but may accept a money commutation of a corporal penance. Even this tenuous limitation was not always observed.[61]

For two kinds of private wrong that we would consider secular, the exclusive redress was with the ecclesiastical courts. One was defamation; the other usury. The lay courts were late in developing their own remedy for defamation, and they did not interfere with the ecclesiastical remedy except where the defamation complained of consisted of a resort to the processes of royal justice.[62] This exception was eventually to swallow up the rule, as we shall see in a later chapter, but for most of the Middle Ages it was applied straightforwardly enough. As for usury, there was no lay remedy outside the City of London until 1494, except in the case where the usurer was dead, and so beyond the reach of the church's moral correction.[63]

There were a few cases of violence in which the lay authorities had to take action, although only the church could afford complete relief. Cases where a woman was coerced into marriage or a cleric into resigning his benefice were the main examples.[64] In the former case Parliament enacted a series of statutes imposing criminal punishments and manipulating property rights in such a way as to make the crime less attractive. Once they even enacted a private bill allowing the victim to bring an appeal of rape even though the rapist had become her husband. But they did not undertake to do anything about the marriage itself. Similarly, in the other case, they allowed the displaced cleric to bring an action of trespass, but they did not attempt to put him back in his benefice.

Where lay and ecclesiastical courts dealt with the same matter from a different standpoint, or afforded a different remedy, there was a problem of the *res judicata* effect to be given by one court to the determinations of the other. The lay courts were generally content to let each system take its own course and reach its own result, whereas the churchmen — owing, it seems to me, to the ideological orientation of their legal system — found it very hard to accept that a given question could be decided one way in one court and another way in the other. In the *Articuli Cleri* of 1315 they made it a grievance that the judgment of a church court in such matters as assault on the clergy should not be treated as *res judicata* when the same matter came up before the lay court, but the king gave them no satisfaction.[65]

B. Misuse of Ecclesiastical Authority.

The persons and offices through which ecclesiastical jurisdiction was exercised were diverse and scattered, and responsible prelates had no adequate resources to keep them all under control. Accordingly, the royal authorities were often called on to protect people against injustice or extortion even where the church had power to act.

In the first place, there were a few cases of what we would call lack of due process — action taken against a person without giving him adequate notice or opportunity to be heard.[66] The lay courts would allow a collateral attack on such action where a case could be made for one under general principles of law. A deprivation of office without due process, for instance, could be complained of as a disseisin, or an imprisonment without due process as a trespass. By way of more direct relief, there was a statute of 1414 under which a defendant in a church court could stop the proceeding until he was given a copy of the pleading (the ''libel'') that he was supposed to answer.

There were also cases of failure of justice in the church courts — cases where the court failed through chicanery or malice to afford a litigant the relief to which he was entitled. Here, the litigant could sometimes persuade the king or the Council to send the ordinary a special order to do him justice.[67] I also have the impression he could seek relief in the Star Chamber after that court was established in 1487.

But the usual case involved not too little process but too much. The Parliament Rolls and the Sessions of the Peace are full of complaints about the actual or threatened use of ecclesiastical process for purposes of extortion.[68] A diocesan official cited a parson to appear before the bishop of another diocese, and so wearied his victim that he paid twenty shillings to be let go. The same official got two days' work a year from a couple of mowers by falsely accusing them of working on Sundays. A dean excommunicated a man, then took money for absolving him. A cleric sued for trespass in the court Christian, and had his adversary cited in three different places on the same day. The courts Christian compounded these mischiefs by issuing blank citations with authentic seals, so that there was no telling who would be cited next, or by whom.

In all these cases, the same remedies were available as would have been available against comparable misconduct by royal officials or abuse of royal process.[69] That is, civil actions of false imprisonment or trespass on the case could be brought, or, if there were two or more persons involved in the spurious proceeding, there could be a writ of conspiracy. Also — and this over the strenuous objection of the prelates — extortions of this kind were rountinely included among the matters to be inquired into and punished on the Eyre and the Commissions of the Peace.

Even where no extortion was intended, the laity were continually unhappy with the high cost of ecclesiastical proceedings, and with the necessity of going hither and thither about the country to have their cases heard. Their complaints were not effectively met until Henry VIII embarked on his confrontation with Rome. In the case of probate fees, one of the main grounds of complaint, a statute was made in 1415 giving a treble damage action to the victim of an overcharge, but this was to run only for a year, and it was not renewed.[70] The king answered most of the petitions in Parliament by offering the prelates one more chance to set their own house in order before he stepped in. The judges may have intervened occasionally without specific statutory warrant. The clergy complained of such interference in the Parliament of 1341, and the king was willing to restrain his judges only if the fees in question conformed to a fixed schedule. But I find no trace in the Year Books of the kind of intervention envisaged in this exchange.

C. Procedures.

1. Prohibition — Where the lay court was willing to intervene directly in an ecclesiastical proceeding, it generally did so by means of a writ of prohibition. This was in origin simply the king's command to a subject to refrain from an unlawful act. It was used to control the actions of lay officials as well as of churchmen, and other writs of similar origin were used for a variety of purposes. For this reason, the scope of the writ always seems a little fuzzy at the edges. Alongside the form writs issued out of Chancery in specific cases, there were always more general writs forbidding the world at large to bring certain kinds of proceeding.[71] In some cases, indeed, it was said that a certain statute, or the common law itself, had the effect of a prohibition.

The form writ out of Chancery was intended to stop a particular ecclesiastical proceeding at the behest of one aggrieved by it. The form books are a little stingy with examples, so it is hard to tell just how it was worded in most cases. For matters such as "debt or lay chattels not touching matrimony or testament," there were evidently rather succinct forms, reciting that such pleas belonged in the king's court, and forbidding them to be held or sued in the court Christian. For more unusual matters (for instance, a defamation action against a man on account of his tampering with a lay jury) there were more elaborate writs. These would have a recital of the salient facts and the governing principles of law (the "surmise") specifically tailored to the case in hand. In most cases where a prohibition was issued, there would be two writs, one telling the plaintiff in the church proceeding not to pursue it further; the other telling the judge not to entertain it.

There was no judicial proceeding leading up to the issuance of the writ. At one time it evidently issued automatically on request, or at least on an appropriate surmise. At some point, however, probably late in the fourteenth century, the chancellor developed a practice of looking at the libel (the plaintiff's first pleading) from the church court before deciding whether a prohibition ought to issue. The prelates requested in Parliament in 1377 that this be done,[72] and by 1414 it had become impossible to get a prohibition without showing a copy of the libel — one reason for the statute of that year requiring the defendant to be given a copy. Even when the chancellor looked at the libel, though, he did not make any judicial determination upon it. The issuance of the writ remained a preliminary step: the serious litigation was yet to come.

When the writ was issued, it would be served in the presence of witnesses. It was then up to the plaintiff and the judge in the church court to decide whether to stop the proceeding or not. They faced a substantial liability if they went ahead with it and were later determined to have acted improperly. On the other hand, there was considerable, albeit not unanimous, authority that if the case actually belonged to the church court, they were entitled to ignore the prohibition, and would have a good defense if they were proceeded against for doing so.

If either the plaintiff or the judge was not willing to take a chance on making good this defense, the ecclesiastical proceeding was temporarily at an end. There would have to be further word from the royal authorities before it could be reopened. In Bracton's time, the usual way to obtain this further word was for the judge to "consult" the king's justices, who would reply with a formal writ telling him whether or not he could hear the case. But the plaintiff had no right to initiate such a consultation: if the judge failed to do so, the plaintiff's only remedy was by a petition in Parliament. In 1290, a plaintiff brought such a petition. The royal authorities ordered it referred to the chancellor or the chief justice to see whether there was a remedy available in the king's courts in the particular case. If the answer was no, they were to write to the ecclesiastical judge and tell him to go ahead with it.[73]

The procedure adopted in this case formed the basis of an ordinance in 1290 and of the Statute of Consultations of 1296. These provided for issuing the so-called writ of consultation, available on the initiative of the plaintiff in the ecclesiastical proceeding. Thereafter we hear no more of consultations being initiated by the judge.

This writ was available from the chancellor or the chief justice, without resort to Parliament. The decision to issue it was evidently taken on the basis of the libel alone — that is all the statute requires the chancellor or the chief justice to look at, and there is no provision for a trial or an adversary hearing.[74]

If a consultation issued, or if the plaintiff and the judge decided to take a chance on going forward without it, the next move of the person who sued out the prohibition was to sue out an "attachment." He could do this whenever he chose, but he often waited for the end of the ecclesiastical proceeding, perhaps in the hope of defending it successfully. After an unfavorable result in the church court, he would have the judgment and consequent excommunication to complain of when he brought his attachment, as well as the proceeding itself. If he prevailed on the attachment, he could recover substantial damages, together with an order to the ordinary to lift his excommunication.[75]

The writ of attachment was in the *si te fecerit securum* form used for writs of trespass and the like. It commanded the sheriff, on receipt of proper security from the complaining party, to bind the party complained of to come before the court on such-and-such a day to answer why he had done such-and-such in violation of the king's prohibition. On the appointed day, the plaintiff (defendant in the ecclesiastical proceeding) would enter a "declaration" setting forth just what the defendant (plaintiff or judge in the ecclesiastical proceeding) had done, adding appropriate allegations about service of the prohibition on the defendant, and about damages.

The defendant, by way of answer, might deny that the prohibition had been served on him, might assert that he had stopped the proceeding when it was served, might claim that the case was a proper one for the church court to hear, or might show that a consultation had been issued. Any of these defenses had a good chance of prevailing, but none of them was absolutely sure.[76] The contention that the prohibition had not been served, or that the proceedings complained of took place before it was served, might be met with the argument that the law itself was a prohibition in a case such as this. The contention that the case was properly in the jurisdiction of the church court might be met with the argument that the defendant should have gotten a consultation before going on with it. Against the consultation, it might be objected that there were conditions that had not been met, that the subsequent proceedings were not in the form the consultation envisaged, or even that the consultation should not have been issued in the first place. The cases I have been able to find do not make it clear when these arguments were accepted and when they were not.

However these attachment cases were argued, the end result was usually for the defendant to deny the plaintiff's allegations in about the same terms in which the plaintiff had made them. Such a denial would bury, rather than resolve, the legal issues presented by the case.[77] If, for instance, a case went to a jury on the question of whether the defendant had sued a plea of lay chattels in the court Christian against the king's prohibition, the jury would have to decide any way it could whether it was a plea of lay chattels when the church court treated it as a plea of sacrilege, or whether it was sued against the prohibition if no prohibition was served. The jurors were permitted, but not encouraged, to pass these questions back to the court by means of a special verdict (a narrative recital of the relevant facts, as opposed to a general verdict, which simply answered yes or no to the issue submitted by the court.) Indeed, in many cases, the trial was by wager of law — the defendant taking his personal oath on the issue accompanied by twelve respectable citizens willing to swear they believed him. He could then of course let his conscience be his guide on whatever legal questions the issue presented. A petition in the Parliament of 1314-15 suggested that the court check defendant's oath against the record of the church proceeding — but nothing came of it.

These prohibition procedures would have worked better if they had not developed haphazardly out of the basically administrative process of ordering the king's subjects to behave themselves and punishing them for their failure to do so. As the process was routinized, and the complexity of the legal questions involved became more apparent, it became clear that in all fairness there should be a judicial determination of the issues before anyone exposed himself to the possibility of heavy penalties. The writ of consultation represented a step in that direction, but it was not altogether successful. The prelates (fairly well reconciled by the beginning of the fourteenth century to the fact that this process would go on in some form despite the canons against it) offered what seems a constructive suggestion — that the scope of the writ of consultation once issued be a matter for judicial determination in the ecclesiastical proceeding.[78] This the laity were not willing to concede. They always insisted that the king's law could be interpreted only in the king's courts; besides, they tended to mistrust the ecclesiastical judges. The best approach would have been for the lay courts to review the ecclesiastical proceeding after it was over, and set aside any improper action of the church court. For some reason, it was not until after the Reformation that they developed a procedure for doing this.[79]

Prohibition proceedings, despite their cumbersomeness, gave rise to very little complaint.[80] The Commons pointed out on one occasion that defendants in ecclesiastical debt suits were too poor to seek the prohibitions to which they were entitled, and the clergy for their part tried to get permission to impose spiritual censures on those who used the process for vexatious delays where the church in fact had jurisdiction, but the king did not find it necessary to give a remedy in either case. The ordinances adopted for the City of London in 1312 provided for the lay judges to impose damages or imprisonment where prohibition was maliciously used "in causes involving the correction of sin and others purely spiritual which do not in any way pertain to the lay court;" but we find no attempt to extend this rule to the rest of the country.

The most persistent complaint about the process concerned its ineffectiveness in cases involving tithes of wood.[81] The problem was the terminological overlap between "great wood," which the laity considered non-tithable because it had been growing so long as to be part of the soil rather than part of the annual increase, and *silva cedua,* or "cuttable wood," which the canonists considered tithable regardless of age. When a parson claimed tithes of *silva cedua,* his libel would say nothing about great wood. Since a consultation was awarded on the basis of the libel, the parson could always get one if his parishioner brought prohibition. The parishioner would then have to show in an attachment proceeding that the suit had really concerned great wood. The parson meanwhile would insist that only *silva cedua* was involved. Since both sides were telling the truth, who would win would depend on how the issue was framed for trial. The Year Book case I have found frames the issue in terms of great wood *vel non,* and therefore favors the parishioner. But the frequency with which the Commons sought some other remedy (always to no avail, incidentally) indicates that the general trend of these cases was not satisfactory to the laity. On the other hand, tithes of wood can hardly have loomed very large in the economic and social picture of the time. If they furnished, as they seem to have done, by far the most serious ground of complaint about the workings of the prohibition process, we will have to say that the process, for all its difficulties, was on the whole a success.

2. Praemunire and other Special Proceedings — The king, by his own letters patent, could have anyone who offended him — any *impugnator juris regis* — seized and kept in prison until he met whatever conditions the king saw fit to impose for letting him out.[82] This power was used freely against anyone who tried to excommunicate a royal official, and against anyone who brought papal process into the country to obstruct the king's courts in enforcing their judgments or the king's clerics in occupying their benefices. The first class of cases was no doubt considered too heinous to be left to the ordinary processes of prohibition and attachment; in the second class, it was probably too hard to serve the necessary writs on the wandering clerics who armed themselves with papal process and the variety of English prelates who might be called on to execute it.

In two classes of case, the king's power to move against users of papal process was routinized in the mid-fourteenth century (though only sporadically enforced until the fifteenth). These were dealt with respectively in the Statute of

Provisors of 1350 and the Statute of *Praemunire* of 1353.[83] The first dealt with benefices provided to by the pope. In addition to various remedies affecting the benefice itself, it enacted that any provisor (I do not know why the beneficiary of a provision is called a provisor instead of a provisee) who disturbed an incumbent was to be arrested along with his proctors and anyone else who assisted him. On conviction, he was to be imprisoned until he satisfied anyone who considered himself aggrieved, paid whatever fine the king wished to impose, and gave security against offending in the future.

The Statute of *Praemunire* applied to anyone who brought a proceeding outside the realm (i.e., in the Roman curia) which should have been brought in the king's courts, or one which was intended to defeat or impeach a judgment of the king's courts. Such a person was to be warned by the sheriff (the statute takes its name from the writ *Praemunire facias* directing the sheriff to do this) to be before the king and Council, or some designated judge on a specified day not less than two months off. Personal service was not required; the warning could be made wherever the offender had lands or possessions, or wherever the subject-matter of the case was found. If he did not come on the day fixed, he, his proctors, and everyone else involved in the execution of his papal process, would be outlawed, and their lands and goods forefeited to the king.

If he did come when he was supposed to, the statute is not explicit as to what his punishment was to be; it merely says he is to be justified by the law and to receive what the court shall award. If the case came before the king and Council, I suppose he could be subjected to whatever conditions they wished to impose. But if the case came before the regular courts, they probably dealt with it in about the same way as they did with an attachment.[84] The lawyers seem to have felt that the main purpose of the statute was not to punish offenders more severely, but to make them easier to catch.

It is hard to see how the wording of this statute, or of its various embellishments in later parliaments, could make it applicable to suits in ecclesiastical courts in England. In the fifteenth century, however, it was held to apply to such suits.[85] The advantage of using it in such a case was that it was available to someone who did not seek a prohibition until the ecclesiastical case against him was over, and so could not have an attachment.

The learning with which the common law courts surrounded the principle of rendering to Caesar the things that are Caesar's may seem needlessly technical at this remove. But after all, the cases did have to be decided, and it would be hard to find a non-technical way of deciding them. It is not easy to turn great principles into practical lines of distinction. It is all very well, for instance, to say that money belongs to Caesar and marriage belongs to God, but someone still has to sit down and decide how you are to collect the £10 I promised you for marrying my daughter.

Technicality, and especially procedural technicality, is the life blood of a legal system. It seems that the more important the underlying values are the more technical the problems are of giving them effect — witness the modern law on searches and seizures by the police. It seems also that the more limited the resources of a legal system are the more technical the problems are of using them to good effect. The king's judges in the cases we have been considering did have important values to deal with, and they had a system whose resources were drastically limited as compared with those of any modern system.

In making the decisions they had to make, they dealt with real problems and they worked with the tools at hand. There were faults in what they came up with, and I doubt if they themselves had any illusions about it. But I think they were honestly committed in principle to giving the ecclesiastical authorities the necessary scope to do their jobs. And I think they made the division of authority more competently and more responsibly than the canonists would have done.

III. Secular Policies — The Amendment of the Realm

The government's Erastian outlook was of course very far from calling for a general reduction of the church to an instrument of secular policy. But it did call for thinking secular policy just as good as any other policy. So the government did not have to feel inhibited about interfering with the church in aid of a particular secular policy when it seemed appropriate to do so. The churchmen, for their part, once they had put their theoretical objections on paper, were fairly pragmatic in their day to day response to being interfered with. The resulting adjustments were complicated, sometimes exquisitely so, but not usually on a high ideological plane.

The greatest complications came in three areas: law enforcement, where public policy had to be squared with the traditional immunities of the church; patronage, where the convolutions of medieval land tenure had to be dovetailed with those of ecclesiastical administration; and mortmain, where the law thwarted both the piety of magnates and the acquisitiveness of churchmen. These will all have to be taken up at some length. Other matters of foreign and domestic policy can be covered more briefly.

A. Law Enforcement.

The king naturally made it of the first order of importance to preserve his own peace, and the good order of his kingdom. To that end, he was willing to intervene in all kinds of matters that belonged theoretically to the church — quarrels between prelates over jurisdiction or protocol, town and gown disputes at the universities, the murder of one professed monk by another.[86] The church's privileges of sanctuary and clerical immunity raised problems in implementing this basic aim of secular government. No one was willing to abolish either of these outright, but neither could have been given full scope without a serious disruption of civil order. The lay authorities developed an ingenious set of procedures to recognize the privileges in principle while meeting the necessities of law enforcement in practice.

1. *Sanctuary* [87] — The general right of sanctuary protected an accused felon who took refuge in a consecrated church. Anyone who removed him would be subject to ecclesiastical censures, and a royal writ would issue to put him back. The procedure for dealing with him was initiated by the local populace, under the supervision of the coroner, surrounding the church so that he could not get out without submitting to arrest. It was provided in the *Articuli Cleri* of 1315 that those keeping watch would not camp on consecrated ground, would allow food and drink to be brought to the suspect, and would give him room enough to relieve himself without befouling the church.

The suspect then had forty days to make up his mind whether to come out, submit to arrest, and stand trial. If he chose not to do so, he had to ''abjure the realm,'' that is, swear to walk straight down the king's highway to a port assigned him, and there take ship for another country, and never come back to England. Once he took this oath, if he either left the highway or came back to England after taking ship, he could be hanged by the king's judges, or slain as an outlaw. In the *Articuli Cleri*, the prelates complained of such people being dragged or inveigled off the highway and so hanged — a practice the king deplored, but probably did nothing much to prevent.

At the end of forty days, if the suspect had neither abjured nor submitted to arrest, the people surrounding the church cut off his food supply. In aid of this treatment, the coroner could evidently have a writ out of Chancery forbidding anyone to assist the suspect; anyone who did so would then be guilty of contempt.

A convicted felon, as opposed to one under suspicion or indictment, did not get the benefit of all these procedures. If taken out of sanctuary, he had no claim to be put back, and if allowed to abjure the realm he could be taken off the highway and hanged in execution of the original sentence. I gather, though, he was still supposed to be starved out rather than seized in the church, so that anyone who took him out could be subjected to ecclesiastical censures despite the general principle of no censure for anything done in execution of the king's business.

Even this protection was not available to a man whose arrest was sought on civil process rather than for felony. Unless there was a service going on, the lay authorities could arrest him in church or even carry him out bodily, and the king would protect them against ecclesiastical censures. There were royal charters, however, generally dating from Anglo-Saxon or early Norman times, that gave certain churches, including Westminster Abbey, the privilege of protecting debtors as well as felons. Such a privilege was open to serious abuse. In 1378, the abbot of Westminster was accused in Parliament of running a virtual hotel for defaulting debtors. Living conditions were so comfortable that servants were moved to make off with their masters' goods and set themselves up with them in the abbey precincts. There was a considerable investigation, in the course of which a group of theologians and canonists informed the king that sanctuary should not by right extend to anyone not in danger of life and member. It was finally decided, however, that debtors who in good faith had not the wherewithal to pay could escape prison by taking sanctuary in the abbey.

2. *Criminal Proceedings against Clergy*[88] — Under the settlement that followed the martyrdom of St. Thomas Becket, a cleric could not be punished for felony in a secular court. The rule extended to felonies only, excluding high treason on the one hand and contempt on the other.[89] I have found no contemporary explanation for drawing the line in this particular way. Perhaps treason was excluded because the king had to protect his own authority, contempt because it did not involve loss of life or member.

The cleric accused of felony could claim his privilege at any stage of the proceeding, apparently even at the foot of the gallows.[90] If his claim was accepted, he was handed over to the ordinary. If he had not yet been tried, however, an inquest was taken to see whether he had committed the crime. If the inquest reported him guilty, or if he had been convicted on a regular trial before claiming his privilege, he was handed over *"tamquam convictus,"* and the ordinary had to imprison him pending further canonical proceedings. Since the church did not recognize the power of the lay court to try him, his status before the ordinary was that of a suspect, not a convict. If he cleared himself in the usual way by a canonical "purgation" — a ritual oath with compurgators — the ordinary would let him go.

The canon law imposed some obstacles to purgation, but not enough to satisfy the laity, who were convinced that serious criminals were regularly going free under the process, and who occasionally urged restrictive legislation in Parliament.[91] There are a few Year Book cases indicating that a cleric who had confessed his guilt in open court before being handed over to the ordinary could not thereafter be allowed purgation, but I doubt if the churchmen followed this rule. Since they insisted that the whole lay proceeding was *coram non judice,* they could not consistently have recognized anything that happened there as a judicial admission of guilt. It seems, however, that when the lay court issued a specific order not to admit a particular person to purgation, the churchmen reluctantly obeyed. These orders issued fairly often, and sometimes the ordinary had to post bond to secure his compliance. But I can find little on the criteria for issuing them.

While the offending cleric was in the ordinary's prison, his status before the secular law was ambiguous.[92] He was imprisoned on canonical, not secular, process, but if he escaped, or was improperly admitted to purgation, the ordinary was fined, as a sheriff or jailer was when a lay felon escaped.

Similarly, the cleric's lands and goods were taken into the king's hands like those of a lay felon, but, unlike those of the lay felon, they were given back if he made purgation, or when he died.

One who wanted to escape the gallows by this route had to begin by satisfying the lay court that he was a cleric. The main things the judges would consider in this regard were whether the ordinary was willing to claim him, whether he wore the clerical dress and tonsure, and whether he could read. Between the mid-fourteenth century and the mid-fifteenth, the criterion of dress and tonsure became less and less important, that of literacy more and more.

The part played by the ordinary in the decision is obscure.[93] It is clear he did more than simply examine his records to see whether the prisoner was incardinated in his diocese. Sometimes he or his representative brought a book for the prisoner to read out of, or otherwise examined him in the presence of the judges. Whatever he did, his decision in the prisoner's favor was not conlusive upon the court. In fact, he could be fined for claiming a man the court decided was not a cleric — in the fourteenth century, a man who did not wear the dress and tonsure, in the fifteenth, a man who could not read.

The ordinary's decision against the prisoner may have carried more weight, at least at one time. There are several mid-fourteenth century cases in which a genuine cleric was hanged because his conduct so annoyed the ordinary that the ordinary refused to claim him. But the situation became more complicated in the fifteenth century, when the clerical privilege was turning into the "benefit of clergy" of later centuries — a mitigation of the criminal law for cleric and layman alike.[94]

Gabel's definitive monograph shows that persons with all kinds of occupational designations — websters, coopers, chapmen, yeomen, and even laborers — began to be afforded the privilege toward the end of the fourteenth century. These men can hardly have been true clerics, though all showed they could read. If the court was minded to spare such persons whether or not they were clerics, it cannot have allowed the ordinary to stand in the way. In 1455, the archdeacon of London greatly embarrassed the judges of the King's Bench by refusing to claim a prisoner who read well enough, simply because the prisoner was not a cleric. The judges kept the prisoner in jail for two terms wondering what to do about him until a new and more cooperative archdeacon came in and took him away. Not long afterward, it was definitely established that if a convict could read the ordinary would be compelled to take him.

The one way a reader could lose his privilege was by being a *bigamus*.[95] You were a *bigamus* if you married more than once, or if you married a widow or other non-virgin. The Council of Lyons in 1274, following a long canonical tradition, excluded *bigami* from all clerical privileges, including this one. The lay authorities, who at that point were restricting the privilege all they could, were quick to embody this rule in the secular law. The question of who was a *bigamus* was tried by a lay jury until 1344, when a statute provided for certifying it to the ordinary like questions of marriage and legitimacy.

When benefit of clergy became generally available to laymen, this exception lost whatever justification it might originally have had. As early as 1376, the Commons were asking to have it abolished, pointing out that some men lived in lechery all their lives rather than take a chance on losing their right to escape the gallows. The king was not impressed, and the exception lingered until the time of Edward VI.

A statute passed in 1487 — without objection from the church as far as I can see — consummated a reform that had been sought for some decades by providing that no one not actually in holy orders — priest, deacon, or subdeacon — could have benefit of clergy more than once.[96] Provision was made for burning the non-ordained offender in the thumb to show that he had had his one time, and for establishing the orders of the ordained offender by showing documentary evidence to the ordinary. This statute initiated for the non-ordained person the transition to the version of benefit of clergy that saved so many post-Reformation criminals from the gallows until its final abolition in 1827.

3. Civil Proceedings against Clergy — While the church was theoretically opposed to making clerics answerable in lay courts, even in civil cases, the English prelates did not take a stand on the point. They even used their own processes at royal command to support the king's civil jurisdiction over their clergy.[97] When a bishop was ordered to bring one of his clerics before the king or a royal court, he would have the cleric cited, just as he would in an ecclesiastical proceeding. He would even excommunicate him if he did not obey the citation. The bishop would also, if so ordered, sequester any benefice the cleric in question might have in his diocese. The sequestration could be used as a form of mesne process, to coerce the cleric into coming to court. Or it might be used as a form of execution, the bishop using the revenues of the benefice to pay off the lay court's judgment against the incumbent.

There was evidently a period at the end of the thirteenth century when the lay authorities expected more of these processes than they were able to accomplish, for they actually penalized the bishop if his cleric failed to show up in court. The bishops pointed out that they had no magical powers over a cleric who did not mind being sequestered or excommunicated, and that it was hardly fair to blame them for being defied. Presumably they made their point, for by the beginning of the fourteenth century they had ceased to complain.

These processes were only supplementary to those used against clergy and laity alike. A cleric could be arrested or outlawed on civil process, or imprisoned for debt, just as anyone else could.[98] The prelates thought of proposing that a cleric, once arrested in this way, be handed over to the ordinary for custody, but I do not find that the proposal was ever formally made. If it had been, the royal authorities would no doubt have turned it down. They must have kept debtors a good deal less comfortably than the ordinaries kept clerical offenders, for there is a case of a cleric trying to avoid a debtor's prison by pleading guilty to a trumped-up felony charge and having the ordinary imprison him as a convict.

Attachments and executions against a man's land could be used to reach a cleric who held "lay fee" — that is, land he had bought or inherited, as distinguished from the temporalities of his benefice or church. The latter could of course be reached by sending the bishop a writ to sequester the benefice, but this would only be done after the sheriff reported that the incumbent had no lay fee. In any event, church lands were not to be directly invaded by royal officials.[99]

Civil processes for reaching chattels were subject to similar rules.[100] As a general matter, sheriffs and bailiffs were not supposed to come onto church land to levy execution, or to take distresses (distress is a form of petty harassment through seizure of chattels; it played a great part in medieval mesne process, and is used for some purposes even today). Exceptions were made in 1315 for lands newly purchased by the church, and in 1341 for goods belonging to laymen who had hidden them on church land to escape the law. But the parson's furniture in his rectory, or the sheep on his traditional glebe land, continued immune. Certain chattels that he held in the right of his church, for instance, the horse he rode on the king's highway, were immune wherever they were found. So were all spiritual chattels — severed tithes as well as chalices, prayer, books and the like.

B. Patronage Rights.

As we saw in the last volume the rights of the patron of a church were reduced for all practical purposes by the beginning of the thirteenth century to that of presenting to the ordinary a fit cleric to occupy the church. Given the need of the upper and middle classes to provide for younger sons, retainers, and bureaucratic staffs, this one right was an extremely valuable one,[101] and one productive of a great deal of litigation in the king's courts.

The "advowson" or right to present was treated as nearly as possible like an interest in land. It was conveyed and inherited like land, and, to a large extent, litigated over like land.[102] The analogy raised problems. You can serve a writ in a land case by nailing it up on the land; can you serve one in an advowson case by nailing it up in the church? No, it was decided, because while the advowson may be a piece of real property, it is something more subtle than the physical church. You claim a statutory forfeiture of land by taking possession of it. But the only way you can take possession of an advowson is by presenting a cleric to the ordinary when the church falls vacant. How can you claim a forfeiture of an advowson if the church is not vacant at the time? This was debated but not resolved.

To be sure, many advowsons were "appurtenant" to other landed estates, so that possession of the one was possession of the other. This must at one time have been the case in most places — the village squire being patron of the village church. But it was fairly easy to convey real property, and the people who could use advowsons were not always the same people who could use land. Many advowsons, therefore, came to be "severed," and held "in gross." It was these that raised the problems of possession.

Severance might raise other problems as well. Here is a case, more difficult, perhaps, than the run of advowson cases, but suitable to put one in the right frame of mind for considering this thorny subject: A man dies owning a manor with an advowson appurtenant. One-third of the whole estate is assigned to the widow for life as dower. Her third of the advowson consists of the right to make every third presentment that comes up. The man's son inherits the rest of the estate, including the other two-thirds of the advowson. He keeps the land, but sells his share of the advowson to a stranger. The stranger makes the next two presentments. By the time the third vacancy comes up, the widow is dead, and her dower land has fallen back into the main estate. The stranger now wants to make the third presentment: he argues that the widow's life interest in her third of the advowson fell into his two-thirds on her death. But the court holds the presentment belongs to the son. His conveyance severed his two-thirds of the advowson from the land, but the widow's third remained appurtenant. Hence, on her death, it fell into the rest of the land, not into the rest of the advowson.[103]

So much for what the lay courts understood an advowson to be. Now let us see how they went about determining who was to have it.

1. Processes[104] — A typical case would begin when the parish church of St. A fell vacant, and B and C each presented to the bishop a cleric to occupy it. The bishop would learn from his routine inquiries that the benefice was "litigious" and would proceed no further on either presentment until the lay court had resolved the dipute. If he failed to suspend proceedings, he could be served with a writ of *ne admittas*, ordering him to keep the benefice open, and could be held liable in an action of *quare incumbravit* if he failed to do so.

When the bishop suspended proceedings, either party could complain that the other had "disturbed" him in his enjoyment of the advowson, and could bring an action to vindicate his rights. If the first one to sue was too slow in prosecuting his case, the other could bring an action of his own.[105] Haste was important, for (as against any patron except the king) the bishop did not have to keep the benefice vacant for more than six months. At the end of that time, if he had not been told which presentment to accept, he could declare a "lapse" and put in his own man, just as if he had received no presentment at all.

Two forms of action were available to the rival claimants: the assize of darrein presentment, and the action of *quare impedit*. Both were analogous to possessory remedies for land. Their main thrust was to determine who had made the last presentment to the benefice (and therfore was seised of the advowson), so that he or his heir might make this one. Darrein presentment was an assize; that is, the jurors stood waiting while the lawyers argued over the pleadings and framed the issues. *Quare impedit* was a full-dress litigation, in which the jurors were not sent for till after the issues were framed. The more summary remedy was slightly more limited in scope. If you had some reason why the person who properly made the last presentment should not make this one, you could defend against an assize of darrein presentment, but you could not bring it. For a grantee against his grantor, a remainderman against the heir of a life tenant, etc., the remedy had to be in *quare impedit*.

The Statute of Westminster II (1285) provided that if a ward had lost the last presentment through the negligence of his guardian, a wife through that of her husband, or the holder of a reversionary interest through that of the person in possession, a possessory action could be based on the last presentment before the loss. Otherwise neither darrein presentment nor *quare impedit* could be based on any presentment but the last. To go farther back, a writ of right of advowson had to be used. This was a real action. You prevailed in it by showing an earlier presentment than your opponent could show, and proving that that presentment was under color of a fee simple estate that had properly descended to you. The proceeding was subject to the same elaborate and archaic procedures — including trial by battle — that hampered other writs of right. So everyone avoided it if he could.

The possessory actions, darrein presentment and *quare impedit*, could not be used unless the benefice was vacant, except that by statute (1285) you had six months to bring suit against a rival whose presentee had just been put in. The plea that the benefice was full more than six months before the writ was purchased (called a plea of "plenarty") was a good affirmative defense. It was sent to the bishop for trial like a question of marriage or bastardy. If the bishop was a party, it was sent to the metropolitan; if the metropolitan was a party, it was tried by the jury with the rest of the case.

Plenarty was not a defense to a writ of right of advowson; the writ could be brought any time. Of course, the successful party could not be given "possession" of the advowson until the next vacancy. At that time if he was disturbed in making a presentment, he could use his judgment to support a proceeding in *quare impedit*. If he failed to consummate his victory at the first vacancy, he lost the benefit of it. A successful presentment by someone else was regarded as disseising him of the advowson, and he had to bring a new writ of right to recover it.

What you recovered in a possessory action was damages amounting to six months' income of the benefice, plus a writ to the bishop ordering him to admit your presentee notwithstanding your opponent's claim. If the bishop did not comply, he was liable for damages in an action of *quare non admisit*. But this form of judgment settled the case only between the parties. If a third person had made a presentment, the benefice was still litigious, and the bishop still did not have to admit anyone.

In any event, if the benefice remained vacant for six months without a final decision as to who was to present to it, the bishop could "collate" — i.e., put in his own man. Once he did so, the patron's right was lost for that time. The litigation, however, could still proceed to judgment, and the winner would be awarded damages equal to two years' income of the benefice. Presumably, he could also use the judgment to support a possessory proceeding when the next vacancy occurred.[106]

2. Problems of Ecclesiastical Authority — If the hierarchy had adopted more ambitious administrative goals — for instance, a rational distribution of church property and revenues — they might have clashed seriously with the zeal of the lay courts for protecting the rights of the patron and the value of the benefice in his gift. But the rudimentary goals they in fact set themselves — keeping benefices filled with men possessing the minimum qualifications to occupy them — were adequately recognized, at least in theory, by the lay courts. The bishop did not have to put a man into a benefice if he was not qualified. Except in a few cases, he did not have to put him in if, under the applicable canon law, the benefice was already occupied. Nor did he have to leave the benefice vacant for more than six months, whatever the state of the patronage rights.

In practice, though, there were problems, mostly procedural. The legal systems of church and state operated with a good deal of mutual mistrust, and certainly without anyone making much effort to harmonize their results. As a consequence, there were a number of situations in which the bishop could get into trouble with the lay courts simply by doing his canonical job.

In the normal course, when a bishop received a presentment, he would order a set of inquiries to answer three questions: (1) whether the person making the presentment was entitled to do so, (2) whether the benefice was vacant, and (3) whether the presentee was qualified. If the bishop received one and only one presentment to a benefice, made these inquiries, and found everything in order, and if he had not been served with a writ of *ne admittas*, he was fairly safe in putting the presentee in.[107] If an adverse claimant to the patronage showed up after the transaction was complete, he might have remedies against the man who made the first presentment, but he had none against the bishop. In an action of *quare impedit*, it would be held that the bishop had not disturbed the claimant because the regular exercise of ordinary jurisdiction could not be a disturbance. In *quare incumbravit*, it would be held that the bishop was entitled to encumber the benefice, because the canonical requirements had been met and he had no notice of an adverse claim. In *quare non admisit,* it would be held that the bishop did not have to admit the second presentee because the benefice was already full with the first one.

So far so good. But suppose the bishop received two presentments at the same time. He had two alternatives, and was not quite safe in pursuing either.[108] One was to hold both presentments in abeyance until the lay court decided which he should accept, or until the benefice had been vacant six months and he could fill it himself because of the lapse. The other was to mount the customary inquiries on both presentments, and confer the benefice on the man whose patron appeared to have the better right. The best Year Book authority supported the bishop in adopting the first alternative: he need not put any presentee into a litigious benefice. But one case seemed to require the second alternative: a bishop who refused a presentee would be liable in *quare impedit* for disturbing the patron unless he could show that he had acted canonically on the presentment. To act canonically on both presentments, the bishop had not only to make inquiries; he had to confer the benefice in accordance with the result. But if he conferred the benefice with notice of an adverse claim, he was open to liability in *quare incumbravit* should the lay court decide he had put in the wrong man. The fact that he had followed proper canonical procedures would probably not help him in such a case: it was for the lay courts, not the churchmen, to determine who was patron of a benefice.

The bishop was still more open to liability if he received a single presentment, and his inquiries showed that the one making it had no right to do so. If he disregarded his own processes and put in the presentee, he would be liable in *quare impedit* if the rightful patron showed up within six months. He had no defense because he had not acted canonically. But if he refused the presentment, he would be liable to the person who made it should the latter persuade the lay court that he was the true patron.[109] Again, the bishop could not use the result of his inquiries to prevent the lay court from making an independent determination of who was patron. And this time, he could not offer the litigiousness of the benefice as an excuse, because only one presentment had been made.

There were somewhat similar pitfalls for a bishop in cases of plenarty — where the benefice presented to was already full. In the first place, there were certain cases, as we shall see, where the lay courts held that a successful patronage claimant was entitled to have his rival's presentee ousted and his own put in. In such cases, the bishop was expected to bring this result about in the teeth of the canonical principles protecting the first incumbent. Nor, for the most part, did the lay courts find it necessary to square matters with his ecclesiastical superior for him when they compelled him to do this.[110]

But the bishop's most serious problem with plenarty was in the trial of it.[111]

As we have seen, if A sued B in *quare impedit,* and B alleged plenarty as a defense, the question would be sent to the bishop for trial. But if A simply made a presentment and the bishop turned it down because the benefice was full, A would not sue B, he would sue the bishop. Then the bishop could not try the question of plenarty because that would make him judge in his own case. The metropolitan would have to try it, or, if the metropolitan was a party, the jury. If they disagreed with the bishop's officials, the bishop would be liable as a disturber.

The same unfortunate application of the rule *nemo judex in causa sua* plagued the bishops in dealing with the fitness of presentees.[112] The lay courts allowed the bishop a good deal of latitude in refusing an unfit man, and in deciding whether or not a man was unfit. The bishop might set an examination, and do nothing further about the presentment if the presentee did not appear. He could have an official examine the presentee, and still fail him after the official passed him. In the case of an ecclesiastical patron, he could even declare a lapse when a presentee was unfit, without giving the patron a second chance. But the one thing he could not do was assert his own determination of unfitness as a defense in *quare impedit* or *quare non admisit*, as that would make him judge in his own case. Rather, he had to allege that the presentee was in fact unfit, and hope that the metropolitan or the jury would agree with him.

The bishop's power to fill benefices for lapse suffered from a tendency to treat it as a property right of the bishop rather than an administrative expedient.[113] It passed to the king during a vacancy of the see. And if the king was the patron responsible for the lapse, the bishop could not take advantage of it because prescriptive rights are not good against the king. These restrictions would have been more serious if the bishop had been seriously concerned with putting people into the benefices to do the work. Actually, he used his powers to support the same kind of bureaucrats the king and other lay patrons supported. Indeed, some bishops were not above creating artificial delays on presentments in order to avail themselves of additional lapses for their staffs.

3. Protection of the Incumbent — The disposition of patronage rights by the lay courts was not supposed to affect the position of a cleric in canonical possession of a benefice. What with one thing and another, however, a substantial body of cases built up in which the incumbent could in fact be ousted.[114] In the first place, if he had been in less than six months, you could bring suit against the patron who presented him, and have him put out if you won. Or, if you met the conditions for an action of *quare incumbravit*, you could get an order to the bishop to disencumber the benefice. Also, the lay court did not recognize a man's tenure of a benefice until he was "inducted" or placed in physical possession by the archdeacon, whereas his canonical right was complete when he was "instituted" or accepted by the ordinary. If something came up (such as the passing of the advowson into the king's hands) after institution but before induction, his tenure might be in doubt.

If the king had an adverse claim to the patronage, the incumbent was always in trouble.[115] If he had been put in by the ordinary for lapse, he was clearly out of luck: as we saw, lapse was treated as a prescriptive right and the king was not bound by it. It is not quite so clear that the king could displace an incumbent who was in by a regular presentment, but the cases indicate that he could — the theory being that the protection of an incumbent after six months was a kind of prescriptive right that did not accrue against the king. The king's claims in cases of this kind were helped along also by the reluctance of the bishops to thwart him. There were several complaints in Parliament of bishops ousting incumbents without any kind of process in order to put in royal presentees.

In other cases the incumbent suffered because of lack of standing in a proceeding that affected his rights.[116] For instance, where the bishop filled a benefice for lapse and was then sued by the patron, if he disclaimed any interest in the patronage, and forgot to plead that he had filled the benefice on account of the lapse, he would be ordered to put in the plaintiff's presentee, and the incumbent would be ousted. There was nothing the incumbent could do to defend his own interest in the proceeding.

The standing problem became more serious when a practice developed of naming the incumbent as co-defendant in an action of *quare impedit*. A successful plaintiff in *quare impedit* recovered a writ ordering the bishop to admit his presentee notwithstanding the defendant's claim, and the bishop evidently interpreted this to mean notwithstanding his claim to the incumbency. The incumbent-defendant would have liked to avoid this result by pleading plenarty, or, failing that, by showing that the plaintiff was not the true patron. But it was argued that he had no standing to do either. Since the litigation was over patronage, only a person claiming the patronage could be heard to offer a plea. It is not clear how far this reasoning was accepted.

A 1350 statute, by expressly authorizing the incumbent to plead against the king in a case of this kind, made his right to plead against a private person even more debatable than it was before. Was the statute limited to proceedings brought by the king because the framers had not wanted such a plea to be accepted in a proceeding by a private person? Or was it because in a proceeding by a private person the incumbent already had the right to plead and did not need the help of the statute? Again, the cases are divided.

To be sure, if the patron who presented the incumbent made a successful defense in the case, the incumbent had nothing to worry about. But the patron might not be as interested in the case as the incumbent was. Or the incumbent might have been put in through a papal provision or a lapse, and have no patron to litigate for him.

The bishop had better luck than the incumbent in establishing his standing to raise relevant issues without claiming the advowson for himself. If he was a party to the proceeding, he could protect the incumbent if he chose.[117] But more often he was not a party, and came into the picture only when a writ issued ordering him to execute the judgment. Here, it was argued that his action was merely ministerial, like that of a sheriff. It followed that he could raise no objection to complying with the writ, and that he had no defense in the action of *quare non admisit* that would be brought against him if he failed to do so. The 1350 statute was evidently supposed to mitigate this situation, but I have not found enough *quare non admisit* cases after 1350 to know how it worked.

There was an action in the church courts for what was called spoliation that served ousted incumbents in some cases.[118] As far as the church courts were concerned, it lay whenever the rightful incumbent was put out of a benefice. But the lay courts restricted its use to cases where the ouster was by a colorable act of ecclesiastical authority, and where the right of patronage was not in issue. Where there was no intervention of ecclesiastical authority, the case was one of trespass for the royal courts; where the right of patronage was in issue, some kind of advowson proceeding should be used.

The spoliation action was used with some regularity in cases where the incumbent was disputing with his own patron over whether the benefice was vacant or not. Suppose, for instance, the parson of St. A took a new benefice. Unless he had a dispensation to hold two benefices at once (pluralism), St. A would become vacant immediately by operation of the canon law, and the patron could make a new presentment. If the bishop instituted the new presentee, whether on his own initiative or on compulsion from the lay courts (as would happen if he rejected the presentee and was not allowed to plead plenarty in the ensuing *quare impedit* proceeding), the old parson could bring a spoliation action, and recover if his dispensation was good.

But the lay courts did not allow the spoliation action to be a general substitute for a plea of plenarty in a lay proceeding. If A's presentee was ousted in favor of B's presentee, he could not bring a spoliation action to get back in. Even though A's presentee was relying solely on his canonical incumbency, and not claiming that A had any title to the advowson, the lay courts would regard the case as involving the advowson, and would issue writs of prohibition to stop it.[119]

The incumbent, in the rather common case where his danger came from a presentment by the king, had a further opportunity to save himself by resorting directly to the king and seeking either a charter confirming his incumbency or a revocation of the new presentment.[120] The latter was evidently the safer. The lay courts did allow royal charters to affect the course of their proceedings, but they did not look on them with favor, and were apt to interpret them as strictly as they could.

The revocation of a presentment, on the other hand, was generally effective, and was easy to come by if the king found on investigation that he had no right to present. By the mid-fourteenth century, a routine system was developed for handling requests for such revocations. The request would be sent into Chancery, where the king's presentee would be sent for to show cause why the presentment should not be revoked. If he had no cause to show, the chancellor would have the presentment revoked. As the king's presentee had probably been the one who brought the benefice to the king's attention in the first place, it was fair enough to impose on him the burden of maintaining the king's right.

A statute enacted in 1389 provided that any incumbent ousted by a royal presentee without due process could sue to get his benefice back.[121] It is not clear from the wording of the statute whether this proceeding for revocation of the presentment was contemplated, or a spoliation proceeding in the ecclesiastical court, or both. I suspect it was both, as once the new presentee was inducted it is hard to see how a revocation of the presentment would get him out.

In any event, the statute applied only to an expulsion without due process. If the incumbent lost a *quare impedit* proceeding, or failed to defend it, the statute would not help him.

4. Appropriation, Election, etc. — Appropriation, as we saw in the last volume, was a process whereby a religious house, cathedral chapter, or other establishment was allowed to occupy a benefice in its corporate capacity. Canonically, the appropriator was both patron and incumbent; in patronage litigation, it was apt to be given the worst of both capacities. Suppose, for instance, a stranger presented a cleric to occupy the benefice, and the bishop was persuaded to put him in. The appropriator had no possessory action in the lay court to stop this presentment and admission from going forward. To bring such an action, it would have to show that it had made a presentment and had been disturbed, whereas it had not made a presentment, and could not do so without losing the benefit of the appropriation.[122]

Nor (and this was the subject of a long debate, first in Chancery, and then before all the judges in the Exchequer Chamber) could the appropriator bring an ecclesiastical action for spoliation. While there was an argument that only the incumbency was in issue — that was all the appropriator was asking for — the successful presentment had disseised it of the advowson, so the judges thought it was claiming that also. Accordingly, the appropriator had to bring a writ of right of advowson first — and then probably a spoliation action as well, since the writ of right did not affect the incumbency.

But suppose on the other hand the bishop rejected the stranger's presentment, and the stranger brought *quare impedit* against the appropriator.[123] The obvious defense, a plea of plenarty, was one the courts were reluctant to accept. The difficulty was that the issue of plenarty would be sent to the bishop for trial instead of being passed on by a jury. In the ordinary case, a finding of plenarty by the bishop would put off consideration of the plaintiff's claim to the advowson only till the next vacancy. But where the plenarty was based on an appropriation, it was perpetual, and the claim to the advowson would never be tried in a lay court at all. So the appropriator might be questioned very closely on its authority for the appropriation, or even be made to deny the prior presentment on which the plaintiff relied.

On the whole, then, appropriators had difficult procedural hurdles to surmount if they were to be sure of keeping what they had. As they were not favorites of either bishops or lay judges, no one felt too sorry about this burden on them. As we have seen, it did not do much to prevent their progress throughout the Middle Ages in reducing the benefices of England to possession.

Another case that presented peculiar difficulties was that in which one side or the other claimed that a benefice was elective.[124] The courts were not willing to treat the right of election as an advowson belonging to the electors; hence, the electors could not bring a patronage proceeding, and had trouble resisting one brought by someone else. If the bishop took their part, they could sometimes prevail on the theory that being elected was a condition precedent to occupying the benefice, but even this was not always sure.

Comparable problems were raised by certain other interests in churches. A makes a presentment to the church of B. You claim that B is not a church, but a chapelry of C, and that you and your ancestors have been presenting chaplains to it for years. But you cannot make the form allegation that your presentees have been instituted and inducted, as that would turn the chapelry into a church. How do you plead your case? (You attack the plaintiff's previous presentment. It seems you are out of luck as regards your own presentments, even if they are later than his.)[125] The king makes a presentment to the vicarage of D. The bishop determines that there is no such vicarage. What is he to do? (Get the king to revoke the presentment.)[126]

C. Mortmain.

A 1279 statute, successor of earlier legislation that had failed of enforcement, forbade any kind of conveyance without a license whereby lands or estates might come into mortmain. Mortmain, or "dead hand," meant simply the hand of a corporation, body politic, or officeholder enjoying perpetual succession — an artificial entity that could not die.[127] The idea was evidently that certain kinds of feudal services would be lost if land fell into the hands of someone who could not be expected to pass it on to his heirs, or perhaps die without heirs and leave his land to escheat.

I cannot see the law as an anticlerical measure. The freedom with which licenses were granted shows that there was no general purpose of limiting church endowments. Furthermore, by the end of the fourteenth century secular bodies politic (city corporations and the like) were expressly subjected to the same rule as church bodies. Conversely, a grant to a man and his heirs for the purpose of having masses said (what we would call today a religious trust) was not within the law unless some body with perpetual succession had the right to enforce the grant.

But whatever the intent of the law, the prelates felt themselves wronged by it.[128] They were accused of believing that they might in good conscience resort to bribery and chicanery to evade its operation — and indeed, they did resort to such things from time to time. If there had to be such a law, they would have liked to have an exception made where there was adequate provision for keeping up the feudal services due from the land. They were not able to get such an exception put into the law, but licenses were evidently granted pretty much in accordance with the criteria they had in mind.

All manner of conveyances and all manner of interests in land were included within the ambit of the act.[129] An advowson, a rentcharge, or the release of one, the imposition on a tenant of a duty to have his corn ground at his lord's mill — all were included. But a pension, as a personal charge, was not included, even though it was a perpetual benefit to a prelate and his successors.

The fact that an interest was already in mortmain did not prevent the act being applied to it —[130] even though the statutory language was "come into mortmain." An exchange of lands between two religious houses was a violation. So was a transfer between a bishop and his chapter or between a chapter and one of its prebendaries. A chapter even violated the act by endowing a chaplain to celebrate in their own cathedral.

It was a transfer of possession rather than a conveyance as such that brought the act into operation.[131] So where devisable land was devised in mortmain, but the heir took possession in violation of the will, it was held that the act did not apply. Conversely, where a bishop made two presentments to a benefice in the gift of a layman, it was held that the advowson had fallen into mortmain, even though there was no evidence that the patron had consented to being thus disseised of it. Presumably, therefore, the act would apply where a churchman disseised a landowner, but not where he bought land and failed to take possession.

Since the act referred to a "scheme or device," it did not apply where land devolved upon a churchman by operation of law.[132] If land escheated to a churchman, or was forfeited to him for failure to render feudal dues, or even forfeited under the Mortmain Act itself (where a layman held lands of a bishop, say, and granted them to an abbot), he could take possession without worrying about the act. The same was true where his villein inherited land from free relatives (generally, a lord could take over any land his villein owned). But it was not true where his villein bought the land — that might be part of a scheme or device.

When the statute was violated, the king or other chief lord had a year to take possession of the land or interest that had been transferred. If the chief lord failed, his chief lord had six months after the year was up, and so on up the line to the king, who could enter "immediately" *(statim)* after the time was up. If no one entered in the prescribed time, the transfer was presumably successful.[133]

This right of entry was the only sanction for violation of the act. It did not avail a litigant in a land case to show that the conveyance on which his opponent relied brought the land into mortmain. Nor could an heir avoid a devise or a villein keep land from his lord on this ground. In all these cases, the law would simply take its course, and the king or chief lord would then take over if the resulting state of affairs was within the statute.[134]

This manner of applying the act invited collusive lawsuits. If you wanted to convey your land to a neighboring abbot, you had only to let him sue you for it, then make a default, and the court would award it to him. The first people to try this (1283) got away with it: the justices of the Common Pleas wanted to stop them, but were told to let the law take its course. In the Statute of Westminster II (1285), however, provision was made for taking a verdict in every such case to see if the churchman was really entitled to the land.[135] If he was not, the king or chief lord was given possession, just as if there had been a conveyance in mortmain. The courts extended this statute from possessory actions to other actions affecting the title to land (e.g., where the defendant was established as the plaintiff's feudal tenant, or where he was required to make good a warranty of title by rendering lands of equal valve), and from default cases to other cases where the merits were not fully litigated (e.g., where the defendant admitted the plaintiff's case, or where he took issue on a collateral matter and lost).

As far as I can see, the statute served its purpose. The various complaints in Parliament about evasion of the mortmain laws do not mention collusive lawsuits, and it is hard to see any loopholes in the statute as administered. The numerous Year Book cases on whether a verdict shall be taken or not seem to involve simply a routine practice that the plaintiff hoped to avoid because it delayed his case.

In the fourteenth century the devices used for evading the mortmain laws were generally informal. A churchyard would be enlarged simply by moving the boundary with the acquiescence of a neighbor. Or a strawman would be enfeoffed of a piece of land, and would turn the rents and profits over to a churchman. Perhaps the rights of the church were enforceable in the ecclesiastical courts in these cases, but more probably the persons involved simply lived up to their undertakings without external coercion. In any event, informal arrangements of this kind were brought under the mortmain laws by a statute of 1391.[136]

For those who wished to comply with the law, licenses were freely available, though rather expensive — fees ranged from six months' to over three years' proceeds of the lands involved.[137] The legal basis for the king's granting these licenses is obscure; there is no provision for it in the statute. Some authors have suggested that the king claimed a general power to dispense from statutes, and used it here, but I think it more likely that his mortmain licenses were simply waivers of his own right to take possession of the land for violation of the statute — comparable to his acceptance of a fine in lieu of a forfeiture after the event. It does not appear that a mesne lord (i.e., a feudal lord between the grantor and the king) was bound by the license, as he would have been if it dispensed from the operation of the statute.

The grant of a license was proceeded by an inquest *ad quod damnum*, taken before the local escheator in response to a royal writ. The inquest determined what loss of services or other damage would befall the king or anyone else if the requested license was granted. Fitzherbert indicates that the same procedure was used if the king wished to make a grant of his own lands to a religious house, if a private person wished to give lands to the king for the purpose of his making such a grant, or if the king wished to accept a fine in lieu of a forefeiture for lands already in mortmain.[138] I have found no indication of what was customarily done with the result of such an inquest after it was taken. Perhaps some arrangement was required to see that the services were kept up; perhaps the damage to the king entered into the fee exacted by him for the license.

A statute of 1292 provided that mortmain licenses would not be issued except on petitions presented in Parliament (rather than in Chancery), and then only on a showing that the churchmen involved could not live without the additional endowments they asked for.[140] There is no indication that this statute was put into effect. Certainly, the number of petitions recorded in the Parliament Rolls does not come anywhere near the number of licenses recorded in the Patent Rolls. As for poverty, there may have been some perfunctory showing required, but there is nothing of it in the records. In fact, it would seem that medieval religious houses habitually lived beyond their means, so that it was always possible to make a showing that there was not enough to live on.

D. Foreign Relations.

During the fourteenth century, there arose in England a national consciousness inimical both to the export of money abroad and to the influence of foreigners at home. The result was a series of inroads on the cosmopolitan character of the church.

The main sources of financial drain were the revenues of benefices whose incumbents lived abroad, the tribute levied on English religious by foreign superiors or motherhouses, and the expenses of doing business with the papal curia.[141] The first of these was dealt with at least as early as 1298, when the king began sequestering the benefices of nonresident aliens. This practice became routine with the outbreak of the Hundred Years War. The Commons would have liked to extend it to the benefices of Englishmen living abroad, but the royal authorities evidently thought this was going too far.

The attack on foreign superiors and motherhouses began in 1298 also, when Edward I tried to stop the English Cistercians from attending the general chapter of their order at Citeaux, and to get them to give him the money they saved by staying home. Then, in 1307, a statute was enacted forbidding all English religious to carry or send payments to superiors or motherhouses abroad, and forbidding foreign superiors to collect anything beyond their expenses when they came to visit. The statute did not apply to revenues held by a foreign community directly, rather than through a daughterhouse. These were evidently seized a little later, along with the daughterhouses themselves (the so-called "alien priories") in connection with the war effort against France. The foreigners made some effort to recover their money by suing in the papal court, where, of course, the seizures by the English lay authorities were not recognized. Such suits were complained of in Parliament in 1373, with no clear result. Presumably they became impossible during the years 1378-1414, when England and France had different popes.

Despite the dim view the government took of papal taxation, they seem to have made no attempt to prevent the incurring of expenses at the curia. A good deal was done, however, to prevent the export of gold and silver to make the payments. A scheme was developed during the latter half of the fourteenth century, and made statutory in 1390, whereby money for use in Rome was procured through letters of exchange purchased from merchants who had to buy English goods with the proceeds.[142]

The work of putting aliens physically out of the English church went a good deal more slowly than that of keeping the money at home.[143] The Commons made a comprehensive proposal for the purpose in 1346, but the king and the great men, with more international concerns, were not enthusiastic in their response. It was not until the last quarter of the fourteenth century that serious measures were finally taken against foreigners as such.

The first such measure, adopted in 1377, provided that alien religious and clergy, except those with life tenure of offices or benefices, and security for their good behavior, were to leave the country for the duration of the war. In 1383, a statute was enacted forbidding aliens to take new benefices, under penalty of *praemunire*. This statute was expressly made applicable to those who occupied their benefices in person (supplementing a 1379 statute that had imposed the same penalties on people who collected revenues for nonresident aliens), and the king undertook not to grant exemptions except to persons to whom he was especially beholden for some cause. Then in 1403-4, provision was made for the permanent expulsion of foreign religious, and their replacement by Englishmen. Exceptions were made for those too infirm to travel, and for those with life tenure of their offices, but these too were to be replaced by Englishmen when they died.

As far as I can see, the prelates made no objection to any of these measures for nationalizing the church. They responded routinely enough to the king's writs concerning the benefices of aliens,[144] and if they did anything to stand up for the rights of their foreign subjects or the revenues of their foreign confreres, they left no record of it. All these measures must have looked at the time like straightforward expedients for economic prosperity and national defense. They left room enough for the exercise of centralized ecclesiastical administration (as long as it was not too expensive), and even for the legitimate financial endeavors of a common Christendom — the funds collected from the English Hospitallers for the last confrontation of their order with the Moslems were not subjected to the laws against exporting money.[145] Whatever effect they had on the fabric of Christian unity was not felt until much later.

E. Economic and Social Order.

The lay authorities did not hesitate to include the church and its institutions within whatever economic and social policies they laid down for the whole society.[146] In some cases, the results were anomalous — as where a sumptuary statute authorized the higher clergy to keep up a style forbidden by the canons. In one case, church and state parted company. The laity tried to prevent married women and villeins from making wills because they were not *sui juris,* whereas the churchmen thought every Christian should make a will for his soul's health. So if a married woman or a villein made a will, the church courts admitted it to probate, but the lay courts refused to recognize the executor.

In most cases, though, the two systems cooperated. For instance, in the aftermath of the Black Death, the prelates assisted in promulgating and enforcing the Statute of Laborers, and adopted measures of their own to control the wages of stipendiary priests. Similarly, the heads of the four mendicant orders took their oath to keep the statute made in 1402 against receiving villeins into the clergy — though they were evidently not vigorous enough about it to satisfy the Commons.

One lay social policy that needed, and got, considerable ecclesiastical support — in the teeth of what would seem to be sound Christian practice — was that of maintaining family and feudal control over marriages. The parents of those who had parents, and the feudal lords of those who had not, habitually married off sons and daughters with more regard for consolidation of landholdings than for domestic felicity, and often took cash payments for doing so.

The secular law supported arranged marriages in a number of ways.[147] It allowed a guardian to exact money damages if his ward refused a proffered match. It allowed a "widow" to recover dower at the age of nine. It allowed the issue to be legitimate when a marriage was dissolved for consanguinity (marrying relatives to each other was a good way to keep landholdings intact), whereas it made the issue illegitimate when a marriage was dissolved because one of the parties had contracted to marry someone else (the family was apt to have more control over betrothals than over marriages). It deprived a woman of her inheritance if she consented to being carried off and married.

The churchmen, for their part, were free with dispensations from impediments of consanguinity, and maintained the rule that a prior betrothal to someone else voided a marriage. Most importantly, they were extremely lax in determining whether marriages were genuinely consented to, and whether consent was free from coercion; I recall no case of a marriage being annulled for lack of free consent.[148]

IV. Religious Policies — The Salvation of Souls

The sampling of parliamentary rhetoric that I offered earlier on shows that the laity saw supporting the customary forms of piety and good works, and maintaining the religious establishment set up by their ancestors, as top-priority goals for the whole society. While the implementation of these goals was primarily entrusted to churchmen, the churchmen could not be left to sink or swim with them as fortune served. The king, his officials and his Parliament, responsible before God for the overall common good, had to take a hand when a hand was needed.

In discharging this responsibility, the government was sometimes able to fall into its canonical role of "secular arm," providing suitable muscle for the judgments and processes of the church. This was how the occasional Lollard was dealt with, or the stubborn excommunicate, or the irascible squire who ran the parish priest or the archdeacon out of town. But the more important cases, and the ones I will take up first, were those in which the government did not wait for the church to act, but moved on its own initiative, with more effective procedures and a more utilitarian outlook than the churchmen had. Here the royal authority was drawn on to keep religious foundations from squandering their resources, to keep the peace in the universities, and to keep up services in the parish churches.

A. Affairs of Monasteries and Pious Foundations.

The medieval laity were generous in endowing both liturgical and charitable functions. The great lords founded monasteries and collegiate establishments, or added lands to those already founded. The growing middle classes set up chantries according to their means, or participated in pious guilds to maintain masses or vigil lights in the parish churches. Some laymen founded "hospitals" for the relief of the poor; others launched educational enterprises ranging from Henry VI's great college at Cambridge to a citizen's £40 a year to support two chaplains and such poor boys as one of them could teach. The masses of the priests, the offices of the religious, and the grateful prayers of the poor men and scholars were all expected (and in some cases elaborate provision was made for them) to redound to the good estate of founders and heirs of founders living, and to their souls' health when they died. Kings not only made such benefactions themselves, but also encouraged them in their subjects. They freely granted mortmain licenses for the purpose, and were generally included in the ensuing spiritual benefits.

It was a fixed policy of the secular law to see that these benefactions were maintained, and used for their intended purposes. To this end, a wide variety of lay processes were made available to the interested parties to prevent waste and alienation, and to insure that the services and charities envisaged were kept up.

1. Rights of the House — Religious houses (and probably other corporate foundations, though the records are not clear) were protected against improvidence by a set of strict rules of agency.[149] The undertaking of a monk could not bind the house unless the other party could show that he had rendered a *quid pro quo* that was of profit to the house. For instance, when a monk bought goods and ran away with them, they never came to the profit of the house, and the house could not be held for the purchase price.

On a simple debt, the abbot was evidently in the same case as the monk. His undertaking did not bind the house unless it appeared that the consideration was to the house's profit. Whether he himself would be liable is a more difficult question. I suspect he would not be, since he had nothing but the house's property with which to pay.

On a sealed instrument, of course, there was no question of consideration, and there was evidently a time when the abbot, or anyone else who got his hands on the seal, could execute such an instrument and bind the house. From the early fourteenth century on, however, anyone suing on a sealed instrument seems to have had to show that it was executed with the consent of the community. There is some evidence that this result was brought about by the Statute of Carlisle (1307), though it is hard to see why it should have been. The statute provides that the house is to have a common seal in the custody of the prior and four monks, and is not to be bound by any other. No doubt, if the seal was kept as the statute provided, it could not be used without the consent of the four monks, but there is no direct provision for showing anyone's consent to the sealing of a given instrument. Nevertheless, the subsequent cases say a great deal about the consent of the community, and nothing at all about the custody of the seal.

Just as the house could avoid a sealed instrument that the abbot made without the consent of the community, so it could recover lands that he sold or leased without such consent. For this purpose there was a writ of entry called *sine assensu capituli* (so called because it was also used where a bishop alienated lands without the consent of his chapter).[150] The most serious hitch in its use to recover land was that no action could be brought during the tenure of the abbot who made the unauthorized conveyance. The house could not come into court without him, and the rule that a litigant cannot deny his own act cut deeper than the policy of protecting the house. It was debated whether a successor abbot who accepted fealty or rent from the grantee of the land was barred by the same rule. The Year Book cases go both ways.

In addition to protecting religious houses against improvident debts and alienations, Parliament tried to protect them against the petty exactions and freeloading that were a constant drain on their resources. A statute enacted in 1275[151] forbade anyone but the patron to lodge in a monastery at the monastery's expense unless he had been invited in advance. If anyone came uninvited, he could be put up if the community was willing, but only at his own expense. An exeption was made for the poor people whom monastic hospitality was intended to relieve. Other popular ways of making free with monastic property were enumerated at considerable length and forbidden. The offended house was given a right to sue for double damages, and the offender was also made liable to fine and imprisonment for contempt of the king.

This statute remained on the books, and was referred to in the *Articuli Cleri* of 1315, but I cannot find any case where it was enforced. There are trespass cases brought by abbots in the Year Books, but I can find none in which double damages were claimed under this statute; still less can I find a case where those who vexed monasteries were fined or imprisoned by the king. Probably religious houses did not wish to risk poor relations with great men by relying on the statute, and the king was not interested in acting where the house did not complain.

2. Rights of Beneficiaries — I have found three cases in Parliament indicating that the beneficiaries of a charity were entitled to have it enforced.[152] In 1278, an inmate of a certain hospital complained that he had been transferred to another institution without a proper hearing, and the hospital officials were ordered to reconsider. In 1330, a petition was brought in the name of the poor of two parishes, complaining of an abbot for failing to keep up the alms to which they were entitled. The king's justices were ordered to call in the abbot and do justice to the petitioners. In 1347, the inhabitants of Latchford, Oxon. complained of the abbot of Thame for not keeping up a chantry, and were told to sue at common law, and before the bishop as well if they wished. The 1347

entry suggests the existence of a routine writ for the purpose, but I have not
been able to find one. The 1330 entry seems to be an ad hoc delegation.

3. *Rights of Private Founder or Donor* — If you or your ancestors before the
statute *Quia Emptores* (1290) gave land to a religious house or other foundation
for pious purposes, you could have it back through a writ of *contra formam
collacionis* if they alienated it. If they kept it, but neglected for two years or
more any specific alms or good works provided for in the grant, you could have
it back with a writ called *cessavit*. Both these remedies were established by the
Statute of Westminster II (1285), and put to regular use thereafter.[153]

The *contra formam collacionis* required a two-pronged litigation. The writ as
set up in the statutue was directed against the religious house that had alienated
the lands, not against the third party who had bought them. So after you got
judgment against the house you still had to get the lands back from the
purchaser. For this you brought a proceeding called *scire facias* to execute the
judgment. In this proceeding, the purchaser was not bound by the result of your
original litigation against the religious house because he was not a party to it.
So you would have to prove your case all over again before you recovered
the land.

Cessavit, like *contra formam collacionis*, returned the land to the grantor or
his heirs, rather than restoring it to the pious use contemplated in the original
grant. The defaulting clerics or religious could, however, save their land by
making a tender of the arrears. This procedure was provided for in an earlier
statute (1278) establishing the writ of *cessavit* for secular services, which
statute was referred to in the 1285 provision. Hence, it was insisted that the
tenant should have the same right in the case of spiritual services that he had
with temporal. The theological problems raised by making a tender of, say, the
two hundred masses and offices of the Blessed Virgin that ought to have been
said every Thursday for the past four years probably did not bother medieval
Catholics as much as they would modern ones.

Both of these remedies, *cessavit* and *contra formam collacionis*, were based
on a conception of feudal tenure. The general benefits of having endowed a
religious house or hospital, or the specific benefits of definite prayers and good
works, were analogized to the feudal services to which a person was entitled
when he bestowed his land on another. The analogy was used in all sorts of
ways, some of them bizarre.[154]

The statute *Quia Emptores* of 1290 did away with feudal tenures on any
subsequent grants. Thereafter, if A held land of B and granted it to C, C would
hold of B on the same terms A had held, rather than holding of A as he would
have done before. Accordingly, it was decided that *contra formam collacionis*
and *cessavit* were not available on a grant made for religious purposes after
Quia Emptores took effect.[155] Other remedies took up at least part of the slack.
Fitzherbert suggests convenant, evidently on the theory that the religious

purpose is a covenant running with the land. It was probably possible also to word your grant in such a way as to distrain for spiritual services on the analogy of a reserved rent, or to exercise a right of entry for condition broken.

4. Rights of the Crown – On the whole, the king did not concern himself with the affairs of foundations other than his own.[156] In dealing with his own foundations, however, he did not limit himself to the remedies available to a private donor. He used flexible, and distinctly governmental, procedures to enforce his religious and charitable purposes. He issued commissions of inquiry to investigate reported derelictions, and he subpoenaed those involved to appear before his commissioners. He issued orders calling on those in charge of his foundations to correct their subordinates, to refrain from waste or alienation, or to undertake no obligation until a proper inquest could be taken. On occasion, he intervened in person or through commissioners to protect exemptions, adjust visitation rights, or distribute monastic revenues between abbot and convent. Breach of his orders in any of these matters would no doubt have been punished as contempt.

The 1285 statute that provided the writ of *contra formam collacionis* for a private donor provided that land granted by the king and alienated by his grantee should be "taken into the king's hands." This provision was enforceable by a proceeding called an "inquest of office" which lay for the assertion of all manner of royal rights. This inquest was held by the king's escheator by virtue of his office (hence the name). Land thus taken by the king did not automatically fall into the royal demesne, as would have happened if the proceeding had been entirely analogous to that brought by a private grantor. The state of being "in the king's hands" was generally conceived of as a temporary one, and the usual direction to an escheator was to hold lands until further order from the king. The procedure looks a little like a distress or an imprisonment for contempt. I imagine that in the usual case the offender was eventually permitted to arrange a money fine, though I have no evidence on the point.

The 1285 statute did not provide the king with a remedy analogous to that afforded the private donor with the writ of *cessavit*. I would be reluctant to suppose that this meant that the king could not seize land if the services for which he gave it were not kept up. Here again, though, he was probably expected to use his powers to restore the services rather than taking the land back in demesne.

To set a religious house back on its proper course, the king had a procedure rather like a receivership. This was often set in motion at the behest of a house unable to cope with its obligations, but it could also be imposed involuntarily on a suitable showing of mismanagement. What it involved was the appointment of a group of custodians (sometimes ecclesiastics, more often laymen) to take charge of the lands and revenues of the house and administer them. They were to recover property improperly alienated, turn out superfluous boarders, provide for the reasonable support of the community, and use the remaining funds to pay off the debts. The arrangement was usually accompanied by a royal protection that prevented anyone from suing the house while it was in custody.

The only serious hardship wrought by this procedure seems to have been on the holders of corrodies. The commission to the custodians would be apt to call for turning such persons out, and the accompanying protection to the house would prevent them from bringing suit. A group of men complained in Parliament in 1402 that they had suffered from such protections, had paid cash down for their corrodies, and had no other way to live. The chancellor was ordered to do right by them in the particular case, but I find no indication that the general practice was ameliorated. In fact, it would have been hard to put a monastery back on its feet financially without some control over corrodies.

Royal commissioners dealt more summarily with hospitals than they did with religious houses. Generally, they came, summoned jurors and witnesses, took specific corrective measures, and got out. The whole process resembled a canonical visitation, and was sometimes called by that name. Since the hospital was more or less a lay foundation (though it was spiritual enough for the ordinary to have some control over it),[157] the commissioners could fire the head and replace him with someone else. Perhaps it was for this reason that they did not need a prolonged custody.

The records show surprisingly little of either cooperation or interference between the royal and ecclesiastical authorities in these matters. If a house had a prolonged spell of trouble, there would probably be many attempts on both sides to cope with it, but not at the same time. The respective approaches to the problems of preventing mismanagement and cutting down expenses were somewhat different, but not radically so. Only the ecclesiastical visitor had power to dismiss the head of a religious house (if he was willing to undertake the difficult canonical processes required), while only the king had clear power to dismiss the head of a hospital.[158] Only the king could protect a house against its creditors, and only the king customarily took custody of its lands and property, though the canonical vistor could probably have done so if he chose.

The churchmen made no difficulty about royal commissioners taking power over monasteries and hospitals. Sometimes protests were forestalled by appointing ordinaries and religious superiors to act as royal commissioners, but often the commissioners were all laymen, or the only clerics included were those of the king's bureaucratic establishment. Evidently, the prelates were simply more interested in rehabilitating the houses in question than they were in excluding the laity.

B. *Affairs of Schools and Universities.*

The lay authorities encouraged and supported education in the same way as other works of charity. Below the university level, I do not find that they went any farther than that in dealing with it. Specifically, they seem not to have interfered with the licensing of schoolmasters — a function that the church took on I do not know when or how.[159] On one occasion (1447) the Commons asked the government to take a hand in the process:

> for where there is grate number of Lerners, and fewe Teachers . . . the Maisters wexen riche in money and the Lerners pouere in connyng, as experience openly showith.

But the king was not willing to supersede the church's jurisdiction in the matter.

In the universities, on the other hand, royal intervention was straightforward and active.[160] The king played a large part in settling a series of late fourteenth-century controversies concerning the position of friars as teachers and students. In 1379, commissioners were appointed in Parliament to settle the rights of the archbishop of York as visitor of one of the Oxford colleges (probably Queens). And in 1411, the king imposed the archbishop of Canterbury as visitor of the whole University of Oxford, overriding a papal bull of exemption which he found to have been granted:

> In prejudice of his Crown, and to the enervation of the Laws and Customs of his Realm, to the favor and audacity of Heretics, Lollards, Homicides, and other malefactors, and to the seeming destruction of the said University.

In all likelihood, the state of the university was not that bad, and a visitation from the archbishop could not have corrected it if it had been. At any rate, the royal authorities were not willing to leave a matter of this much public importance to the vagaries of papal exemption and canonical litigation.

C. *Affairs of Parishes.*

The disparate interventions of lay government for the purpose of keeping up the parish ministry included a statute (1307) forbidding rectors to chop down trees in their churchyards except to repair their churches; orders maintaining the tithes from royal estates and supplementing them when they were unduly diminished by changing land use (if you changed, say, a field to an ornamental park, you had no legal obligation to compensate the parish priest for his loss of tithes, but it was considered decent to do something for him); a series of judicial decisions preventing the alienation of parish endowments or the imposition of pensions without the joint consent of patron, ordinary, and

incumbent; a legislative effort (1400-6) against religious orders like the
Cistercians who tried to enforce papal bulls exempting them from the payment
of tithes on certain of their lands.[161]

The most important item of this kind was the control the government took
over appropriations.[162] It was evidently supposed when the Mortmain Act was
adopted in 1279 that a religious house needed a license under the act to
appropriate a benefice. In the case of *R.* v. *Prior of Worcester* (1304) it was
decided that the act did not in fact apply to appropriations, but that because of
the practice since 1279 the king was seised of the right to require a license, and
an appropriation made without one was void. Licenses continued to be issued
regularly, and the prices charged for them show that the necessity of having
them was taken seriously.

In 1391, in response to a typically plaintive petition of the Commons, a
statute was enacted to the effect that royal licenses for appropriations would no
longer be given out except on condition that the bishop set up a suitably
endowed vicarage, and make provision for the distribution of "a convenient
sum of money" to the parish poor. The condition appears fairly regularly in
licenses thereafter. The king waived compliance with the act occasionally until
1402, when, in response to a further complaint in Parliament, he agreed to
stop. It seems likely that this strict enforcement of the 1391 act played a large
part in checking a practice that the popes fell into late in the fourteenth century
of allowing rectories to be appropriated without vicarages, or allowing
vicarages to be appropriated by the houses that had already appropriated
the rectories.

The Commons would have liked the king to take a stand against pluralism
and nonresidence as he did against appropriations without vicarages, and
against religious houses getting exemptions from paying tithe. In fact, they
made out a fairly convincing case. The practice depended on papal
dispensations as the others did, and the same lugubrious effects on the parish
ministry could be pointed out. But the king was not prepared to supersede the
authority of the churchmen on this point. Parliamentary petitions that he do so
were turned down on five separate occasions between 1400 and 1425.[163] The
reason for the refusal was no doubt the importance of pluralism and
nonresidence to the bureaucratic establishments of the king and other magnates
of the realm.

D. Solicitation, Doctrine, and Preaching.

It appears that in the mid-fourteenth century the government concerned itself
with charitable solictations. The Patent Rolls for 1348 show a number of royal
protections to individuals and institutions engaged in soliciting alms for various
charitable purposes at home and abroad.[164] It is not clear to me what these

protections accomplished for the people who got them. I know of no law you would have violated by soliciting without one. Perhaps they relate in some way to the concern about sturdy beggars that led to the enactment of legislation on the subject in 1349. In my periodic sampling of the documents, I find nothing of the kind in other periods.

The advent of Lollardy in the latter part of the fourteenth century put the royal government in the business of enforcing the doctrinal commitments of the church.[165] A statute briefly in force during 1382 provided that heretical preachers and their accomplices should be arrested by the sheriffs on a certification into Chancery by any prelate. An act of 1400 provided the same treatment for all unlicensed preachers, heretical or not, as well as a procedure for burning anyone finally convicted of heresy. Finally, an act of 1414 ordered judges and justices of the peace actively to seek out heretics. All these statutes, however, left the actual trial of heresy to the ecclesiastical authorities. The enforcement of these laws had its ups and downs, depending on the political situation, but their presence on the books showed that the orthodoxy of the English people was of more than ecclesiastical concern.

E. Assistance and Protection.

Maitland's famous book on canon law in England argues persuasively that no specific legislation was needed to authorize the lay authorities to enforce ecclesiastical jurisdiction and canonical rights. The Patent Rolls and the Parliament Rolls bear out this view.[166] Here an abbey is invited to enroll its papal privileges in Chancery so it can have royal process if they are violated. There a sheriff is told to assist the Primate of Ireland in asserting his right to have his cross borne before him. Some procedures start as special ones and ultimately become form writs out of Chancery. That for apprehending apostate religious seems to be an example.

Some remedies available to laymen and churchmen alike were given to churchmen in special ways.[167] They got special treatment, for instance, in the matter of purveyances — more or less compulsory purchases of supplies for the king's use — which was a common grievance. Similarly, by a statute of 1377, judges and litigants in church courts were given a special remedy against those who had them indicted for spurious crimes. Finally, through the mid-fourteenth century, commissions of oyer and terminer for non-routine handling of serious cases of armed invasion (an alternative to the Chancery writ of trespass) seem to have been given to churchmen somewhat more freely than to laymen.

But the two most important ways in which the state assisted the operations of the church were in the enforcement of excommunications and in the prevention on violent interference with ecclesiastical jurisdiction.

1. Excommunication – The two secular sanctions visited on the excommunicate were his disability to litigate in the king's courts and his liability to be seized by the sheriff. The disability to litigate was narrow.[168] It did not permanently bar a suit; the plaintiff, once absolved, could proceed anew on the same writ. The disability, such as it was, had to be asserted by the defendant, and had to be supported by the certificate of an English bishop not a party to the case. A foreign bishop (even the pope), or a prelate of lesser rank, even if he enjoyed an exempt jurisdiction, would not do. Nor, in most cases, could the suit be stopped if the defendant had anything to do with getting the plaintiff excommunicated.

The seizure of the excommunicate by the sheriff was initiated by the ecclesiastical authorities filing in Chancery a document called a signification (sometimes called *significavit*). On the basis of it, the royal writ *de excommunicando capiendo* would issue, commanding the sheriff to seize the excommunicate named, and hold him until he made satisfaction to the church.[169] This satisfaction could take the form either of actual complicance or of an undertaking for future compliance fortified with a suitable "caution" in the form of a pledge, an oath, or a set of sureties. If the church court regarded the proferred caution as insufficient, he would not be absolved, but he could seek release from a custody through a royal writ *de cautione admitenda*. It is not clear how the sufficiency of the proposed caution could be tried in the proceedings on this writ, but the prelates were outraged that the writ should issue at all.

Another way the offender could be released from custody, or could avoid being taken in the first place, was by appealing from the original sentence of excommunication. He could then have a supersedeas out of Chancery on undertaking to prosecute the appeal and return to court if he lost. The supersedeas could also be had on a showing that the excommunicate was prosecuting an attachment on a prohibition based on the proceedings that led to his being excommunicated.

Here again, it was only an English bishop who had a general right to have his excommunications enforced. A few exempt prelates of lesser rank (most notably the chancellor of Oxford) had special grants from the king; otherwise, they were excluded. So was the pope. Evidently the officials who held a bishop's court could be received more freely for this purpose than they were for the purpose of disabling a plaintiff in the lay court. Fitzherbert says that a signification from the bishop's vicar-general will do, but he seems a little dubious about an official or an archdeacon.

2. Lay Force – The king maintained as a general matter that a large enough use of armed force in his dominions was a violation of his authority, which required neither a form process nor a special complainant to redress. Some outbreaks of violence in ecclesiastical disputes were dealt with under this principle, either by bills in Parliament or by prerogative proceedings in the courts.[170] I suspect that the king proceeded more readily in this way where one of his own clerics was involved.

For certain cases in which force was not sufficient to threaten the authority of the crown, but was sufficient to interfere with the ordinary processes of the church, there was a form writ available in Chancery, the writ *de vi laica amovenda*.[171] This perhaps evolved out of the general royal prerogative at a relatively late date, for I find cases in the Close Rolls of 1248 where the form writ as Fitzherbert describes it would have served.

The writ evidently lay with respect to a specified church, at the request either of the ordinary or of the incumbent or would-be incumbent. The sheriff in executing it was to do what the writ said, and remove the lay force. He was not to put anyone out of possession, but simply to let the ecclesiastical processes take their course with the lay force out of the picture.

The form writ given by Fitzherbert refers only to *lay* force where the writ is issued in response to the bishop's request. On the other hand, where the writ is given to protect a man presented to a benefice by the king, it refers to lay force *and armed force*. Perhaps, therefore, where the bishop was resisted by, say, a body of armed monks, the form writ would not serve.

The form writ, then, must have been a good deal narrower than the possibilities for forcible intereference with ecclesiastical process. In cases not covered, I suppose that the ecclesiastical authorities would have to proceed by excommunicating the offender and then seeking a writ *de excommunicato capiendo*, or else by actions of trespass or other appropriate common law proceedings. If all else failed, they might have to seek a remedy in Parliament. It does not appear that an ecclesiastical judgment as such could be enforced by routine secular process.

V. Crown Versus Papacy — The Advancement of Holy Church

A. Sources of Conflict.

Although there was no secular law against papal process as such, the authorities were sensitive, and not altogether predictable, in seeing particular uses of it as contempts of the crown.[172] Those who got into trouble ranged from a man who procured an order excommunicating the unknown persons who broke into his house (presumably because housebreaking is a crime punishable in the king's courts) to a dependent priory that was made into an abbey by the pope (because the worth of the king's patronage of the motherhouse was diminished). In many cases, the only way you could be entirely safe in using a papal rescript was to get a royal license in advance.

As might be expected, the serious quarrels, except in isolated cases, involved finance or personnel.[173] The various forms of papal taxation clashed with lay policy by making the clergy less willing to be taxed by the king, by taking money out of the country, and by diverting lay benefactions to purposes not contemplated by the donors.

Further, during the years when the pope sat at Avignon, it was suspected, no doubt with good reason, that the funds he was taking out of England were assisting the king's enemies in France. The royal authorities asserted themselves sporadically against the levying of special taxes, or the introduction of new general ones. Sometimes they were successful; other times they were persuaded to drop their opposition or at least look the other way. They did not really develop a coherent policy of opposition to papal finance, much as the Commons would have liked them to. The situation probably presented political ambiguities not apparent on the face of the record.

More straightforward, but still complex enough, was the royal attitude toward papal placement of personnel.[174] In the beginning, the clash was between king and pope over the fairly narrow class of benefices in the gift of churchmen whose temporalities were in the king's hands. As we have seen, the king claimed that the advowson was a temporality, and was therefore in his hands, so that he could present to the benefice if it fell vacant. The pope claimed — and increasingly exercised — a right to provide a cleric to any benefice in the gift of a churchman. Battles between royal presentees and papal provisors in cases of this kind appear in the records at least as early as 1298. Up to the mid-fourteenth century, I cannot see that action was taken against papal provisions in any other cases, except on one or two occasions when a private party had recovered a judgment in the king's courts, and interested the royal government in protecting his rights under the judgment. An ordinance was made in Parliament in 1306 against provisions generally, but it seems not to have been enforced.

In the course of the fourteenth century, however, the Commons began to take a new interest in provisions. From the tenor of their petitions, they seem to have supposed, first, that many if not most provisors were aliens, and second, that most of the evils of nonresidence were due to provisions. Neither of these suppositions was true. Pantin made a careful check on the incidence of foreigners in English benefices at the time, and found it negligible. As for nonresidence, as long as bureaucrats were put in benefices, they could hardly have resided, whoever put them there. In fact, as we saw in the last volume, papal provision was a fairly efficient way to recruit and place bureaucrats. It is not surprising, therefore, that kings, lords, and prelates — that is, the employers of bureaucrats — were less enthusiastic than the Commons were about cracking down on papal provisions.

Accordingly, there was a good deal of backing and filling. The Statute of Provisors was passed in 1350, imposing penalties on provisors, and authorizing the king or other lay patron to make a presentment where ecclesiastical electors or patrons were shut out by a provision. It was reenacted in 1389, and again in

1407, each time with a pardon for those who had violated it in the past. As late as 1409, it was contended in court (unsuccessfully, to be sure) that the statute had never been enforced.

Meanwhile, in the last years of Edward III's reign and all through Richard II's, negotiations were undertaken with the papacy to mitigate the supposed evils of provisions. The Commons felt, probably rightly, that these negotiations were being blocked by the great lords who wanted to advance their own clerics. In any event, partial agreements were reached on a couple of occasions, but no permanent accomodation was arrived at.

Richard II was evidently rather free in licensing exceptions to the Statute of Provisors, and in 1391 he received from the Commons the authority to modify the actual terms of the statute. Although the Commons made Richard's favoring of provisors one of the grounds of impeachment against him, they gave Henry IV still broader powers to do the same. In 1402, however, Henry revoked the licenses he had previously granted; then, in 1407, he gave up his right to modify the statute. He evidently reserved some kind of right to grant licenses in individual cases, but both licenses and provisions became fairly rare after this time.

A royal license to use a provision could make trouble if the benefice affected had already been filled by a regular presentment. By the beginning of the fifteenth century, the statute was evidently being so well enforced that the ordinaries would put a presentee into a benefice despite the fact that there was a provision outstanding. But when the royal license made the provision enforceable, the presentee could be ousted by the ordinary processes of church law, which had regarded him as an intruder from the start. A response in Parliament in 1406, and then a statute of 1415, dealt with this situation by making the royal license void if the benefice was full when it was issued.[175]

B. Procedures.

After the interdict imposed by Innocent III on England from 1208 to 1213, none of the differences between crown and papacy was pursued by a direct power confrontation. Rather, the two parties negotiated with one another, while each brought as much pressure as it could on the third parties involved.[176] In 1346-48 for instance, when the king opposed the collection of procurations for certain papal nuncios in France, the pope threatened to excommunicate any bishop who did not make the necessary collections; the king threatened to impose forefeitures on any bishop who did. In a battle between a papal provisor and a royal presentee, the presentee would have the provisor imprisoned, and the provisor would have the presentee excommunicated. Who won in the long run would depend on who could hold out the longest.

The royal authorities made a good deal of effort to stop papal process at the seaports, and to prevent Englishmen from going abroad to get it. Once it came in, they could still imprison people for using it, but there was not much they could do to keep it from taking effect. They did not find it possible simply to treat such process as nugatory. It appears from the Year Books, for instance, that a person in a benefice by papal provision was generally considered a proper incumbent, despite the Statutes of Provisors.[177] The provision would support a plea of plenarty in a *quare impedit* proceeding, and a provision imposed upon a religious house would count as a presentment by the house to show its possession of the advowson.

The pope, on the other hand, treated all royal process in violation of his rights as absolutely void. For instance, when the king took over the alien priories, the pope entertained suits by their motherhouses to collect the customary dues, and would not allow them to defend themselves by showing that these dues had been confiscated by the king.[178] Similarly, the pope regarded as absolutely void any presentment to a benefice after he had provided to it or reserved it for future provision.

Let us see how all this worked out in a concrete case — for instance, a mid-fourteenth-century provision case.[179] The vacant benefice of St. A, let us say, is in the gift of the prior of B, whose temporalities have just been in the king's hands on account of a vacancy of the priory. The king has made a presentment of X, and Y has come forward with a papal provision. The provision and the presentment are both in the hands of the bishop of C as ordinary.[180]

The first move is the bishop's. I think he is probably better off to put the provisor in first. If he does not, he will hear in no uncertain terms from the pope. The king will write a letter for him to the pope, but this will probably do him no good. On the other hand, if he puts in the provisor, he will probably not be held in contempt of the king (although I suppose he could be), but will be subject only to the ordinary processes of royal patronage litigation.

This means the king will have to bring a *quare impedit*, charging the bishop and the provisor with disturbing him. The bishop will say that he claims only as ordinary, and will probably be let off on this. The provisor's only defense, however, will be plenarty, which, as we have seen, is probably not available against the king. Accordingly, the king will prevail against the provisor, and will recover a writ ordering the bishop to admit the king's presentee notwithstanding the provisor's claim.

At this point, the bishop had better let the presentee in; otherwise he will be liable in an action of *quare non admisit*. It seems reaonable to suppose that this is one of the *quare non admisit* cases in which plenarty will not be a defense, since the incumbent is the very person whose claim the bishop is ordered to disregard. On the other hand, the bishop cannot get into too much trouble if he does let in the presentee. He does not have to throw out the provisor; he can simply put one on top of the other and let the two of them fight it out. I gather that the provisor will have no canonical grievance against the bishop if this is done, since the putting in of the presentee will be canonically nugatory, and the bishop will have done nothing to oust the provisor physically from the benefice.

The next move is up to the parties. The provisor has to get to Rome before the presentee can catch him. The presentee has to get to the king's Chancery and get as many writs as possible to prevent this happening. The provisor has already incurred the penalties of the Statute of Provisors by reason of his disturbance of the presentee. It seems that he cannot be attached for this by ancillary process in the *quare impedit* proceeding,[181] but by a new writ he certainly can be attached, and imprisoned until he makes satisfaction to the king, and also gives surety not to meddle further with the benefice. By attempting to take his case to Rome, the provisor also incurs the penalty of the Statutes of *Praemunire,* with rather more summary remedies. It is not clear whether these can be invoked on a showing that he is about to go to Rome, or only on a showing that he has gone already. But if he gets away, they will be waiting for him when he comes back. Meanwhile, without any statute at all, the king can and will issue a writ ordering his sheriffs to stop the provisor at any seaport from which he is planning to depart to litigate in derogation of a judgment of the king's court. Once stopped, he may be required to put up bond not to go.

But if the provisor or his proctor can get to Rome and back, he can have a canonical spoliation suit which he will almost certainly win. The suit cannot be heard in England because the king's prohibition will stop it. But in Rome he will get a judgment excommunicating the presentee, and probably ordering the bishop to sequester the benefice. If he can then get back to England without being arrested, and have the order delivered to the bishop, he can have the benefice sequestered. He can also make good the excommunication of the presentee, which will not only trouble the latter's conscience, but will make him canonically incapable of saying mass, and therefore of occupying a benefice with cure. The papal judgment may also be fortified with a specific provision depriving the presentee of whatever preferment he holds — which may be more than the benefice in issue. As far as I can see, there is no secular process to protect the presentee against these consequences.

When all this has been done, assuming the sheriff has caught up with the provisor in the meanwhile, both sides will have done their utmost. The case will remain in this posture until it is settled. The chances of settlement are generally good. Both parties are bureaucrats of the same kind; neither king nor pope wants to be too hard on either of them, nor do they want to be too hard on each other. One or the other of them can be bought off with another benefice. If the king's man gives in, he will simply be absolved by the pope, and the provisor will receive a royal pardon for taking out the provision, together with a royal license to use it. The king may also write the bishop revoking the original presentment. If the provisor gives in, he will receive a royal pardon, give bond not to meddle with the benefice, and send his letter of resignation to the pope. The pope will then make a provision of the king's presentee, reciting that the benefice is vacant by reason of the resignation. This the presentee will get a royal license to use.

My guess is that before the crackdown in 1407 the king's man prevailed in 50 to 75 percent of these cases. Thereafter, there hardly were any cases; the vigorous enforcement of the statute all but did away with provisions. We can find somewhat the same situation with respect to licenses to appropriate without vicarages, or with respect to the imposition of papal income taxes on the clergy. Where the royal opposition was half-hearted or tempered by political considerations, the pope had a good chance of having his way; where the royal opposition was coherent and vigorous it was generally successful.

C. Recognition.

It cannot be inferred from any of these maneuvers that the English government took a generally skeptical attitude toward the pope, or required royal approval before giving his mandates effect. Even in the most outspoken protests against him, he was *"Nostre Seint Piere le Pape."*[182] He was not allowed — nor was anyone else — to impinge on the customary rights of the crown, but where these were not involved, he did as he pleased. The royal courts applied many of his judgments and processes quite routinely, and on no authority but his.[183] The disabilities of an excommunicate — both his inability to proceed in court and his liability to arrest on secular process — were suspended pending an appeal to the pope. The deprivation of a benefice by the pope was regarded as creating a vacancy that the patron could fill. Conversely, the pope's reversal of a deprivation imposed by someone else was recognized as doing away with a vacancy. By the same token, a papal dispensation was recognized as a basis for holding a benefice which the general law made vacant — as long as the rule dispensed from was one of church law only, and not part of the "law of the land."

It was sometimes said in the Year Books, to be sure, that the pope's seals would not be recognized in an English court because the pope was not an English prelate.[184] But in many cases where papal judgments were given effect it is difficult to suppose that they were proved in any way except by looking at the documents with their seals.

If we are to find foreshadowings of the Reformation in the late medieval attitude toward the papacy, I think we must find them in this — that the position of the pope, although fully recognized in theory, was not fully integrated into the increasingly coherent structure of the church-state nexus as the royal authorities envisaged it. Theology and custom required a pope, but the internal logic of the institutional system did not. When the time came that the English were prepared to break with theology and custom, they could do so without too much wrenching of their institutional forms.

VI. Conclusion

All these ideological and administrative patterns have a fairly clear affinity for the Erastian outlook as I have described it — the view that God is honored through the overall conformity of a given society to an image of His will, and that the church is only one of the institutions of society through which that conformity is to be achieved. The outlook was both cause and effect of the technical and utilitarian character of the legal forms. The understanding of the work of government came from centuries of experience of government at work, and in turn affected the new ways in which government defined its task.

The work of government in this understanding was skilled, technical, and, above all, pragmatic. The presence of a variety of institutions, lay and ecclesiastical, each with its claims to independent life, increased the complexity of the technical problem without altering its basic terms. All the organs of society were to operate together to the honor of God and the salvation of souls. The work of imposing the requisite order was technical because such questions as when a given sheaf of wheat ceases to be lay chattel and becomes tithe cannot be other than technical. Expecially is this so when the question has to be decided by a system with fairly limited resources. The painful development of a writ here and a process there to cover this case or that comes of an instinctive awareness of technical limitations, and of the need for keeping everything in mind.

All this is in marked contrast to the High Church ideology that dominated ecclesiastical administration. The churchmen had a theoretical neatness that the laity could not match, but they maintained it at the expense of their overall view of what they were about. Their tendency was always to accept one set of claims on its theoretical persuasiveness without regard for competing claims or for the limitations of their resources. Their general church-state approach was one of insisting on a theoretical symmetry for the concerns of the institutional church without regard to the effect on the other institutions of society. The High Churchmen would have the church intervene in temporal affairs whenever a spiritual matter was involved, and yet take no responsibility for the temporal affairs in which they intervened.

As a result, the tension between High Churchmanship and Erastianism tended to be expressed in a difference of attitude toward theoretical considerations as such. Erastianism was not without its theoretical articulations;

I described some of them at the beginning of this chapter. But on the whole, Erastian sentiment tended to be impatient with the higher reaches or the subtler refinements of theory. Therein, it seems, was its weakness. The English Erastian (that is, the typical English layman) was prepared to see the church as having a job to do, but he was not prepared to accept it in its self-chosen role as standing witness through its institutional forms to the transcendant sovereignty of God. When he came to see this witness as blocking the way to the immediate goals of a Christian society, there was nothing to stop him from letting it go down the drain.

2. Utility and Reform

I. King Henry's Reform

A great many ordinary Englishmen seem to have gone through the Reformation more firmly committed to the Erastian system I have been describing than to any of the doctrines or practices that came into issue. Such people played, it seems to me, a rather consistent part in the whole affair. Guided by a kind of foursquare undifferentiated Christianity, and a general attachment to the traditional order of things, they picked their way through the niceties of theology and politics alike, and probably came out in the end with more of what they wanted than anyone else got.

A. The Medieval Commons.

Their ideas of reform are expressed as early as the fourteenth and fifteenth centuries in the parliamentary material we considered at one point and another in the last chapter, especially in the petitions submitted by the Commons. To be sure, we must not regard the medieval Commons as unfailing guides to grass-roots sentiment among the laity. But they probably reflected accurately enough in the long run the major interests of the townsmen and landed gentry who were their constituents. Certainly, they were not mere mouthpieces of the government — as is shown by the frequency with which the government turned their petitions down. As for the peasants and petty artisans, they certainly had their differences with the classes represented in the Commons, but when they had their one moment of articulation in 1382, they did nothing to indicate a radically different attitude toward church-state relations. We may suppose, then, that the Commons, while they did not fully live up to their name, at least reflected a broad base of public opinion.

Their views indicate a general agreement with the Erastian policy of controlling ecclesiastical institutions in the interest of the overall common good of a Christian realm. At the same time, they show a good deal of impatience with the political and administrative limitations the government imposed on itself in implementing that policy. What the Commons felt about the complex arrangements of the medieval church-state nexus was generally that they did not go far enough in the direction of royal control.

To be sure, the Commons were doctrinally orthodox. They could oppose heresy as stoutly as anyone. They accepted the prelates and clergy as a proper estate of the realm, and they reverenced the pope, or were willing to say they did. But they expected the king, not the pope or the prelates, to check clerical pretensions and see that clerical functions were efficiently performed. They had a low regard for French and Italian Christianity, and made it clear that they did not want their church run directly from Avignon or Rome.

They seem to have regarded the exising apparatus of ecclesiastical autonomy as unqualifiedly irrelevant, a system that served God but little and man not at all. They saw their English prelates as a privileged estate, loth to bear their fair share of the common burdens of the kingdom, but astute to bring in new laws to bind the laity without their consent; vigorous in finding new and unheard-of sources of revenue, but feeble in keeping up the ministrations of the church. They saw the great prelate-bureaucrats who served the king as men of divided loyalty, ready in crucial matters to support their clerical brethren against their royal master. They saw the international ecclesiastical establishment headed by the pope as drawing currency out of the country and sending nothing back, as peopling the land with French and Scottish spies to search out the secrets of the realm, as supporting the French war effort with English gold. They looked back to a golden age when every benefice in England was staffed with a faithful and competent teacher of God's law and dispenser of alms to the poor; they felt that a little positive action by the royal authorities would bring that age back again.

The royal authorities, for their part, shared the general ideological orientation of the Commons, but as more sophisticated statesmen, they preferred diplomacy to confrontation. Also, when it came to implementing the common ideology, the kings and great lords had more reason than the Commons for feeling ambivalent. The system of papal provisions offered them a better way of staffing their bureaucratic establishments than local ingenuity could match. The international character of Christianity furnished essential diplomatic underpinnings for their military ventures on the Continent. The Italian bankers whose chief business was supplying the English with money to spend in Rome evidently spread their assets judiciously on the local scene as well. And the pope's part in turning English benefices to the support of English bureaucrats and religious houses served to take the onus off the English lords and prelates for whose benefit he acted.

Hence, there were a wide variety of grievances on which the Commons never got full satisfaction from the government. These included procedural irregularities and financial exactions in the ecclesiastical courts, unaccustomed tithes, overpaid chaplains, aliens in English benefices, usury, failure to keep up services in chapels, failure to augment vicarages, and pluralism, nonresidence, incontinence, or failure to take orders on the part of parish incumbents. In all these matters, the Commons asked for lay remedies, enforceable in the king's courts, bypassing the ecclesiastical authorities. In each case, the government turned them down, sometimes referring to a concern for ecclesiastical prerogatives, sometimes expressing a desire to use diplomacy, sometimes contenting themselves with a mere *"le roy s'advisera"* or a statement that the existing law will do. The government also rejected attempts of the Commons to exclude churchmen from high offices of state, to exclude the laity from the operation of ecclesiastical legislation, to make grants of money conditional on like grants from the clergy, and to prevent English clerics from residing abroad. In short, it appears that from the mid-fourteenth century on, the Commons (and presumably their constituents) were prepared to make a sharper break with international Christianity, to undertake a more drastic administrative reform along national and utilitarian lines, than the kings and great lords were prepared to countenance, and to give the secular government more control over the church than the secular government was prepared to accept.

B. St. Germain.

At the very moment of the Reformation, the attitude that had dominated the Commons for two centuries found something like a theoretical synthesis in the work of Christopher St. Germain, an elderly (1460?-1540), and not particularly distinguished scholar of the common law. Besides having a solid knowledge of the laws of the realm, he seems to have been familiar with the commonplaces of ecclesiastical rhetoric, and was able to draw upon several current canonical compilations as well as the writings of the French theologian Jean Gerson (1363-1429). Thus equipped, and with the medieval world by way of crumbling about his ears, he set himself the task of showing how the laws of England might stand with conscience.

The resulting work, *Doctor and Student,* is a classic among lawyers, although it has received scant attention from anyone else. It consists of a series of dialogues between a Doctor of Divinity and a Student of the common law. One part was published in Latin in 1518, and then in English in 1523. The rest was published in English only in 1531 and 1532. The work is no abstract exercise in the meaning of law and conscience; the thorniest technicalities of English law are analyzed against the sharpest tenets of a schoolman's conscience:

> If a man enfeoff other in certain land upon condition, that if he enfeoff any other, that it may be lawful for the feoffor and his heirs to re-enter, etc., whether is this condition good in conscience, though it be void in the law?[1]

A rent is granted to a man in fee to perceive of two acres of land, and after

the grantor enfeoffeth the grantee of one of the said acres; whether is the
whole rent extinct thereby in conscience, as it is in the law?[2]

If a man steal a horse secretly in the night, it is used that thereupon he shall
be indicted at the king's suit, and it is used that in that indictment it shall be
supposed that he such a day and place with force and arms, (that is to say)
with staves, swords, and knives, etc., feloniously stole the horse against
the king's peace; and that form must be kept in every indictment, though
the felon had neither sword nor other weapon with him, but that he came
secretly without weapon: how can it therefore be excused, but there is
an untruth?[3]

In the course of all this, St. Germain picks up quite naturally a number of
traditional areas of disagreement between the laws of the church and those of
the state — patronage, bastardy, tithe, alienation of church property — and
asks where conscience stands on these matters. By appealing to a conscience
whose dictates are the same for everyone, he precludes in each case the
medieval solution whereby each body of officials follows its own law. Rather,
he insists that the temporal law must govern in each case because the
subject-matter is a temporal thing. The Student brushes aside the Doctor's
objections that a thing can be spiritual by reason of the use to which it is put or
by reason of its traditional subjection to ecclesiastical law. He is quite sure that
anything you can count out or put your hand on is temporal, and that any
control the church has over it is by custom or concession. As for the spiritual
object, "the king, which hath the rule and governance over the people, not only
of their bodies, but also of their souls,"[4] may be expected to direct his laws to
that object as fully as the church does its laws.

A little more is made of the Doctor's view that learning the secular law is a
harder task than the ecclesiastical judges can be expected to undertake. The
Student is sympathetic, but inexorable. If the temporal law applies, they must
give judgment according to it or they offend in conscience. If they cannot learn
it themselves, they must consult with learned men.[5]

The later edition of the second part of the Dialogue was fortified with a
substantial "Addition", setting forth the author's views of the power of
Parliament over the church and its affairs. An intriguing array of possibilities is
meticulously laid out, supported by analogues in old legislation, by the lay
power over temporal things, by the common good, and even by the canon law
itself (which sometimes forbids a practice, but does not set a sufficient
remedy). Parliament, according to the arguments set forth here, may:

1. Displace with secular proceedings the ecclesiastical remedies for
   dilapidations, pensions and annuities, and defamation (except as regards
   the personal correction of the offender). These all involve the payment
   of money, and the lay claim to exclusive jurisdiction goes back to
   Circumspecte Agatis.

2. Forbid all appropriations of benefices and all alienations in mortmain. It has long regulated them; also, the lands alienated and the advowsons appropriated are both temporal estates of inheritance.

3. Alter or abolish rights of sanctuary and benefit of clergy. These do not exist "by the spiritual authority", as the Doctor supposes, "but by the old customs and maxims of the law of the realm."

4. Provide for the distribution of church property and revenues between churchmen, and that even in the case of consecrated ground. The Student grounds himself on a statute of 1307, concerning the purposes to which trees growing in a churchyard might be put, and a statute of 1391, which has the effect of deconsecrating any land consecrated in violation of the mortmain laws.

5. Regulate the cost and character of funeral rites, impose sumptuary laws on the clergy, and regulate the wages of domestic chaplains. All these are temporal matters, and the matter of chaplains' wages has in fact been dealt with by Parliament in the past. Regarding funerals, the Doctor tries to make a distinction between "such things as be ordained to the service of God, or to the relief of the soul" and "such . . . things as be but worldly pomps and be rather consolations to the friends that be alive than any relief to the soul that is departed."[6] But the Student insists that Parliament can regulate both classes. "For such statutes be for ordering of temporal things, and to force that the king's subjects should not be charged but as the Parliament should think expedient for the wealth of the realm."[7]

6. Forbid ecclesiastical visitors to take money from those they visit. This would be in keeping with the general good of the church, and has a precedent in the statutes of Edward I concerning alien visitors.

7. Regulate the age of reception into religious houses. The religious life, like marriage, is basically a spiritual matter, but, like marriage, it can be subjected to incidental regulation.

8. Impose secular penalties on bishops who ordain men who lack sufficient learning. This is already forbidden by church law, but the sanction imposed by the church is inadequate. The Student's chief problem with such a law as this is to determine who will try the case.

9. Regulate the spreading of ill-founded reports concerning miracles, and make those who profit from shrines and the like take steps to see that the faithful are instructed concerning the proper place of such devotions in the Christian life. Statutes of this kind would be analogous to one enacted in 1400 which forbade preaching without the license of the bishop. "And under this manner the Parliament may ordain many good laws for strength of the faith, and for the good of all the people, as well spiritual as temporal, though it judge not upon the right of things that be

mere spiritual.'' For, while Parliament has no direct power over the
laws of God, "to strengthen them and to make them to be more surely
kept it hath good power.'"[8]

10. Determine the reasons for the heresies and charges of heresy that are
abroad in the realm, and devise a suitable remedy. This would be
analogous to the act of the Parliament of 1378 in determining which of
two claimants was to be considered the lawful pope. In such
determinations as this, Parliament is evidently to consider the laws of
God and of the church, but may make its own judgment as to what
those laws provide. It seems that part of the reason why St. Germain
gives Parliament such latitude in dealing with heresy is that he does not
take the doctrinal aspect of heresy very seriously:

And verily if it be true that some have reported, many of them
[heresies] be so far against the truth, that I suppose no christian man
will hold them, believing them to be true: but that they do it for some
other consideration. . . .[And] therefore if it were ordained for a law,
that every curate at the death of every of their parishioners, should say
for their souls in audience *Placebo* and *Dirige*, and mass, without
taking anything therefore, and that they should also at a certain time,
there to be assigned by Parliament, as it were once in a month, or as
shall be thought convenient, do in likewise, and pray especially for the
souls of their parishioners, and for all christian souls, and for the king
and the whole realm: and religious houses to do after the same manner,
I suppose, that in short time there would be but few, that would say,
there were no purgatory. And in likewise if it were ordered so by the
pope, that there might be certain general pardons of full remission in
divers parts of the realm, which the people might have for saying
certain orisons and prayers, without paying any money for it, it is not
unlike, but in short time there would be very few, that would find any
default at pardons: for verily it is a great comfort to all christian people
to remember, that our Lord loved his people so much that he would to
their relief and comfort, leave behind him so great a treasure, as is the
power to grant pardons . . . And I think verily, that if the king's grace,
and his Parliament, look not upon these matters, it will be hard to tell
who shall be able to do it.[9]

In 1532, St. Germain published anonymously *A Treatise Concernynge the
Division Betwene the Spiritualtie and Temporaltie,* in which he developed
certain themes that had been touched on in passing in *Doctor and Student.*
This launched an exchange of pamphlets with St. Thomas More, in which
More, in my judgment, came off second best.[10] In the series of pamphlets,
St. Germain complained about lack of procedural safeguards in heresy trials,

and about the menial conditions under which so many clergy served in the households of lay employers or patrons. But his most serious complaint was that the clergy were continually dissipating their influence in the maintenance of their own prerogatives. He regarded these prerogatives as the chief source of the current religious disagreements — the doctrinal controversies like faith versus good works not being really serious. For the most part, he was pointing to a problem rather than urging a solution; but insofar as he had recommendations, they involved more active intervention by king and Parliament.

The corpus of St. Germain's writings is completed with another pamphlet, again published anonymously, called *A Treatise Concerninge the Power of the Clergye and the Lawes of the Realme*. This is not dated, but it must have been written after 1535, as it mentions the royal supremacy established at that time. Most of this pamphlet is a series of statements on the power of Parliament, rather like that in the last part of *Doctor and Student*. St. Germain takes the royal supremacy in his stride, insisting that it does not extend to spiritual matters (in his rather narrow conception of what is spiritual), and that it is really nothing new.

But what is most interesting in this document is its treatment of the claims of the clergy to an autonomous jurisdiction. St. Germain rehearses all the clichés of medieval clericalist rhetoric, and demolishes them on their own terms:

1. The text "whatsoever thou shalt bind on earth shall be bound in heaven" must be interpreted in the light of the Lord's statement that His kingdom is not of this world. It means that the clergy have power to separate evil men from the communion of the faithful, nothing more.
2. The text about the two swords being enough refers not to the temporal and the spiritual power, but to the number of swords required on the occasion of our Lord's passion. It means that two swords would serve His purposes as well as a thousand.
3. The text instructing a person wronged by his brother to "tell the church" refers not to the clergy but to the whole Christian people, who constitute the church. Thus, the text means for one aggrieved to tell the person, lay or clerical, whose duty it is to hear the matter and punish the offender.
4. The text to the effect that the spiritual man judges all things and is judged of no one refers to the follower of the Spirit, not to the member of the spiritual estate.
5. The text "you will judge angels; how much more secular things" was addressed to the whole congregation at Corinth, not just to the clergy.
6. The text about God making the sun and the moon cannot be used to support the dependence of lay power upon clerical power without some proof that mention of these celestial bodies is meant to be taken in other than a literal sense.

7. Grants to the church by secular rulers on the Continent do not apply in England; nor does the king of England have the right to grant away his own powers.

8. The text from Deuteronomy that hard and doubtful cases should be decided by the priests cannot apply to priests of the New Law. Their superiority over the Aaronic priesthood does not, as they argue, give them a better right to judge such cases; rather, it makes it less suitable that they should meddle in worldly affairs. Here St. Germain refers to Acts: "It is not meet that we forsake the Word of God and serve tables."

9. It is argued that emperors lost their rights through mistreatment of the church, and that those rights then devolved upon the church. But these rights came not from the church but from God. Even if they had been forfeited, they would have returned to God, not passed to the clergy.

10. The text "All power is given to me . . . ." cannot support attributing all Christ's powers to the Apostles and their successors, as it is clear that they do not have his power to work miracles. He gave them power to administer the sacraments; there is no reason to suppose he gave them other powers that would distract from their doing so.

11. The text "He who heareth you heareth me" was spoken to the disciples when they were sent forth without scrip or staff and were told what to preach. Hence, it means simply that those who truly preach the Gospel must be reverently heard.

All this is not as revolutionary in practice as it seems to be in theory. The concrete suggestions accompanying it are mild enough, and leave the main body of clerical privileges fairly well intact. What is important is that the whole argument makes all such privileges depend for their existence on the state.

Despite the timely support all this might have given King Henry, I think it is fairly clear that St. Germain was not a royal propagandist. He gives unobtrusive but persuasive evidences of sincerity and piety in many places. He is entirely silent as to the king's divorce. And he is extremely reticent in dealing with any matter in immediate controversy. For instance, in taking up the powers of Parliament, when he comes to the subject-matter of the 1529 act on mortuaries, he says:

> I hold it not best to reason, or to make arguments, whether they had authority to do that they did or not. For I suppose, that no man would think that they would do anything that they had not power to do.[11]

Neither is he one of those followers of Marsilius of Padua who began to appear in connection with King Henry's proceedings. He is not for giving the temporal authorities a blank check in regulating the affairs of the church. Radical as his proposals are, he takes each one up point by point and decides it on its own merits. Whatever we may think when he has finished, he himself never ceases to believe that he has left intact the authority of the spiritual estate over matters merely spiritual. Also, he is very clear that whatever powers king and Parliament possess are not to be exercised for secular political ends. The king "hath the rule and governance over the people not only of their bodies, but also of their souls." It is his business to order the temporal affairs of his subjects so that they may prosper both in this world and the next. Parliament, also, is to exercise its powers "with a charitable intent" for the improvement of the whole church. If St. Germain had his way:

> . . . then would all men, as well spiritual as temporal, rather take heed to themself, to see that they did nothing to give occasion to the parliament to extend his power upon them or their possessions, than to resist or deny the authority of the parliament.[12]

The problem for St. Germain was the "division" between the lay and spiritual estates of the realm, a problem continually exacerbated by the jealousy with which the clergy maintained their own prerogatives. The solution as he saw it was in having a law superior to both estates. To this law clergy as well as laity ought in conscience to submit:

> Wherefore it seemeth that they that have the greatest charge over the people, specially to the health of their souls, are most bound in conscience to look to this matter, and to do that in them is, in all charity to have it reformed, not beholding the temporal jurisdiction or spiritual jurisdiction, but the common wealth and quietness of the people: and that undoubtedly would shortly follow, if this division were put away, which I suppose verily will not be, but that all men within the realm, both spiritual and temporal, be ordered and ruled by one law in all things temporal.[13]

He seems to suppose that the whole division can be resolved by merely allowing the temporal authorities to have power over temporal things, the spiritual authorities over spiritual — a simple matter of rendering to Caesar. He is not unaware of the problem of deciding what things are temporal, but he tends to minimize it. He rejects out of hand the Doctor's notion that the ecclesiastical authorities must pass judgment on this question because their institution serves the higher end: in this he follows the position taken by the lay authorities since the thirteenth century. But he does not substitute an absolute right of the lay authorities to make the determination for themselves. Ideally, he would like the two sets of authorities to agree.

> And if spiritual men, and temporal men, would charitably lay their heads together, and fully determine what the parliament may do . . . . I think verily that there would nothing do more good to appease such variances, schisms and divisions as be abroad in the realm.[14]

But of such an eventuality he has little hope, given the predilection of the
clergy for maintaining their own power. Failing that, men must work things out
in conscience as best they can — presumably following reason and precedent as
St. Germain does in his book.

Curiously enough, he considers and rejects, in passing, a suggestion of the
Doctor's that looks very like the modern solution whereby the authority of the
church operates in an area of personal freedom left open by the state. He refers
to an act that an abbot cannot do under the canon law without consulting the
members of his house, but which by the laws of England he can do alone. The
Doctor suggests reasonably enough that the laws of England do not forbid him
to consult the members of the house, and therefore that he should do so and
thus comply with both laws. The Student says that he may consult if he will,

> but if he takes their assent, . . . thinking that he is so bound to do in law and
> conscience, setting a conscience where none is, and regardeth not the law of
> the realm, that will discharge his conscience in this behalf . . .; there is an
> error and offence of conscience in the abbot.[15]

In the last analysis, then, St. Germain is a medieval thinker. He sees the
temporal and spiritual estates as two sets of powers, each with its proper
jurisdiction in a unified Christian society. If he gives more scope to the
temporal, less to the spiritual, authority than others would do, it is partly
because he is looking at matters from the standpoint of a temporal man, and
partly — perhaps mostly — because it is the temporal authorities that show
some promise of doing the job that needs to be done. Here also he harks back
to the Commons of the preceding two centuries.

His intellectual enterprise throughout is that of a lawyer, not a theorist. His
theories emerge only gradually out of a series of single instances in which he
moulds both principle and precedent to the meeting of felt needs. We can
never be sure he realizes just how far his reasoning has taken him. The church
must have some kind of freedom of action in the temporal sphere if it is to
discharge its task of spreading the Gospel. By the same token, if everything
you can see, feel or walk on is "temporal", the church cannot fulfil its mission
of proclaiming the physical presence of the spiritual in the world. Of all this,
St. Germain seems oblivious. The arguments for ecclesiastical authority that he
sets himself to answer are all on the level of rhetoric, not of policy, whereas
the arguments he puts for temporal authority are ultimately all on the level
of policy.

His approach, then, is all of a piece with his refusal to take seriously the
theological questions that he finds agitating Christendom. He cannot get excited
about the difference between justification by faith and good works and
justification by faith alone. He cannot believe that a man would throw over
such comfortable doctrines as purgatory and indulgences unless his pocketbook
was at stake. He has, in short, a typical Englishman's impatience with theory, a

typical English desire to get on with the job.

St. Germain, for all his erudition, does not impress one as a particularly creative thinker. Even if we had no evidence on the point, we would be inclined to think that his work involved a synthesis of views that were commonplace in the circles in which he moved. But in fact, we do have evidence, a great deal of evidence, in the history of the previous two hundred years. St. Germain shares with his forefathers the Commons of England their rough and ready piety, their utilitarianism, their impatience with the niceties of theology, their exasperation with the pretensions of clerical power, their insistence on a unified Christian society in which the clergy could not claim to be the church, their wholehearted support for the basic patterns of governmental interference in ecclesiastical affairs, their belief that in more of the same lay the answer to all the problems of the church.

C. King Henry.

I do not mean by all this to minimize the importance of King Henry's religious innovations. It is only that when he came to innovate he had a living tradition of two centuries and more to which he could look for a supply of rhetoric and a measure of popular support. His major pieces of Reformation legislation were fortified with preambles that harked back to appropriate elements in the tradition. They were accompanied by administrative measures which, if they did not meet all the traditional grievances, were at least developed with the traditional grievances in mind.

1. Ministry and Services – One of the first pieces of Reformation legislation, enacted in 1529, dealt with pluralism, nonresidence, and secular occupations on the part of the clergy.[16] The canonical rule that automatically ousted a man from one benefice when he was inducted into another was made a rule of secular law if the first benefice was worth more than eight pounds a year. The rule was put beyond the reach of ecclesiastical dispensation, and anyone accepting a purported dispensation was liable to a forfeiture of twenty pounds. Anyone seeking to evade the law by leasing or farming a second benefice instead of being inducted into it was to forfeit ten times the annual value. All the forfeitures provided for might be sued for by anyone who cared to litigate, who would then divide the proceeds equally with the king.

A number of exceptions were made. The king could bestow on his own chaplains as many as he chose of the benefices in his own gift. A privy councilor might hold up to three benefices with cure. Other officers of state, holders of academic degrees, and brothers and sons of lords or knights could all hold two. The various lay and ecclesiastical magnates were allowed to have chaplains (from one to eight, depending on rank) with two benefices apiece.

The provisions on nonresidence were comparable. Anyone who did not reside on his benefice (or one of his benefices if he was lawfully a pluralist) was to forfeit ten pounds. A further forfeiture of twenty pounds was provided for anyone procuring a dispensation of nonresidence if the act required him to reside. Exceptions were made for the king's chaplains with his permission, and for pilgrims, students, (a provision of 1536 limited this exception to persons under forty, and required them to attend lectures regularly)[17] diplomats, specified bureaucrats, and chaplains dwelling in the households of the various magnates of the kingdom.

In the line of secular occupations, the statute forbade any spiritual person, again on pain of suitable forefeitures, to keep a tannery or brewery, to traffic in goods for profit, or to occupy lands as a farmer or lessee unless he needed them to maintain his household.[18]

Pluralism and nonresidence had been a concern of the Commons since before 1400. The 1529 statute contained nothing on these matters that was not adumbrated in one or another of the four petitions they filed on the subject between 1400 and 1425. The matter of secular employment is harder to pin down. There was a great deal of canonical legislation on the subject in the medieval period, but I find nothing to indicate that the lay authorities concerned themselves with it. One petition on the subject of nonresidence (1410) seems to treat secular occupation as a source of nonresidence, but it is academic and bureaucratic, rather than commercial, activity that is envisaged:

> some now occupy offices either in your Court or in the courts of other lords, and others sojourn at London, Oxford, or Cambridge, or in Abbeys, or priories, or in various other places, spending little or nothing for good purposes attending in no way to their cures, or to doing the things they are supposed to, so that (*issint q̃*) the riches of the realm are now in their hands.[19]

What happened, I suppose, is that the same qualities of literacy and lack of feudal attachment that made the clergy successful bureaurats in an earlier period were now in the process of making them effective middlemen in the growing commerce of the period, including the commercial exploitation of land.

Other improvements in the ministry were less important.[20] The draconian measures against clerical concubinage in the Six Articles Act of 1539 evidently reflected Henry's theological interest in celibacy rather than the traditional concern of the laity for clerical morals. An act of 1545 providing for the union of poor benefices probably added nothing to the canonical powers of the ordinary. The establishment of five new bishoprics pursuant to a statutory grant of power in 1539 was a reform three centuries overdue, but it was hardly generous in view of the amount of monastic endowment the king could have devoted to such purposes. A statute of 1534 providing for suffragan bishops with see titles taken from English cities merely replaced the bishops *in partibus infidelium* formerly appointed by the pope for the same purpose.

One perennial concern of the medieval Commons, the failure of religious houses to keep up the services and good works for which they were founded, was radically dealt with — the houses were confiscated.[21] The lesser monasteries were taken over in 1536, the others in 1539. An act was passed in 1545 taking over hospitals, chantries, and collegiate establishments as well, but this was not implemented until the following reign. None of these acts made any pretext of restoring the endowments to the purposes for which they were originally given. The 1536 act contained a provision for keeping up hospitality on the sites of the suppressed monasteries, but this was evidently never implemented. The 1539 act was accompanied by another which authorized the king to put the proceeds into new bishoprics, but only a fraction was actually devoted to that purpose. The 1545 act simply recited that the endowments of the suppressed establishments could be better used in helping the king sustain the financial burdens of the state.

None of these measures was rested on any theological argument like those that accompanied similar measures under Edward VI. While some advantage was taken of the newly established supreme headship, most of the justificatory language in Henry's acts spoke of the intentions of the founders, the moral and financial irregularities of the suppressed establishments, the fact that they had been set up under mortmain licenses from the king's ancestors — traditional medieval arguments in favor of lay intervention in their affairs. What was new was not the intervention by the government, but the radical form that intervention took. Even here, though, there was medieval precedent, at least in theory. The Statute of Westminster II (1285), as we saw in the last chapter, provided that a private donor could have his land back if the religious house alienated it or failed to keep up the services. Provision was made for lands held of the king to be taken into his hands under such circumstances: while it was evidently expected that he would restore them to a religious use, there was nothing that required him to. Further, in 1324, when the Templars were dissolved, it was determined in Parliament that the king and other lords might take their lands back by escheat, although "for the health of their souls and discharge of their consciences" they decided to turn them over to the Hospitallers for the carrying out of the pious purposes of the original grantors. Finally, in 1371, Edward III, in ordering the Bishop of London to correct the irregularities of the canons of St. Paul's stated that these irregularities gave him every right to take back the possessions granted by his ancestors, and that he only refrained out of piety from doing so. In short, while the medieval lay authorities were disposed to maintain ecclesiastical endowments in their original purposes, they claimed a right to take them back if they were misused.

How the Commons felt about Henry's wholesale exercise of this right is hard to say. Those who participated in the Pilgrimage of Grace (in 1536, after the suppression of the lesser monasteries and before that of the greater) took up the cause of the monasteries.[22] Robert Aske, their leader, put the case in terms of intercessions, ministry, good works, and esthetics, giving, it seems to me, greater emphasis to the intercession than the good works. Henry responded by alluding to the vices and improvidence of the monks, so that God was not well served in their houses, but quite the opposite, and their funds were better spent in helping to meet the great expenses of the king for the public good than in supporting the "unthrifty life" of the religious. With whatever value there might be in the prayers and masses of the monks, and with their contributions to the rural ministry, Henry concerned himself not at all.

I doubt if either Henry's argument or Aske's found general acceptance among the people. Rather, I should suppose that the ordinary citizen was sympathetic to the ideals represented by monasteries and kindred institutions, but saw little worth taking up the cudgels for in these institutions as they stood. He would probably have liked to see Henry reform them instead of cutting them down, but as that was not to be, he was prepared to acquiesce in abolishing them rather than letting them go on as they had been.

What surprises me most in the liquidation of these establishments is how little was made of the profanation of sacred objects and consecrated ground. Aske alluded to the matter:

> . . . the temple of God ruined and pulled down, the ornaments and relics of the church of God unreverent used, the tombs and sepulchres of honourable and noble men pulled down and sold . . .

but even he made less of it than of other things. It is the law of England to this day that consecrated ground cannot be secularized except by Act of Parliament, [23] and I find nothing on the point in any of the suppression acts. Nor do I find any legal writer from that day to this who addresses himself to the question of how consecrated monastic land became secular. Yet we know that it was done all over England.

In fact, though, even in more pious times there appears to have been no systematic provision made to preserve sacred ground from profanation when a change was made in its use. It is related that when Henry VI appropriated Sherburne Priory to Eton:

> . . . oon Benet, then priour there, and all the Monkes Ministers and Servauntes of the said Prioury . . . were put oute, and from the same taken almaner Goodes, Catalx, Juelx, Reliquiez and Honourmentes . . . and the moost parte of the edefying thereof drowen down, caried away and destrued, not abhored to lye Cornes, Hay, and to suffre booth Horses and Cartes dayly to go uppon the sepultures of Christen people, in grete number buried in the Chirch there, whereof moo than XXX symtyme were worshipfull Barons, Knyghtes and Squyers . . .[24]

Someone (perhaps the local populace) had to take the matter into Parliament to have it set to rights. Here too, then, what was done under Henry had been done before, albeit on nothing like a comparable scale.[25]

The suppression of the monasteries brought no direct alleviation of the Commons' old grievance against monastic appropriators who failed to keep up services and hospitality in their appropriated churches. The rights of the appropriators were taken over by the king and bestowed on his grantees to hold as fully and as irresponsibly as the monasteries had held them — if not more so. But the laicization of these rights seems to have had the effect of turning an important class of the laity from victims to beneficiaries of appropriation. From Henry's time on, it is the laity who favor the status quo on this point, and the clergy who complain.

2. *Finance* – Another of the acts that inaugurated the royal program in 1529 dealt with mortuaries.[26] It fixed the amount that could be taken on a sliding scale ranging from ten shillings where the deceased left more than forty pounds' worth of movable goods to nothing if he left less than ten marks. Subject to these limits, mortuaries could be taken only where customary, and only where the deceased was a householder residing in the parish where the mortuary was sought. Anyone taking more than the act allowed was to restore it, and in addition forfeit forty shillings to the person aggrieved.

I do not find mortuaries among the grievances advanced by the medieval Commons, although the desire to limit ecclesiastical exactions in general is familiar. It was over a mortuary that the London merchant Richard Hunne had come to grief in a notorious case in 1514; it may have been this that made mortuaries temporarily the most unpopular of ecclesiastical dues.

Henry's legislative program made no general provision for controlling the exaction of tithe.[27] The tithes of wood that had constituted a particular bone of contention in the parliaments of the fourteenth and fifteenth centuries were dealt with by reviving a statute of 1371 providing for a prohibition when tithes were sought for trees more than twenty years old. This statute was evidently not much enforced before the Reformation. As late as 1414, the Commons were still complaining about the matter, and getting no satisfaction from the government. Coke, anxious as always to show the antiquity of the practices of his day, is able to show a steady incidence of cases beginning in 33 Henry VIII (1541), but only one before then.[28]

The most important of Henry's effects on tithe was the laicizing of large amounts of it in conjunction with the dissolution of the monasteries. Whatever tithe revenue a monastery had possessed devolved on the king by the dissolution, and passed from him to his lay grantees. An act of 1540 provided that for most purposes any tithes or similar ecclesiastical revenues "which now be, or hereafter shall be made temporal, or admitted to be, abide and go to or in temporal hands and lay uses and profits by the law or statutes of this realm" might be held, conveyed, and litigated over like other temporal estates in land.[29]

For the actual collection of tithe, however, the traditional ecclesiastical proceedings were preserved, with somewhat more effective enforcement.[30] Laymen were given access to the ecclesiastical courts by the 1540 act for the purpose of bringing such proceedings. The preamble to that act recites that they had not had such access "by the order and course of the ecclesiastical laws of this realm." As to this assertion, I am a little dubious. It does not seem to me that tithes could have been farmed to laymen as often as they were if the laymen had not been able to bring proceedings to collect them.

By turning tithe into a lay hereditament, and making the church courts enforce it in that capacity, Henry swept away five hundred years of ecclesiastical tradition concerning the sacred character of this form of revenue. How far he was departing from medieval lay tradition is more problematical; still, it would seem that the departure was not small. The medieval Commons insisted, as I have pointed out, that tithe was a customary payment and not a radical tenth of the gross national product; in this, they had the support of the government as often as not. Logically, if tithe has no higher origin than custom, it cannot be of divine right, and must be a payment that the community can grant or take away. What the divine law requires is merely that the clergy receive sufficient funds for their support, and tithe is no more sacred than any other funds allocated for that purpose.

Logically, this is true. But I find no one in the mainstream of medieval English lay opinion who drew the logic out. The medieval Commons recited on a number of occasions that tithe was a payment with which no layman could meddle; on a number of occasions they took measures to keep tithes in ecclesiastical hands. Not until St. Germain was the secular character of tithes articulated. St. Germain had theologians to back him up, but no one in his own tradition. The Commons were prepared to recognize that tithes, whatever their origin, had a sacred character and should not be in lay hands.

The lay farmer has often been pointed to as the man who smoothed over the transition of monastic tithe from the sacred to the profane. The practice of farming appropriated churches to laymen had been growing apace for a century and a half; by the end of the fourteenth century, the popes were supporting the practice with wholesale dispensations from a canonical prohibition that cannot have been too well enforced in the first place. We may suppose that these sturdy businessmen came and carried off their property in a way that made it easy to forget the sacred character of what they were about. We may suppose also that when the dissolution came they made arrangements with the king or his grantees that left the practical situation in the appropriated parishes much as it was before.

Henry's financial program for the church included one set of statutes giving him a permanent share of ecclesiastical revenues as such — first fruits and tenths.[31] The first fruits were a full year's value (according to the valuation in the royal survey of 1539, which soon became much less than true value, on account of inflation) of every benefice to be paid by each new incumbent on taking over. The tenths were a tenth part of the same value to be paid in every year but the one in which first fruits were paid. Except during Mary's reign, these revenues continued to be part of the general funds of the state until 1702, when they were devoted to ecclesiastical purposes under the name of Queen Anne's Bounty.

The traditional Anglican account of these revenues has it that they had long been collected by the pope, and were transferred to the king in connection with his newly established supreme headship.[32] Lunt has pointed out how little this tradition is supported by the facts. The pope exacted first fruits only of benefices filled by his provision; as we saw in the last volume, these included by the late fifteenth century only the bishoprics and a handful of lesser benefices. Tenths the popes had endeavored to obtain from time to time either by grant of Convocation or by exercise of their own authority, but what with one thing or another they had only succeeded five times in two hundred years. These exactions, however they were regarded by the English, can hardly be equated with the year-in-year-out levy that replaced them.

In fact, the act imposing this levy makes no reference to the former papal taxes. It simply sets forth what a good king Henry is, and has been these five and twenty years, and how much it has cost and still costs him to do his job so well, and says that his loving subjects

> do therefore desire, and most humbly pray, that for the more surety of continuance and augmentation of his Highness' royal estate, being not only now recognized (as he always indeed hath heretofore been) the only supreme head on earth, next and immediately under God, of the church of England, but also their most assured and undoubted natural sovereign liege lord and King, having the whole governance, tuition, defence and maintenance of this his realm, and most loving and obedient subjects of the same: it may therefore be ordained and enacted . . .

While this mentions the supreme headship, it mentions it only in the context of the other duties and prerogatives of the king. To me it seems reminiscent of the Commons' request in 1344 that the king take the fruits of aliens' benefices for the defense of the realm *"et de Seinte Esglise d'ycelle."*[33]

The substantive provisions of the Act for First Fruits and Tenths may be set beside the two attempts of the Commons in Richard II's reign to condition their subsidies on like subsidies by the clergy, and their request in the same reign that the king take first fruits from clergy advanced by royal patronage as the pope did from clergy advanged by papal provision. Henry's levy of first fruits and tenths may be patterned on papal models, but it rests its main bid for justification of the traditional desire of the Commons to have the church assume a larger share of the common burdens of the kingdom.

    3. Ecclesiastical Administration – Henry opened his attack on the administrative autonomy of the church with a statute in 1529 that limited the probate fees in the ecclesiastical courts.[34] The amount fixed varied with the value of the movable goods in the estate, ranging up to five shillings (or two shillings sixpence plus a penny for each ten lines of the will, at the option of the scribe) for an estate worth more than forty pounds. Violators were to make restitution, and forfeit ten pounds besides, half to the victim, half to the king. The fees thus regulated had long been a sore point with the Commons. They had been asking for some such measure as this since 1347. In fact, a statute was made on the point in 1415, but it was worded to expire in a year, and was never renewed. Much of this history was recited in the preamble to the 1529 act.

    Another grievance similar to that concerning probate fees involved the practice of the church courts concerning citations. The medieval Commons had succeeded in obtaining legislation to insure that a defendant in an ecclesiastical proceeding was given a copy of the libel in his case. They had also wanted the government to intervene to prevent a defendant's being cited out of the vicinity of his home, and to prevent the issue of citations in blank which inferior clergy or apparitors could use against anyone they chose. These grievances were met in part by an act of 1532 which forbade any person to be cited out of the diocese or peculiar jurisdiction in which he lived.[35] Suitable exceptions were made for wrongs committed in another diocese, and for the appellate jurisdiction of the metropolitan courts. Violators were subject to double damages to the victim plus ten pounds' forfeiture, half to the informant, half to the king.

    The Submission of the Clergy, adopted by Convocation in 1532, and made a statute in the following year,[36] bound the prelates not to legislate for the English church without submitting their enactments for the king's assent, and also to submit to the king's pleasure all provincial legislation then in force. Nothing came of the ensuing project for revising the existing canon law, but the requirement that new English canons be submitted for the royal assent endures to this day.

    The legislative autonomy of the prelates was a grievance in the Commons' petition of 1532, and it had been brought up once before, as early as 1376. But the emphasis was sharply altered. What the Commons were worried about was that the ecclesiastical legislation took effect, it seemed to them, as part of the law of the land without their — the Commons' — assent. The king's assent was mentioned, along with that of the Commons, in the 1532 petition; in 1376, the Commons mentioned only themselves. Also, the Commons were not concerned about ecclesiastical legislation governing the internal affairs of the church; their grievance was with being themselves subjected to it when they had had no part in its enactment. So Henry's provision that ecclesiastical legislation should not take effect even within the church without his — the king's — assent related to the Commons' grievance, but can hardly be said to have met it. It remained for an eighteenth-century court, relying on one Year Book case and a few passages from Coke, to establish that ecclesiastical legislation does not bind the laity unless confirmed by Parliament.[37]

Aside from the matters just discussed, the only interferences of Henry's program with the internal workings of the machinery of ecclesiastical government were those necessitated by the abolition of the papal jurisdiction. Acts, mostly adopted in 1534,[38] gave the pope's routine dispensing power to the Archbishop of Canterbury, his non-routine dispensing power and his power to grant indulgences to the King in Council. The powers of the pope, and of foreign superiors as well, over English religious houses were transferred to the king. Appeals that formerly went to Rome were to be heard in Chancery by the king's delegates.

Evidently it was not contemplated that the papal power to displace local ecclesiastical courts of first instance with judges-delegate would be kept up under the new arrangement. The Court of High Commission that exercised analogous powers by royal authority in Elizabethan and early Stuart times was not fully in operation until Elizabeth's reign.

The pope's part in the election of bishops was eliminated rather than replaced.[39] The old procedure of election by the cathedral chapter with a royal *congé d' élire* was retained, and the displacement of the election by papal provision was done away with. The custom of the chapter to elect the person nominated by the king was made a statutory duty; on failure to comply, the electors were made subject to *praemunire* and the king was authorized to fill the see by letters patent.

4. Secular Policies – The medieval ecclesiastical privileges of sanctuary and clerical immunity received a far less sympathetic treatment under Henry than they had had in earlier times.[40] The sophisticated evasions of the earlier period gave way to frontal attack. The first invasion of sanctuary came in 1531, with an act that substituted confinement at designated places in England for the old abjuration of the realm. The criminal was not exactly imprisoned in the designated place, but he was subjected to periodic muster, and other irksome restrictions on his activity, on pain of losing his right of sanctuary. On the whole, after this act, all a man got by taking sanctuary was a reduction of his punishment to life imprisonment. In 1540, even this privilege was taken away from anyone who committed murder, rape, burglary, robbery, or arson.

The medieval concern for starving out the offender rather than invading the physical precincts of the church was a good deal less noticeable in Henry's legislation. It was expressly provided in the 1531 act that if a person who took sanctuary came out, committed further felonies and returned to sanctuary, he could be forcibly taken out. It seems likely also that the 1540 act contemplated the physical removal rather than the starving out of classes of offenders excluded from the benefits of sanctuary.

It is not entirely clear to me how radical a departure this was from medieval practice. Cox quotes a passage from the late thirteenth-century *Mirror of Justice* to the effect that certain types of felons may be physically removed from sanctuary, including those who ''have offended in sanctuary, or joined upon this hope to be defended in sanctuary.''[41] We saw also that a man once convicted could be taken out of sanctuary for the execution of the sentence — though those taking him out may have been subject to ecclesiastical censures. Certainly, there was a shift of emphasis between the medieval and the Henrician practice; certainly, the exquisite formalism of starvation went gradually out of use at this time. But again, there is no reason to suppose that the change was wholly without precedent.

An act passed in 1532, and made perpetual in 1540, made important changes in benefit of clergy. It began with a recital of the evils of allowing purgation to clerical convicts, and some of the efforts that had been made in previous centuries to get ordinaries to keep their convicts in prison. It followed with a list of crimes, including murder and most kinds of robbery, for which benefit of clergy would not be allowed except to men in major orders. Those allowed clergy for such offenses because of their major orders were to be kept without purgation, unless they gave bond with substantial sureties for their future good behavior. This was followed by acts punishing specific offenses (sodomy in 1534, embezzlement in 1536, horse stealing in 1545) without allowing benefit of clergy for anyone. Finally, a 1536 act (also made perpetual in 1540) imposed on clerics in major orders the same rules that applied to everyone else. That is, they were not allowed to escape punishment for the crimes listed in the 1532 act, and they were allowed clergy only once, as was provided for other men in an act of 1487.

These acts completed the transition of benefit of clergy from a privilege of the church to a mitigation of the rigors of the criminal law for everyone.[42] The transition was in process all through the fifteenth century, as we have seen. The church had presumably acquiesced in it, since the ordinaries generally cooperated in the claiming of spurious clerics, and appeared to make no objection to the restrictions of the 1487 act. The only real innovation under Henry VIII was the subjecting of clerics in major orders to the same treatment as their spurious brethren. I find no case before the 1536 act in which real priests, deacons, or subdeacons were subject to capital punishment for any secular crime except high treason. Indeed, not since Becket's time had anyone suggested that they should be. The medieval laity had shown considerable willingness to inflict violence on priests, but never before by process of law.

Henry's legislation took major steps toward the ultimate secularization of usury and poor relief, two matters, logically secular, that had been of ecclesiastical cognizance all through the Middle Ages.[43] There had been a concurrent secular remedy for usury since 1494 — something the Commons had long desired. An act of 1545 initiated the modern pattern of making interest lawful up to a certain amount (in this case, ten percent), and imposing a secular penalty on any higher rate. As for poor relief, an act of 1536 made systematic provision for collecting and administering the alms of the people for this purpose. It left the parish minister and churchwardens with a significant part to play, but mainly under the supervision of the justices of the peace. Both these subjects had a complicated history in the ensuing reigns, as we shall see, but they were never again to be regarded as matters primarily for the church.

5. *The Supreme Headship* – The justifications offered for shaking off the pope's authority over the Church of England and binding on the king's gravitated between the realm of traditional grievance and the realm of high doctrine in the course of four acts passed between 1532 and 1534. The first of these did away (subject to further negotiations between king and pope) with the payment of "annates" or first-fruits to the pope in connection with the conferring of English bishoprics.[44] Its preamble simply recites the magnitude and injustice of the payment in question; it might have been written in 1307, or at any time since. The substantive provisions of the law (forfeiture of all the temporalities of the see of anyone making the payment in question) were perhaps more drastic than earlier generations would have demanded, but both the seizure of temporalities and the prohibition of papal taxes had been familiar in one form and another for centuries. The provision for negotiation, with the act to be suspended if negotiations were successful, also had precedent, especially in the debates over provisions.[45]

The next step, taken in the following year, was the Act for the Restraint of Appeals.[46] Its fundamental purport was that all ecclesiastical litigation was thenceforth to be heard and determined within the realm, and that no papal or other foreign process was to be executed in England, on pain of *praemunire*.

The most important thing in the act is the preamble, which served for centuries, and to some extent still serves, as the main official formulation of the Anglican claim to historical continuity. Here it is in its entirety:

> Where by divers sundry old authentic histories and chronicles it is manifestly declared and expressed that this realm of England is an empire, and so hath been accepted in the world, governed by one supreme head and king, having the dignity and royal estates of the imperial crown of the same; unto whom a body politic, compact of all sorts and degrees of people, divided in terms, and by names of spiritualty and temporalty, been bounden and owen to bear, next to God, a natural and humble obedience; he being also institute and

furnished by the goodness and sufferance of Almighty God with plenary, whole, and entire power, preeminence, authority, prerogative and jurisdiction, to render and yield justice, and final determination to all manner of folk, resiants, or subjects within this his realm in all causes, matters, debates and contentions, happening to occur, insurge, or begin within the limits thereof, without restraint or provocation to any foreign princes or potentates of the world; the body spiritual whereof having power, when any cause of the law divine happened to come in question, or of spiritual learning, then it was declared, interpreted, and shewed by that part of the said body politic, called the spiritualty, now being usually called the English church, which always hath been reputed and also found of that sort that both for knowledge, integrity and sufficiency of number, it hath been always thought, and is also at this hour, sufficient and meet of itself, without the intermeddling of any exterior person or persons, to declare and determine all such doubts, and to administer all such offices and duties as to their rooms spiritual doth appertain; for the due administration whereof, and to keep them from corruption and sinister affection, the King's most noble progenitors, and the antecessors of the nobles of this realm, have sufficiently endowed the said church, both with honour and possessions; and the laws temporal, for trial of property of lands and goods, and for the conservation of the people of this realm in unity and peace without rapine or spoil, was and yet is administred, adjudged and executed by sundry judges and ministers of the other part of the said body politic called the temporalty; and both their authorities and jurisdictions do conjoin together in the due administration of justice, the one to help the other.

And whereas the King his most noble progenitors, and the nobility and commons of this said realm at divers and sundry parliaments, as well in the time of King Edward the First, Edward the Third, Richard the Second, Henry the Fourth, and other noble Kings of this realm, made sundry ordinances, laws, statutes, and provisions for the entire and sure conservation of the prerogatives, liberties and preeminences of the said imperial crown of this realm and of the jurisdiction spiritual and temporal of the same, to keep it from the annoyance as well of the see of Rome as from the authority of other foreign potentates attempting the diminution or violation thereof, as often, and from time to time, as any such annoyance or attempt might be known or espied; and notwithstanding the said good statutes and ordinances made in the time of the King's most noble progenitors in preservation of the authority and prerogative of the said imperial crown as is aforesaid; yet nevertheless sithen the making of the said good statutes and ordinances divers and sundry inconveniencies and dangers not provided for plainly by the said former acts, statutes and ordinances have arisen and sprung by reason of appeals sued out of this realm to the see of

Rome in causes testamentary, causes of matrimony and divorces, right of tithes, obligations and obventions, not only to the great inquietation, vexation, trouble, cost and charges of the King's highness and many of his subjects and resiants of this his realm, but also to the great delay and let to the true and speedy determination of the said causes, for so much as the parties appealing to the said court of Rome most commonly do the same for the delay of justice. And forasmuch as the great distance of way is so far out of this realm so that the necessary proofs nor the true knowledge of the cause can neither there be so well known, ne the witnesses there so well examined as within this realm, so that the parties grieved by means of the said appeals be most times without remedy: in consideration whereof, the King's highness, his nobles and commons, considering the great enormities, dangers, long delays and hurts, that as well to his highness, as to his said nobles, subjects, commons, and resiants of his realm in the said causes testamentary, causes of matrimony and divorces, tithes, obligations and obventions do daily ensue, doth therefore by his royal assent, and by the assent of the lords spiritual and temporal, and commons . . .

This language, setting forth as it does the claims of the Henrician Parliament, naturally invites comparison with the preamble to the Statute of Provisors of 1350,[47] in which are embodied the claims of the medieval Parliament. Some similarities are obvious. The most striking is in the emphasis on the role of the clergy in teaching or interpreting the laws of God. Their role is expressed in both documents in strictly utilitarian terms. They are established not to be ornamental, but to do a job. Both documents go on to stress the material endowment that has been bestowed on the clergy so that they may be adequately supported in discharging their utilitarian function. Each document describes in great detail the "inconvenience" from a utilitarian standpoint of the papal intervention which the statute is about to forbid.

The two documents are similar also in the character of their appeal to history. Both begin by alluding to the original settlement of Christianity in the kingdom. Both follow through by showing how the kings and Parliaments of other generations endeavored to preserve that settlement in its pristine state.

The language in the 1533 act about "a body politic, compact of all sorts and degrees of people, divided in terms, and by names of spiritualty and temporalty" seems to have no counterpart in the fourteenth-century language. It does, however, correspond to the general run of medieval lay opinion, as I tried to describe it in the last chapter. This is the fundamental Erastian insight, as I have defined it.

The 1533 language presents a little more of an innovation in the position it assigns the king. This is subtle, but I think the emphasis has changed. That is, the fourteenth-century Commons might have attributed to the king (albeit less fulsomely)

> plenary, whole, and entire power, preeminence, authority, prerogative and
> jurisdiction, to render and yield justice, and final determination to all
> manner of folk, resiants, or subjects within this his realm, in all causes,
> matters, debates and contentions, happening to occur, insurge, or begin
> within the limits thereof . . .

But they would hardly have said that the realm was

> governed by one supreme head and king . . . unto whom a body politic
> compact of all sorts and degrees of people, . . . been bounden and owen to
> bear, next to God, a natural and humble obedience . . .

This reads as if the king were above the law, whereas the king was told in 1350

> that since the right of the crown of England and the law of the said realm are
> such that upon the mischiefs and damages which happen to his realm, he
> ought, and is bound by his oath, with the accord of his people in his [*son* =
> its?] parliament, to make remedy and law . . .

There is lurking in Henry's legislation, then, along with traditional themes,
certain elements of the divine right learning that was to have such important
consequences for the Church of England before its final rejection in the
following century.[49]

The Act for the Restraint of Appeals was followed in 1534 with the Act
Concerning Peter-pence and Dispensations,[50] which transferred the dispensing
power of the pope to the king and the archbishop of Canterbury. This act begins
like the one on annates by referring to financial exactions, but it turns quickly
to a different note:

> . . . wherein the bishop of Rome aforesaid hath not been only to be blamed
> for his usurpation in the premises, but also for his abusing and beguiling
> your subjects, pretending and persuading them that he hath power to
> dispense with all human laws, uses and customs of all realms, in all cases
> which be called spiritual, which matter hath been usurped and practiced by
> him and his predecessors for many years, in great derogation of your
> imperial crown and authority royal, contrary to right and conscience; for
> where this your Grace's realm recognizing no superior under God but only
> your Grace, hath been and is free from subjection to any man's laws, but
> only to such as have been devised, made, and obtained within this realm, for
> the wealth of the same, or to such other as by sufferance of your Grace and
> your progenitors, the people of this your realm have taken at their free
> liberty, by their own consent to be used amongst them . . . etc., etc.

After a good deal more preamble to the same effect, the dispositive portion of
the act is set forth in considerable technical detail. In the midst of this appears
the following curious protestation:

> Provided always, That this act, nor any thing or things therein contained,

shall be hereafter interpreted or expounded, that your Grace, your nobles and subjects intend by the same to decline or vary from the congregation of Christ's church in any things concerning the very articles of the catholic faith of Christendom, or in any other things declared by holy scripture and the word of God, necessary for your and their salvations, but only to make an ordinance by policies necessary and convenient to repress vice, and for good conservation of this realm in peace, unity and tranquillity, from ravin and spoil, insuing much the old ancient customs of this realm in that behalf; not minding to seek for any relief, succours or remedies for any worldly things and human laws, in any cause of necessity, but within this realm at the hands of your Highness, your heirs and successors, Kings of this realm, which have and ought to have an imperial power and authority in the same, and not obliged in any worldly causes to any other superior.

By contrast, the act, later in the same year, in which the royal supremacy is officially established is succinct, not to say cryptic. This is all of it:

Albeit the King's majesty justly and rightfully is and ought to be the supreme head of the church of England, and so is recognized by the clergy of this realm in their convocations, yet nevertheless for corroboration and confirmation thereof, and for increase of virtue in Christ's religion within this realm of England, and to repress and extirp all errors, heresies, and other enormities and abuses heretofore used in the same: be it enacted by authority of this present parliament, That the King our sovereign lord, his heirs and successors, Kings of this realm, shall be taken accepted and reputed the only supreme head in earth of the church of England, called Anglicana Ecclesia; and shall have and enjoy, annexed and united to the imperial crown of this realm, as well the title and style thereof as all honours, dignities, preeminences, jurisdictions, privileges, authorities, immunities, profits and commodities to the said dignity of supreme head of the same church belonging and appertaining; and that our said sovereign lord, his heirs and successors, Kings of this realm, shall have full power and authority from time to time to visit, repress, redress, reform, order, correct, restrain and amend all such errors, heresies, abuses, offenses, contempts and enormities, whatsoever they be, which by any manner spiritual authority or jurisdiction ought or may lawfully be reformed repressed, ordered redressed, corrected, restrained or amended, most to the pleasure of Almighty God, the increase of virtue in Christ's religion, and for the conservation of the peace, unity and tranquility of this realm; any usage, custom, foreign laws, foreign authority, prescription, or any other thing or things to the contrary hereof notwithstanding.[51]

Taking this legislative package as a whole, it seems to establish the royal supremacy in as conservative a fashion as the nature of the case admitted.

There are elements of high Renaissance kingship doctrine but they are suitably muted with medieval grievances and medieval conceptions of a Christian body politic. Fundamentally, the royal supremacy is conceived not in philosophical or theological, but in juridical and utilitarian terms. It consists of "honours, dignities, preeminences, jurisdictions, privileges, authorities, immunities, profits and commodities." It is to be exercised to "visit, repress, redress, reform, order, correct, restrain and amend" whatever may lawfully be so dealt with "by any manner spiritual authority or jurisdiction," all "to the pleasure of Almighty God, the increase of virtue in Christ's religion, and for the conservation of the peace, unity and tranquility of this realm."

The medieval church had been conceived of as a body of officials in a unified society; it was in this capactity that the head of that unified society took control of it. Henry was far from claiming sacerdotal powers for himself — a point adumbrated in the famous language from a 1545 statute about "your Grace being a layman," and finally spelled out in the provision in the Thirty-nine Articles "On the Civil Magistrate."[52]

On doctrine, a traditional concern of the *sacerdotium,* where there was little medieval precedent for his concern, Henry was especially circumspect in exercising his supremacy. He was quite content to take his own divorces at the hands of English prelates,[53] and he would move nothing in matters of doctrine without taking their advice. Further, in doctrinal questions, he attributed his intervention to a traditional concern of secular rulers — a desire to keep the peace:

> Where the King's most excellent majesty is by God's law supreme head immediately under him of this whole church and congregation of England, intending the conservation of the same church and congregation in a true, sincere and uniform doctrine of Christ's religion, calling also to his blessed and most gracious remembrance as well the great and quiet assurance, prosperous increase, and other innumerable commodities which have ever insued come and followed of concord, agreement and unity in opinions, as also the manifold perils, dangers and inconveniencies which have heretofore, in many places and regions, grown sprung and arisen of the diversities of minds and opinions, especially of matters of christian religion, and therefore desiring that such an unity might and should be charitably established in all things touching and concerning the same as the same so being established might chiefly be to the honour of Almighty God, the very author and fountain of all true unity and sincere concord, and consequently resound to the common wealth of this his Highness' most noble realm and of all his loving subjects and other resiants and inhabitants of or in the same; hath therefore caused and commanded this his most high court of parliament, for sundry and many urgent causes and considerations, to be at this time summoned, and also a synod and convocation of all the

archbishops, and bishops and other learned men of the clergy of this his realm, to be in like manner assembled.[54]

This, the preamble to the Six Articles Act of 1539, goes a little farther than St. Germain went with his analogy of Richard II deciding who was pope, but the general idea is there. The idea that Anglican doctrinal formulas are established not for spiritual edification, but for temporal peace is not inescapably established in this language, but it is available for later generations to elicit.

But while the prelates' doctrinal authority was preserved under the royal supremacy, it may have shifted its ground somewhat. The preamble to the Act for the Restraint of Appeals refers to the "knowledge, integrity, and sufficiency of number" of the spiritual estate. In the language quoted above the king speaks of consulting with "the archbishops, bishops and other learned men of the clergy;" further on in the same act, we are told that he

> most graciously vouchsafed, in his own princely person, to descend and come into his said High Court of Parliament and council, and there, like a prince of high prudence and no less learning, opened and declared many things of high learning and great knowledge . . .

It would seem, then, that the interpretation of doctrine had become a matter not of charisma, but of scholarship. Needless to say, a clerical prerogative based on learning was more compatable with the new state of affairs than one based on charismatic gifts would have been.

How much of a departure it was from medieval conceptions is problematical. Certainly the Gregorian theology of medieval High Churchmanship attributed powers to the clergy by reason of Him Whom they served and Whose livery they wore. But just as certainly the Gregorian conception was not generally accepted in the community. We saw that the physicians in 1421 believed that the soul should be ruled by Divinity as the body was by Physic, and worldly goods by Law "and these conynges should be used and practised principaly by the most conyng men in the same Sciences." Perhaps the proponents of such sentiments as these would not have found it entirely strange for Henry to take his doctrine from the "learned men of the clergy,"

It is difficult, even today, to comment on the elements of historical continuity in Henry's program without falling into some kind of special pleading. For my own part, the most I can say of the situation is this: It seems to me that a fair-minded man, not committed a priori to the theological claims of the papacy, need not do violence to his conscience in regarding the whole program as a continuation of the medieval dialectic between church and state on terms more favorable to the latter.

Whether I am right or wrong in this regard, there are two things the program clearly achieved with its adherence to precedent. One was that no dissenter knew exactly where to draw the line and take a stand; the other was that no dissenter found a juridicial or institutional alternative to the established church. Those who took up arms against the king's proceedings failed in their purpose precisely because they were never quite sure what their purpose was. Of the few who went to the block, some went for one thing, some for another, but none for the Catholic faith as such. Those who died for the Roman primacy died not for refusing to acquiesce in Henry's supreme headship, but for refusing to swear that they believed in it. The pope excommunicated Henry in 1535 for taking his kingdom into schism, but I find no evidence that any Englishman on that account withdrew from the sacraments of the English church.

Meanwhile, the ordinary citizen, attending mass in his parish church as he had always done, paying his tithes to the same lay farmer who had collected them in the past, weighing the ruin of his local monasteries and shrines against the reform of one or another of the ancient grievances he had suffered at the hands of the church, listening to sermons against a papal jurisdiction he had reverenced but not understood, and a papal corruption he had understood all too well, may have marvelled at the changes going on around him, but I doubt if he can have thought that the foundations of his religion had fallen away.

D. Edward and Mary.

The legislation of the suceeding reigns need not detain us long.[55] Edward's reign began with the taking over of chantries and collegiate establishments — a step envisaged in an act late in Henry's reign, but never carried through. Edward's statute differs from Henry's in carrying a theological justification (denial of the sacrificial value of the mass), and in making provision for keeping up the ministerial and charitable functions of the suppressed establishments.[56] In the following year came the first of the Acts of Uniformity, imposing an English liturgy, purged of crucial references to Catholic eucharistic doctrine, to Purgatory, and to the invocation of saints. The Catholic-minded bishops of Henry's reign made some efforts to live with the new liturgy, but all of them finally fell away from the establishment on one point or another of eucharistic doctrine.[57] Again, the Catholics did not set up a competing ecclesiastical organization. Adherents of the old liturgy mounted one armed rebellion in Cornwall, and probably a good deal of passive resistance elsewhere

Edward's other major change was in legalizing the marriages of the clergy. This act was conservative enough in tone, reciting traditional arguments in favor of celibacy, pointing to experience as shwoing that the clergy should not be held to the ideal and ending with a judgment that:

> it were better and rather to be suffered in the commonwealth, that those which could not contain should after the counsel of scripture live in holy marriage, than feignedly abuse with worse enormity outward chastity or single life.

The general view people took of this act seems to have been that it embodied, rather than modified, the contemptuous tolerance with which the ordinary Christian had always regarded the carnal lapses of the clergy. Another act had to be passed four years later to make it clear that the children of such unions were no longer bastards.

Other liturgical adjustments were minor. The work of taking down images and the like, begun by exercise of the supreme headship in Henry's time, was completed with a statute of 1549. The same statute sent the Catholic service books the way of the images. The calendar was reformed to abolish all but the major feasts and fasts, and those that remained were given a suitable doctrinal explanation. In case of fasts, the traditional ecclesiastical censures were supplemented with secular penalties. The doctrine on the subject as set forth in the preambles to the statutes was one familiar in later Anglican apologetic — that days and foods are matters indifferent in themselves, but that a particular church may make its own arrangements about them for purposes of edification, worship, or discipline. The importance of the traditional fasts to the fishing industry was also pointed out.

The protestantizing tenor of Edward's rign was not reflected in any statutory doctrinal test beyond that implied in the acceptance and use of the Prayer Book liturgy. The Reformers repealed Henry's statutory impositions of Catholic doctrine, but did not replace them with formulas of their own.

The general upheaval of religious affairs led to legislation strengthening or supplementing ecclesiastical processes in some areas. A law against reviling the Sacrament carried imprisonment at the king's pleasure as a punishment. Brawling and similar unbecoming behavior in church were subjected to specific ecclesiastical censures — a measure probably necessitated by the increased tempo of liturgical disagreements. If the brawling extended to the drawing of a weapon, the offender could be summoned before a justice of the peace and have an ear cut off. A new act to improve the collection of tithe authorized the ecclesiastical court to give double damages in certain cases. It also empowered the person entitled to the tithe to enter another person's land and see to the setting off of his tithe form the nine parts.

An act of 1547 gave a new and more or less definitive shape to benefit of clergy. In connection with a general revision of the criminal law, it listed certain offenses not clergyable — a somewhat narrower list than Henry's legislation had provided — allowed all other offenders to have benefit of clergy, and privilege of sanctuary as well, in the same manner as in the first year of Henry's reign. Hence a priest or deacon could again have benefit of clergy more than once. This act also put an end to the anachronistic rule, discussed in the last chapter, that a *bigamus* or twice-married man could not have benefit of clergy.

The provision of this act concerning sanctuary is a little difficult to understand. In terms, it applies only to one arraigned or found guilty, whereas the privilege as it existed in the first year of Henry's reign was available only before arraignment. I cannot believe that this act revived the whole medieval apparatus of abjuration and starving out, and I can find nothing to indicate just what it did do. One way or another, the whole law of sanctuary appears to have been moribund long before it was finally abolished under James I.[58]

Mary, as is well known, renounced the supreme headship, revived Catholic doctrine, and undid all of what Edward had done with the liturgy, and much of what Henry had done with the administration of the church. But it is not quite accurate to say that she restored the status quo as it had existed before Henry began his work. In her first session of Parliament, she had attempted to do just that, and the Commons had refused to pass her bill. When they were finally persuaded to return to the papal allegiance, they were willing to acknowledge that they had been in schism since 1528, but not to repeal the administrative interventions that had initiated the schism. They also were explicit that they were not restoring to the pope any jurisdiction he had not had when the schism began.

A specific rehearsal of which of Henry's innovations they left intact may be instructive:

1. The 1529 legislation on pluralism, nonresidence, and secular employment was left in force, except for that part which penalized the seeking of papal dispensations. It would seem that the use of a papal dispensation was no longer to be an offense in itself, but that it would not protect the pluralist or nonresident from the penalties otherwise incurred.
2. The new bishoprics created by Henry were retained, with papal permission, although the provision for suffragans was repealed.
3. The confiscation of the endowments of monasteries, chantries and collegiate establishments was confirmed, and expressly accepted by the papacy as a fait accompli. The penalty of *praemunire* was provided for anyone molesting the holders of such lands. However, the mortmain laws were suspended for twenty years in case anyone who had them was minded to give them back.
4. The 1529 act regulating mortuaries was retained in force. The policy, inaugurated under Henry, of enforcing the 1372 statute on tithes of wood was continued.
5. The 1529 act limiting probate fees was retained, although the 1531 act on citing a person out of his home diocese was evidently repealed.
6. No change was made in the laws concerning sanctuary and benefit of clergy.

The Commons, in short, left off the work of Reformation in the same spirit in which they had taken it up. They had no quarrel with Catholic doctrine or with the spiritual primacy of the Roman see. But from the institutional apparatus of the church they wanted better and less expensive service than their ancestors had had, and they looked to the intervention of the royal government to secure it for them.

II. The Elizabethan Settlement

The Reformation program was restored, of course, and given pretty much its final form in the first years of Elizabeth's reign.[59] The main features of the legislation by which this was accomplished were these:

1. The supreme headship was restored about as it had been claimed in Henry's time, but shorn of some of the more exuberant caesaropapism of Henry's rhetoric. Elizabeth ended up not as Supreme Head on earth of the Church of England, but as "the only supreme governor of this realm . . . as well in all spiritual or ecclesiastical things or causes as temporal." Provision was made for the exercise of her powers through commissioners, who became the Court of High Commission of early Stuart times.
2. The liturgy was established as it had been planned in the last year of Edward's reign, subject to a couple of small concessions to residual Catholic sentiment. Serious penalities were provided for those who used any other form of corporate worship ("common prayer"), old or new.
3. The punishment of heresy was limited to doctrines expressly denounced in scripture or in the early general councils, unless Parliament with the consent of Convocation should extend it to others (which, needless to say, no Parliament has ever done). This met the last of the major grievances of the pre-Reformation Commons by depriving the clergy of any serious control over the doctrinal deviations of the laity. The laws for burning heretics endured till 1676,[60] but this limitation prevented any significant body of English laymen from being subject to them. Through an act of 1571, the prelates of the Reformed establishment were allowed to impose their Thirty-Nine Articles (adopted in Convocation in 1562) on the clergy, but not on the laity.[61] The maintenance of papal authority was taken fairly seriously, but was treated as a political, not a doctrinal, offense.
4. First fruits, tenths, and appropriated rectories in royal hands, all of which had been renounced by Mary, were resumed, subject to an endeavor, largely abortive, to restore them to clerical hands without loss to the royal revenues by swapping them off for temporal holdings of the church.

A. Parties.

This arrangement has often been spoken of as a compromise. After hearing so long of Anglicanism as a *via media,* it is easy enough to regard the situation in that light. It is less easy, though, to determine who compromised with whom. To understand the settlement, we must explore this point a little. As I see the situation when Elizabeth came to the throne, the preceding decades had more or less divided the nation into three main parties, each of which had to be coped with in one way or another in any permanent settlement of the church.

1. *Protestants* – Those whose religious convictions committed them to a radical alteration of the traditional order of the church were led in the main by intellectuals who had come under the influence of Continental doctrines in the universities, had risen to positions of power in Henry's reign, and had more or less had their way with matters in Edward's. Under Henry, these Protestant intellectuals had provided the theological props for the king's divorce, and for much of the rest of his program; hence, their power and influence had been quite out of proportion either to their numbers or to the sympathy the king had for their doctrines. Henry had on the whole protected them from being called to account for their heterodox beliefs. He had encouraged them in their zeal for distributing English Bibles and enhancing the preaching ministry. Especially had he encouraged them in pulling down shrines and images that had been "abused" by "superstitious worship" in the past — and turning over the resulting loot to the royal treasury. Many of these measures Catholics of the "New Learning" also supported, but much of the rhetoric and élan with which they were pursued was Protestant.

Under Edward, the Protestant leaders had come into power, and had succeeded in putting much of their rhetoric into the statute book. They imposed a liturgy pretty much to their liking, but were unable to establish the disciplinary processes that were part of the Continental program they sought to emulate. Their liturgical strictures had been generally obeyed, and the accompanying modification of the church fabric (pulling down the rest of the images, substituting tables for altars) carried out, but there was no general enthusiasm for the underlying doctrines.

Most of the leaders of the movement went into exile under Mary. In the process, they absorbed a good deal of the doctrine of the Continental reformers who took them in. These reformers, especially Calvin, looked for a church polity derived entirely from their own perusal of scripture. It seems to have had no place for bishops, ceremonies or vestments of any kind, or even for set prayers. The Marian exiles were to scruple in one way or another at all of these.

Meanwhile, the rank and file of the Protestant party had been gradually gaining ground. The nucleus was a handful of humble people who had kept alive the Lollard tradition of an earlier time, reinforced by readers of the new English Bibles in the middle years of Henry's reign. Others had been won over by preaching and propaganda as events wore on. Some of these converts had worshipped in clandestine congregations in Mary's time; others had lapsed into surly conformity, or had simply kept their religion to themselves. When the lid came off, they constituted a powerful and well organized pressure group (though by no means a majority) in Elizabeth's first Parliament.

2. *Roman Catholics* – Those who had a religious commitment to the papacy included all but one of the bench of bishops, for all but one of them were to give up their sees rather than swear to Elizabeth's supremacy. The exact nature of the spiritual odyssey of these men — conformists all under Henry, deprived under Edward, restored to the papal allegiance under Mary, and now intransigent in that allegiance — has been the subject of a certain amount of debate among historians. Smith, in his engaging *Tudor Prelates and Politics,* makes out a persuasive case for the view that the experience of a generation of royal supremacy had left them convinced that the essentials of Catholic faith and worship could not stand without the pope, that the papal authority "holdeth up all." Hughes, on the other hand, insists that "a return in this spirit, from such a motive, would not . . . have been a true return at all."[62] In his view, these men had obeyed Henry through mere cowardice. He shows that many of them admitted as much in Mary's time, and expressed sincere repentance for their weakness.

My own guess is that the truth lies in some kind of combination of these two points of view. I should think that these men, renouncing the papal allegiance in their youth, had had some pangs of conscience, but had held no convictions on the point strong enough to put their careers and their lives on the line for. In those days, the nature of the pope's authority was a matter of academic debate; only later did experience show it to be of the essence of the Catholic faith. These were men of rugged loyalty, but no great spiritual insight; it seems reasonable enough to suppose that they came only slowly to realize what was really at stake. There is many a man who bitterly repents in his old age what seemed a reasonable course of action in his youth.

In any event, one of the facts of life when Elizabeth came to the throne was that most of the higher positions in the church were filled with men who had spent much of their lives trying to maintain the Catholic faith without the pope, and were not minded to try the experiment again.

How many of the lower clergy or the laity felt the same way is hard to say. The Marian settlement had been fundamentally medieval in outlook. No one had tried to bring over the disciplined Catholicism of the Counter-Reformation that was already developing on the Continent. So conformity, even sincere conformity, under Mary could not be taken as the mark of an intransigent papist. There were, to be sure, a good many people whose loyalty to the old religion made them ready to defy the government in modest ways. You can see them floundering about in the first decade or so of the new reign — laymen who went to the official services and said their rosaries, priests who said mass in their parsonages after reading the Prayer Book services in church. But the welding of these into a Roman Catholic party, and later into an English Roman

Catholic church could not really begin until the 1570s when the pope made it clear that his followers had to stay away from the official services, and when he began sending priests trained on the Continent to minister to them.

3. Ordinary Englishmen – The one thing we can be pretty sure of when we speak of the ordinary Englishman of the period is that he was a man who would not go to the wall with either papist or Protestant. The great mass of both laity and lower clergy were remarkably docile toward all the different changes back and forth. We have great trouble saying what this uncommitted majority actually believed in, or, indeed, what they can have supposed was going on. If we can judge by their representatives in Parliament, they saw in Henry's legislation the redress of grievances that had weighed on them for two centuries, and on these matters they stood their ground in Mary's reign. But what did they think of the changes in polity, doctrine, and worship that went along with the redress?

In the first place, a good many of them, if they had their choice, would probably have accepted the jurisdiction of the pope in matters merely spiritual, though they might not have allowed the extensive papal jurisdiction exercised before Henry's time. This was St. Germain's position before the supreme headship was established by Parliament. It was the position taken by the Pilgrimage of Grace, and probably by many who opposed in Convocation and Parliament the settlement of 1559. The reservation built into Mary's restoration legislation of 1554 seems to indicate that the same attitude was at work in Mary's reign.

But even those who accepted the *de jure* authority of the pope were generally prepared to accept the *de facto* authority of the crown, and even swear to it when the occasion arose. We may suspect, for instance, that a good many people who venerated the handful of martyrs that Henry's reign produced were not yet prepared to follow in their footsteps. As we have seen, there was much in medieval piety that led the ordinary Christian to suppose that the higher reaches of sanctity were not for him. Anyone who thought that martyrdom under Henry's law was the prerogative of a spiritual élite would be following in the pattern his forefathers had handed down.

As for the doctrinal changes, whatever they were, there must have been a great many people who neither understood nor cared about them. The average person had probably lost patience with heresy prosecutions in Mary's reign, if he had not done so earlier at the time of the Hunne affair. The desire to be free of such prosecutions is reflected in Elizabeth's first Supremacy Act. But once the stake was out of the picture, it must have been easy for ordinary people to lose interest in the niceties of doctrine — especially in a society where such matters had long been left to professionals. We have seen that St. Germain could not take seriously the doctrinal issues of his day; there must have been many others who felt as he did.

Some of the more moderate reformers evidently felt the same way. Bernard Gilpin, for instance, the famous and saintly North Country parson, whose ministry lasted from Henry's reign through much of Elizabeth's (ordained 1541, died 1583), seems to have been extremely chary of doctrinal formulas, because they troubled men's consciences, and interfered with the important work of the ministry.[63] He became legendary for his charity, his pastoral zeal, and his scathing denunciations of corruption in the church, without ever taking a stand on matters like justification, or even the Eucharist. Disgust with practical abuses seems to have contributed as much as anything else to his parting company with the pope. He appears, in short, to have carried into the new settlement of the church a traditional English impatience with theory, a traditional English concern for getting on with the job. We can hardly call Gilpin an ordinary man, but it is reasonable to suppose that he reflected many ordinary men's concerns.

Liturgical change would of course have more popular impact than doctrinal change. Experience under Edward indicated that a good many of our ordinary Englishmen did not care for the new liturgy. It seems likely, though, that men who lacked the training for close analysis of the language of the Canon did not have a clear idea that their traditional mass was being taken away and replaced by something else. Their opposition may have been more like that of the Latin mass enthusiasts of the late 1960s to the current changes in the Roman Catholic liturgy. Of the protesters who left specific objections for posterity, I find none below the rank of a bishop who referred to the language of the Canon. Further, under the Elizabethan settlement, a number of traditionalists were to interpolate Catholic forms of reverence (including the elevation) into the Prayer Book rites[64] — a practice that would have been pointless, not to say idolatrous, if they had not supposed that the traditional Eucharist was being offered. So it seems likely that many opponents of the Prayer Book were defending not the theological purity of the Sacrament, but simply the rites they had been brought up on.

For one of the most pervasive sentiments among the ordinary Englishmen of the time was attachment to their folkways, to traditional ways of doing things. Here, the attitude toward the new liturgy is sharply illuminated by the pathetic efforts of the York Corporation in the ensuing years of the Elizabethan settlement to preserve their great cycle of mystery plays from the prevailing deluge.[65] They changed the name from Corpus Christi plays to Creed plays to Pater Noster plays. They begged the dean and the archbishop to revise the texts. They kept trying to put the plays on in some form as late as 1580. But their tenacity in holding onto the ancient pageantry was matched by their total apathy toward the beliefs that pageantry embodied. They were willing to put in whatever doctrine the local prelates cared to give them as long as they could keep the plays.

Other aspects of the Reformation were to be met with similar nostalgia at one point or another.[66] It seems to have been harder to get people to stop ringing bells for the dead than to get them to stop praying for them. A priest in 1576 "said De profundis in Latin in the church . . . and said it was a good prayer and had not been used many aday." As late as 1604 a countrywoman was had up in Lincolnshire for putting on a minister's children the medieval epithet of "priest calves."

These bits and pieces of evidence hardly provide a general answer to how ordinary Englishmen took the Reformation as a whole. They do suggest, though, a rather broad popular base for certain attitudes, carried over from medieval Erastianism, toward the role of government in religious affairs. That is, to the extent people were conservative, they were conservative of a whole social order, a whole pattern of Christian living, rather than of particular tenets of the church. And to the extent they were for changes, they were apt to be more concerned with the redress of specific grievances, the elimination of specific abuses, than with the scriptural basis of any given doctrine. It seems, then, that the ordinary Englishman of 1559, like his ancestors the medieval Commons, saw the church in contingent and utilitarian terms, as an institution which the royal government should take in hand, for the honor of God and the overall amendment of the realm.

B. The Anatomy of Compromise.

We may suppose that Elizabeth's own affinities were with the group I have characterized as "ordinary Englishmen." She had political problems her subjects did not, but in general sentiment she must have been pretty much at one with them — if not from personal inclination, then from an instinctive judgment of political expediency. What little we know about her personal religious convictions bears this out. Her attachment to certain non-essentials of the old religion is well known — her contempt for priests' and bishops' wives, and her crucifix in her private chapel. So is her impatience with the subtleties of doctrine.

Now, to anyone studying the history of the preceding reigns, it must have been apparent that the ordinary Englishman and his queen, if they were to have an orderly settlement of their religious affairs in 1559, would have to make common cause with one or the other of the religiously committed groups. The Roman Catholics and the Protestants would tear the country apart with their dissension unless one or the other was accommodated. Furthermore, there was not a trained ecclesiastical administrator in the country who did not belong to one camp or the other.

As between the two, there were a number of reasons for choosing the Protestants. In the first place, they seem to have been a more violent and troublesome minority than their rivals were. A peace with them might have looked (erroneously, in the long run, I suspect) more conducive to national unity than a peace with the Catholics would have been. Also, they provided contacts with anti-government forces in France and Scotland that could be useful in the game of international politics.

Roman Catholicism, on the other hand, while it might have been closer to the heart of the ordinary Englishman than Protestantism was, may well have been personally repugnant to Elizabeth by reason of its insistence that she was illegitimate. It also had against it the experience of Mary's reign, with the unpopular heresy persecutions and the unpopular Spanish marriage. Nor were the traditional grievances about papal corruption and Roman politics dissipated by recent experience. Finally, there was still probably some doubt about whether the pope's followers had really and permanently renounced the church's claim to the endowments confiscated under Henry and Edward.

In any event, the crucial decision was made. The settlement was to be one which the ordinary Englishman and the religiously committed Protestant could accept, and accept it they did — the ordinary Englishman with grumblings and fits of nostalgia, the Protestant after great soul-searching and lengthy correspondence with Geneva. Let us see, then, just what it was that they accepted.[67]

On the whole, the Protestants had their way on doctrine. The liturgical texts were set up to support, if not to require, a Protestant doctrinal interpretation. And the Protestant prelates were allowed to impose on the clergy, with the Thirty-Nine Articles, a doctrinal test that was generally Protestant in tone, although not entirely free from ambiguity. On the other hand, the view espoused in Henry's statutes that doctrinal tests are developed not for edification but for peace seems to have motivated the government still. Efforts to impose more rigorous patterns of Calvinst orthodoxy than the Thirty-Nine Articles required were effectively sidetracked by the queen.

Meanwhile, the reformed liturgy (which, unlike the reformed doctrine, was quite coercively imposed) probably had more in it for the ordinary Englishman than for the Protestant. Calvin's followers favored a public worship consisting of extempore prayers and a sermon; they were not comfortable with the use of any form of set prayers. Particular aspects of the Prayer Book service especially offended them: the use of the sign of the cross in baptism, the reception of Communion kneeling, the wearing of the surplice by the priest. For the ordinary Englishman, these gave a certain quantum of unity and continuity to the whole settlement, and gave him some opportunity to put the new services into the rhythm of his daily life in about the place the old had occupied.

Further, the set prayers and the limitations on preaching assured the traditional status of the parish clergy and the local gentry who were their patrons. Any man who could read the Missal could read the Book of Common prayer, whereas if ministers were to preach and pray in terms of their own devising, they would have to meet a standard of learning and zeal that they had never met in the past, and would scarcely meet in the future unless the manner of their recruitment were to be altered drastically.

Also, if every parish were to have a preaching minister, the government could hardly control what they would preach, and the ensuing controversies would set the whole country by the ears. Experience dating back to the fourteenth century taught the government that such a state of affairs would be inimical to the public peace.

The institutional forms of the medieval church were left almost entirely intact by the Elizabethan settlement. Here, the Protestants would have liked to go back to the scriptural first principles put into operation by Calvin at Geneva and Zwingli at Zurich. These envisaged a presbytery, or collegiate body of parish ministers, to replace the bishop as the central authority in a diocese, with elders and deacons exercising a subordinate ministry under the ordained minister in the parish. The proponents of this polity rejected the episcopate as having no scriptural warrant to support it. The apparatus of subordinate diocesan officials they rejected on the same ground, adding to their objections the debilitated state of this apparatus and its origin in the popish canon law. Nevertheless, they took on the whole apparatus, and even accepted episcopal office themselves — on the theory that they could advance a more perfect reformation from the positions of influence thus acquired.

The government's or the ordinary Englishman's espousal of episcopacy seems to have had no theological apologist in the first generation of Elizabethans.[68] Even a good deal later, the apologetic contended itself with defending the permissibility, rather than the necessity, of episcopal ordination. I think it likely, though I would be hard put to prove it, that the ordinary Englishman preserved from his medieval past the view that a true Eucharist required an episcopally ordained priest. Whether I am right in this, of course, depends in great part on whether I am right in my other speculations about how the ordinary Englishman took the Prayer Book services.

But whatever religious sanction he attached to the episcopate can hardly have extended to the rest of the apparatus — say, to the archdeacon, for whom, as far as I know, no one, whatever his religious persuasion, had said a good word since the twelfth century. Here, I think, two forces were at work. One was the inertia characteristic of any bureaucratic establishment. If a substantial bureaucracy is really shaken up, no one can tell exactly what will happen, because no one can really penetrate its workings far enough to see that its necessary functions are provided for in some other way. By the same token, its ramifications are apt to take in enough vested interests to generate a good deal of political opposition to cutting the structure down. We can never be quite sure what these vested interests are, but they never fail to make themselves felt. We may suppose that a government that was feeling its way in so many matters was not disposed to take on the entire ecclesiastical bureaucracy if it did not have to.

The second force for the maintenance of the traditional apparatus of ecclesiastical government was the character of the alternative offered by the Protestants. Accompanying the Genevan polity was always the Genevan "godly discipline," whereby the moral lapses of the laity were ruthlessly brought to light and rigorously reformed. This program was no more attractive to the ordinary Englishman than the fires of Smithfield had been. As early as 1378, the Commons had stated in no uncertain terms that they had no intention of being any farther subjected to ecclesiastical judgment than their ancestors had been. To be sure, the traditional mechanism of parochial visitation was supposed to serve the same ends as the godly discipline, but it had its inefficiency to recommend it.

In any event, the Calvinist procedure for establishing a church polity had little attraction for the ordinary Englishman. We have seen that the medieval Commons had insisted that the form of the church-state relation was to be determined not by first principles but by precedent, and that Henry had been careful to assimilate this view of matters by building suitable appeals to precedent into his legislation. The view in question was as hostile to the Calvinist reliance on first principles as it had been to the Gregorian reliance on different first principles in an earlier time. In the reforming of the church, as in other public affairs, the English were to proceed by way of specific revisions of the existing order to meet specific needs.

III. Theory And Public Policy

The better part of a century after the Elizabethan settlement was devoted to bringing a certain intellectual order to the new form the English church-state nexus had taken. This order was more a rationalizing upon the original settlement than a creative following of the Spirit. But insofar as the settlement itself reflected the genuine needs and aspirations of the ordinary Englishman, the rationalizing of it produced an effective and plausible foundation for the religious life of the nation. This intellectual edifice — whose crowning achievement was the great period of Caroline piety — has been reviewed many times from many standpoints; we need not take it up in detail another time. I mean here only to touch on certain aspects that show in what spirit the institutional patterns of the medieval church were carried through the Reformation.

A. Revisionism.

Next to the confutation of the papacy, the most serious intellectual task the

Anglican apologists set themselves was that of meeting the reproaches of their Continental brethren, and of the radical Protestants in their own midst. These reproaches were addressed in form to specific matters — vestments, ceremonies, episcopacy, and the medieval apparatus of ecclesiastical government. But beneath them lay the radical difference between the methodology of reform as conceived at Geneva and that imposed by the government upon the English church. The Genevans would have nothing of liturgy or polity that was not expressly referred to in the scriptures, whereas the ordinary Englishman, as we have seen, would have no changes except those he was persuaded were required. I have tried to show, beginning with the medieval Commons and St. Germain, how much it was the view of the ordinary Englishman on this point that dominated the actual settlement of the church. It remained for the divines to justify the approach as best they could.

They took two lines. One, which had its most sophisticated formulation from Hooker, was that the forms of liturgy and polity were matters of theological indifference, and therefore appropriately regulated by any church as it saw fit. It followed that those who would introduce new forms must sustain the burden of anyone who would alter the positive law — that of showing what was wrong with the law as it currently stood. The Genevan endeavor to place on the proponent of existing forms the burden of showing a scriptural warrant for them was therefore entirely wide of the mark.

The second line occupied rather a secondary position among the Elizabethans, rising to prominence with Laud and his fellow Carolines. It sought a warrant for existing practices in their conformity to the usage of the primitive church. Proponents of this line tended to accept the Calvinist's pessimistic view of history, for they saw as essential only what had been in existence from the beginning. But they did not agree with the Calvinist that primitive usage was to be found only in scripture; they were prepared to accept the witness of Christian antiquity, and to devote their scholarship to finding that witness out.

The two lines are of course not mutually exclusive. Jewel, in fact, managed to get them both into a single sentence, when he said that the Church of England kept all ceremonies delivered from the Apostles, and

> some others too besides which we thought might be suffered without hurt to the Church of God: because that we had a desire that all things in the holy congregation might (as St. Paul commandeth) be done with comeliness and in good order.[69]

The same two lines had appeared in various combinations for centuries, from the parliamentarians of 1307, who presumably held orthodox Catholic views of papacy and episcopate, yet thought that the Church of England had been founded in the state of prelacy by the kings and great men, through Laud himself, who asserted at his trial "that bishops might be regulated and limited by human laws in those things which are but incidents to their calling: but their calling, as far as it is *Jure Divino,* by divine right, cannot be taken away."[70]

In fine, the traditional forms of the Church of England were compounded of two elements. One was of historical provenance, and not be altered without good reason. The other was of apostolic provenance, and not to be altered at all. One could combine the two elements in a number of ways, any of which would furnish him with an apologetic maintainable with equal force against either Geneva or Rome.

B. Historical Continuity.

A corollary of the revisionist approach was that the Church of England after the Reformation was the same institution as the Church of England before the Reformation. I have already alluded to the manner in which this view of the matter was embodied in the legislation, and the extent to which it was accepted by the ordinary Englishman.

The divines were divided on the point. Those of the Genevan persuasion — including most of the first generation of Elizabethan bishops, as we have seen — were not enthusiastic about either the royal supremacy or the settlement it had brought about, but simply accepted them, *faute de mieux.* At the same time, they did not share the tendency of the laity to minimize the theological significance of breaking with the pope. Their language about the Antichrist and the Whore of Babylon was not the mere tasteless vituperation the more urbane Carolines supposed it to be. It was their justification for breaking out of the historical unity of Christendom.

With this viewpoint, they were reluctant to see their church as in historical continuity with the established institution of the past. Rather, they considered themselves the spiritual and ecclesiastical successors of the Lollards, and the other dissentient groups of the Middle Ages. This view of historical continuity is implicit in Foxe, through whom it must have gained a certain hold on the popular conception. The nearest it came to official status was in *A Treatise of the Perpetuall Visibilitie and Succession of the True Church in all Ages,* published in 1624 by George Abbot, James I's archbishop of Canterbury. By then the theological contest was pretty much over. The repudiation of papal jurisdiction had long been consummated, and Anglicanism no longer felt the necessity of justifying a breach with the past.

Meanwhile, there were not lacking divines of less rigorous Calvinist bent to support the popular and governmental view. Matthew Parker, Elizabeth's first archbishop of Canterbury, evidently a decent cleric without strong opinions on the doctrinal issues of the day — an "ordinary Englishman" that is — in his *De Antiquitate Ecclesiae Britanniae* traced historical continuity through the institutional past. The same view, of course, is implicit in Hooker.

On this point it was the lawyers, not the divines, who had the last word. A series of cases in the 1590s established that the scope of the royal supremacy was to be defined not by the Reformation legislation, but by the pre-Reformation ecclesiastical law.[71] The supremacy, according to the courts, had always existed *de jure;* only in particular places the pope had been allowed *de facto* to trespass upon it. In general, then, the powers of the crown over the church were those powers the pope had exercised *de facto* before the Reformation.

In 1606 Coke lent his learning and his authority to these cases by publishing one of them, *Caudrey's Case,* [72] in his Reports, in Latin and English (whereas the rest of the reports were in Law French, a language comprehensible only to lawyers), fortified with a monumental appendix in which he set forth instances from every period of English history of the exercise of ecclesiastical jurisdiction by the crown. His compendium began with the early Anglo-Saxons, and ended with the preambles to Henry's and Elizabeth's Reformation legislation. In between was every manner of royal intervention in the affairs of the church.

Needless to say, Coke's use of the authorities was tendentious. It is a lawyer's business to find precedent for what he does, and Coke was above all else a master of his trade. Anyone who has followed this and the preceding chapter can judge for himself how far Coke was right in saying the royal supremacy was nothing new. What matters, of course, is not so much that he was right or wrong as that he was generally accepted. His vast store of learning and his commanding stature in his profession set the final seal of intellectual respectability on the conservative version of the Reformation. From his time on, it became the Church of England's usual account of itself that it was the same church it had always been, only purged of usurped authority and doctrinal innovations. [73]

C. The Royal Supremacy.

It was Coke also in great part who established the mainstream Anglican understanding of what it meant for the sovereign to be head of the church. We have seen that Elizabeth moved away from the elements of Renaissance kingship doctrine that appeared in Henry's legislation, and relied on the medieval juridical elements — jurisdictions, powers, preeminences and the like, supreme governorship of all causes including spiritual, rather than supreme headship under God of the Church of England. The cases just alluded to moved in the same direction by using the medieval scope of ecclesiastical authority to measure the newly established powers of the crown.

There was a certain tendency among the divines, however, to think of the royal supremacy not as something derived from medieval law, but as something inhering in the nature of a Christian prince. This tendency took on new force with the coming of James to the throne in 1603, for it fitted well with James's divine right conceptions of kingship. Ultimately, it became something of a rallying-point for Stuart High Churchmanship.

The difference between the two approaches was of more than academic concern. To the extent that the royal supremacy rested on the divine commission to the monarch, it was a personal supremacy of his, and left the church, under its divinely appointed head, as free of interference by the secular government as it had claimed to be under the headship of the pope. Whereas to the extent the royal supremacy rested on medieval legal precedents, it was a supremacy of the monarch *qua* civil magistrate, and exercisable only under appropriate legal forms.

Early in James's reign (1606), there came a confrontation between the two approaches, represented respectively by Richard Bancroft, archbishop of Canterbury and Coke as chief justice of the Common Pleas. Bancroft, on behalf of all the clergy of England, submitted a set of articles complaining of abuses of the writ of prohibition. The judges, led by Coke, responded to them one by one. Coke finally published the articles with the responses as a preface to his commentary on the *Articuli Cleri* of 1315 — thus putting the whole situation in the historical continuity established by him in *Caudrey's Case*.[74]

Most of the articles are technical and need not concern us at the moment. The first two, however, are very much in point. One shows how the prelates felt jurisdictional disputes should be decided. It begins by reciting that the king has both temporal and spiritual jurisdiction annexed to his imperial crown — official doctrine since the time of Henry VIII. It goes on to draw the conclusion that the king has "sufficient authority in himself, with the assistance of his Council, to judge what is amiss in either of his said jurisdictions, and to have reformed the same accordingly." With this contention, the judges are very short:

> No man maketh any question, but that both the jurisdictions are lawfully and justly in his Majesty, and that if any abuses be, they ought to be reformed; but what the Law doth warrant in cases of Prohibitions to keep every jurisdiction in his true limits, is not to be said an abuse, nor can be altered but by Parliament.

The second article complains of the form of the writs of prohibition, which recite that the prohibited proceeding is being carried on "against the crown and dignity of the king." Since the ecclesiastical courts are as much the king's as any other courts are, the prelates argue, it cannot be against his crown and dignity to try a case in them. The judges are aware that all courts are the king's courts, but insist that the writ must have the form it has always had unless it is changed by Parliament. Furthermore, it is *contra Coronam & Dignitatem Regium* for any to usurp to deal in that, which they have not lawful warrant from the Crown to deal in, or to take from the Temporal jurisdiction that which belongeth to it.

What this means is that for Coke the supremacy of the king over the church is the supremacy of the temporal law over the spiritual, and that the common law judges, subject only to Parliament, have the final say in applying the temporal law. It follows that they have the final say in setting the limits to the spiritual law. These points Coke was to argue over and over — in protesting being made to argue a jurisdictional point versus the prelates before the king instead of deciding it judicially from the bench; in keeping the Statute of *Praemunire* in force; in allowing the king's High Commission no more power than medieval ecclesiastical judges had had; in insisting that the interpretation of an act of Parliament belonged to the common law courts even if the act itself concerned the church.[76]

All this was part of the general confrontation between the common law judges and the Stuarts; Coke's stand on ecclesiastical jurisdiction was part of his stand on other matters. As a result of the Civil War and the Restoration, Coke's stand was the generally accepted one. The opposite view as Bancroft presented it remained a High Church doctrine till recent times, but it was long tied in with the fading fortunes of the House of Stuart, and had no real vogue from the Revolution of 1688 until the Tractarians revived it in the nineteenth century. It was accepted by the generality of churchmen, as well as by the agencies of secular government, that the royal supremacy represented a continuation of medieval Erastianism, through which the church, as one of the institutions of a Christian commonwealth, was controlled in the interest of the overall society.

D. Uniformity.

Both under Edward and under Elizabeth, the only firmly coercive element in the ecclesiastical settlement was the liturgy. I have already alluded to the practice, beginning in Henry's reign, of imposing doctrinal formulas not for edification but for peace. As events progressed, it became more and more apparent that peace was best to be had by reducing, rather than multiplying, such formulas. By the time the Stuarts came to the throne, the influence of the government was generally directed to discouraging positive stands on controverted questions, rather than to examining such questions and settling them.[77] After the Thirty-Nine Articles, no attempt was made at a coercive imposition of doctrine. Even those Articles, as we have seen, were not imposed on the laity.

But at the same time, increasingly severe and ingenious penalties were being devised for those who spoke against the Prayer Book liturgy, absented themselves from the Prayer Book services, or held alternative services of their own. All this was in the teeth not only of the Roman Catholics but also of an increasing number of Protestant Dissenters. Diversity of doctrine and uniformity of worship continued to be a central characteristic of the Church of England until the ritual controversies of the nineteenth century.

It was not inevitable that the unity of the Church of England should have been grounded in this way on liturgy instead of doctrine. Henry's efforts at unity were generally directed at doctrinal formulas. Divines have not been wanting from Elizabeth's time to the present who thought it outrageous for people who shared the Protestant faith to be excluded from the national church on a point of ceremony. Indeed, under the Commonwealth, an attempt was made to define the national church through a united profession of doctrine, and let the members worship as they pleased. But the main current of Anglican policy was all the other way.

Accordingly, one would think that at some point fairly early in the game there should have been an articulated decision to press liturgical uniformity, and let doctrinal uniformity go. But I find no evidence of how or by whom such a decision was made, or even that it was made at all. I find no Anglican apologist before the Restoration who addresses himself to the question of why doctrinal deviation is to be tolerated whereas liturgical deviation is not.[78] It would seem, then, that this most important characteristic of the Anglican settlement came about not through deliberate choice but simply through the logic of events.

Why the logic of events required doctrinal flexibility we have already seen. The laity were not prepared to support a rigorous suppression of heresy, and, absent that, peace and concord could best be achieved in the church by allowing each to go his own way within the broadest possible limits. What is hard to see is why the same logic did not support a comparable flexibility in liturgical observance. Here we can only guess.

My own guess is that it was first of all a matter of peace. The concern of the ordinary Englishman with the liturgy, if I read him right, was not to have it accurately reflect the nuances of Eucharistic theology, or the proper balance between faith and works, but simply to have it contribute an element of piety and order to the recurring rhythm of his days and works. This meant that he did not want it perpetually changing, and he did not want his more theologically zealous neighbors forever quarreling about it. Many of the laws and royal injunctions of the period seem to bespeak a condition of turbulent debate over the forms of public worship. It may well have been felt that only by fixing these forms beyond the possibility of debate could the general uproar and confusion be controlled.

Akin to the goal of peace was that of good order and decorum — a value stressed by those Anglican apologists who wished to make it clear that the retention of certain popish ceremonies did not imply the retention of any popish illusions about the supernatural value of such ceremonies. But decorum in the sense envisaged was probably somewhat foreign to the medieval approach to the liturgy. The medieval priest and his parishioners were concerned not with the beauty and dignity of public worship, but with the mechanical formalities attached to the supernatural work they were about. The shift in theological emphasis required the substitution of an esthetic for a mechanical understanding of liturgical forms.

But, given the decision that the parish clergy were not to be held to the standards of learning and high-mindedness envisaged by the Protestant party, the requisite esthetic standards would have to be enforced by the central machinery of ecclesiastical administration. That machinery, as we have seen, could not be expected to enforce anything beyond a mechanical conformity to external standards of performance; nor were the laity prepared to have it strengthened. Hence, it seems likely that a rigorous external standard of observance was required if there was to be any order in the liturgy at all. If a puritan could read the services without his surplice, a country priest could read them without his shirt.

In addition, I suppose that there were elements in the political background of the settlement that required that the external manifestations of conformity be rigorously imposed. The Protestant-minded clergy had to be made to keep up a state that befitted the essentially conservative role in which they had been cast. The Catholic-minded had to be restrained from those liturgical practices whose abolition was the price of Protestant participation in the settlement. To the government, the balance may well have appeared too delicate to allow any play for private choice.

Finally, underlying all these considerations, it seems to me, was an inchoate, and essentially medieval, sense of the religious unity of the nation. Where Protestant and Catholic alike saw the liturgy in the light of the broader question of how a person may be saved, the ordinary Englishman persisted in looking at it with an ancestral vision of a Christian nation's corporate response to God. There was to be a uniform liturgy because it was a national, not a personal, piety that the liturgy was to express.

The church-state nexus that emerged from the English Reformation seems to me to be more than anything else a monument to the English genius for good government. It is good government to discern the historical forces at work in a given time, and to update the institutions of society to embrace them. It is good government to balance the competing interests in society and to develop a synthesis by which the whole community can be at peace. It is precisely these things that were done — whether instinctively or of set purpose — by the architects of the English Reformation.

The English churchman of the seventeenth century — say, Sir Thomas

Browne — could see in his church an institution as fully up-to-date as any in Europe, yet one firmly rooted in the highest antiquity of his race and nation; an institution purged of the corruptions of the immediate past, yet fully embracing the religious achievements of his own forefathers and the Fathers of the church; an institution with strong affinities for his ancestral lifestyle, yet entirely open to new expansions of the quality of life; an institution, in short, through which he could face both past and future with equal urbanity.

Basic to this achievement was the persistence and viability of the medieval Erastian outlook in the religious and national sensibilities of the ordinary Englishman. It was this Erastian outlook that furnished the element of continuity between the pre- and post-Reformation settlements. It was this outlook also that furnished the requisite position of detachment from which both new and old theological commitments could be evaluated and assigned appropriate places in the scheme of things.

The achievement was not without a price. The historic role of the church as an institutional and liturgical embodiment of the corporate religious life of the nation was preserved, as we have seen, at the expense of the most religiously committed elements of the population, both Protestant and Catholic. Anglicanism was to develop its own patterns of personal commitment in due time, but even today it is safer to say that England is a Christian nation than to say that the average Englishman is a Christian.

Also, even in the corporate religious life of the nation, the response to the forces of history was perhaps too complete. History does not stand still, and what changes once can change again. It was to take a High Church revival in the seventeenth century, and another in the nineteenth to provide any kind of theological check upon the historical erosion of the church's witness; and even then the check would not be as powerful as many wished it to be.

Meanwhile, the work of administration went on under the new circumstances, putting flesh on the settlement as it had emerged. It is this work we have now to consider, first from the church's side, then from that of the state.

3. By Law Established

Two pages from the register of Thomas Cooper, who held the see of Lincoln from 1571 to 1583, epitomize the difficulties of administering the *via media* of Anglicanism in the first century of its existence. On page 135, we find the case of the rector of Congerston, Leics. After being found out in a false statement that he was licensed by the bishop to preach, he insisted that the text "Go into the world and preach the gospel." gave him and every Christian man having sufficient ability by learning the right to preach without a license. The bishop, no doubt with a certain amount of arm-twisting, persuaded him to back down from this uncanonical interpretation and admit that he ought to have a license. He was then made to acknowledge before two named persons that he had acted slanderously in saying that he was licensed when he was not. Until he made this acknowledgement, he was to be suspended from his ministry.

He represents one side of the coin. For the other side, we have the case of the rector of Sherington on page 136. He was testified against by his parishioners on eight articles: He was a common drunkard. He was a great swearer and blasphemer of God's name. He said *De Profundis* in Latin in the church on the 24th of June and said it was a good prayer and had not been used many a day. On the 26th of May, he tried to take a man's wife away from him by the highway, and used such filthy speech that they banished him out of their company. Another time, he tried to ravish a parishoner's maid. He plucked off her kerchief, and she had to call for help. One day, when he had finished half the service, he stopped and sat on the church wall saying he tarried for one who should have been there; then he clapped up the book and went his way without any more service. Another time, he stopped evening prayer in the middle when he heard a child cry. Yet another time, he took some exception to the bell-ringer, and said no service at all. The bishop took evidence on all these articles — with what result does not appear.

These two rectors, one with his Gospel, and the new-found freedom of the sons of God, the other with his nostalgia for Latin prayers and his tendency to slight the services and attack the serving-maids, represent the scope of the church's administrative task.[1] On the one hand, there were those who would scrap the whole ecclesiastical apparatus, and erect in its place the unadorned Gospel as they had received it, probably from Geneva. On the other hand, there were the festering abuses of the medieval clergy, which no administrative power from the *plenitudo potestatis* on down had been able to eradicate. Between were the bishops, charged with imposing a purified Christianity on the nation, while retaining much of the medieval lifestyle and most of the medieval polity.

They approached the task with more zeal and resourcefulness than they are generally given credit for. Whatever their personal preferences — and most of them had had puritan learnings in their younger days — by and large they carried out the office they had undertaken in enforcing the official policy of the realm. The resources available to do the job were mainly those inherited from the medieval church. The crown and its officers were prepared to supplement these to some extent out of the royal supremacy — a partial analogue of the *plenitudo potestatis* of old — but the Commons and the lay courts were no more friendly to extensions of ecclesiastical jurisdiction than they had been in their fathers' days.

So you find the traditional mechanism of visitations and presentments, articles and injunctions, courts and processes being put to work for a variety of purposes, new and old.[2] Among old purposes the maintenance of clerical morals, the imposition of penance on fornicators, the keeping up of church fabric and services, were pursued in pretty much the old ways. Other old purposes, church attendance, the suppression of conventicles and irregular ministrations, the learning and orthodoxy of the clergy, were pursued with new emphases, and often with new zeal. Other purposes, defacing the monuments of popery and superstition, enforcing reverence and attentiveness in church, could be considered altogether new.

The personal, loosely institutionalized agencies of the royal supremacy — the sovereign herself or himself, the Council, and a loose-knit group of royal commissioners who gradually became the hated Court of High Commission — dealt with matters of more than parochial concern. There were the especially recalcitrant or the especially eloquent among the nonconforming clergy. On the other side, there were the new breed of Counter-Reformation Catholics fresh from the Continent with their Spiritual Exercises and their papal bulls; these were felt, no doubt with good reason, to be more of a danger than the medieval holdouts in the country parishes. In addition, before these agencies of the royal supremacy came cases of marriage, adultery and what-have-you, drawn out of the routine channels of litigation in ways that are not clear. They seem to have nothing to distinguish them from routine cases except that those involved in them were generally rich.

Besides taking some cases for non-routine treatment, the supreme authority was occupied in a good deal of instruction as to how routine cases were to be handled. The "Injunctions" issued by Elizabeth to her commissioners in the first year of her reign were the foundation of episcopal administration in the parishes for many a year.

I. Functions

A. Clergy.

1. Qualification – Needless to say, the problem of providing the church with a qualified ministry was not created by the Reformation. On the other hand, the change in Eucharistic theology gave the problem a new kind of urgency. True, the reformed Church of England continued to hold that the unworthiness of the ministers hindered not the effect of the sacraments, and continued to insist on the efficacy before God of set prayers which any literate minister could read. But the awesome objectivity of the traditional mass doctrine was no longer available to sustain the worth of the unlearned or unedifying priest.

Nor were the Protestant critics of the settlement slow to point out the resemblance between the discredited mass-priest and the unlearned minister, ordained with no specific cure, who read the Prayer Book services for his hire. They were continually pressing for rigorous examination of ordinands — preferably by working preachers rather than by bishops or archdeacons — and for ordaining no one who did not have a specific benefice with cure awaiting him.

There was a good deal of pressure, though, in the other direction. The church was committed to keeping up services in all the parishes, and there were not enough qualified men to go around.[3] Some effort was made to take up the slack with lay readers, but a good deal of it was done by ordaining insufficient men. This arithmetical necessity was supplemented by pressure from influential laymen who wanted clerical posts for superannuated retainers of one kind or another.

On this point, Strype preserves an exchange of letters between John Parkhurst, the amiable and not terribly competent bishop of Norwich from 1560 to 1575, and one William Heydon, patching up a quarrel over the bishop's refusal to ordain a man presented by Heydon for the purpose.[4] "You bring unto me," says the bishop,

> a simple old man, spent with labours and turmoils of the world, who through his age and other imperfections, is no longer able to labour for his living (for so he himself hath reported,) that he should now enter the ministry: his knowledge in the Latin very small; in the scriptures as little: by occupation a husbandman. . . . Oh! Mr. Heydon, I and all other bishops have made too many such. Necessity drave us to do the same. But to continue so doing, it

were a fault too heinous. Of late years I have had great care in this behalf; and do intend so to continue by God's grace.

To cope with the situation thus presented, the prelates took four main lines of canonical approach, all more or less rooted in pre-Reformation precedent, but rather ingeniously reworked to meet their current needs. These were:

1. The traditional qualifications for ordination, with the procedures for determining whether the ordinand possessed them.

2. The traditional right of a bishop to reject an unqualified candidate for a benefice.

3. A requirement, first enacted in 1408, that preachers be licensed by the bishop.

4. A system of what we would call "continuing education" for clergy lacking full educational qualifications.

On qualifications for orders,[5] the Elizabethan bishops in the first few years of the settlement evidently contented themselves with the standards inherited from their predecessors. These, it may be recalled, were fairly explicit on secondary matters like age, title, and ceremonial irregularity, but extremely vague on all-important matters of morals and learning, and equally so on the procedures for determining if the ordinand possessed such qualifications as a given bishop saw fit to require of him.

It was not until 1571 that an attempt was made to specify canonically what a man must know to be ordained in the reformed Church of England. Even then, the provisions were vague enough. If the ordinand was not trained in letters either in an academy or in some inferior school (*in academia vel in inferiori aliqua schola*), he must know Latin well enough (*satis commode*), and be "skilful in sacred letters."

Beyond these intellectual requirements, such as they were, the 1571 canons imposed traditional requirements of age and title. They required that the ordinand present testimony of his life and innocency from grave and pious men known to the bishop. Finally, they excluded anyone brought up in agriculture or in any "vile and sedentary trade."

Later canons were more specific, but if anything less exacting. The exclusion of men brought up in agriculture or trade was not repeated — whether because the putting forward of such men ceased to be a problem or because it became impossible to do without them we cannot say. Meanwhile, in 1584, the requirement of sufficient knowledge of Latin and scripture became a requirement that the ordinand give an account in Latin of his faith according to the Thirty-Nine Articles. In 1604 he was made to fortify this account with scriptural references. In 1585, the requirement of testimonials from men known to the bishop was dropped. Either the man's college or his local justices of the peace, and "worthy men" would do. In 1604 the justices were replaced by "three or four grave ministers."

One addition in the 1604 canons was the first specific provision for examining an ordinand.[6] It was laid down that the bishop must examine him personally in the presence of at least three ministers of the cathedral, who would then participate in the laying on of hands. This was perhaps as much a concession to Presbyterian sentiment as a means of seeing to the qualification of the ordinand, but it probably did insure a more competent examination.

The main trouble with all this, it seems to me, was that, like the medieval system, it did not provide for any examination of the ordinand until the day he came forward to be ordained. The serious consequences to him and his patron or employer of disqualifying him at that late date must have put many a man through whom a conscientious bishop would have discouraged from applying if he had seen him sooner.[7]

Whatever standards might be set up for ordination were apt to be undermined if a candidate was able to shop all over the country for a bishop willing to overlook his defects.[8] The medieval canon law had attempted to meet this difficulty by requiring the candidate, whoever ordained him, to show "letters dimissory" from the bishop of his home diocese. This rule, for a variety of reasons, seems not to have accomplished the purpose. Accordingly, the Elizabethan bishops, in the first year of the reign, determined that everyone except a university graduate would have to be ordained in the diocese where he lived. In 1571, however, they abandoned this rule, and adopted a new policy of requiring everyone to be ordained in the diocese in which he was to minister. This seems a logical approach, as it gives every bishop a chance to set the standards for his own diocese, and makes him live with the men he has seen fit to ordain.

This shift of emphasis from residence to employment was pretty well without canonical precedent. It was given a familiar look by being tied in with the traditional concept of "title." It had always been required that the ordinand show some means of livelihood in his chosen profession; now it would have to be a means within the diocese of the ordaining bishop.[9] This showing was to be over and above the traditional letters dimissory from the diocese of his residence, and other suitable testimonials to his life and conversation.

After dealing with standards for ordination, the various Reformation canons addressed themselves to maintaining a second line of defense — against unqualified men who had already been ordained. These men were either presented to benefices or hired as stipendiary curates. As to the first category, the bishop inherited considerable powers from his medieval predecessor; as to the second category, he inherited scarcely any.

The routine inquest on presentment to a benefice was used in about the same form after the Reformation as before.[10] It was intended primarily to determine questions of vacancy and patronage, but it could also be used to elicit whatever the local clergy and parishoners knew about the qualifications of the presentee.

In addition, the bishop could examine the presentee in any way he cared to, and reject him if he found him in any way unfit. So the Reformation canons on admission to benefices probably served more to set standards for a careless bishop than to enhance the powers of a careful one. They provided that a presentee to a benefice must exhibit the same qualifications as a candidate for orders.[11] By implication, they required the bishop to conduct in every case an examination at which the requisite showing could be made — though this was not made explicit until 1604.

Whatever improvement these canons made in the standards for admission to benefices was rather hampered, it seems, by the judiciary. There was a proceeding called *duplex querela*, or "double quarrel" available to the rejected presentee in the archbishop's court. I have not been able to determine just what the trouble was with this proceeding, but the prelates had so little confidence in its being carried to a just result that they required the archbishop to intervene personally when it was brought by an unsuitable person. The lay courts also were not very receptive to the imposition of more exacting standards by the bishops. In 1568, for instance, they held that a "haunter of taverns and illegal games" could not be excluded on that ground from a benefice, evidently because it was nothing but a canon that he was violating.[12]

The most important improvement made by the Reformation canons in the standards for the ministry involved not the beneficed clergy but the stipendiary curates — the clerical proletariat.[13] The medieval bishops had exercised virtually no control over the migration and employment of these men. The Elizabethans based their powers on one of the queen's Injunctions of 1559. This referred to the unlearned persons, barely able to read the mass and prayers, who had been ordained in previous reigns, and directed the ordinaries not to admit such men to any spiritual function. The bishops interpreted this Injunction as requiring them to examine every minister before allowing him to serve as a curate — presumably to determine whether he was such a man as the queen had ordered them to exclude. From the necessity of examining him, they had derived by 1571 a requirement that no one be admitted as curate unless he could show the churchwardens a specific license from the bishop — as an indication, no doubt, that he had passed the examination.

In the nature of things, a curate could not be as strictly examined as a candidate for orders or a presentee to a benefice. Rightly or wrongly, he had been ordained, and the canons forbade him to use himself as a layman. Unless he was entirely impossible, he had to be given a chance to earn his living in the ministry. So the qualifications for a curate were never spelled out in the canons. The bishops in 1561 envisaged a sliding scale "having respect to the greatness of the cure, and the meetness of the party." The Articles of 1575 merely directed the bishop to "cause straight and diligent examination to be used" in making sure he was not one of the "unlearned" persons referred to in the queen's Injunctions. The Canons of 1604, the last word on this and most other subjects, went back to the language of 1561.

With these differing standards, one flexible for low-level employment, one more rigorous for entry and preferment, the hierarchy probably achieved as much control over the quality of the clergy as the situation permitted. Indeed, given the available personnel, they probably had to be more flexible in practice than they were on paper. A certain number of positions had to be filled, even if fully qualified men were not forthcoming.

Meanwhile, the prelates made a kind of clerical élite out of those who actually possessed the qualifications nearest to their hearts — the licensed preachers.[14] The requirement that a preacher have a license was first enacted in England in 1408, as part of a campaign against the Lollards. It was probably in the same spirit that the queen continued the requirement in her Injunctions of 1559. Making an itinerant preacher show a license from the ordinary was a good way to insure the orthodoxy of a class of clergy who were particularly influential with the people, particularly hard to control, and particularly prone to doctrinal error or institutional disaffection. The requirement as thus conceived was not imposed on a parson, vicar, or curate preaching in his own cure.

But by 1566 the prelates had begun taking a new approach, concerned as much with the moral and intellectual qualifications of the preacher as with his orthodoxy. Archbishop Parker's "Advertisements" of that year called for an examination of the would-be preacher, and provided for calling in all outstanding licenses so that their holders could be examined. In 1571, and again in 1575, outstanding licenses were recalled for further re-examination, presumably with a view to tightening the standards still more.

Meanwhile, the pastoral functions of a minister who lacked the preaching license were being restricted in ways both vexatious and humiliating. By 1571, he was forbidden to preach even in his own parish. When reading scripture to the congregation, he was to make no comment whatever on the text. By 1604, he was expected to leave to others the task of arguing with the popish recusants in his parish, and even to confine himself to the Prayer Book texts when comforting the sick.

To some extent, this increasingly sharp distinction between preachers and non-preachers was a product of a traditional desire to forestall heterodoxy and disaffection. But I suspect it had affinities also for the militant Protestants' view that only the preacher was truly a minister.[15] The same canons that restricted the pastoral activities of the non-preacher had to censure the parishoner who refused to receive the sacraments from him. We may suppose that the working out of the distinction between preaching and non-preaching ministers was part of the general tension between traditional and reform elements in the settlement.

In aspiring to an élite status within the clergy, the preachers placed themselves in competition with the traditional occupants of that status, the overendowed and underworked higher clergy carried over from the Middle Ages. These men had done bureaucratic work before the Reformation; in Elizabeth's time, as far as I can see, they did nothing at all. They were evidently expected to contribute elements of aristocracy and book learning to the clerical body.[16] The government steadfastly refused (in the face of a good deal of pressure) to deprive them of their economic base by doing away with pluralism or turning cathedral revenues to the support of preachers.

Taking the non-preaching degree holder as the prototype of this class of unreconstructed higher clergy, it seems that he finally came off second best to the preachers.[17] At first, the honors were even: a statute of 1571 reserved all benefices with cure worth more than £30 (in the queen's books; the actual value would have been greater) for men who had either a license or a degree. And after 1585, a pluralist had to have both. But after 1586 only the preacher was exempted from the program of continuing education the bishops imposed on the clergy; previously, the degree holder had also been exempt. The program, which I will take up below, would not have been difficult for the degree holder, but it would certainly have been humiliating.

The cathedral prebends that were the staple diet of the higher clergy could in theory be occupied by anyone.[18] Cathedral statutes, however, tended to require the prebendaries to preach. Some episcopal visitors, beginning in the 1570s, required this preaching to be done in person and not by deputy, a rule that was made universal in 1597.[19] Presumably this would have excluded non-preachers from the affected prebends.

So by the end of the reign it was pretty clear that a man who preached and had no degree stood higher in his calling than a man who had a degree and did not preach. I suspect, though, that by then there were few in either category — that a man who aspired to the higher ranks of the clergy equipped himself with both qualifications. The various political and canonical maneuvers had brought about not a triumph but a synthesis.

For clerics below this level of learning and eloquence, the prelates had a program of continuing education.[20] Their predecessors had from time to time imposed further study on individual members of the parish clergy, but had never attempted to do anything for the whole class. The Elizabethans began feeling their way toward a systematic program from the beginning of the reign. Their efforts took two main forms. One, involving assignments and examinations, was evidently favored by the government; it first appeared in the queen's Injunctions of 1559 and the bishops' Interpretations of 1560-61. The other, called an "exercise" or a "prophesying" (if it happened today, we would call it a "preach-in"), was more in the Genevan fashion, and aroused more general enthusiasm until the queen suppressed it. There exist fairly elaborate descriptions of both forms.

The exercise, which dominated the field through the mid-seventies, was a public meeting, probably monthly or fortnightly, involving the clergy from a specified area and such of the laity as cared to come. The leaders of the program, presumably qualified preachers, were called moderators. The other participants were assigned to be either speakers or writers. In advance of the meeting, the moderators chose a series of texts from different parts of the Bible. Each text was then broken up into verses, and each verse assigned to a moderator, a speaker, and a writer. At the meeting, after the opening prayer, the first moderator would read the verse assigned him. Then the writer would read observations on that verse, which he had gathered and written down (the description does not say from what source). Then the speakers could add brief observations if they cared to. Then the moderator would deliver a critique of the proceedings on his verse. When each verse of the several texts had been given this treatment (the speakers and writers taking notes all the while), the moderators would use the occasion to correct moral offenses that had come to their attention, and fine absentees from the previous meeting. Finally, the meeting would close with a prayer, having occupied pretty much the whole day.

The queen had two objections to this strenuous program. The first was technical, but serious enough in view of the form the settlement had taken — the exercise violated the Act of Uniformity by being a public service not provided for in the Prayer Book. The second objection was more practical. The unlearned laity were resorting in great numbers to these meetings, and it was not expedient for them to spend their time listening to disputations on abstruse points of divinity. It is hard to believe Elizabeth was not exaggerating the number of laymen who turned out for this exegetical marathon. On the other hand, those who did turn out must have been fairly fanatical believers in a preaching ministry, and therefore apt to be disaffected toward the settlement. We may suspect that this was equally true of the more zealous clerical participants. So it appears to have been chiefly as rallying-points for the expression of dissident views that the queen decided to suppress the exercises.

Archbishop Grindal attempted to save them with a set of orders he put out in 1576. The local ordinary was to determine the time and place of the exercises and to appoint the moderators. Only fit men, listed in advance, were to be speakers; others were to be assigned written tasks, and were to read them out of the presence of the laity. Laymen, or clerics who had been deprived or inhibited, were not to speak. Anyone who spoke against the laws of the realm, the discipline of the church, or any specific person was to be silenced on the spot, and not allowed to speak again till newly admitted by the bishop. These orders eloquently bespeak the nature of the queen's objections; needless to say, she was still not satisfied. In 1577 (displacing Grindal, who had refused on grounds of conscience to obey her on the point), she ordered all bishops to do away with the exercises.

To compensate, the prelates turned to a system of assignments and examinations. Programs of this kind had been going on alongside the exercises from the beginning of the reign. Their exact form varied, but they generally involved reporting at one synod or visitation on an assignment given out at the previous one. The form that was finally made universal was, with some modifications, that adopted in 1577 by Bishop Cooper of Lincoln, who had been a vigorous supporter of the exercises until they were suppressed that year. Cooper provided that every parson or vicar, and every curate in a parish where there was no preacher, unless he had an M.A., an LL.B. or a preaching license, should buy a Bible and a copy of the *Decades,* a book of sermons by the Swiss reformer Henry Bullinger. He was to read and take notes on one chapter of the Bible every day, and one sermon of Bullinger's (there were fifty all told) every week. The archdeacon, with the help of one or two of the local preachers, was to examine the clergy at his visitation, and presumably look at the notebooks.

The final development of this program is embodied in a set of rules agreed on in the Convocation of 1586. These improved on Cooper's scheme without radically departing from it. Each preacher was assigned the regular supervision of specific ministers in the neighborhood, instead of being called on from time to time to participate in an examination. He was to report annually on whether his charges did their work. A delinquent was to be admonished once; the next time, he would be censured if he was beneficed, or inhibited from the diocese if he was a curate. All the exemptions except that for licensed preachers were taken away. Finally, a kind of practice preaching (limited to exposition of the catechism, and not to be done from the pulpit) was provided for to help prepare men to be licensed. All this was to be supervised by the archdeacon if he himself was a preacher; otherwise the bishop had to do it.

No one can say that all the measures we have been considering provided the Church of England with a well-qualified ministry. Hughes gives several pages of discouraging statistics, culled from various visitation returns, and he quotes a number of contemporary bishops who take as dim a view as he does.[21] On the other hand, it would be hard for anyone who had studied the medieval situation to think that the Reformation had made it any worse. If you suppose (as I do) that in 1559 the English parish clergy had nowhere to go but up, and if you grant (as everyone seems to) that it was a time when the pay was low, and the kind of religious spirit in short supply that moves people to work for low pay, the record of the prelates in raising standards is really not bad at all.

Taking the Lincoln diocese records that Hughes uses, for instance, we find that in 1576 about one-fourth of the clergy reported on had degrees. In 1585, it was about 40%; in 1603, more than half. Meanwhile, the number of licensed preachers went up from between eight and thirteen per cent (depending on the archdeaconry) in 1576 to between 27 and 32 per cent in 1603.

I suspect that the continuing education program had a good deal to do with such improvement as there was. There is evidence that at least some of the unlearned clergy did their homework. Kennedy gives a set of statistics on the task assigned the clergy of Durham diocese of 1578.[22] 130 of them were supposed to do it; 62 in fact did it, and 29 more at least tried. This is scarcely impressive, but if it happened every year it must have helped.

2. Status and Deployment – The system of clerical employment left over from medieval times continued to force the lower clergy into abjection and tempt the higher into parasitism. Short of scrapping the system entirely, only palliatives were possible. These the prelates attempted, mostly with indifferent success.

First, they tried to provide some measure of stability and security for the stipendiary curates.[23] Only two of their measures for this purpose seem to have had a permanent effect. One required a curate to be licensed for a particular cure, rather than for the diocese at large, so that he had to take out a new license when he changed employment, even in the same diocese. The other forbade him to serve more than one cure at a time. These must have given him a rudimentary local identification.

Other measures, built on sporadic and abortive medieval precedents, fell gradually by the wayside as they came up against the realities of patronage or of supply and demand. One such rule, embodied in the Canons of 1571, forbade any curate to accept a stipend of less than £10 per annum. This was not picked up in any of the later canons, and it is clear that by the end of the century many curates (and many incumbents for that matter) were getting a good deal less. Also, it seems that in the seventies and eighties, the bishops were willing to set the stipend for a curate where the incumbent was nonresident, and set it at a good deal more than the £10 minimum, whereas by the end of the century they were not.

Similarly, there are traces of an effort to protect the curate against arbitrary dismissal by the incumbent. Laud as late as 1633 was of the opinion that an incumbent had to have a grave cause to dismiss his curate — though he would have had to go back to 1214 to find an English canon on the point. In 1588, the bishops made a rule that a non-resident incumbent could not "place or displace" a curate without the bishop's permission, but this too failed to gain full canonical status. My guess is that both medieval and Reformation bishops looked favorably on the principle of employment security for curates, but were unwilling to put their full weight behind it. Given the kind of man the curate was apt to be, we can sympathize with their ambivalence in his regard.

Turning from the lower clergy to the higher, the prelates concerned themselves with controlling the traditional evils of pluralism and nonresidence.[24] These came in for heavy attack from the puritan wing of the church, just as they had from the utilitarian laity of medieval times. Their abolition was resisted by the bishops and the government on the ground that they were needed for the support of learning among the clergy, and to hold out rewards for high achievement in a clerical career — pretty much the same rationale used by Innocent III with his reference to ''sublime and literate persons'' in the Fourth Lateran Council.

The prelates did, though, adopt a few mitigations. They made sure that the pluralist was in fact sublime and literate by requiring him to be both a master of arts and a preacher. They provided that his cures must not be more than thirty miles apart, and they ordered him to preach eight sermons a year in each of them. In the Canons of 1571, they limited his cures to two all told — though this provision dropped out in the later canons.

As for nonresidence, they developed a variety of ways to tighten up the traditional excuses. The main grounds for dispensing from residence were study, service in a cathedral, pluralism, and service as chaplain to the queen or certain specified magnates. The prelates made the student submit to an annual examination on his progress. They made the cathedral prebendary reside on his cure except during compulsory periods of residence imposed by the cathedral statutes. They tried to make the chaplain reside on his cure except when he was in personal attendance on his patron. The pluralist, of course, could not be fully resident on both his cures, but he was expected to reside a ''reasonable time'' on each of them. After 1604, he had to post bond conditioned on his doing so.

When he was legitimately absent, the nonresident was expected to leave a ''sufficient'' curate to take his place. The Elizabethan prelates regularly reiterated this ancient rule. By the turn of the century, they were requiring the curate in question to be a licensed preacher, at least if the benefice could afford one. They also called on the absent incumbent to maintain hospitality on his cure for the local poor (failure in this regard had been a leading grievance against the medieval nonresident), and in some cases to make them a cash contribution as well.

Along with these improvements in the rules governing pluralism and nonresidence, the Elizabethans mounted a more vigorous enforcement of such rules as there were.[25] The numerous visitation articles of the period are full of inquiries on the subject — not routine or perfunctory ones, but detailed questions, bespeaking an intention to act on the information obtained:

> Whether your parson or vicar have any more benefices than one; how many and in what country they be, and what are their names, and whether he be resident upon his benefice and keep hospitality or no; and if he be absent, whether he doth relieve his parishioners, and what he giveth them. . . .
>
> Whether is your parson or vicar resident and keepeth hospitality on his benefice; and if he be not resident whether he doth place a sufficient minister, well able to preach or catechize the youth, and orderly, distinctly,

and reverently to read prayers and administer the Sacraments or no. . . .

Nor can any medieval register show the wealth of monitions to reside, orders to put in curates, and deprivations or sequestrations for nonresidence that appear in the register of Thomas Cooper.[26] There are not sufficient records for us to tell whether Cooper was typical. After reading his register, I would be surprised if he were not a better than average administrator; but he was not far enough out of the ordinary to gain any great reputation either among his contemporaries or among historians. His colleagues must have been working on about the same lines as he.

In the realm of all pay and no work, the pluralists and nonresidents shared the honors with the cathedral prebendaries. In general, the organization and functions of the medieval cathedral establishments had been unaffected by the Reformation. Their main work was liturgical, and only a few of the canons themselves had a hand in it. For the most part, when the employment of clerical bureaucrats went out of style, the cathedral prebends became sinecures in the popular, as well as the canonical, sense. But the authorities declined the invitation to do away with them; like pluralities, they were to provide rewards for the higher clergy.[27]

We have already considered in passing what the prelates did about them. Those who did not have to reside in the cathedral they made reside on their cures (every prebend had a benefice with cure appropriated to it). As only a handful of them had to reside in the cathedral at any one time, this provision must have covered most of them most of the time. Then, those who did reside in the cathedral were made to preach there in person, as well as in other places from which the cathedral drew income. The idea was presumably to make the cathedral a center of the preaching ministry, as it had always been of the liturgy. I doubt if it accomplished quite this. But most of John Donne's sermons were preached as Dean of St. Paul's.

3. Morals and Deportment[28] – The Reformation did little to alter either the official standards of clerical behavior or the prevailing departures from those standards. The most important change, of course, was in allowing priests and deacons to marry. Edward VI's statute on this point had been repealed by Mary, and was not revived as long as Elizabeth lived. She did, however, in her Injunctions of 1559, reluctantly permit a minister to marry, provided he had permission of his ordinary, based on suitable testimonials to the life and conversation of the bride.[29] I have found only a few of these licenses in the records; if the requirement had been systematically enforced, there ought to have been more. The bishops had no sympathy with Elizabeth's scruples in favor of clerical celibacy, and I can find no records of any of them inquiring after or punishing violations of her Injunction on the point. So I suppose the clergy married about as freely as other men did, although their right to do so was restricted on paper until 1604.

A good many, though, must still have preferred to burn. The Elizabethan records disclose, it seems to me, about the same character and incidence of sexual irregularities on the part of the clergy as the medieval records do.[30] The bishops and archdeacons on their visitations asked the same questions as their predecessors had been asking for three centuries and more — whether the minister is incontinent or reputed so to be; whether (being unmarried) he keeps a woman in his house who is not too old or too near of kin to be suspected. Before the Reformation, a number of the clergy had maintained stable, if illicit, unions, as did the miller's father-in-law in Chaucer's Reeve's Tale; others had been more casual. Evidently the two types persisted under the new dispensation, one taking advantage of the queen's Injunctions, the other continuing to engage the disciplinary machinery of the church.

Wenching continued to be linked in the various strictures with other traditional forms of misbehavior — drunkenness, dicing, gaming, haunting taverns and alehouses. Sometimes hunting — equally uncanonical but less indecorous — was added to the list.[31] Along with the old vice of haunting taverns and alehouses, the prelates had to deal with a new one of keeping taverns and alehouses at home.[32] If the medieval clergy offended in this way, I can find nothing in the records to show it. This was the only means of supplementing clerical incomes that regularly engaged the attention of the Elizabethan prelates. Sporadically, they tried also to discourage manual crafts, and even the too vigorous pursuit of agriculture.[33] As far as I can see, none of these pursuits — not even the running of a tavern if the cleric brewed his own beer — would have been condemned by the pre-Reformation canons. We may suppose that the Reformation ideals of scholarship and decorum, rather than the earlier canons, were behind such measures as the hierarchy took in this regard.

Clothes were a traditional concern.[34] The medieval cleric was expected to wear his official habit as a kind of livery to identify him as God's servant. He was also supposed to abstain from extravagance in dress and show himself more sober and modest than a layman. Elizabeth insisted in her Injunctions that the clergy continue to wear a distinctive habit, so that they might receive the reverence due them as "special messengers and ministers of Almighty God." Her prelates, more Protestant minded than she, could perhaps have done without the special messenger status, but they were very concerned about sobriety in dress. Between them, therefore, they made "clerkly and decent apparel" a regular element in their program. Sometimes the authorities went on from the minister's dress to consider that of his family:

> and that their wives, children, and families be apparelled handsomely, without vanity and great charges, fit for the calling of their husbands.

There are a few traces, attenuated to be sure, of the ancient forms of ritual purity.[35] Cooper may have had something of the kind in mind when he forbade one of his clerics to practice medicine. Parker may have been stating a simple moral qualification when he forbade any homicide, felon, or other person disabled by ecclesiastical laws to minister, but I suspect he was alluding to the traditional body of canonical irregularities, in which anyone who kills another is a homicide, even if he is not a felon. Some years later, in 1621, George Abbot, one of Parker's successors, came very near to ruining his career through killing a man in a hunting accident. He himself and a number of others thought there was no irregularity because he was innocent. But it was finally thought appropriate to arm him with a royal dispensation, and even then Laud seems to have scrupled to be consecrated by him.

To these traditional concerns was added a new one — brawling or railing at the parishioners.[36] The medieval authorities were willing to proceed against a person reported to them as a common defamer or a sower of discord, but I find no record of the parish priest or his curate being dealt with in this way. Certainly, no medieval bishop asked in his visitation "Whether your minister or curate . . . is slanderous in any part of his conversation, fighting quarreling, picking and peace breaking." The medieval clergy were surly enough in their own way, but they did not have the spur of theological divergency, or the opportunity afforded by the new emphasis on preaching. The redoubtable controversialists of the reformed church had to be told to keep their feuds and disputations out of the pulpit, and had sometimes to be brought to book for inveighing against their colleagues as unfit ministers, or their captive audiences as adulterers and whores.

B. Ministry and Worship.

In the enforcement of pastoral standards, the reformed church authorities took from their medieval predecessors a preoccupation with external conformity, and a general understanding of what kinds of external conformity they should expect. Such changes in emphasis as they introduced were due in part to their holding a different doctrine, in greater part to their encountering a different type of offender.

Their first concern, like that of their predecessors, was to see that the prescribed round of liturgical observances was kept up, and the prescribed occasional offices available at need.[37] The liturgical package (mattins and evensong every Sunday and holy day; litany every Wednesday and Friday; monthly or quarterly communion) probably suffered as much and as little neglect as the mass had suffered before the Reformation. If a minister bothered to be in residence at all, he probably went through the motions with only occasional lapses (Hart refers to one who found it necessary one Sunday morning to go and look for his lost dog). Sometimes, though, he might be late starting. Sometimes, too, he had to be reminded to read so the congregation could understand him, and not to mutter like a popish mass-priest. Especially was he subject to these vices when he served two cures — rushing every whichway through the service at one in his haste to be off to the other, and even so not getting to the other on time.

The occasional offices (baptism, churching of women, and burial of the dead) were rather less apt to be neglected — the minister got paid for them. The counterpart of the medieval curate who slighted the burial services was not unknown, but this form of laxity was comparatively rare.

A new and more serious problem in maintaining the prescribed liturgy was presented by the minister who departed from the set forms not through sloppiness or haste, but through conviction. If he was tradition-minded, he might elevate the Host at the communion service, or offer prayers for the dead. If he was oriented toward Geneva, he might refuse to wear his surplice, or he might distribute the Sacrament to parishoners sitting in their pews. As the Prayer Book rubrics represented a hard-fought compromise, it was felt that no such deviations could be tolerated, and the authorities attempted to root them out. In the resulting controversies, there developed a set of shibboleths, all trivial enough in themselves, but accepted by general consensus as showing where a man stood on the matters in issue.

Prominent among these were the standards of eucharistic reverence.[38] The authorities had occasionally to forbid elevating the Host, or otherwise "counterfeiting the popish mass." More often, they had to make sure the minister made the communicants kneel.

The wearing of the surplice was evidently considered about equally important.[39] Enforcing the use of this garment seems to have been a compromise between Elizabeth, who was for more elaborate vestments, and the prelates, who were for no distinctive vestments at all. It was galling to the more militant reformers to be dressed in any way like popish priests. I suspect, though, that a good half of the surplice violators were more lackadaisical than reformist. In many cases, there was no surplice in the parish, or the only one available was too small or too threadbare. Sometimes the minister and the churchwardens could not agree on who was to buy a new one, so neither of them did. Where there was a surplice, the offending minister was apt to wear it sometimes and leave it off others, not evincing any consistent stand on it.

A third major concern involved the faithful departed.[40] Nowhere did the Reformation clash more sharply with parish folkways than in its uncompromising abolition of prayer for the dead. The authorities had to deal with all kinds of survivals — the celebration of communion at funerals (evidently this savored too much of a requiem mass even if it was conducted in strict Prayer Book form), the use of candles on biers, and the like. For some reason, the chief bone of contention was bells. "Superfluous" bells at a funeral (short peals at passing, and before and after burial were allowed), or any bells at all on All Souls' Day were regularly inquired after and reported on parish visitations.

Next came a set of rules concerning baptism.[41] Children were to be baptized at the traditional font; godparents were to answer for them; and the minister was to make the sign of the cross over them when he was done. All of these occasioned great scruples and had to be enforced by the authorities. This was especially true of the sign of the cross. Evidently the prelates felt quite defensive about it, for they devoted almost four pages to its justification in one of the Canons of 1604 (c. 30).

Somewhat less serious problems were presented by holy days and rogation processions.[42] Many, but not all, of the traditional holy days had been suppressed. The authorities had to exert themselves both against traditionalists who kept the suppressed ones and against purists who kept none at all. There was also a rule that a holy day be announced on the preceding Sunday; this seems to have been harder to enforce than the actual celebration.

Rogation processions were retained probably because they served the secular purpose of preserving parish boundaries. As they were the only survivor of a variety of medieval processions, there was some tendency to make a larger production of them that the prelates considered appropriate. They forbade at one time or another the wearing of surplices, the carrying of candles, the pausing at wayside crosses. At the same time, they had to keep both the lazy and the puritanical from omitting the procession entirely.

Most liturgical violations, however they were in fact motivated, seem to have been treated as matters of neglect. The typical offender did not go to the wall for his conscience, if his conscience was involved. He temporized, made what excuses he could think of, and at least made gestures in the direction of not offending again. The authorities, for their part, were usually ready enough to let him off with an admonition, or at worst an apology to his parishoners.

The Elizabethan bishops were more concerned than their predecessors (and probably more concerned than the queen) with preaching.[43] The weekly sermon had evidently been recognized as an ideal by the fifteenth century, but a medieval pastor could probably have kept out of trouble with as few as one or two sermons a year. Elizabeth on her accession set a goal of quarterly sermons for an incumbent who was a licensed preacher. As for other incumbents, she was content if they gave place to a licensed preacher when one showed up.

The prelates were stricter. They insisted on quarterly sermons everywhere, which means that the non-preaching incumbent had to hire a preacher four times a year — though poverty was sometimes accepted as an excuse for not doing so. The bishops tried to make preachers available for this purpose by cutting down on their price. Archbishop Parker's Advertisements of 1566 forbade "unreasonable" exactions. The Canons of 1571 limited the preacher to food and a night's lodging. Presumably this spartan measure was not fully enforced, and there were still parishes that could not afford preachers. In 1586, it was provided that the bishop should actually assign preachers to cover the quarterly sermons for non-preaching incumbents. These were presumably to be drawn from the neighborhood, for their compensation was limited to dinner, food for their horses, and substitutes to serve their cures while they were gone.

By the end of the century, the bishops were trying to move from quarterly to monthly sermons. In connection with this development, they evidently allowed preachers to take cash stipends again. The Canons of 1604 made monthly sermons compulsory, but only if the bishop found that the parish benefice could afford them. The 1586 arrangements were not carried on.

Meanwhile, the licensed preacher was being put to more work. Where Elizabeth had ordered him to preach quarterly in his cure the bishops in 1586 made him preach twelve sermons a year, eight in his own cure. In 1604 he was told to preach every Sunday in his own cure unless he was filling in for an unlicensed colleague somewhere else.

Sundays and holy days when there was no sermon, the minister was supposed to read his congregation a homily from a book of them put out in Edward VI's time, and augmented in 1563.[44] He had also a variety of announcements to make — the holy days for the ensuing week, the names of excommunicates, etc. Once a quarter, he was to read off the queen's Injunctions of 1559. It was haste, not theology, that made problems in enforcing most of these rules. If you were in a hurry, the Homilies and the queen's Injunctions — dull fare by and large — were particularly attractive candidates for omission.

For the licensed preacher, who made up his own sermons instead of reading the Homilies, the prelates had a good deal of advice, some of it enforceable.[45] He was to exhort people to contribute to parish poor relief instead of spending their money on shrines, pilgrimages, and the like. He was to extol the settlement, and exhort his hearers to obedience. Specifically, he was to tell them not less than quarterly that all foreign ecclesiastical jurisdiction was rightly taken away. In his doctrine, he was to stick to the scriptures, the Thirty-Nine Articles, and the Fathers, eschewing subtleties and deep points of doctrine. He was to avoid matters of state except such as were encompassed in the prescribed strictures on obedience. He was not to stir up controversy, or make "odious invections and undiscrete discourses by name or by plain circumstance to defame any person." Most of this of course was unenforceable. Preachers, however, who neglected the quarterly denunciation of foreign jurisdiction, or who descended to specific personalities, were corrected from time to time.

After his liturgical and homiletic responsibilities, the next duty of a minister was to instruct his flock in the rudiments of the Christian religion[46] The development of an official Catechism made it possible for the Elizabethans to make this duty more specific than the medieval canons had. The minister was told to drill people in this document for at least half an hour every Sunday afternoon. The parishioners were to send their children and servants to him for this purpose, and, if necessary, come themselves. Neglect on either side would be inquired after and reported on parish visitations. In addition, the minister was supposed to examine everyone seeking to marry, to be a godparent, or to go to communion, and repel anyone who did not know his Catechism.

The only more or less pastoral function with which the authorities were concerned was, as it had been before the Reformation, the visiting of the sick.[47] It continued also to be liturgical as well as pastoral. The minister was encouraged to memorize scriptural passages with which to console the sick person. The Prayer Book provided a service, including a substantial Exhortation (mercifully, it could be cut short if the sick person was "very sick") for the minister to read. Anointing, and something rather like auricular confession and absolution, were provided for on request. The communion service would be celebrated in the bedchamber (as a substitute for the theologically objectionable communion from the reserved Sacrament — which seems to have been practiced sometimes despite the theology). The rubrics gave some room for the minister to deal personally with the sick person, but the liturgical framework was probably not too encouraging. It seems that only a licensed preacher could scrap the prescribed service entirely, if, indeed, anyone could. Presumably, it is this semi-liturgical package that is envisaged when various visitation articles inquire whether the parish minister visits the sick when requested. Failure to do so was not common.

After making the clergy conduct the prescribed services, the authorities concerned themselves with making the parishioners attend.[48] The Elizabethans did not invent compulsory church attendance, but they encountered new kinds of difficulty in enforcing it. For the occasional Lollard of medieval times who stayed away from conviction, there was now the whole body of popish recusants, as well as the odd puritan who could not bring himself to hear a service without a sermon. In addition, the upheavals of the times (or the introduction of the Book of Homilies) had considerably swollen the ranks of those who were absent from apathy or perversity.

So, where the medieval ordinaries were content to process such cases of non-attendance as the parish churchwardens brought to their attention, the Elizabethan ordinaries were continually after the churchwardens themselves to make sure they rooted offenders out. Not only did they check up on the churchwardens at visitations, they tried to have them reminded of their duty every Sunday from the pulpit. The churchwardens, for their part, canvassed the alehouses, and even the homes, of the vicinity from time to time to turn out the absent brethren. Three or four other parishioners, called swornmen, were assigned under the queen's Injunctions to help them in this work.

The Act of Uniformity of 1559 set a penalty of 12d for each absence. This was to be given to the churchwardens for the relief of the local poor. Evidently, if the offender could be persuaded to pay voluntarily the matter would go no further. Otherwise, the churchwardens could proceed either before the ecclesiastical courts or before the justices of the peace. One churchwarden was made to collect the statutory sum from nine men who went bowling with him of a Sunday evening instead of attending evensong, and to add another twelvepence for himself.

On paper, of course, this penalty fell on the recusant for conscience sake — usually a Roman Catholic, though non-attending Protestant sects were beginning to appear — in the same way as on the man who preferred to bowl or snare rabbits of a Sunday. In practice, though, the result was a little different. The full-fledged recusant, not a mere misliker of the queen's proceedings, but a person fully committed to an institutional church that was not the Church of England, developed his own ways of coping with the devices set up to turn him from his resolve. The ordinary machinery of ecclesiastical administration was probably the least formidable of those devices, although it served well enough to turn his more frivolous neighbors out of the alehouse.

When they got the reluctant parishioner into church, the authorities' next concern was to make him behave. The ideal, as set forth in the queen's Injunctions was

> That no man, woman or child, shall be otherwise busied in the time of the service, than in quiet attendance to hear, mark, and understand that is read, preached, and ministered.[49]

This appears to set a new standard of reverence. The medieval parishioner, it seems, if he was devout, prayed his beads, read his primer, or looked at the pictures and statues about the church. If he was more secular, he chatted with his friends and neighbors — a practice condemned by medieval moralists, but not, as far as I know, by the authorities. He recognized the sacred place and action by appropriate gestures, kneelings, crossings, knockings on the breast, at specific places in the service. Also, he moved around fairly freely, because in most churches there were no seats.

The Reformation took away his pictures and statues, and often his beads and his primer also. The crossing and knocking (the kneeling was all right if done at the prescribed time) were not expressly forbidden, but they were not encouraged. One minister was so engaged in reproving his flock for idolatries of this kind at communion, that he himself got in trouble for forgetting to kneel.[50] So, the Elizabethan parishioner, maintaining the drily mechanical reverence of an earlier time, was apt to be wandering about the church talking, and waiting for an especially solemn moment that the Prayer Book services did not provide. The "quiet attention to hear, mark, and understand" — or even the external appearance of it — was hard to inculcate. Indeed, the Reformation brought new departures. A parishioner who did not care for the Prayer Book services might set out to disrupt them by boisterousness or ridicule. Of, if he heard, marked, and understood the sermon, he might express his opinion on the spot.[51]

The filling of churches with seats — a process which had been going on for more than a century, and was now virtually complete — must have increased the sleeping while it cut down on the walking about. More important, it gave a new reason for creating a disturbance in church.[52] Quarreling over seats is mentioned in an English canon as early as 1287; presumably, it developed as rapidly as the seats themselves. It has an important place in Elizabethan disciplinary records. The law on the subject almost invited dispute. You could come by a particular seat in church either through prescription or through assignment. The assignment was made by the churchwardens in accordance with your social position. If the churchwardens did not consider your prescription as effective or your social position as high as you did, you might find yourself displaced at any time. If this happened, you could go to court if you wanted, but it was easier to express your annoyance by digging your elbow into your supplanter, trying to sit on his lap, or even jabbing him with a pin in the middle of the service.

It was the business of the churchwardens and their helpers to keep their unruly congregation in order.[53] They were supposed to make everyone sit in his proper seat. If somebody was loitering about the church door, they were to make him come in or go away. If he was asleep they were to wake him up. If he was walking about they were to make him stay put. If he was talking they were to shush him. If he left during the service, they were to know the reason why. If he made a disturbance they were to subdue him. If he resisted their efforts or failed to amend, they were to present him to the authorities for correction. If they failed in any of this, they were subject to correction themselves.

Needless to say, they got small thanks for their efforts. It is recorded that one sleeper had "hard speeches" for the churchwardens who woke him up. Another man, walking out of the service, presumably to relieve himself, used "unrevevent talk" when the churchwardens asked him where he was going. And one garrulous lady:

> called one of the churchwardens prating Jack and said she would talk and ask him no leave when he reproved her for talking in sermon time.

While these things were going on in church, the Lord's Day was supposed to be being observed outside.[54] Despite the objections to putting days of men's devising on the same footing with the scriptural Sabbath, the handful of holy days retained in the Prayer Book were kept in precisely the same way as Sundays. Canonically, the observance in question involved abstaining from secular amusements in service time, and from certain forms of trade and labor all day.

During service time, the queen's Injunctions and various subsequent documents expressly required the closing of inns and taverns; the courts added prohibitions of cards, hunting, dancing after a piper, and the like. Naturally these offenses involved absence from service (though in theory they could be committed by someone from another parish after he had attended services at home), and they might be visited with the statutory twelvepenny fine. But it appears that they were also considered active profanations of the day. The stricter moralists of the Reformation, like those of the Middle Ages, would like to have forbidden secular amusements all day Sunday, but they never succeeded in getting their views into the canons. So the strictures governing service time may have been a kind of compromise. At any rate, I find no official document before the Reformation that forbids secular amusements on Sundays at all, and none afterward that forbids them except during service time.

Some authorities, however, took it upon themselves to impose a more rigorous standard. James I in 1618 found it necessary to restrain "the prohibiting and unlawful punishing of our good people for using their lawful recreation and honest exercises upon Sundays and other holydays" after they had attended the proper services. This "Declaration of Sports" pained the puritans greatly; one of the paving-stones on Charles I's road to the scaffold was his reissuing of it in 1633.

What the canons did forbid for the whole day Sunday was work. Shops were specifically ordered to be closed, and the medieval rules on artisans and husbandmen were regularly enforced. Elizabeth in her Injunctions made a general exception for harvesters, but I cannot find that this was given effect. In fact, the Elizabethan authorities seem to have been a bit stricter than their predecessors in passing on excuses for Sunday work.

Sacred places, like sacred times, were an old concern.[55] Altars, shrines, images, rood-lofts, vigil lights and the like "momuments of superstition" were in the process of being replaced by communion tables, Bibles, lists of Commandments, the royal arms, and a great chest under three locks to collect offerings for the poor. Missals, grails, altar cloths, vestments, and the rest of the apparatus of popish worship had given way to Prayer Books, tablecloths, and the battered and ever-contentious surplice. But the duty of the churchwardens to see to all things needful, and the work of the parish visitors in checking up, were going on just as they had always done.

Equally enduring was the problem of dilapidation.[56] The churchwardens were supposed to keep up the nave at the charge of the parish, levying a rate for the purpose if other funds failed. The chancel was the rector's responsibility. It appears that rectors were more remiss than parishioners, so more chancels than naves were in disrepair. It may be that the parishioners were more interested in repairs because they had to use the church every Sunday; it may be simply that they were easier to catch. The rector might be an Oxford college or a cathedral chapter; he might be a great lord who had displaced a monastic appropriator in King Henry's time. In many places, the queen herself had the responsibilities of the rector — and tended to be slow in discharging them.

Except for the replacement of monasteries by lay impropriators, all this was equally true before the Reformation. There is nothing to indicate that the laymen, bad as they were, were any worse than their monastic predecessors, or that dilapidation generally was any worse than it had been at other times. Taking for comparison a consecutive set of Oxfordshire parishes in an episcopal visitation of 1519,[57] I find rather more than half of them complain of dilapidation, broken windows or something of the kind. And about three chancels are complained of for every nave.

Churchyards also continued in a familiar way.[58] Either the parishioners or particular adjoining landowners were supposed to keep them fenced. Some complaints mention only the lack of fencing. Others specify that cattle and swine have defiled the churchyard because of the lack. In still other cases, the incumbent, or an agressive neighbor, has turned his animals into the churchyard on purpose to pasture. There was no century from the thirteenth through the nineteenth in which parish visitations failed to turn up matters like this.

The Reformation seems to have brought an increase in official concern with secular goings-on in the church precincts.[59] Certainly it brought a change in emphasis. Fairs and markets received about the same attention as before, courts and musters a little less. But festivities and games of all kinds were a good deal less tolerated than they had been. Bowlers and cricketers in the churchyard were corrected by the authorities. Church ales, the counterpart of modern ice cream socials or jumble sales, were banished to a secular building. Puppet plays, morris dances and the like were repeatedly forbidden, and a set of disguised merrymakers called Lords of Misrule came in for an especial ban. Rushbearings, the festivities connected with strewing the church floors, had to be rescued by King James in his Declaration of Sports. We can document prohibitions of this kind of thing since the thirteenth century, but no sustained or systematic effort to suppress it. Any dozen years or so of Elizabeth's reign will yield more material on the subject than the whole medieval period.

In some cases the authorities set out to correct those responsible for such misbehavior. More often they turned their attention to the minister and churchwardens who allowed it to go on. These were apt to be caught in the middle between sportive parishioners and stern authorities. In one case we see a rector being made to apologize to his congregation (and pay 3s. 4d. to the local poor in token of his repentance) for suffering "the Church of God and house of prayer to be profanely abused with Puppet plays." In another case a curate was beaten up by a group of bowlers in the churchyard for trying to stop them.

C. Lay Morals.

For Calvin and his followers, the "godly discipline" by which the elders of the church corrected sinners was just short of being an essential mark of the true church. They were much disappointed, therefore, to find they could not introduce the system into England. The traditional ecclesiastical discipline, which the reformed Church of England had inherited in working order, had little consolation for them. Aside from the various corruptions and inefficiencies endemic to this system, the militants were not interested in having a fornicator put to penance in a white sheet.

> For what great thing is it to go ii or three days in a white sheet before the congregation, and that sometimes not past an hour or two in a day having their usual garments underneath, as commonly they have? . . . I have heard some miscreants impudently say, that he is but a beast that for such white livered punishment would abstain from such gallant pastime . . .[60]

They were for the death penalty, or at least branding on the cheek.

But the old machinery rolled on for all their protests. Sexual offenders were presented on parish visitations and put to penance. Defamers, scandal-mongers and sowers of discord were admonished. Husbands and wives were reconciled. Quarrels were patched up.[61] Sorcerers were turned up rather more than they had been before — perhaps because the change in religion broadened the appliction of the term. Most of those presented for this offense had done no worse than mutter prayers over their sick neighbors, (serious witchcraft had been dealt with as a secular offense since 1540). It went a little harder than before with drunks, blasphemers, and singers of ribald songs — in the old days most churchwardens would not have bothered to turn them in.

In fact, it seems to me that a good deal of work was done to try to catch sinners who would not have been caught before. Perhaps the bishops were stung by their Calvinist brethren; perhaps their own nostalgia for Geneva moved them. In any event, the dominant impression I get from the medieval materials is that people were turned in only when their neighbors were annoyed at them, whereas the Elizabethan materials show the neighbors being systematically prodded to turn people in.

This impression is a little hard to document directly, for of the articles put to pre-Reformation parishioners, there seem to be none extant after the mid-thirteenth century. It has been suggested that these (deriving ultimately from Grosseteste) were used throughout the Middle Ages, but that would involve a good deal of conjecture. For what it is worth, though, compare Grosseteste's

> An adulteria et crimina publica et notoria laicorum sint rite per archidiaconum correcta?[62]

with Elizabeth's

> Whether any have committed adultery, fornication, or incest, or be common
> bawds, or receivers of such evil persons, or vehemently suspected of any of
> the premises.[63]

Note in the first place that Grosseteste's article in terms asks not who is
committing offenses in the parish, but whether the archdeacon is doing his job.
It can be read not as inviting new presentments, but as asking whether the
presentments made on the previous visitation have been processed. There are a
number of Elizabethan articles meant to check up on court officials, but the one
just quoted is clearly seeking new presentments.

In the second place, Grosseteste is looking for "public and notorious"
offenses, whereas Elizabeth seems to be asking if the ministers and
churchwardens to whom her articles are addressed know of any offenses at all,
or even a general suspicion of any. The post-Reformation canons continued to
envisage reporting notorious sinners, offensive to the parish community,[64] but
individual prelates, like the queen, tended to go farther:

> Ye shall diligently inquire and faithfully present all such faults as you shall,
> *either upon your own knowledge* or by public fame, understand to be
> committed within your parish. . . .[65] (my italics).

This is from an oath administered to churchwardens and sidesmen by Bishop
Bickley of Chichester in 1586. Note that it requires them not only to report
such offenses as they know of, whether publicly or privately, but also to make
diligent inquiry in order to learn of more.

Not only was the Elizabethan churchwarden asked specifically about his
neighbors' offenses, and oath-bound to report them; he was also checked up
on himself:

> Whether you know or have heard that the churchwardens and swornmen of
> your parish the last year have left any person or persons, punishable for any
> offence by the laws ecclesiastical, unpresented; whether they have escaped
> unreformed and by whose default; and what are the parties' names that have
> so offended, and wherein have they offended?[66]

This is no empty language; churchwardens were in fact corrected for failure to
report offenders. The medieval records show nothing of the kind.

The Elizabethan authorities, then, by keeping after the churchwardens, strove
to bring offenses to light that the offender's neighbors would have been willing
to leave private. In the case of sexual offenses, they were not content even with
this. Efforts to cover these offenses, or at least keep them a little out of the
public eye, were inquired after as offenses in their own right. So "bawds and
receivers of such incontinent persons" — in other words, anyone who gave the

illicit lovers a place by the fire — were subject to reporting and correction. People who took in unwed mothers from other parishes, and let them be delivered and go home without doing penance, came in for special attention. One bishop even mounted a general inquiry about people suspected of incontinence who had left the parish, and where they had gone.[67]

The same desire to ferret out offenders seems to me to be reflected in a new concern about matrimonial irregularities.[68] A table of prohibited degrees of kindred was put up on the wall in every church. Licenses to marry without banns were the subject of numerous restrictions, designed to insure that the marriage was legitimate, public, and not without parental consent. Marriages contracted in secret or otherwise illegally were regularly asked after on visitation, and punished when caught. Conversely, those who published banns and then failed to marry were subject to correction.

If a marriage was found to be invalid, rather than merely illicit, the ordinary would evidently break it up on his own initiative, and would check on his parish visitations to make sure the parties did not come back together again. On the other hand, if people were validly married, he would make them live together. After 1597, they could not have a judicial separation without posting bond to live chastely.

In short, where the medieval church was satisfied to leave matrimonial problems to private litigation between the parties except in cases of open notoriety in the parishes, the Elizabethan church attempted to see that no improper marriages took place, and that no man and woman lived together who were not truly married in the eyes of God.

In connection with these efforts to police the morals of the laity, the Elizabethans dusted off an old discipline about excluding public sinners from communion.[69] This discipline is to be distinguished both from the judicial sentence of excommunication and from the automatic excommunication visited by the canons on certain kinds of misbehavior. It involves a judgment made by the minister, on his own responsibility, as to the sinner's status on the particular occasion when he seeks to communicate. It does not make him an excommunicate for any other purpose; indeed, it does not prevent his receiving communion in another parish in which he is not known.

This discipline has been set forth in a Prayer Book rubric ever since 1549. It applies to "notorious evil-livers," and to persons out of charity with one another. It requires the minister to inform the bishop within a fortnight of invoking it against any of his parishioners. As far as I can see, the principle behind this rubric is ancient. It seems though, that putting persons out of charity in the same position as notorious evil-livers was an innovation, as was the provision for resort to the bishop.

But the most important innovation was the systematic enforcement of this rubric by the higher auhorities in the church. The bishops regularly asked on their visitations whether the minister was admitting offenders to communion. In fact, some of them went rather beyond the rubric:

> Whether [the ministers] have admitted any notorious offender, or malicious person, or any notoriously known to be out of charity, or that hath done any open wrong to his neighbour either by word or by deed, to the Holy Communion, without open acknowledging of their fault and reconciliation?[70]

In the same vein, the Elizabethan bishops began worrying about ministers churching unwed mothers — a problem that seems never to have concerned the medieval churchmen one way or the other.

The extended application of this kind of discipline would have given the parish ministry a judicial power akin to that of the bishop's commissaries and officials.[71] It was one thing to repel the town whore from communion, or a man who lived openly with another man's wife — which must have been all a medieval priest did (and I find no record of his doing even that). It was quite another to decide who was a malicious person, or who had done any open wrong to his neighbor by word or deed. Also (as with the inquiries to churchwardens) the requirement of notoriety, which would have provided some safeguard against arbitrary action by the minister, was slighted at one point or another in a number of the documents, including one of the Prayer Book rubrics themselves:

> The same order shall the Curate use with those betwixt whom *he perceiveth* malice and hatred to reign . . . (my italics).

The bishops, again no doubt under Genevan influence, seem not to have objected to giving the parish clergy this kind of power. One or two of them sought to temper it, though, by involving the parishioners in its exercise. For instance, in 1577, Thomas Cooper provided for the Lincoln diocese that no one should be repelled from communion until the minister had "opened the whole cause to the churchwardens and some other of the best-staid of his parishioners, whom he shall think meet to call thereto."[72] If any of them objected, the whole matter was to be referred to the ordinary. Arrangements of this kind probably took their inspiration from the "elders of the church" envisaged in the godly discipline of Geneva. They were never taken into the canons.

D. Institutional Concerns.

The processes of the reformed church, like those of the medieval church, were used with varying degrees of felicity to protect the persons of the clergy, and see to the integrity and right use of the revenues. I discern, though, a somewhat less exalted (perhaps I should say romantic) view of these functions after the Reformation. Churchmen had become less impressed with the sacredness of the interests they were protecting, and less impressed with the transcendent significance of their processes. They went about their business more as practical men pursuing practical goals.

1. Abuse of the Clergy – It had always been the law, and was the law still, that anyone who laid violent hands on a cleric could be corrected by the ecclesiastical courts. I find a few cases invoking this principle, but not a lot of them. The cleric who had suffered in a private quarrel probably did better taking his case before the justices of the peace or the civil courts. The prelates were more interested in his ministry than in his person. It was the people who did him violence when he was trying to conduct services, or correct their behavior, or defend the rights of his church that engaged the attention of the parish visitors, or even the High Commission.

The shift of interest from the sacredness of the priest's person to the dignity of his ministry led the authorities to take verbal abuse of the clergy more seriously than the medieval authorities had done.[73] Calling the local minister a "plain fool" or saying he "were more meet to stand in a swine sty than in a pulpit" or calling his children "priest calves," would all get you called up before the parish visitors and made to apologize. A number (but not all) of the visitation articles asked after offenses of this kind. Such offenses were probably taken the more seriously because they often bespoke a certain disaffection with the settlement.

This extension of the church's power to verbal offenses, or indeed, any application of it beyond cases of actual physical violence, was a clear violation of secular law, for which the lay courts would grant a writ of prohibition if asked.[74] Evidently they were not asked very often. It was no doubt easier to apologize to the parson than to go litigating in the royal courts.

A somewhat unnoticed change from the medieval practice was the limitation of the church's protection to priests and deacons. Minor orders went out at the Reformation; so, evidently, did the setting apart of clerics by first tonsure. Thus, for most purposes no one could claim to be a cleric until he had been ordained at least a deacon. The "benefit of clergy" in secular criminal cases persisted, but, as we have seen, it had not been confined to true clerics since the fifteenth century. The "parish clerk." who received some kind of stipend from local church funds, for ringing bells, saying responses, and cleaning up the church, retained his ancient office, but had no longer the status of a cleric in the medieval sense.[75] Doing away with this level of the lower clergy must have made a substantial change in the medieval scene, and put a very different face on ecclesiastical protection of the clergy.

2. Collection of Church Dues – Tithe litigation was carried on in the church courts in about the way it had always been. The royal courts ranged wider with their writs of prohibition than they had before, and occasionally (under an ambiguous statute of Edward VI) entertained tithe suits in the first instance. But on the whole the customary tithes were collected in the customary way. It was the attempt, mainly in the seventeenth century, to go beyond custom and claim a radical tenth that produced the church-state disputes, just as it did in the Middle Ages. The jurisdictional difficulties were largely ancillary to the difficulties of substance.

Mortuaries and the like were collected in the church courts. Sometimes also those who failed to pay were presented on parish visitations, though I do not find that they were inquired after by the visitors. The same was true of church rates levied by the parish vestry to repair the fabric; the controversies that figure so prominently in later centuries were just beginning to arise. Occasional payments — offerings by those who received particular ministrations — seem to have been less litigated over than before. Some of them went out with the ministrations that supported them when the new liturgy came in. But mainly, the reformed clergy and their ecclesiastical superiors seem to have been less scrupulous about withholding the service until payment was made — a practice which the medieval canons had stigmatized as simony. The clergy did, however, litigate with those who tried to escape the payment of the fee by omitting the service. Especially was this the case with the churching of women; a number of more advanced thinkers did not see the need to be churched.

3. Leakage of Revenues and Endowments – In addition to dues and offerings, churches and ecclesiastical benefices were still supported by a variety of other resources which the churchmen had to be at best vigilant, at worst mean, to keep intact. In the first place, there were parish funds and parish goods, given, collected or bequeathed for the poor or for the services of the church. The minister and the churchwardens were to watch these, and watch each other; the parish visitors watched them all.[76] Alms for the poor were kept in a chest with three locks, a requirement of the queen's Injunctions. The minister had the key to one, each churchwarden the key to another, so the box could not be opened unless they were all together. The churchwardens accounted to their successors and to the parishioners for the funds in their hands. They reported to the visitors if the minister was wasting them or if an outsider was into them or holding them back.

A more serious problem was keeping the benefices intact. The Canons of 1571 and 1604, and a number of bishops in between, urged the parish incumbent to get together with his churchwardens and the more substantial of his parishioners and make up a ''terrier'' or list of his landholdings, lest any of them stray out of ecclesiastical hands.[77] How they strayed is not altogether easy to determine. But for the terrier, I suppose, during a vacancy of a parish benefice a neighbor might move into a bit of the glebe without the successor incumbent being any the wiser. Or a patron might take property from an abject or complaisant incumbent. Or a man holding church lands on a long lease might get away with neglecting to pay the rent till people forgot whose the land was. But most depletions of church lands were not inadvertent. The usual means of accomplishing the purpose was a long lease. It was customary to grant such leases not at the fair rental value of the lands involved, but at much less, the difference being reflected in an "entry fine," or lump sum payment, made to the landlord at the commencement or renewal of the tenency. For some reason, it was considered reprehensible to set rents at "rack-rent", i.e. what the traffic would bear, but less so to negotiate entry fines on the same basis.

The art of accountancy in the period was not up to taking the entry fine into income pro rata over the life of the lease, as a modern accountant would do.[78] It was treated like income for the year it was paid. So, if church land was let out on a long lease, the incumbent who entered into the lease would pocket the fine, while his successors would bear the burden of the low rent — compounded by an inflationary trend that made all fixed money payments less valuable year by year.

A number of bishops, and perhaps some lesser clergy, got rich by invading capital in this way. But not all leases were made with negotiated fines. In many cases, bishops were dragooned into making favorable leases to the queen or her favorites; sometimes they had to promise to do so before being put into their sees. The lower clergy were often served in the same way by their patrons.

The queen, at least, was not at all underhanded about any of this. There is preserved a document that looks very like a form writ, ordering the dean and chapter of York to consummate a lease in due form giving her certain property for thirty-one years at the customary rental plus one year's rent as a fine.[79] Her more informal requests were also straightforward enough. As Robert Cecil put it on her behalf, having bestowed all, she was entitled to take part back.

She also had a right by Act of Parliament (1559) to exchange her impropriate rectories (left over from the dissolution of the monasteries) for secular estates of a bishopric whenever the latter came into her custody through vacancy of the see.[80] This, although a plausible enough way of putting church revenues back into church hands, was highly damaging for the bishops, who were swapping good land of their own for the right to collect produce from other people's land. I do not find that the queen used it very often except perhaps at the beginning of her reign; generally, she took long leases instead. She did use it though to separate the rich manor of Crediton from the see of Exeter. Gervase Babington, bishop-elect at the time, was blamed for parting with the manor, but I do not see where the Act of Parliament gave him a choice.

A series of acts in the course of the reign sought to limit ecclesiastical leases to three lives (i.e. until the death of the last survivor of three specified persons living when the lease was made) or twenty-one years — at the customary rent.[81] Leases by bishops, except to the queen, were subjected to this limit in

1559, leases by other churchmen in 1571. The exception for the queen does not appear in the 1571 act, but she evidently took long leases of deans and chapters as well as of bishops. She could assign her leases to others, and often procured them at the request of her courtiers, so it has been suggested that the whole effect of the legislation was to centralize, rather than to prevent, the plunder of the church through long leases. James I at the beginning of his reign gave up his right to reward his favorites in this way; legislation passed that year extended the three-lives-or-twenty-one-years rule to all ecclesiastical leases.

Even when this legislation was complied with — as often it was not — it was not an adequate solution to the problem. Three lives could be quite a long period if the three persons were chosen carefully, and even the twenty-one year alternative could run a good deal into a successor's time if an elderly bishop made the lease. Sometimes also a bishop about to be translated to a new see would make a batch of leases just before parting with the old one. Richard Montagu, the Laudian Bishop of Chichester, found he had to "pick holes" in his predecessors' leases in order to make anything of his endowments.[82] Many of his colleagues must have been in the same case. The only real solution to the problem would have been to do away with entry fines. Then no bishop could have left his successor with terms he would not be content with for himself. This solution seems not to have been thought of till the nineteenth century, perhaps because of the later development of the relevant accounting principles.

Parish incumbents — parsons and vicars — were not as much affected by long leases as the higher clergy were. Their leases, even if they otherwise complied with the law, would not bind their successors unless confirmed by the patron and the ordinary. The patron — if indeed he was not himself the lessee — could probably be gotten around, but the ordinary was another matter. He had no ulterior motive to countenance the venality of his clergy, and the Canons of 1571 instructed him not to confirm long leases for them.[83] There was also an Act of Parliament of 1571, designed to check nonresidence, that provided that a lease of lands belonging to a parish benefice should be effective only so long as the lessor resided.[84] Later on in the reign, the common law courts decided (a rather strained interpretation, it seems to me) that the lessor was no longer resident if he was dead, and residence by his successor would not do.

Some bishops attempted on their visitations to uncover violations of the various statutes by parish incumbents. Others took up the long and unavailing medieval battle against "farms." A lease of tithes or other church revenues, but not a lease of secular landholdings, would fall within the original meaning of the medieval strictures on the subject. One bishop in 1569 required all farms to be approved by the ordinary — as a number of medieval bishops had done.[85] Bishop Barnes of Durham admonished his clergy in 1577

 . . . that their houses and chancels be forthwith repaired, and that they settle themselves to the uttermost of their ability to keep godly hospitalities, and do not let out, lease out, or tavern out, their livings under pain of deprivation, and other censures ecclesiastical.

I have not been able to determine what those bishops who concerned themselves with clerical leases did about them. If the lease was void by secular law, they could get the incumbent to avoid it, or, more likely, to renegotiate it on more favorable terms. If it was merely uncanonical, they could punish the man who made it. If they sequestered a living for nonresidence, they could put out the nonresident's lessees. But I have found no examples of their in fact doing any of these things.

At any rate, it was not long leases, but a variety of other devices, more audacious than clever, that did most of the eating up of parish benefices. Often, the patron was the villain. In a number of cases — how he got away with it I have no idea — he simply kept the benefice vacant and pocketed the revenues. In such a case, he might hire a chaplain to hold services, or he might even send a layman to do the job.

When the patron was also the impropriate rector of the parish— a cathedral, a college, the crown or other lay successor to a former monastery — he was especially well placed for a coup of this kind. Sometimes, there had been no endowed vicarage before the Reformation; in that case, the impropriator would have the right to serve the cure with a stipendiary priest. In other cases, he may have simply used his position as rector for a kind of ecclesiastical coloration to move into the vicar's endowments while the vicarage was vacant.

Of course, the patron who kept a benefice vacant in order to absorb the revenues was taking a chance. If the bishop caught him after six months, there would be a "lapse" and the bishop would put his own man into the benefice, leaving the patron nothing. Visitations were frequent enough so one would think the bishop could have caught him fairly quickly. Even if the visitation articles did not include some question like:

Whether your patron suffer his benefice to be void, in the mean season take the fruits and commodities to himself?[86]

it would be hard to get through an ordinary visitation without finding out that the benefice was vacant.

So, while some patrons invaded vacant benefices, it was more usual to present an incumbent after coming to an understanding with him.[87] This might involve giving the patron a favorable lease of part of the endowment (not a long one, just a favorable one), foregoing some or all of the patron's tithes, or even marrying the patron's daughter. In other cases, a cleric, or someone else on his behalf, might pay straight cash to the patron for presenting him.

All of this, of course, was unmitigated simony. There was both a traditional objection to it as sacrilege, and a contemporary objection that godly ministers were losing out to their more venal brethren in the competition for suitable benefices. Archbishop Courtney in 1392 had provided that everyone presented to a benefice should take an oath that neither he nor anyone on his behalf had given or promised anything for the presentment. This oath was sometimes reworded during Elizabeth's reign to make it more specific — though the final form it took in 1604 was about as general as the 1392 form had been.[88] The bishops in 1561 proposed to replace the mere oath with a set of interrogatories, to be answered under oath, concerning secret compacts for alienation of the glebe, for forgiving the patron's tithe, for imposing pensions on the benefice, and "for sums of money and other contributions." I do not find that anything quite so elaborate was carried into effect. The straight oath, though, was regularly imposed.

Parish visitors inquired regularly whether the incumbent was suspected of having come to his place through simony. However, the visitation returns I have examined do not show anyone presented on this account. If the protest literature of the period is to be believed, there were plenty of violators, so we may suppose that the visitations were not as effective at turning up simony as they were at turning up other forms of clerical misconduct.

A statute of 1589 may have been a little more effective. It provided that a presentment or institution tainted by simony was totally void.[89] This meant that the cleric involved could not be the legal incumbent of the benefice. His leases were not binding, and he had no right to his parishioners' tithes. The statute, unlike the canonical provisions, applied even if the cleric himself was innocent, as where his friends had bribed the patron without his knowledge. Also, unlike the canons, it punished the patron: the right to present for that time was forfeited to the queen. Thus, the statute motivated people to take simony cases to court, and a number of them did so in the ensuing decades.

As in the Middle Ages, the sale of the next presentation was considered akin to simony, but was quite legal unless the benefice was vacant when the sale was made. The bishops agreed in the Canons of 1571 that they themselves would eschew such transactions as contrary to charity and good morals.[90] The bishops of Lincoln, beginning in the late 1400s, undertook (I do not know by what authority) to keep a register of sales of next presentations affecting benefices in their diocese, perhaps so they could check how the purchasers used their rights. The printed records from Thomas Cooper's tenure of the see show an enormous number of such sales. In some cases, the buyer may have been providing for a friend or relative; otherwise, he must have been making an investment that could not be recouped without simony of some kind.

The measures taken to protect the revenues of the church against simony, long leases, and the like were not particularly bad as measures go. They did not differ radically from those that served the purpose well enough in the Middle Ages, or from those that serve the purpose well enough today. It is just that in this particular time they were overwhelmed by the general prevalence of the practices they sought to control. With the passing of the clerical bureaucrat out of the picture, patrons from the queen on down began finding ways to take financial profit from benefices that they would previously have given intact to clerics in their secular service.

E. Civil Concerns.

There was sporadic medieval precedent for marshalling the pastoral resources of the church behind a secular economic policy — the most important example being the implementation of the Statute of Laborers in 1348. Something of the sort was attempted by Archbishop Whitgift at the queen's request during a grain shortage in 1596.[91] The change of times is reflected in his use of preaching rather than anathemas to move the faithful. This kind of thing was infrequent, and probably not much use, in the Middle Ages; it was less frequent, and probably less use, after the Reformation. Certainly, the reformed bishops were even less interested than their predecessors had been in any general use of the powers of their office to christianize the economic and social life of the community.

In fact, the two areas — usury and poor relief — in which medieval ecclesiastical administration had impinged most closely on what we would consider Christian social concerns were in the process of passing out of ecclesiastical hands.[92] In the case of usury, this process was begun as early as 1494, with a statute giving the lay courts concurrent jurisdiction over the offense. Thereafter, an act of Henry VIII (1545) legalized interest of up to ten per cent, and one of Edward VI (1552) forbade all interest again. Neither of these mentioned ecclesiastical jurisdiction one way or the other. The Elizabethan act on the subject (1571) afforded a kind of compromise between Henry's commercial realism and Edward's fundamentalist doctrine. It limited its serious penalties to interest of more than ten per cent, because the blanket prohibition had proved to be unworkable. But it provided a token forefeiture (the amount of the interest if anyone cared to sue) for interest taken at lower rates, because all usury was sinful. Ecclesiastical jurisdiction was expressly preserved where the ten per cent limit was exceeded, but the statutory forefeiture was made the exclusive remedy where it was not.

It is hard to determine just how the church responded to this course of secular legislation. The clergy in the first Convocation of Mary's reign speak as though the canonical punishment for usury had lapsed by that point.[93] But a number of Elizabethan bishops both before and after the 1571 statute dealt with usury in their visitation articles. The Canons of 1571 and 1604 both mention people who offend their brethren by usury, along with those who offend by adultery, drunkenness, brawling, and the like, as proper people for the churchwardens to present.[94] After the 1571 act, some of the bishops limited their inquiries to usurers who exceeded the statutory ten per cent. Others, like the canons, continued to speak of usurers in general. Purvis's compilation of the York diocesan records yields a couple of cases from 1586 in which the interest taken was five per cent or less. To process these cases was a clear violation of the statute, but they seem to have been processed all the same.

But the prelates could not go on indefinitely administering moral correction in an area that had become one of mere commercial policy. We may suppose that they were out of the picture by the time Parliament next dealt with the subject, in 1624.[95] At that time, the limit was lowered to eight per cent, and the forefeiture of interest within the limit was dropped. Nothing was said about ecclesiastical jurisdiction, although there was a protestation that Parliament did not mean to authorize usury "in point of religion or conscience."

The secularization of poor relief had also begun in earlier reigns. An act of 1536, the culmination of almost two centuries of legislation on the subject of "sturdy beggars," had made systematic provision for sending poor people back to their home parishes, putting everyone to work who was able to work, and collecting alms to relieve everyone who was not.[96] The system was administered by churchwardens and other parish officers under the supervision of the parish priest and of the justices of the peace. Almsgiving extraneous to the statutory system was restricted (as it had been to some extent since the mid-fourteenth century) to prevent the enouragement of sturdy beggars. Otherwise, the system supplemented, rather than displaced, existing arrangements.

The parish collections which this system envisaged were an old feature in the life of the church, but they had served in the Middle Ages as a last resort when all else failed. Not until the 1536 act did they become the primary means of relieving the poor. Various expedients were tried to make them sufficient for the purpose. The 1536 act required the parish clergy to preach on the necessity of contributing. Elizabeth's Injunctions (following those of Edward VI, which in turn had picked up a practice sometimes resorted to by medieval parishioners collecting for their fabric fund) provided for placing a conspicuous chest in the parish church to attract contributions. It was contemplated that people could be persuaded to put in this chest the sums they would formerly have spent for masses, indulgences, tapers, and the like.[97] The contributions elicited in this way were to be supplemented by one-fortieth of the income of the incumbent if he was wealthy and nonresident, and by the twelvepenny fines collected for not attending church.

But still there was not enough. Either people were not willing to spend as much on the poor as they had formerly spent on keeping out of Purgatory, or the amount they had spent for the latter purpose had been exaggerated. By 1552, it had become necessary to report noncontributors to the bishop, so that the bishop might

> send for him or them to induce and persuade him or them by charitable ways and means, and so according to his discretion to take order for the reformation thereof.[98]

Nothing was done until 1562 about people who could not be induced or persuaded by the bishop. In that year it was provided that the bishop should turn such obstinate ones over to the justices of the peace, who would fix a sum and collect it. Finally, in 1572, the bishop and his charitable ways and means were taken out of the process altogether; it was provided that the parish collectors would report noncontributors directly to the justices of the peace.

Although the levying and administration of these funds was shifting from an exercise of Christian charity to a statutory duty, the bishops continued to concern themselves with the process. They made it their business (probably on medieval precedent, for the statutes and Injunctions are silent on the point) to check on the accounts of the poor funds with the rest of the churchwardens' accounts. They also inquired from time to time whether the chest was set up in the church, whether preachers exhorted the faithful to contribute, whether collectors were appointed pursuant to statute, whether nonresidents paid their compulsory fortieths. Or, they asked more generally:

> whether ye have provided for the poor of your own parish according to God's word, charity, and the laws of this realm?[99]

Until the justices took over in 1572, they also sometimes asked for the names of obstinate noncontributors.

Besides these collections, most parishes had available for poor relief a number of legacies and endowments. Some of these produced unrestricted cash income, which went into the chest with the rest; others involved houses for the poor to live in, often connected with elaborate provisions for further indoor relief. The statutes contemplated meshing these resources with the main parish collections, or, where appropriate, with statutory provisions for putting the able-bodied poor to work. The bishops contributed to the process by seeing to it on their visitations that the churchwardens collected the legacies, and that specific foundations were administered according to their terms. An act of 1597 gave the lord chancellor concurrent jurisdiction over the latter function through commissioners of which the bishop of the diocese was to be one.[100] This gave permanent form to a measure that was taken often enough ad hoc in the Middle Ages, and once (1414) by Act of Parliament. There was nothing in the 1597 act that directly displaced the parish visitors, but I cannot find that they concerned themselves with the matter thereafter.

Casual, occasional, or indiscriminate alms, which must have played a major part in the relief of the medieval poor, had been drastically restricted by the 1536 act. While it was no longer contemplated that the ordinary poor should be relieved by this kind of almsgiving, special collections continued to be taken up for the victims of specific disasters — especially fires, and the capture of relatives by pirates — as well as for church repair and other public purposes.[101] Licenses to solicit for such purposes, or ''briefs'' requiring parish clergy to take up collections, had been issued concurrently by popes, bishops, and sometimes kings in the Middle Ages. The pope's functions in the matter were taken over by the crown at the Reformation, and gradually routinized in Chancery. The bishops kept, and sometimes used, their own concurrent powers, but were gradually displaced by the routine resort to the royal Chancery.

One other form of relief, a venerable one, was neither taken into the statutory system nor displaced by it. That was the exercise of hospitality by parish clergy. Whatever this function involved, the Commons from the fourteenth century on took it very seriously, and their interest in it was in no way diminished by the Reformation. Failure to keep hospitality had always been a major grievance against appropriators and nonresidents. The Elizabethan bishops recognized the grievance by mentioning hospitality in most of their canons on residence:

> So we exhort all the pastors of the churches in the Lord Jesus that they return immediately to their several parishes, diligently teach the Gospel, feed their families in accordance with the measure of their fruits, and render hospitality to the poor . . .[102]

The bishops evidently supposed that if a cleric was in fact in residence you could tell whether he kept hospitality or not. The matter was inquired into in several visitations, and in a couple of reports on the state of the clergy the hospitable and the inhospitable are distinguished in the same way as the learned and the unlearned.[103] But what made a cleric hospitable or the opposite I have not been able to determine. We cannot suppose that the bishops tried to hold the whole parish ministry to the standards of the saintly Bernard Gilpin, who treated his whole parish to Sunday dinner all winter every year. Gilpin's example leads me to suspect that the parson's hospitality was looked to generally as a mitigation of the marginal life of the average parishioner, rather than as a form of relief for the wholly destitute. Perhaps this is why the Commons set such store by it, and why it was not integrated into the statutory scheme. But as to how it could be formulated specifically enough to be enforced by the church authorities, the records give no clue.

While the church was in the process of shedding its traditional concerns with usury and poor relief, it was expanding its concern with education. The licensing of schoolmasters was a function that the church had evidently carried out in the Middle Ages without attracting any particular attention. But the Reformation produced a great increase in the number of schools to be coped with. It was partly that other traditional pieties had been done away with, and partly that learning was more important to people who read the Bible and listened to sermons than to people who said the rosary and went to mass. By the same token, it was more important to radical Protestants and Counter-Reformation Catholics than to moderate conformists — so the new schools bore watching to make sure no disaffection was taught in them.

Accordingly, the Elizabethan church put forth a great many canons and visitation articles aimed at making sure that no one taught publicly or privately without a license from the bishop, that no one was licensed who was not a sound churchman, that teachers, once licensed, attended services and brought their pupils, that they taught the lawful catechism, and that they used no grammar but the one put out by Henry VIII and continued by Edward and Elizabeth.[104] Professional qualifications (the Canons of 1571 require learning and fitness; those of 1604, like the queen's Injunctions, add "dexterity in teaching") were evidently not inquired into on parish visitations as religious qualifications were. The bishops did, however, try to examine those seeking licenses and refuse those who were not qualified. As with ordinations, though, they sometimes had to make do. There is a record of one schoolmaster being found insufficiently learned, but left in his position until a qualified replacement could be found.

The parish clergy were supposed to share the educational work of the schoolmasters. Not only were they to teach catechism to all the children of the parish (a work which they sometimes tried to fob off on the schoolmasters) but if they were not preachers they were to teach the children to read.[105] The Canons of 1604 developed an expedient for expanding their educational functions still farther, and augmenting their incomes at the same time. It was provided that unless there was a public school in the parish, the curate would have first chance at a schoolmaster's license. In some cases at least, curates took advantage of the opportunity.

Perhaps it was a concern with education, or perhaps it was a concern with putting down witchcraft, that gave the church the function of licensing physicians, surgeons, and midwives. In the case of physicians and surgeons, the requirement of a license from the bishop is provided for in an early statute of Henry VIII (1512).[106] In the case of midwives, I can find no canonical or statutory basis for it. I suppose there must have been some kind of medieval precedent in both cases, for the Tudors were not apt to bestow new and unprecedented powers on the church. In any event, the Elizabethan prelates regularly issued licenses to physicians, surgeons and midwives, and regularly corrected unlicensed practitioners.

Physicians and surgeons, once licensed, were evidently interfered with no further; but the lowlier midwife was checked up on from time to time.[107] The authorities were particularly concerned lest she invoke the supernatural to assist her in her efforts, though they took some interest also in professional competence, baby-switching, and, I gather, the opportunities for ribald talk that the occasion presented. Also, if the child was begotten out of wedlock, it was felt that the midwife would be a good person to find out who the father was and let the churchwardens know.

Completing the list of the church's civil concerns were the two traditional ones of marriage and decedent estates. The jurisdiction of the church in these areas was about what it had been in Edward I's reign, and was to go on being until Victoria's. It was exercised not only in the courts at the instance of interested parties, but also by the parish visitors on their own initiative. I have already alluded to the efforts made to ferret out matrimonial irregularities in this way. Similar efforts were made to find people who withheld legacies or otherwise obstructed the distribution of estates. The probate violators, unlike the matrimonial ones, had been equally a concern of the medieval parish visitors. The fact that these matters were dealt with in visitations as well as in private suits must have kept them from being as esoteric as they became in later times.

F. Enforcement of the Settlement.

In general, it was considered the work of ecclesiastical authority to maintain the church in the posture it had assumed in 1559. The papists, who had, or were supposed to have, ambitions to overrun the country with Spaniards and put Mary of Scotland on the throne, came in for a good deal of attention from the secular authorities, but even they were as apt to hear from the Ecclesiastical Commissioners or the archdeacon as from the Council or the justices of the peace. Those disaffected in a Protestant direction were, except on one or two occasions, left to the disciplinary forces of the church.

The authorities addressed themselves mainly to overt behavior. They did make the clergy subscribe to the doctrinal formulas of the Thirty-Nine Articles, and every so often they would quiz a man on his beliefs.[108] But for the most part, they contented themselves with reaching the misbeliever on the basis of what he did, or at least of what he said. We have seen that they corrected ministers who disobeyed the rubrics, and laypeople who stayed away from church, or who came and disrupted the services. They also tried to catch anyone who spoke too vigorously against the settlement or the services, who kept the books of exiled dissidents, or who hid vestments, missals and images in his house in the hope that they would come back into use.[109]

The prelates' ingenuity was more seriously taxed by organized nonconformity, which might have remade the Church of England in a different

and extralegal form, or else introduced a plurality of churches — as indeed it
ultimately did. The menace, as the prelates were seeing it by the middle of
Elizabeth's reign, took the following forms:
1. "Conventicles," or private assemblies for nonconforming worship.
2. The intrusion of nonconforming ministers into the parish churches.
3. Selective church attendance by parishioners, based on their opinion of the
   minister or the form of service.
4. The extralegal establishment of Genevan institutional forms — the
   presbytery or *classis* on the diocesan level, the eldership or the godly
   discipline on the parochial.

Conventicles had been forbidden since the early fifteenth century, when the
Lollards' gatherings were called by that name. The Reformation brought no
change in the rule, and Elizabeth referred to "unlawful conventicles" in her
visitation articles of 1559.[110] The original idea, I gather, was to reach
gatherings at which unlawful doctrines were propounded or unlawful services
carried on. But if you once let people hold services in private houses at all, you
will not have much way of knowing whether they malign the Prayer Book,
leave off their surplices, or violate the Act of Uniformity. So it was determined
early on that no services should be held in private houses except where there
was someone too sick to come to church (carrying the reserved Sacrament to
the sick was considered theologically objectionable), or where there was a
domestic chapel canonically established.[111] On the surface, this represented no
departure from the medieval canons; it had never been lawful to minister in a
parish without permission from the bishop and the incumbent. But the medieval
law was mainly concerned with protecting the incumbent's collection plate,
whereas the Elizabethan measures were aimed at preserving the unity and
uniformity of the church. The bishops were fairly regular in asking about
violations.

The laws requiring preachers and curates to be licensed were evidently not
sufficient to prevent nonconforming ministers from being intruded into parish
churches. Some of the concern about whether ministers were properly ordained
was evidently directed to the same end (not all, though; much of it was aimed
at mere slovenliness in the administration of parish cures). It was provided in
the Canons of 1575 that no one could be licensed to preach who was not in
orders.[112] This presumably kept out people who were totally alienated from the
system or total strangers to it.

But the most important measure for control of the preaching ministers was to
require them personally to read the Prayer Book services a certain number of
times a year.[113] This device seems to have been invented by Thomas Cooper,
who required it of all resident incumbents in his diocese in 1577. Archbishop
Whitgift in 1584 imposed the same requirement on all preachers. At a time
when opinion was not fully polarized, there were evidently a number of

nonconforming incumbents who would not have scrupled to hire conforming curates, and a number of conforming incumbents willing to give their pulpits to nonconforming preachers. These measures were an ingenious and effective way of reaching such men. The visitation articles of the latter part of Elizabeth's reign show considerable effort to enforce them.

While nonconforming clergy tried to maintain themselves in the parish ministry, like-minded parishioners tried to seek out their ministrations. To many of the reformers, it was outrageous that a mere ceremony, or, worse, a popish ordination in Queen Mary's time, could make a "dumb dog" or a superannuated pastrycook into the equal of a preaching minister. Those who felt this way, if their incumbent was no preacher, were apt to go on Sunday to another parish where there was preaching. Others of similar disposition cast about for a parish with a minister who did not wear the surplice, or one who would baptize their children without the sign of the cross. Still others went to sermons wherever they were held, but did not attend the regular Prayer Book services at all.

The authorities endeavored to deal with these people at first by keeping everyone in his own parish, and later by singling out for special attention those whose wandering was motivated by contempt for the nonpreaching or the conforming clergy. The rule that you were to attend services in your own parish church rather than elsewhere was another medieval rule for the protection of parish revenues that became an Elizabethan rule for the preservation of unity and uniformity.[114] It was included both in the queen's Injunctions and in the Act of Uniformity. Violators were specifically inquired after in the queen's 1559 visitation, but generally they were dealt with through the regular processes for enforcing attendance — going to another parish was not taken as an excuse for not going to your own.

At the end of the reign, the authorities began distinguishing more carefully between disaffection and wanderlust. In his frontal attack on the puritans of London in 1601, Bishop (later Archbishop) Bancroft demanded

> Whether any do refuse to receive the Holy Communion at their own minister's hands either because he is not a preacher or because he duly observeth the order of ministration appointed in the book; and who they be that do go from their own parish to receive at any other minister's hands?

And, immediately thereafter:

> Whether any of your parishioners having a preacher to their parson, vicar, or curate, do absent themselves from his sermons and resort to any other place to hear other preachers?

Immediately following this was a question (copied from models earlier in the reign) as to whether all the parishoners came to "their" parish church on

Sundays and holy days. Immediately preceding all of these was a question about "popish or sectary recusants" who considered it "unlawful to come to our assemblies as the church of England now standeth established by her Majesty's authority." In another part of the questionnaire, Bancroft asked about various irregularities in baptism, including

whether any do carry their children from the parish they are born in to other parishes to be baptized, and so refuse their own parish . . .?

Putting this material together, we can say that for Bancroft at the turn of the century there were three kinds of parish-hoppers. First, there were those who refused the ministrations of the parish priest on the ground that he was no preacher, or that he followed the Prayer Book rubrics — the question refers to refusing communion, but those who "refused their own parish" for baptism must have done so on the same grounds. These were specifically asked after, and no doubt specifically corrected — probably along with the popish or sectary recusants of the previous question. Second, there were those who would rather hear Preacher A than Preacher B. They must have been specifically corrected too; I cannot find how severely. Finally, there were those who preferred a preacher to a non-preacher, but were willing to receive communion from the latter. These were evidently treated like other absentees from their own parish — those who did not like the vicar's face, and those who would rather fish on Sunday mornings.

The Canons of 1604 were a good deal simpler than Bancroft's strictures. One of them (c. 57) excommunicated anyone who refused to receive the sacraments from a non-preacher, and suspended any priest who ministered baptism or communion to people from outside his parish who approached him for such a reason. This provision referred to the doctrinal error involved in believing that the ability to preach was required to make a man a valid minister of the sacraments. Those who refused the sacraments from a minister who used the Prayer Book services were not covered in this canon; presumably the general canons against denying the lawfulness of these services would cover them.

The 1604 canons said nothing about the man who went to another parish merely because he liked the sermons better. They continued to provide for churchwardens making parishioners come to "their" church (c. 90), and they carried over from the 1571 canons a provision (c. 28) against admitting strangers to communion. I suspect that the latter provision was to prevent the undermining of any disciplinary measures that might have been taken against a person at home.

The erection of a Genevan polity in and around the Establishment seems to have become a problem in the 1580s. The prophesyings or exercises that had been suppressed in 1577 had carried on a certain amount of disciplinary work along with their exegetical activities. After the suppression, clergy in some places kept up the organization and the discipline. These groups, under the name of *classes* (singular, *classis*), advised their members on various points of doctrine or discipline, and encouraged them to put up a common front on the issues of the day.[115] In some cases, the *classis* would give advice on how to respond to a particular order of the bishop, or would present a joint address to the archdeacon. Some of them would screen candidates for orders, and even lay hands on an ordinand before he presented himself to the bishop. Because they gave advice, not orders, and often checked with counsel before they acted, they considered themselves to be within the law. They hoped for changes in the law that would permit them to complete their organization at the national level.

In the parishes, meanwhile, the power of the minister to exclude notorious evil livers from communion, coupled with the powers of the churchwardens to root out offenders, could sometimes develop into something rather like the godly discipline of ministers and elders. One or two bishops actually encouraged this development insofar as it associated the parishioners with the minister — I have already quoted Bishop Cooper's provision on this point. But the bishops always envisaged themselves or their officials as having the final say. The real Genevans evidently ignored the bishop and heard charges or imposed penances on the spot.

Generally, the prelates did not go out of their way to suppress these Genevan organizations. Bishop Aylmer of London (1577-94) asked in his 1577 visitation "whether any new presbytery or eldership be lately among you erected," and in 1586 asked whether the local ministers belonged to a group where they "set down any orders contrary to the orders observed in the Queen's book."[116] Otherwise, there is nothing in the articles before Bancroft's London visitation of 1601. The *classes* were strongly attacked on political grounds (publishing seditious books and plotting against the queen's life) in the late eighties and early nineties but not by ecclesiastical authority as such.

Bancroft, for his part, did not find it necessary to say anything about *classes* among the numerous nonconforming practices covered in his 1601 articles. He did, however, include two articles designed to check on the use of the godly discipline in the parishes.[117] One asked whether the minister had put anyone to penance "without the consent or the privity of the ordinary." The other asked whether the minister or churchwardens called parties before them in the parish vestry "and so do use a kind of presbytery or censuring over your neighbours under pretence of your vestry meetings."

The Canons of 1604 deal with the problem of paralegal organizations in language that seems calculated to embrace both *classes* and parish discipline at once:

> Whosoever shall hereafter affirm, That it is lawful for any sort of ministers and lay-persons, or either of them, to join together, and make rules, orders, or constitutions in causes ecclesiastical, without the king's authority, and

shall submit themselves to be ruled and governed by them; let them be excommunicated *ipso facto,* and not restored until they repent, and publicly revoke those their wicked and anabaptistical errors. (c. 12)

The preceding canon (c. 11) similarly excommunicates those who hold that meetings, assemblies, or congregations other "than such as by the laws of this land are held and allowed" may "rightly challenge to themselves the name of true and lawful churches." The whole idea, then, seems to be to put conventicles and other Genevan manifestations into a single category.

II. Resources and Techniques

The manner of discharging ecclesiastical functions was basically inherited, like the functions themselves, from the pre-Reformation church. But the old system seems to have become a shade less formidable and more effective. At particular points, its efficiency was enhanced by emancipation from Gregorian ideology, or by absorption of Tudor administrative innovations. The displacement of the prelates from their traditional roles in secular administration gave the church, for the first time in centuries, something like a full-time episcopate. At the same time, the desire of the prelates to commend themselves as Protestant pastors made them a bit less mechanical in going about their administrative tasks than their predecessors had been.

A. Agencies.

1. The Royal Supremacy – The Act of Supremacy of 1559 gave the queen power, generally speaking, to do anything that might lawfully have been done by any kind of ecclesiastical authority in the past. She herself was a bit more cautious. She expressly disclaimed the power to determine matters of doctrine — even her more doctrinaire successors were more concerned to suppress controversies than to resolve them. She made a few cautious liturgical changes on her own authority at the beginning of her reign, but generally she thought of her job as merely to enforce the Act of Uniformity and the Prayer Book rubrics. In her personal apologia, published in 1569, she described her function as seeing that the laws of God and man were obeyed in her realm, and providing for the government of the church according to its ancient polity.[118] It can be argued with a certain amount of ingenuity (I have seen it done) that even in bringing about the settlement of 1559 she did not depart from this conception of her role. In any event, once the reformed church was in operation, her part in it (James's and Charles's part in it also) was fairly well in accord with what she said.

This left no room for the sovereign to be a theocrat, as Henry VIII had sometimes tried to be, but it did leave room to be a vigorous executive.

Elizabeth, James, and Charles all controlled the legislative and administrative processes of the church as fully as those of the state, and often more fully. They had the entire say in appointing bishops. Having no secular parts for their bishops to play, they were free, unlike their medieval predecessors, to consult only their ecclesiastical interests in deciding whom to appoint. Through their control of bishops and higher clergy, they had so much informal leverage in Convocation that they scarcely needed the veto power that they had under the laws of Henry VIII. Moreover, it was generally conceded that they could legislate for the church on their own authority, without resorting to Convocation at all — though this power was fully exercised only in the Injunctions of 1559.

On the administrative level, they could order the archbishop of Canterbury to implement specific laws or policies, just as the pope had done before them, or as they themselves did with their secular ministers of state. They could invest the archbishop with new powers so he could carry out their orders, or they could suspend him from his office if he failed to carry them out. Finally, they exercised as full a dispensing power as the pope had ever enjoyed, and they pardoned ecclesiastical offenses as freely as temporal.[119]

Not all the royal power was exercised by the sovereign in person. There was for each province, and for some dioceses as well, a body of Commissioners in Ecclesiastical Causes, broadly deputed to do whatever might be done by ecclesiastical authority (and a few other things besides), and deriving its powers from the queen's or the king's commission. In the last half of Elizabeth's reign, the Canterbury commissioners developed the apparatus, the continuity, and the élan of a full-fledged and vigorous court. Under the name of the Court of High Commission, this court took a leading part in the controversies of James's and Charles's reigns. It was ultimately abolished by the Long Parliament on the eve of the Civil War.[120]

The commission was a kind of ecclesiastical analogue of the Star Chamber. It was provided for in the Act of Supremacy of 1559, but the sovereigns maintained that they set it up by prerogative, not by statute. In fact, Edward VI and Mary had both used comparable commissions. Bodies of this kind were a stock Tudor administrative device, developed to deal with legal matters having political overtones, and with resistance too strong for the ordinary powers of justice. Like other such bodies, the commission started out as an arm of the Privy Council, and gradually developed a life of its own.

The great advantage of the commission over other ecclesiastical courts was its power to fine and imprison, rather than going through the process of excommunicating offenders and suing out writs *de excommunicato capiendo*. Other features common to the canonical system (e.g., the *ex officio* oath) were made formidable by this one. Thus empowered, the commission or commissions (the commissioners were many and the number required for a quorum was small, so there was a good deal of flexibility as to who sat at a given time and place) carried out with considerable efficiency their assigned task of overcoming politically significant opposition to the settlement. They played a great part in the hunting of popish recusants (the pursuivant of English Catholic martyrology was their official). They fairly well broke up the presbyterian *classes*. And they turned an occasional heretic over to the secular arm for burning in the traditional way (by the Act of Supremacy, only those who held doctrines condemned by the early General Councils were eligible).

They also did a considerable business in ecclesiastical cases of no political significance at all that I can see. These included not only surplice violations and intemperate sermons, but also adultery, drunkenness, misapplication of charitable legacies, and all manner of matrimonial disputes. There was no hard and fast rule for dividing cases of this kind between the commission and the ordinary ecclesiastical courts.[121] The prelates had no reason to be jealous of the commissioners, since most of them were commissioners themselves; they probably regarded the commission as a way of coping with people too powerful, too important, or too rich for the parish visitors or the local judges to handle. Prospective plaintiffs probably took the same view of it: it was more expensive and less convenient than the local church courts, but a great deal more efficient. Coke argued that the 1559 act restricted the commissioners to cases of major importance, and excluded them from cases involving property rights. The commissioners, much as they fought with Coke, must have used rather similar criteria in deciding for themselves what cases to hear. Certainly in the records there is a predominance of cases involving knights, gentlemen, aldermen, patrons of rich livings, and people who can afford £500 fines.

2. *Diocesan and Provincial Organization* – Of the prelates as ecclesiastical administrators only a little can be said that would not be equally true of their medieval predecessors. The main thing is that they were generally full time men. They could mount parish visitations on a scale unheard of in the old days. Also, they had more freedom of action. While the Reformation had diminished their status, it had diminished that of their rivals still more. The proud and vigorously exempt religious houses had been disposed of by Henry VIII. The cathedral chapters, no longer financial supports for royal or papal officials, tended to drop into their primordial dependence on the bishops.

Some of the bishops at least took on a more informal style. They had neither the clothes, the status, nor the theology to be as remote and splendid as medieval bishops were, and besides, they did all their work under the censorious eyes of their puritan brethren. So it was, for instance, that Thomas Cooper took to hearing cases, some of them very petty ones, in person, on live evidence, in his parlor.[122]

This informality in their own business seems to have affected the attitude of the bishops toward their judicial officers. The bishop's consistory court and the men who held it had on paper the same powers and functions they had always had; their commissions read almost word for word like the medieval ones. However, they were now laymen, often holding lifetime commissions, rather than clerical followers of the bishop, holding office at his pleasure and hoping for further preferment from him. My impression is that they played a more peripheral and esoteric part than they had formerly done, that somehow only the more routine or the more technically exacting cases came their way.

The archdeacon, by contrast, seems to have taken a new lease on life at the Reformation.[123] He maintained such traditional functions as checking up on candidates for orders and inducting incumbents into benefices; he added new ones such as recommending would-be curates for licensing and seeing that the unlearned clergy did their homework. His parish visitations became frequent and serious, and his courts bore the brunt of the new emphasis on seeking out and correcting offenders. A few presbyterian-minded clergy even thought of turning him into a moderator for their meetings.

The position of that other familiar medieval figure, the rural dean, is more problematical.[124] His traditional function of denouncing excommunicates was gradually taken over by the parish priest, that of serving process by the apparitor (indeed, one set of visitation articles seems to regard him as another kind of apparitor). Here and there, he continued to be assigned supervisory functions in his deanery, especially in connection with the upkeep of the church fabric, but he evidently had no systematic part to play. The Canons of 1571 seem to envision using him as a moral leader among the clergy, but they give him no administrative function. A couple of puritan disciplinary proposals speak of reviving the office of rural dean, as if it had died out. That was probably not quite the case, but Burn's statement that "the little remains of this dignity and jurisdiction depend now on the custom of places, and the pleasure of diocesans" was probably about as true of Elizabethan as of Georgian times.

Two now familiar offices seem to have made their first or nearly first appearance in this period. One was that of the bishop's legal secretary.[125] The role of a legal secretary was to act as the bishop's legal adviser, to guide him through the complexities of his paperwork, and to supervise his court system. Having such a person to cope with his legal problems probably helped the reformed bishop take on a more informal and pastoral stance than his medieval predecessors had done.

The other new office was that of the examining chaplain. Edmund Grindal, when he was archbishop of York (1570-75), put his domestic chaplains to examining presentees to benefices, and on one occasion sent them out to report on all the clergy of the diocese, parish by parish.[126] This is the earliest example I have found of a bishop's chaplains being deputed to that kind of work.

The reformed bishop did not do as many things through special commissions or ad hoc delegations as a medieval bishop did. Working full time in his diocese, he was more apt to be familiar with the regular machinery of administration and the people who ran it. Also, he had a more active set of archdeacons to work with, and he had the Ecclesiastical Commissioners to fall back on if all else failed. When he did have occasion to use a special commission for some purpose, he was apt to give it to one of his regular officers. For instance, when Thomas Cooper visited his cathedral in 1580, he had his vicar general and one of the archdeacons act as his commissaries.

The province, as such, played less part in the church after the Reformation than it did before. The routine functions regularly performed by the see of Canterbury were the following (most of them were performed on a smaller scale by York also):

1. Metropolitan visitations.
2. Custody of the spiritualties of suffragan sees, *sede vacante*.
3. The operation of the traditional provincial courts.[127] The Arches was still the best ecclesiastical court in England; both Parker and Whitgift adopted new rules to maintain its standards. It heard appeals from local courts, and cases brought in the first instance by permission of the local ordinary, who presumably considered them too difficult for his own courts. The Prerogative Court had jurisdiction over the estate of anyone who died leaving *bona notabilia* (defined by the Canons of 1604 as goods worth £5 or more) in more than one diocese.
4. Licensing preachers for the whole province, a power concurrent with that of the bishop in his own diocese.
5. Granting certain dispensations.[128] This work was done in a tribunal called the Court of Faculties. The dispensations customarily considered were for pluralities, holding benefices or taking orders below the canonical age, eating meat in Lent and on fast days, marrying without banns, and being ordained outside one's own diocese. Archbishop Grindal was questioned about his practice in granting these dispensations, and was rather proud of the exacting standards that prevailed.
6. Holding Convocations. These continued to be the church's official legislature, though they were very much supplemented by informal directives from the government and understandings among the bishops.

Needless to say, it was not the performance of these functions in his name that made the archbishop of Canterbury a power in the kingdom. Rather, it was his traditional position as middleman between the hierarchy and the crown. Naturally, this aspect of his job was vastly magnified by the advent of the royal supremacy. The archbishop typically received general directives from the sovereign, and translated them into specific directives for his suffragans — usually, to be sure, after consulting with such of them as he found to hand. These directives were treated as binding on the suffragans, and on the inferior clergy as well, even though they exceeded the canonical powers of the archbishop. In other cases, the archbishop evidently initiated directives of this kind. His recital that he had cleared them with the sovereign was sufficient for them to be put into effect.[129] As a result, when there was a good working relationship between archbishop and queen or king, as most of the time there was, the archbishop's word was very nearly law for his suffragans. Conversely, when there was not a good relationship — chiefly in the case of Charles I and George Abbot, whom he had inherited from his father — the archbishop was little more than a petty official.

3. Churchwardens – The parish churchwardens represented the local community in its ecclesiastical affairs.[130] Their most important duties — administering parish funds, keeping up the fabric (except the chancel) and furniture of the church, and responding to the bishop or the archdeacon concerning parish morals or affairs — were all established long before the Reformation. Although their work was primarily ecclesiastical, a few secular functions had come their way by custom or statute. It is not clear whether their office was originally set up by the church authorities, or whether it arose, like other parish offices, out of the primordial capacity of the English village for self-government. The lay courts tended to treat it as a lay office, whereas the prelates thought of it as part of their machinery for running the church.

The Canons of 1571 provided for the election of churchwardens by concurrence of minister and parishioners. Those of 1604 added that in case of disagreement the minister should choose one and the parishioners the other. It soon became the practice for each to choose one without any attempt to reach agreement. Where there was a custom of doing something different, that took precedence over the canons. Thus in most London parishes the parishioners elected both churchwardens, and a few other parishes had peculiar arrangements of their own.

However the churchwardens were chosen, they were sworn in by the archdeacon, held office for one year unless re-elected, and laid their accounts before the minister and parishioners at the end of each term. As with other parish offices, anyone chosen for the churchwardenship could be compelled to accept it.

I have already dealt in passing with most of the churchwardens' functions. The main ones were:

1. Collecting, keeping, disbursing, and accounting for parish funds. These included a fund for the poor, one for the fabric and whatever specific legacies there were for religious or charitable purposes in the parish.[131]
2. Seeing to the repair of the church (except the chancel) and the fencing of the churchyard. Removing and defacing the apparatus of Roman Catholic worship, and installing the apparatus of Anglican worship. Providing bread and wine for communion, and a surplice for the minister.
3. Preventing secular business or games in the church or churchyard.

Keeping order during the services, and seating the parishioners. Closing down the pubs during service time, and enforcing church attendance. Collecting 12d a Sunday from those who did not attend.
4. Reporting moral and disciplinary offenses to the appropriate authorities at their request.
5. Checking up on the liturgical deviations of the minister. Viewing the license of anyone who presented himself to preach or serve as a curate. Keeping a register of strange preachers to show the bishop.[132]
6. Representing the parish in lawsuits or contracts.[133]

A good deal of effort was made to hold the churchwardens to these duties. The visitation documents constantly show churchwardens made to go home and see to the repair or furnishing of their churches and report back, churchwardens corrected for failing to keep order and report offenders, or churchwardens checked up on for whether they have rendered proper accounts.[134] Derelictions were reported by the parish minister or the successor churchwardens, or even elicited by cross-examination of the delinquents themselves.

This external compulsion was supplemented by elaborate oaths. On taking office, the churchwarden was made to swear to see that the laws and the queen's Injunctions were obeyed, and to render a true account. On making his presentments, he was further sworn to present all offenses without fear or favor. If he failed in this, the Canons of 1604 required him to be repelled from communion as a perjurer.[135]

Despite all this, I think we should take with a grain of salt Kennedy's description of the churchwardens as "non-commissioned officers in the army of the new Divine Right of Kings."[136] They had after all an ancient office, and one more firmly rooted in parish tradition than in Tudor absolutism. It does not stand to reason that they took an administrative line that was not fairly well supported by the community that set them up. Most of the time, they probably did as their medieval predecessors had done, and presented only matters that concerned or annoyed the general parish community. Certainly, it would be ludicrous to imagine that they put a real dent in the rural high spirits of Shakespeare's England.

B. Legislative and Administrative Techniques.

1. Legislation – Both the logic of the Reformation and the governing statutes called for leaving in effect so much of the traditional canon law as was not inconsistent with the new state of affairs. Henry VIII's legislation had envisaged a commission (eight bishops, eight theologians, eight civilians, eight common lawyers) to revise and codify the whole system. Such a commission had actually met and reported toward the end of Edward's reign. Their draft, the famous *Reformatio Legum*, mainly Cranmer's work, was a good deal too rigorous for the English layman to put up with. Nothing came of it, though

the puritans continued pressing for it or something like it well into
Elizabeth's reign.

So it was the old canon law, supplemented by new provisions of the same
kind, that governed the reformed church. Once the original settlement had gone
through Parliament, Elizabeth insisted, as did her two immediate successors,
that it was for sovereign and prelates, not for Parliament, to legislate for the
church. They blocked most of the extreme Protestant measures that might
otherwise have been carried by the Commons. Elizabeth, however, had the
sense to give way when the pressure was too great. There were one or two acts
of Parliament in her reign affecting the internal operation of the church — the
most important being that of 1571 concerning clerical subscription to the
Thirty-Nine Articles.

It was debatable how far a new provision could be given effect without an act
of Parliament. The common lawyers were already beginning to argue that a
canon, as such, cannot bind the laity because they are not represented in
enacting it. On the other hand, a custom based on a canon was as binding as
any other custom. Thus, old canons were binding on everyone because it had
been customary to follow them, whereas new canons were sometimes thought
to bind only the clergy. Given the scope of the actual canons, the issue
remained more or less academic.[137]

Against this background, Elizabeth and her bishops embarked on a vigorous
course of canonical legislation calculated to revive the ancient apparatus of
ecclesiastical government and make it effective for governing the reformed
church. Some of what they did related to the settlement, but much of it was
theologically neutral. In fact, some of their most useful innovations had
made their first appearance in 1530 under Henry or in 1557 under Mary and
Cardinal Pole.

There were a great variety of processes by which new provisions made their
way into the canon law.[138] The highest authority belonged to full-fledged
canons, adopted by both houses of Convocation, and fortified with the Royal
Assent. This was the case with the Canons of 1604, and probably with the
adoption of the Thirty-Nine Articles in 1562. The Canons of 1597 were
properly enacted for Canterbury province, but imposed on York by the personal
order of the queen. Canons enacted in 1575 and 1585 seem to have received
some kind of written approval by the queen, but not under the Great Seal. The
Canons of 1571 emanated from the upper house (i.e., the bishops) of the
Canterbury Convocation only. Elizabeth allowed them to be put into effect, but
never signed them — evidently because their stand on vestments was one she
was willing to tolerate but not to approve. Grindal, then Archbishop of York,
suggested to Parker that he might incur a *praemunire* for putting them into
effect without the Royal Assent, but Parker must have persuaded him that he
was safe, for he allowed Parker to sign them on his behalf.

Elizabeth's Injunctions of 1559 took their force from the royal authority
alone. So in a way did Parker's famous Advertisements of 1566 and Whitgift's
Articles of 1584. The status of the former has been much debated. They were
drawn up at the queen's direction, and enforced with her permission, but she
resolutely refused to put her name to them. The bishops who signed them did
so as her Commissioners in Ecclesiastical Causes, that is, as agents of the royal
supremacy. Whitgift's Articles were promulgated on his own authority, but
he added:

> whereunto it hath pleased her majesty of her princely clemency to yield her
> most gracious consent and allowance, to the intent the said articles may take
> the better effect throughout my province.

Traditionally, the archbishop must have had some authority to implement a
policy on his own. There is no indication, for instance, that Archbishop Islip
had anyone else's approval for his directive of 1350 on stipendiary priests.[139]
But Whitgift preferred to have the royal power behind him. So did Laud.

When the bishops were minded to make general rules without drawing on the
royal power, they did so by unanimous consent. Their Additions and
Interpretations put onto the queen's Injunctions in 1559 and 1561 took this
form. The implementation of such rules would be undertaken by each bishop in
his own diocese on his own authority. The power of a single bishop to legislate
for his own diocese had never been defined, but it had always been very broad.
It was used in this period not only to give force to common determinations, but
also to establish injunctions for particular dioceses. These were typically set
forth after a bishop's visitation, and dealt with things the visitors had found to
be generally amiss.

I suspect also that some rules of higher provenance took their technical
canonical validity from the authority of the bishops who submitted to them.
This may be why no one questioned those canons that did not receive the
fulness of the Royal Assent. It is significant in this regard that Whitgift's
Articles, a year after their appearance, are referred to in a Convocation
document not as the archbishop's or the queen's orders, but as the practice in
most dioceses.[140]

This mass of legislation and quasi-legislation is not really intelligible except
in connection with the canonical tradition of which it forms a part. A canon, as
I tried to show in the last volume, is not like a statute that either is or is not in
force, that you either obey or disobey. Rather, it is a measure, a guideline, a
support of one man's pastorate by the collective witness of his colleagues and
his forebears. One does not care where it comes from in quite the way one does
with a statute; one accepts it for such guidance as it has to offer. The
Elizabethan bishops, whatever else they were, were heirs of the canonical
tradition. They were sufficiently of one mind (or sufficiently over-awed by

those who were) to make a common front in most ecclesiastical affairs. It is as embodiments of their collective experience, rather than as emanations of this or that authority, that their various provisions took effect.

The Canons of 1604 are a little different from their predecessors in this regard. Apparently intended to inaugurate King James's reign with a permanent settlement of the problems confronting the church, they seem to draw up and codify all the experience under Elizabeth. The approaches worked out since 1559 are restated with uncompromising clarity and rigor. The punishments for violations are made clear. Whatever is tentative or hortatory in the language of earlier canons is pruned away. The whole is topped off with a firm statement of the authority with which it is enacted. It is not the complete code of canon law that Cranmer had in mind, but it codifies everything that had been done since the Reformation. For all practical purposes, it marks an end of the legislative activity of the reformed church. There were further efforts in Laud's time, but nothing much came of them except the ill-fated Canons of 1640.

The reformed legislators did not neglect the traditional means of bringing their provisions to the attention of those subject to them. The archbishops circularized the bishops, the bishops the clergy. Compliance was asked about on parish visitations. Especially, provisions were read off to the parishioners at their compulsory Sunday services. Not only were the people apprised of their own duties in this way; they were also informed from time to time of the duties of their minister and churchwardens — perhaps in order to put delinquents to shame, or perhaps in the hope that someone would report them.

Medieval authorities had also felt that announcement in churches was a valuable way of insuring the enforcement of their mandates. But generally they were content with paraphrases. The reformed prelates and sovereigns, with their newfound emphasis on the ministry of the word, went in for the *ipsissima verba* of their strictures.[141] Grindal ordered the Thirty-Nine Articles to be read every year in the churches of the province of York. Cooper expected his injunctions to be read within a fortnight after his parish visitations. Elizabeth, following her brother's (i.e., Cranmer's) lead, ordered the parish clergy to read her Injunctions once a quarter

> that both they may be the better admonished of their duty, and their said parishioners the more moved to follow the same for their part.

The requirement was still being enforced at the end of her reign, and to some extent thereafter.

King James put the final touch on this form of dissemination by requiring that the Canons of 1604 — all 141 of them, eighty pages in Cardwell's *Synodalia* — be read off every year in every church or chapel. Mercifully, he allowed two Sundays to complete the task. More mercifully still, his command seems not to have been enforced, not even by Bancroft in his first metropolitan visitation after the canons were enacted (though he made sure that every parish bought a copy), not even by Laud at the height of his power. To this extent at least, the flexibility of the canonical tradition survived the more rigid formulations of 1604.

2. *Supervisory Techniques* – Licenses, scrutiny of licenses, and sometimes the wholesale cancellation and reissue of licenses, gave the ecclesiastical authorities their chief device for supervising individuals, both before and after the Reformation. In Elizabeth's reign, you had to have a license (or a dispensation, which comes to about the same thing) to be a pluralist or nonresident, to preach, to serve a cure, to solicit alms in church, to marry without banns, to be a physician, surgeon or midwife, to teach school, or to print a book. I have already taken up most of these requirements, and the medieval precedents for them. Taking them as a whole, they show a vigorous expansion of medieval practice, but no radical departure from it.

The various licensing requirements were probably a little better enforced than they had been. The rule that you had to show the churchwardens your license before you were allowed to preach or hold services was new. The scrutiny of licenses on visitations was not new, but was carried out a good deal more systematically than before. It is hard to say, of course, how effective the enforcement was, because a person who got away with not having a license would not appear on the records. On the whole, though, it is significant that there was little complaint. The people who thought it was too easy to get a preacher's license would presumably have said so if they had thought it was too easy to preach without one. The same can be said of pluralism and nonresidence. The man envisaged in the polemics on the subject was not a man escaping the vigilance of the authorities; he was a man with a dispensation he should not have had.

As in the Middle Ages, the authorities did not fully exploit the potentialities of the licensing laws for controlling the behavior of licensees. I find no example of a schoolmaster, a physician or surgeon, or a midwife having his or her license revoked for misbehavior subsequent to licensing. An occasional curate had his license revoked — or was inhibited from the diocese, which amounted to the same thing — but generally for conduct which would warrant suspending a beneficed clergyman. Preachers were corrected in a number of ways for their conduct in the pulpit, but I do not find that any of them had his preaching license revoked. Whitgift's Articles of 1584 and the Canons of 1604 provide that a man is not to preach unless he conforms to the Prayer Book liturgy, but they make no provision for actually taking away his license.[142]

The main use of licensing, of course, was to control the qualifications of those involved. To this end, the prelates had a set of devices which they used in passing on license applications, and for a number of other purposes as well. These devices can be broken down into (1) examinations and testimonials,

(2) evidences of orthodoxy, and (3) promissory oaths, undertakings or bonds.

Examinations and testimonials, as we have seen, were used in varying combinations for ordinations, admissions to benefices, and issuance of preachers', curates' and schoolmasters' licenses. A careful ordinary evidently used similar techniques in passing on routine dispensations; so did a parish priest in admitting people to communion. So did Archbishop Parker in licensing a midwife.[143] She came in with eight "honest matrons" who "greatly commended her as expert, and as discreet and provident." He examined all of these, and also "diligently examined" the candidate herself "concerning her practice and experience in the obstetric art." Parker's procedure here is instructive, in that it has resonances of the academic examination, the testimonial, the examination of witnesses, and the official inquest — the whole stock, in short, of medieval precedents out of which the later procedures were drawn.

As far as I can see, the wholesale imposition of proofs of orthodoxy was a product of the Reformation. No sooner had Henry VIII established his supremacy over the Church of England than he was making people swear to it. The Roman Church followed suit with an elaborate Profession of Faith, drawn up at the Council of Trent, and imposed on nearly everyone by a decree of Pius IV (1564). Elizabeth's church was fertile in comparable devices, beginning with the Acts of Supremacy and Uniformity in 1559.

Generally, as the system was worked out, a man showed the soundness of his doctrine by putting his name to a suitable formula and he showed the soundness of his liturgical practices by taking part in a sound observance. For the layman, this meant that he went to church and received communion, or braved the various penalties for not doing so. For the clergy, the problem was more subtle, and the expedients more complex. Subscription to the Thirty-Nine Articles was imposed by the Canons of 1571 on all ecclesiastical judges, on all ordinands (together with a public manifestation of assent to them), and on all would-be preachers. A statute the same year duplicated the requirement for ordinands, and imposed it also on those already ordained if they had received their orders in popish times. Whitgift in 1584 provided a streamlined subscription that incorporated the other by reference. This involved three points:

1. That the subscriber accepted the royal supremacy
2. That he believed the Prayer Book to have nothing in it contrary to the word of God and that he would use it and no other form of service
3. That he "allowed" the Thirty-Nine Articles, and considered them all to be agreeable to the word of God.

This subscription was enjoined upon everyone admitted to any place in the ministry. Evidently, then, from 1584 on (Whitgift's requirements were reiterated and made more explicit in the Canons of 1604), a clergyman would have to sign the Thirty-Nine Articles word for word on ordination, as required by the 1571 statute, and thereafter would have to sign Whitgift's three articles whenever he changed jobs or took out a new license.[144]

The use of the services themselves as a touchstone of clerical conformity was, as I said earlier on, adopted by Thomas Cooper for incumbents in his diocese in 1577, and taken up by Whitgift for preachers in 1584.[145] It was applied by the Canons of 1604 to all incumbents, and to any preacher with a fixed position. The affected cleric had twice every year (by the 1604 canons; Whitgift and Cooper said quarterly) to read the entire morning and evening prayer services, and to administer baptism and communion, "in such manner and form, and with the observation of all such rites and ceremonies as are prescribed by the Book of Common Prayer in that behalf." This meant that anyone who had conscientious scruples against wearing a surplice, against making communicants kneel, or against using the sign of the cross in baptism would be found out twice a year.

Oaths and the like were used in about the same way after the Reformation as before. They were a favorite device. I have already discussed the oaths against simony, exacted on institution to a benefice. Oaths as to future conduct were required on various occasions.[146] One for persons admitted to ecclesiastical positions of any kind appears in Parker's Advertisements of 1566. One for lay readers was adopted in 1561. There is one for midwives in Parker's Register. Others (e.g., the oath of canonical obedience to the ordinary) were carried over from medieval times.

The use of oaths or undertakings fortified by pecuniary penalties was also copied from medieval practice.[147] It seems, though, that secular penalty bonds of the kind used by contractors, fiduciaries, and public officials today were substituted for undertakings with penalties collectible in the ecclesiastical courts. With this modification, the device was used in the traditional way for such purposes as binding adulterers to avoid one another's company. The most notable expansion of its use was in the area of marriage. Whitgift's Articles of 1584 provided that everyone dispensed to marry without banns would have to post bond conditioned that the marriage not be affected by any impediment or any pending litigation, that it not be solemnized without the consent of the parties' parents or guardians, and that it be openly solemnized in church. The Canons of 1597 required that married persons obtaining a judgment of separation from bed and board post bond to live chastely. Both of these requirements were carried over into the 1604 canons.

The 1604 canons also carried the same device into the area of clerical abuses. They provided that no one should be dispensed for pluralism unless he posted bond to reside for a reasonable time on each of his benefices. The use of the device for this purpose raises the question why it was not used for others along the same lines — to enforce residence in general, for instance, or even the use of the surplice. Since the penal sum would be the object of a secular judgment,

more severe and better enforced than anything the ecclesiastical courts were apt
to impose, it would seem that any rule maintained in this way would have been
hard to violate with impunity. In any event, there was no wholesale use of
bonds to keep the clergy in line. In fact, I doubt if the bond was regularly taken
even in the one case where the canons provided for it.

With their other administrative innovations, the reformed prelates effected a
modest improvement in the keeping and distribution of records.[148] The parish
register of births, marriages, and deaths, compiled weekly by the parish priest
under the eyes of the churchwardens, was first imposed by Thomas Cromwell
in 1538, evidently to check the incidence of spurious matrimonial impediments.
The Elizabethans found the system more or less intact, and kept it going. They
added in 1597 a provision for keeping the records on parchment instead of
paper, and a provision for putting a transcript in the diocesan archives every
year.

Other kinds of records were pretty well initiated by the Elizabethans. Glebe
terriers were not unknown before the Reformation, but the systematic
compiling of them dates from this period. A book in which churchwardens
were to enter the names and licensing authorities of outsiders who preached in
their church was provided for in the Canons of 1571, and again in 1604, no
doubt as an adjunct to the other measures for the control of preaching. A
comparable adjunct to the measures against ill-advised ordinations was afforded
by a provision of the Canons of 1597 making every bishop forward annually to
the metropolitan a list of the men he had ordained, with their qualifications.

None of these measures came at all close to modern standards of record
keeping. For instance, ordination records were still so ill-kept that a man who
misplaced his own letters of orders was in danger of being put out of the
ministry.[149] But we do see here a few halting steps in the direction of
recognizing that records should be assembled in the light of the administrative
purposes they are to serve, and then kept in a place where it is convenient to get
at them.

3. Visitation and the Like –[150] The Reformation saw a great drop in
non-routine handling of problem situations, and a corresponding increase in the
vigor and flexibility of the routine devices for handling them. Thus, the
traditional visitations were much more frequent than they had traditionally
been, and were put to new uses. Especially, they were used a good deal more
for checking up on the internal affairs of the church. Inquiries as to corruption
and dereliction of duty by the ecclesiastical courts went far beyond
Grosseteste's casual question as to whether the archdeacon was correcting
offenders. Curates' licenses were looked at rather more frequently than their
letters of orders had been in the past. Several of the schemes for training the
unlearned clergy envisaged checking on their progress at visitations. Bishop
Neile of Lincoln (later a rigorously Laudian archbishop of York) in the course

of a visitation of 1614 even had his commissaries report on the sermons that they heard as they went about, and on the doctrines expressed in the dinner-table conversation where they were put up.

Bishop Barnes of Durham in 1577 seems to have tried to combine archidiaconal visitations with deanery-wide conferences of the clergy so that lay and clerical failings could be dealt with at once. The resulting amalgam must have looked rather like the recently suppressed prophesying, so I suspect it did not take hold; but it gives evidence of the fertility of the period in finding new ways of using the old device of visitation.

Somewhat akin to visitation was the procedure used in responding to specific inquiries from the archbishop or the queen concerning ecclesiastical affairs. Parker, evidently on more than one occasion, asked his suffragans for lists of the clergy in their dioceses, with an account of the learning, doctrine, and conduct of each of them.[151] Similarly, the queen in 1561 asked for a report on the state of all the hospitals and endowed schools in the several dioceses. In each case, the writ was passed by the archbishop to the bishops, and by the bishops to their commissaries or other officials, who actually made the rounds and compiled the lists. Such medieval precedent as there was for this kind of thing is found in royal, not ecclesiastical, practice — e.g., the king's request in 1346 for a list of all the aliens beneficed in the different dioceses. But the kind of examination required to get the information was that used on the visitations.

The financial controversies that made medieval visitations a bone of contention seem to have abated after the Reformation. It appears that Parker made a number of metropolitan visitations without complaint from his suffragans, and, indeed, when he died was about to make one at a suffragan's request.[152] Hill, in an exhaustive account of the church's financial troubles from 1583 to 1640, makes no mention of any attempt to resist a visitation. The only complaint I have come across about procurations was from the remote and poverty-stricken diocese of St. Asaph.[153] The abuse complained of — dining at the expense of those visited, while still exacting cash procurations — would have been considered a mild one in the Middle Ages.

My guess is that the main reason for the change was that the inflation characteristic of the period made the fixed cash procurations no longer worth fighting over. Also, it seems that in a good many places the archdeacon at least had become entitled to his procurations whether he visited or not. This would mean that the procurations were no longer a reason for resisting the visitation. To some extent, procurations were replaced as a source of complaint by court fees in connection with the processing of presentments. These, as far as I can see, were new in Elizabeth's time. They were paid not by the minister, as procurations were, but by the parish. They contributed to the prevailing disaffection with the whole ecclesiastical apparatus, but evidently did not lead anyone to resist being visited on any given occasion.

The canonical ideal had always been a visitation by the bishop every third year, and one by the archdeacon in each of the two intervening years. There is no way of knowing whether the Elizabethans measured up to this ideal, but it seems likely that they came close to it. As the process became more routine, however, it evidently became more and more usual to have it done by deputy, rather than by the bishop or the archdeacon in person. When Bishop Wickham visited the Lincoln diocese in 1585, he and his vicar general split the work. Bishop Barnes seems to have phased out his personal attendance in the course of his three visitations of Durham (1578-84). In Bishop Redman's visitation of Norwich (1597) and Bishop Neile's of Lincoln (1614), there is no indication that the bishop himself took any part. As for the archdeacon, before the Reformation he had evidently needed (at least in theory) a papal indult if he was not going to make his visitation in person. But the Canons of 1571 provided that he might send his official if the latter met specified standards of age (24), learning and deportment.[154] We have no way of knowing how often he took advantage of the permission, but there is no reason to suppose he was more zealous for personal attendance than the bishop was.

Whoever conducted the visitation, the procedure became pretty well cut and dried. The clergy and parishioners of a given deanery would be given about a month's notice of a place and date to attend. At the appointed time, all the clergy would come in with their licenses to preach or to serve as curates, their letters of orders and of institution into their benefices, their dispensations, if any, for pluralism or nonresidence, their notebooks on the Bible and Bullinger's Decades if they were obliged to a program of study. Schoolmasters and surgeons might bring in their licenses, too. The churchwardens would come in with their answers to the articles propounded to them (these had been distributed either at the previous visitation or with the notice of this one), and two to six of their fellow parishioners to back them up.

The proceedings might begin with a sermon and end with a clerical dinner. Somewhere along the line, the younger clergy might be put through their paces. But the main business of the day was looking at documents (and collecting a fee for each one in accordance with a fixed schedule). At the same time, the first steps were taken in bringing offenders to book. If an offense was reported against the minister or churchwardens, presumably it could be dealt with on the spot — unless they were contumacious, they were already in court. Other parishioners, however, would have to be cited at this time and dealt with later.

The follow-up on the visitation was usually in the regular courts — the consistory for the bishop's visitation, the archdeacon's court for his. Some cases, though, the bishop might deal with personally, either because they were referred to him or because he had personally performed the visitation or gone over the returns. Still others might be referred to the royal commissioners. In any event, the medieval practice of appointing someone ad hoc to follow through on a particular visitation was no longer followed.[155]

It was evidently envisaged that presentments made by the churchwardens (the Canons of 1604 c. 113 gave a concurrent power to the parish priest) on these occasions should be the exclusive means of bringing ordinary parish offenders before the courts. This was a great departure from medieval practice, where most proceedings seem to have been set in motion by court apparitors on their own initiative. After the Reformation, even the most zealous corrector of offenses did not think the apparitor was the right person to have this kind of power. Provisions of the Canons of 1597, repeated in 1604, forbade apparitors to act as informants or "promoters of office," and did away with the blank citations that they used in this work.[156] Archbishop Sandys of York in his metropolitan visitation of 1578 had made a start in the same direction with his inquiry:

> Whether the archdeacon hath any somner or apparitor that doth weekly find out offenders and convent them before the archdeacon; and whether the archdeacon do hear and determine any matter other than such as are presented by the churchwardens and swornmen in his visitation . . .?

These measures were not entirely successful, as we shall see.

The Elizabethan visitation involved less travelling about than did its medieval counterpart. As always, the fundamental unit was the deanery, but where the medieval visitor spent some time at the head church of each deanery and may even have made side trips to other churches, the Elizabethan visitor set himself up at a central location and dealt with the deaneries in batches, often making people come considerable distances to see him. This attenuation of close local concern probably did not keep the bishop's visitation from being a special event in the life of the local community, but in the case of the archdeacon, who had a smaller circuit in the first place, it probably made his visitation look a good deal like a regular session of his court.

This may have something to do with the fact that by the end of Elizabeth's reign the archdeacon was often taking churchwardens' presentments in regular court sessions rather than on visitations. It was simply a matter of holding terms of court at two or three different places in his archdeaconry, circulating the articles of inquiry, and telling the churchwardens when to come. Once the presentments were in, the procedure would be the same in any event. The churchwardens would not have to come any farther than they would to a visitation. The change in practice is shown by a comparison of the Canons of 1571; (p. 124):

> aeditui. . .in episcoporum et archidiaconorum visitationbus patefacient . . .

with those of 1604 (c. 109):

> the churchwardens. . .in their next presentments to their ordinaries, shall
> faithfully present . . .

The change no doubt produced a more efficient system of dealing with
offenders. The trouble with it was that it left nothing to check the zeal of the
court officers for collecting churchwardens' presentments (at 4d. a time). A
complaint was made in the Parliament of 1597 that some archdeacons' officials
were holding court every three weeks, compelling the churchwardens to come
in each time (penalty: excommunication, with 2s. 4d. fee for absolution), and
collecting 4d. for the presentments even if there was nothing to present.[157]
Besides the fourpenny fee, the parish had to pay 12d. for their dinner — to say
nothing of the loss of a day's wages each time, which came out of their own
pockets. Meanwhile, if the court got hold of an offender, it would remit him
from session to session, ostensibly in hope of his reforming. Thus, while never
being put to penance, he would be put to attending court every three weeks at
sixpence a time. All to the enrichment of the court personnel and the
impoverishment of her Majesty's good subjects. The Canons of 1604 (c. 106-7)
met the situation by providing that churchwardens should not be required to
make presentments oftener than twice a year, plus an additional time if the
bishop made a visitation. If they saw fit to make additional presentments, they
were to pay no fee for doing so.

Looking at the whole development of visitation and kindred procedures
through almost half a century between Elizabeth's accession and the Canons of
1604, one cannot help feeling a certain disappointment. Not that an overall
scheme for making sin, as such, illegal could ever have worked. But a program
of systematic personal contact between bishop and archdeacons on the one
hand, clergy and people on the other has a good deal to recommend it.
Watching Barnes or Cooper working to reshape the traditional material, one can
almost envisage such a program coming to pass. But in the end, it was
administrative efficiency, rather than pastoral edification, that prevailed. As the
routines became perfected, the life went out of them.

C. Formal Procedures.

1. Organization of the Courts[158] — Those matters requiring some formality
in the handling were dealt with in one or another of the ecclesiastical courts.
These varied greatly from one diocese to another, though the patterns were
similar everywhere. Aside from the royal commissioners, or Court of High
Commission, whose jurisdiction I have already dealt with as best I can, the
tribunals available for hearing a case in the first instance were roughly these:

1. The diocesan bishop himself, who evidently needed only a notary to
   constitute a court in his own person.
2. A consistory court (in some dioceses, it went by a different name),

exercising powers derived from the bishop, but delineated by ancient tradition. This would be held by the bishop's chief judicial officer: chancellor, commissary general, or official principal, depending on the diocese.

3. In some dioceses, particularly those of the archbishops, one or more other courts, carved out of the area originally delegated to the consistory, or else out of the area the bishop reserved for himself when the consistory was first set up. Some of these courts had well-defined areas of concern (e.g., probate); others overlapped the consistory or each other, creating jurisdictional conflicts that were often coped with by making the same man judge of several courts.

4. A court for each archdeacon, held by his commissary or official, with an indeterminate amount of supervision from the archdeacon himself. In the absence of a special custom, this court would be mainly limited to probate matters and to correction of offenders. There would be some kind of rule governing whether the archdeacon's or the bishop's court had jurisdiction in a particular probate case. An offender belonged to whichever caught him first. The Canons of 1604 (c. 121) provided for cross-registration of proceedings to save people from being called into both courts for the same offense.

5. Courts of various peculiars, or exempt localities. Within their territories, these displaced the archdeacon's court and to some extent, the bishop's.

6. In Canterbury Province, the Court of Arches. This was basically an appellate court, but it heard cases in the first instance at the request of a subordinate court, or under a license given the plaintiff by his own bishop. There is no evidence of a comparable practice in York Province.

7. In probate matters where there were valuable goods (£ 5 worth by the 1604 canons, c. 92) in more than one diocese, the Prerogative Courts of the two provinces. Canterbury had this right by long tradition; York took it up in the 1590s. By the Canons of 1604 (c. 93), a diocesan or archidiaconal court had to examine every case to see if the prerogative jurisdiction applied, and, if so, to refuse jurisdiction on its own motion.

This is the medieval court system pretty well intact. The main differences in operation, to which I have already alluded, are that the archdeacon's court did a brisker business in correcting offenders, and that some bishops at least heard more cases in person.

The judges of these courts were generally career lawyers, trained in the civil law. Their qualifications were laid down in the Canons of 1571, and again in those of 1604. Aside from the necessary training, they had to be zealous for religion, and had to subscribe the Thirty-Nine Articles. Most of them were laymen. In the first part of Elizabeth's reign, some of them had had cathedral benefices nevertheless — it being supposed that a layman could have a benefice

as long as there was no cure attached. But as the reign progressed, the practice
of giving benefices to laymen died out, and the judges had to live on their fees.
Most of them lived fairly well (twenty-five or thirty pounds per annum for an
archdeacon's commissary, anywhere from one to four hundred for a diocesan
chancellor).

The judge could depute a "surrogate" to take over for him on occasion. The
person chosen could be either a fellow law-trained man or a minister (graduate
or preacher) with a benefice in the neighborhood. My impression is that service
as a surrogate was usually rather casual — that no one person served habitually
unless he had been a regular judge or was being groomed for one.[159]

If the judge was a layman, he would probably have with him a clergyman to
pronounce sentences of excommunication for him. The wholesale use of
excommunication to enforce judicial process scandalized the puritans anyway,
and having the sentence pronounced by a layman magnified the scandal as they
saw it. So a series of canons, beginning in 1571, provided for having a minister
prounounce sentence. The Canons of 1604 did not repeat the rule, but the
minister was still used through the 1610s. He was supposed to be deputed by
the bishop, but in practice he might be anyone in orders who happened to be on
hand. Or the judge himself might make some minister his regular associate.

Besides the judges, every court had a registrar, whose duty was to keep
records, furnish transcripts when required, and in some courts to act as a
general secretary to the judge. What with one thing and another, the position
was a fairly responsible one, and paid about as well as the judgeship. The
registrar was probably responsible for the notarial staff that figures in various
ways in the documents.

The lowest echelon of court officials was that of the apparitors or
summoners. These men were originally mere process-servers, but rather early
on, certainly by Chaucer's time, they had taken on the function of finding out
offenders and turning them in on their own initiative. To assist them in this
function, they were provided with blank citations which they could fill in at
need. This function was greatly resented as unscriptural, haphazard, and open
to all kinds of bribery and extortion. I have already alluded to the measures
taken to eliminate this role of the apparitors, and make presentment by minister
or churchwardens the exclusive means of bringing offenders to book.

But the implementation of these measures was merely technical.[160] While the
apparitor finally did stop bringing prosecutions on his own initiative, he was
still expected to seek out offenders and report them to the churchwardens for
presentment — and it would take some courage for the churchwardens to
refuse. Also, in some dioceses the apparitor was expected to report on certain
matters directly to the bishop. For the Norwich diocese, his oath of office, as
prescribed in 1603, lists a number of matters on which he is to make a quarterly
report; liturgical violations and nonresidence by the ministers, and interference
with the regular processes of the courts are the most important.

In theory, there was one apparitor for each deanery; in practice, there tended to be more, because of the size of some deaneries, and because each court tried to employ its own apparitors in order to be sure of getting its share of the business. The Canons of 1597 provided for limiting the number to what it had been twenty years before (the Canons of 1604 went back thirty years), and there is some evidence of compliance.

The whole court apparatus was served by a reasonably competent and well-organized bar. They were divided between advocates and proctors, a division which corresponds somewhat to the modern one between barristers and solicitors, but is a good deal more complicated. Most of the advocates and some of the proctors got their training by studying civil law in the universities — the study of canon law having been abolished by Henry VIII. The rest learned their trade through a substantial apprenticeship. They served their clients in the admiralty courts as well as in the ecclesiastical, and served the government in its diplomatic relations with civil-law jurisdictions on the Continent. At the top of the profession was a kind of Inn of Court, called Doctors' Commons, founded about 1508, and set up in permanent quarters in 1565. The judges and advocates of the courts around London (who had to have doctorates, though those in other courts did not) belonged to it.

Except for the apparitors, all the people I have been describing belonged to a fairly unified career. While a judge did not often have as much experience at the bar as a common law judge did, he was usually admitted as an advocate, and had the same educational background as those who practiced before him. Also, he might practice in one court while he was judge or registrar of another. Similarly, the registrar or one of the notaries of a court might be waiting for an opening as a proctor, or might work his way up to be judge of that court or another. There were still some clergy introducing new blood to this professional body; also, there were a few men who made their way within it on patronage from without. But on the whole, it was getting to be a fairly inbred and esoteric body that staffed the ecclesiastical courts. The Dickensian image was already taking shape.

2. Handling of Business – The cases threaded their way among the different courts in pretty much the traditional ways, but modified, it seems to me, by the new emphasis on discipline, and by the new pastoral orientation of some of the bishops. The old distinction between office and instance business was preserved. The one invoked the office of the ordinary to correct his flock; the other was undertaken at the instance of a party. Outside these categories, there were still a small number of cases that came in from the lay courts. The question of marriage when it came up in a lay proceeding was evidently still sent to the ordinary for trial. Also, the ordinaries continued to process felons who had claimed benefit of clergy in the lay courts until a statute of 1576 provided that they should be let go without further ado.[161]

Instance business mainly involved probate, marriage, collection of
ecclesiastical dues, or rights to ecclesiastical positions. It was conducted on the
basis of formal pleadings and canonical proofs, and, for aught that appears,
went off as well and as badly as proceedings in the lay courts.[162]

Office business was either *ex officio promoto* or *ex officio mero*. The former
class involved a promoter or accuser with pretty much the full rights of a party
litigant. The most important kind of case in this class was defamation. It was
office, not instance, business because it aimed at correcting the offender, rather
than at making the victim whole; its usual result was a public apology. It was
promoted because the victim, not the community, was seeking redress.

Disciplinary proceedings based on a canonical presentment and disciplinary
proceedings set in motion through the personal initiative of the bishop or the
judge were both, properly speaking, *ex officio mero*, though some people
evidently used the term to indicate the absence of a presentment. Terminology
aside, there were the two kinds of cases. It appears that the archdeacon was
expected to act only on a presentment, that the bishop could act when he
pleased, and that whether the diocesan chancellor ought to act as freely as the
bishop was debatable.[163] I suppose the general idea was that no one should be
put to answer for an offense without either a canonical presentment or an
exercise of discretion by a responsible prelate — hence the objection to letting
the apparitor cite in offenders on his own.

The types of case in which it was thought necessary to proceed on occasion
without presentment were, naturally enough, those in which the authorities
were more interested than the parishioners. These were listed by Chancellor
Redmayne of Norwich for the benefit of Bishop Jegon in 1603 as nonresidence
or pluralism, liturgical violations, recusancy, popish or sectary, unlawful
marriages, profaning of churches (morris dances, church-ales and the like, I
presume), bribery and extortion on the part of apparitors, and improper keeping
of parish registers.[164] In addition, there were some cases where the pastoral
interest of the bishop was engaged by a matter that would normally be the
object of a presentment or even of an instance proceeding.

The procedure for handling the normal disciplinary case was quite summary.
A person came in in response to a citation, was sworn, was told what he was
supposed to have done, and responded in his own words. His response was
paraphrased in a few lines, and entered in the record. If it amounted to an
admission of the offense, he was given one of the available punishments,
usually a warning or a penance. If he denied the offense, he was either put to
purgation or let go. When one and when the other is not clear to me; I gather it
depended on what kind of evidence there was against him, and whether he
admitted to having a bad reputation in the matter. Also, as a fee was charged
for compurgators by the head, a man might be let out of supplying them if he
was poor.[165]

There were a number of possible variants on this normal and summary procedure.[166] In the first place, the court might have a better way of finding the facts than taking the oath or purgation of the accused. For instance, when a curate was accused of mumbling the services, he was set in the choir of York Minster and made to show whether it was true or not (it was). Or if a man's status (ordination, institution to a benefice, etc.) was in issue, he was expected to have the appropriate documents to show the court. Or if his accusation was accompanied by a letter from the justices of the peace, the letter would be read and acted upon. Or if it was brought in by a delegation of irate parishioners, they would be heard.

Second, in some cases, the accused was supplied with "articles", an itemized statement of the charges against him, to which he and the witnesses could address themselves one by one. Whether he had a right to this procedure if he requested it, or whether it was only used in more complicated cases, is not clear.

Third, cases requiring special pastoral finesse came in one way or another before the bishop in person. By the Canons of 1604 (c. 122), only the bishop could suspend or deprive a minister. Even before those canons, it seems that parishioners who were really put out at their minister tended to take their complaints direct to the bishop rather than proceeding in court. Other cases were referred to the bishop by parish visitors. For instance, when a Leicestershire vicar was accused at the archdeacon's visitation of seducing a young woman on a promise of marriage, he and the woman and the churchwardens were all brought into Thomas Cooper's parlor to have the affair sorted out.

Finally, it seems that cases involving difficult legal questions were channelled into the consistory or some other regular diocesan court. For instance, the parish visitors for the archbishop of York refused to settle a dispute over whether a certain man was required to provide the parish with eight shillings a year out of a certain piece of land to buy drink for those who perambulated the boundaries. As soon as the claim was contested, they dismissed the presentment "unless the churchwardens wish to prosecute this cause against him in the Consistory Court." Similarly, Cooper, who heard all kinds of cases in person, as I have said, called in his official when he found a legal problem in a case. I suspect also that cases on presentments in the archdeacon's courts were sent to the consistory for trial if they raised any legal problems — though this is more difficult to establish.

Once a disciplinary offense had been made out, the devices for dealing with it were about what they had always been. Monition, penance, and, for the clergy, suspension, deprivation, etc. were the canonical forms generally used. The important changes were a development of the concept of monition to secure a more sophisticated control over future behavior, and a routinization of the forms of penance to cope with the increased volume of cases. Let us consider briefly how these sanctions were applied to the different types of offense.[167]

In the case of clerical offenders, a minister who made a fool or a nuisance of himself would probably have to apologize from the pulpit, though he might get off with a warning (monition) not to do it again. I have the impression that ribaldry or suspicious conduct with women fell into the same pattern, though a minister found guilty of actual incontinence would probably be deprived or made to resign. All this was a considerable departure from medieval practice. Now that a minister could marry, there was evidently less tolerance for his sexual lapses. Also, under the new conception of his position, there was less inclination to cover up for him — it was his ministry, not his person, that was now considered sacred.

Pluralism, nonresidence, and neglect of duty, though ferreted out more systematically, were accorded the traditional leniency when caught. An occasional man might be deprived of a benefice or put out of a curacy when he was first found missing or negligent, but usually he was warned to return by a certain day, or to start doing his job. A pluralist who had no dispensation might be told to get one, or he might be subjected to the old canonical rule that acceptance of a second benefice automatically vacates the first. The Canons of 1604 provided specific periods of suspension for performing clandestine marriages, and for certain types of neglect;[168] these were probably enforced, at least at first.

Liturgical violators of course presented a new problem. They were dealt with rather circumspectly.[169] If they offered an excuse (e.g., that there was no surplice in the parish) steps were taken to remove it (the churchwardens were told to buy a surplice). If they offered to conform in the future, they were dismissed with a warning, sometimes coupled with a requirement that they furnish a certificate of having conducted a conformable service by a specified time. If they insisted that they could not in conscience conform, divines were assigned to persuade them to change their minds. Only when all else failed were they deprived. Even then, they might be allowed to take other positions and go through the whole process again.

Failure, usually on the part of the churchwardens, to repair the church or keep the articles of worship on hand was usually dealt with by a monition ordering the offenders to do their duty and report back. Most administrative irregularities were also dealt with in this day.

Other lay offenses were the object of some kind of penance.[170] Pursuant, perhaps, to the new views of justification, Elizabethan penances had more in them of apology and less of atonement than medieval ones. They fell roughly into three categories. The first was a simple apology, announced sometimes before those who had witnessed the offense, more often before the whole congregation in church of a Sunday. This was the usual sanction in cases of defamation, and in minor forms of misbehavior — drunkenness, swearing, Sabbath-breaking, and what-have-you. Next came semi-public penance, a formal acknowledgement of a fault before the minister, the churchwardens and three or four parishioners. This was evidently used with matters that were not of common knowledge. A married couple that had anticipated the ceremony were apt to be allowed this form of penance rather than the full treatment accorded most sexual offenders.

The fornicators or adulterers who provided by far the bulk of the correction business were subjected, along with a few other serious offenders, to the full-dress (or perhaps we should say full undress) public penance. This varied a little from one court to the next, but in a given court it was about the same for all offenders. The form used in the 1580s and nineties in the diocese of Ely was as follows: Three Sundays in a row, the offender was to stand at the church entrance wearing a white sheet covering her (I say her because all the cases in the record I am following involve women; perhaps the details would be different if a man were involved) clear to the ground, and carrying a white wand in her hand. She was to stand there from the second peal of the bell calling to prayers until the end of the second lesson, asking for the prayers of the worshippers as they came in. After the second lesson, the minister was to lead her into the church, reciting the Miserere in English while doing so. She was then to kneel in the front of the church till the place in the service where the Commandments were read. She would then confess her misdeed in specified and suitably edifying language. Finally, the minister would read a homily — that on fornication the first week, that on repentance the last, presumably one of his own choice in between.

This performance, whatever its deterrent effect (I have already quoted a skeptical view on this point) was sufficiently burdensome to offenders so that wealthy ones were willing to spend money to get out of it. If this did not take the form of a bribe to the apparitor or the judge, it took the form of a commutation. Commuting penances for cash was an old medieval custom, the pros and cons of which were exactly the same as they had always been. The main pros were that the money could be put to a good use, and that it was disruptive of the social order to have the natural leaders of the community standing around in white sheets. The cons were that the payment involved was hard to distinguish from a bribe, and that it made an invidious distinction between rich and poor. As might be expected, the puritans were very much opposed to the practice, but the authorities contented themselves with regulating it.[171] It was provided as early as 1571 that it should be done only for grave reasons and with the personal approval of the bishop. Whitgift's Articles of 1583 added that the money should be publicly devoted to the poor or to some other godly use, and that if the offense was notorious, the fact of the offender's repentance and the amount of his payment should be announced to the congregation. Of these rules, the one about disposing of the money was medieval. The publicity and the personal involvement of the bishop were new. They probably represented a compromise with puritan emphasis on edification as a function of discipline and puritan mistrust of professional church judges.

These rules seem to have been only partly complied with in practice. If there were grave reasons for the commutations allowed, they were not made a matter of record. Some courts at least were strict enough in referring commutations to the bishop, but I suspect his review of the cases was fairly perfunctory. The money was in fact put to legitimate purposes and entered in the records of the court. The requirement that the disposition of the money be made public was not complied with except to the extent that court records were public, or to the extent that money went into parish poor funds that were publicly accounted for. The announcement in church that the offender had been corrected was not, as far as I can see, regularly provided for by court orders in commutation cases. Perhaps the churchwardens were expected to arrange for the announcement themselves if they were worried about in the scandal in the parish.

Neither these rules nor any others on commutation were included in the Canons of 1604. Nevertheless, the practice fell off drastically at about that time, and what commutations there were tended to be more, rather than less, in accordance with the rules.

The most burdensome aspect of the whole disciplinary system was not in the sanctions it imposed but in the incidental expenses it involved along the way. Every appearance in court meant a number of miles traveling back and forth and a good day lost out of your other affairs. Every appearance, and every document as well, had a fee attached to it. On the whole, it would seem that neither the time spent nor the fees charged were unreasonable given the work the courts had to do. There were complaints of oppressive postponements of cases, but most proceedings were in fact disposed of with one or two appearances. Fees had been a subject of complaint since the fourteenth century, but Marchant's recent study shows that they cannot have been generally oppressive. They were brought under systematic central control during Whitgift's primacy (1583-1604), and provision was made for posting a table of approved fees in every court.[172] Also, a poor man could often have all or part of the approved fees remitted at the request of his parish minister.

But the judges and other court personnel did have to live, and they no longer had benefices to live on. As long as the business of the courts was supposed to pay for itself, it could not be done on the cheap. For someone litigating over a fair-sized estate, or for a person of substance litigating over his marriage, this was no problem. But for the peasant facing the consequences of an unguarded moment last Christmas the price could be very oppresive indeed — even if he had enough, strictly speaking, to pay it. This was the bite in the disciplinary system. Where the penance was light, where the offender was let off with a warning, or even where he succeeded in establishing his innocence, there were always fees to be paid.

For many, the solution lay in abandoning the proceedings when they got too expensive, or even in not coming to court in the first place. Marchant finds that of persons cited for disciplinary offenses never more than three-fourths, seldom more than half, often as few as one-fourth, came in, abided the proceedings, and complied with the final judgment. Evidently, the means available to compel compliance were not sufficient.

Here again, the problem was money, The only thing an ordinary ecclesiastical court could do on its own in a case of contumacy was excommunicate the offender. He would then be denounced in his parish church, and excluded from the services. In theory, people were then to avoid his company, but they probably did not pay much attention. If there was no one to testify to his repentance, he could not be buried in consecrated ground when he died. That was all. For a secular-minded person, it was not a lot. For a papist or a sectarian, it was an improvement; he had an excuse for not going to church.

These inconveniences, such as they were, coupled perhaps with the traditional dread of being cut off from Christ's flock, and the persuasions of more devout friends or superiors, put a few people back on the straight and narrow — say one-fourth to one-third of all those excommunicated. Perhaps more would have come back were it not for the fee for being absolved. This again was not heavy, except in the light of the means of those having to pay it. One document mentions 2s. 4d., as compared with sixpence for appearing in court.[173] A fee like this was probably self-defeating. If you were once excommunicated for missing your first court appearance, it paid you to continue staying away.

The traditional means of invoking the secular arm, through a writ *de excommunicato capiendo,* involved another financial roadblock. Marchant figures the standard fees in the lay courts at not less than 30s. In addition, if the original proceeding was in the archdeacon's court, there would be the cost of getting process out of the bishop's, for the lay courts would not issue their writ unless the excommunication was signified by the bishop. There was no hope of getting this kind of money out of ordinary parish offenders, and the courts were not about to absorb it themselves. The Canons of 1604 (c. 65) express a wistful hope that someone who hears the offender denounced will be moved to come forward and set the process in motion, but it is hardly likely that anyone was.

In a few cases, the royal commissioners could be called on. They had power under their commissions to imprison for disobeying their mandates, and would sometimes order obedience to one of the regular church courts. But I doubt if their services were free either, and in any event, they would have been overwhelmed if they had tried to handle all the contumacy cases there were. It was also possible in some cases to refer the offender to the justices of the peace. They had concurrent jurisdiction over some types of offense — notably, fornication if a bastard resulted. They went in for the cat-o'-nine-tails and the stocks, and were willing to absorb the costs of proceeding if need be, though they lacked the churchmen's general mandate for putting down sin. Marchant notes that the bishop of Ely, who had his own justices of the peace, had especially good luck in securing obedience to his ecclesiastical processes.

In light of all this, what can we say about the general effectiveness of the church courts? In the first place, cases involving ministry and worship or the fabric or furniture of the church were probably not seriously hampered. The minister had a stake in his ecclesiastical status, and could probably be brought to terms through excommunication, or if need be replaced with a more docile colleague. The churchwardens were representatives of the parish. The parish paid for their coming to court and obeying the mandates; they were generally obedient, and had no reason not to be.

Next, in an ordinary private litigation we may suppose the court was usually obeyed. There would be enough at stake to make it worthwhile for a party to pay for a writ *de excommunicato capiendo* against his opponent if one was needed, and the costs were comparable to those of other lawsuits. Also, in serious offenses or offenses by prominent people, there might be someone outraged enough to foot the bill, or the royal commissioners might take a hand in the matter.

So the real problem was in petty cases, as it has been in all court systems, even to this day. It would be hard to collect a few shillings of tithe or church rate, or to bring the garden variety parish sinner to book. Even at these points, the church's discipline was not negligible, but it fell a good deal short of either the Laudian or the Genevan ideal.

3. Abuses – The foregoing account may enable us to evaluate the stock complaints that were made in the period about the church courts. Many of these went back to the fourteenth century, though they grew increasingly vociferous as opinion became polarized between the Reformation and the Civil War. About most of them the prelates were no less concerned than the puritans; the measures they took to meet them have already shown up at one point or another in this narrative. At this point, let us bring the whole indictment together and see what response can be made to it.

The most serious count is one of wholesale corruption:

> Soon after the visitation or synod, the petit-bribing sumner, rideth forth laden with excommunications, which he scattereth abroad in the country, as thick as hailshot. . .[174]

Even the innocent must pay to keep out of his toils. As for the guilty, here is a puritan version of how they are dealt with. Sponge the proctor and Hunter the apparitor are reminiscing on the eve of the abolition of their functions by Parliament (1641):

Sponge: Country wenches would sell their petticoats rather to pay us than to endure a white sheet; how have we thriven by their wantonness! We would take what we pleased; 'twas but complying with the surrogate, or bribing the judge's clerk . . .

Hunter: . . . all grists came not to your mills; if the wenches were either willing, or rich, or handsome, we gave them liberty to use their own by our concealment, we had ways enough to keep them out of your purlieus; but if they were old, deformed, and half rotten, and poor, then we would put them into your places of trial; so that alas! we gave you the offals, but kept the choice bits for our own palates, thinking that old bawds and crafty proctors were best bawling together.[175]

All this is great fun, but it has to be taken with a grain of salt. About the apparitor it says nothing that Chaucer did not say, and the literary tradition on the subject was old in Chaucer's time. A few incidents go a long way in the development of this kind of polemic. We must remember also that we are reading biased testimony. Even if the system had been incorruptible, the puritans would not have liked it, because it was wholly incapable of the severity or sureness of the Genevan discipline, and because it was regularly invoked against ministers of their party for liturgical violations.

No doubt there were a number of cases of the kind of corruption envisaged. In the diocese of Gloucester, under two aggressively venal and well-entrenched chancellors who between them held the office for thirty years, such cases seem to have become the rule rather than the exception.[175] On the other hand, the dioceses of York and Norwich, with which Marchant deals in his study, seem pretty clean. In other dioceses, there has not been enough work done on the records for us to be sure how bad things were. Still, it seems to me that if things had been as bad as they were in Gloucester the records that do appear would give more evidence than they do. The prelates evidently attempted in good faith to find out and correct abuses in the disciplinary process; there is no reason why parish churchwardens should not have come forward with any they knew of. The published court and visitation records that I have seen show cases of corruption, but not a lot of them.

Besides, it is hard to see that there was either an economic base or a power base for a really vigorous corruption. The standard proctor's fee, corruption entirely aside, was surely a good deal more than a country wench could get for her petticoat. The appearance of a proctor in an ordinary white sheet case must have been a considerable rarity. Nor can the apparitor have collected any great sums in the way of bribery or extortion. The cost and inconvenience of a disciplinary proceeding were, as we have seen, not negligible, but they can

hardly have been sufficient to elicit substantial bribes to get out of them —
especially when straight contumacy was so easy an alternative. If a person was
rich enough or important enough to be a suitable object for extortion, he could
probably do more harm to the apparitor than the apparitor could do to him. The
whole process had neither the power to coerce nor the power to overawe that it
had in Chaucer's time.

Other grounds of complaint were a little less serious, but a good deal better
made out on the facts than that of wholesale corruption. The most inclusive was
that of wholesale inefficiency:

> So that it is a common saying in the Country, when the presentment is once
> received, they shall never hear more of it.[176]

In fact, as we have already seen, a substantial percentage of the disciplinary
proceedings once begun were never brought to any kind of conclusion. The
puritans were sure that in most of these cases someone had been bought off, but
the amount of contumacy found by Marchant would provide an adequate
explanation by itself. Certainly, the Geneva-type discipline envisaged by the
puritans would have been more efficient — if there had been a real public
demand for efficiency in matters of this kind.

Commutation of penances was another thing the puritans saw as standing
between the typical sinner and the just retribution they had in mind. Despite
their rhetoric, there is not much evidence (except again in the Gloucester
diocese) that funds received from commutations were systematically
misapplied. It does seem though that the process was often more routinized and
the accompanying manifestation of repentance less insisted on than either the
canons or edification required.

While some complaints involved people not being brought to court, others
involved harassment of those who were brought. The canon law had a
proceeding called the *ex officio* oath, whereby a person could be sworn to
answer truthfully the matters objected against him before he was told what the
matters would be. People, especially common lawyers, were unhappy with this
device because it did not allow a defendant to test the legality of the charges
against him before answering them, and because it did not protect him against
self-incrimination.[177] Both complaints and writs of prohibition go far back into
the Middle Ages. The attack bespeaks a preference for common-law over
Roman-law forms of criminal process. While I share the preference, I do not
suppose it has anything to do with ecclesiastical corruption. It is well to
remember here that the common law had its own ways of being unfair to
criminal defendants, and that the puritans might have objected less to the *ex
officio* oath if it had not been the chosen means for bringing men of their
persuasion to book.

There were a number of other ways in which ecclesiastical proceedings could be vexatiously used. The overlap of jurisdictions made it possible for a man to be cited into several courts for the same offense, or into a court where it was extremely inconvenient for him to go. An apparitor might choose his own time to serve a citation, and might choose it for maximum annoyance to the person cited. Or he might use his knowledge of legal technicalities to prolong an unjust suit or to hinder a just one. Even if these things were not done for purposes of out-and-out extortion, they could be used to favor one party litigant over his opponent, or to bring more business and more fees to the apparitors and proctors involved.

Here again, complaints go back to the Middle Ages. We have seen how writs of prohibition and proceedings before the justices of the peace were invoked to protect the victims of these practices. The Elizabethan prelates, unlike their medieval predecessors, made earnest efforts to stop this kind of thing — by limiting the number of apparitors, by abolishing blank citations, by requiring cross-reporting of presentments, by controlling original proceedings in the metropolitan courts, and by checking on apparitors, officials, and proctors in the course of their visitations. The abuses in question are harder to do away with than they look. Indeed, few modern court systems are free of them.

Finally, there was the matter of fees. The charge that these were generally excessive or extortionate seems not borne out on the facts. But we must take more seriously the charge that people were kept excommunicated for not paying even though they could not afford to pay. While Marchant shows that many fees were remitted in whole or in part for poor people, it is not clear that the remissions were sufficient to meet the need. For one thing, many of them were granted at the request of the parish priest; you may have had to be on the right side of him to be considered. Also, I have not found any indication of what standard of poverty you had to meet. I suspect it was one of total abjection, that the court would not have been satisfied with a showing that you had better things to do with the few shillings you possessed. If the standard had been at all lenient, the court personnel would have become pretty well impoverished themselves. Even today, people who concern themselves with the legal problems of the poor find it hard to formulate standards of eligibility that will meet the whole need, and to apply those standards in such a way as to make it easy for those who meet them to come forward.

Taking the court system as a whole, I cannot do better than to repeat the conclusion of Dr. Marchant, whose work I have drawn on many times in this description of it:

> The main criticism of the Church of England at that time was not that it was corrupt, but that in a missionary situation it presented a picture to the world of a vast property-owning organization, with an infinite hierarchy of officers, endlessly absorbing tithes, fees and "offerings", regulated by a man-made law, existing only with the support of the State. It was a home for

hundreds of officials and their underlings, clerical and lay, who made a good living not by extortion but by drawing the legal fees to which they were perfectly entitled. It is no wonder that many who had read their New Testament sought escape from this colossus. . .[178]

III. Conclusion

I tried to show in the previous chapter that the settlement of 1559, whatever one may think of it theologically, represents a decision that the moribund synthesis of medieval Christanity should be updated and revived, rather than scrapped. It was this decision that set the task of ecclesiastical administration during the period we have been considering in this chapter. The prelates had to put new life in the old system, and had to maintain it against challenges far more formidable than any it had faced before. These prelates have had a bad press, both in their own time and ever since. But their administrative achievement, for all that, is impressive. It gives evidence, it seems to me, of a good deal of dedication, resourcefulness, and hard work.

It was by a creative use of medieval devices that they accomplished what they did. None of their expedients would have seemed at all alien to a medieval church administrator. Chichele, Grosseteste, or even Hugh of Wells used many of the same ones; others we feel they would have used if they had thought of them. Of the 141 canons of 1604, for instance, a good 62, by my count, could have been enacted almost verbatim in 1400, and would have made a great improvement in church administration if they had been. At least another 26 were in fact in force in 1400.[179]

What distinguished the Elizabethans, and to some extent the Jacobeans and Carolines as well, from most of their medieval predecessors was their vitality, their fertility in trying out new ideas to cope with old abuses and new needs. Where they came by their administrative skills is hard to see; none of them had gained distinction as a canonist or administrator before the Reformation. But their work shows a considerable familiarity with the existing state of the art, and an equal sophistication in putting it to use.

I suggested in the last volume a threefold critique of English ecclesiastical government as it had developed in the Middle Ages:

1. Considered as an administrative system, it lacked freedom of action. The zeal of the canonists, combined with the decentralization of offices and endowments, had articulated almost every aspect of the structure in terms of personal or property rights protected under legal forms and therefore immune to administrative intervention.

2. Considered as a legal system, it suffered from a pastoral orientation that disposed it to excessive leniency and ineffective sanctions, and from

political and financial pressures that had to be met extralegally as there were no legal forms to provide for them.

3. Considered as a pastoral system, it was straitjacketed by legal forms, and further hampered by social and economic barriers to effective pastoral communication.

The resourcefulness of the prelates, coupled with a change in circumstances at the Reformation, afforded a good deal of improvement as to each of these points of criticism:

1. Many of the legal and proprietary rights that had hampered the administrative action of the medieval church were dissipated by the Reformation. The monasteries were gone, and the other exempt establishments lacked the powerful patrons who had protected them against the bishops in order to support their personal bureaucratic staffs.

2. The legal institutions of the church were freed from the Gregorian romanticism that was reponsible for a good deal of their pastoral orientation. The canons expressed practical goals in the real world, and practical devices for achieving them. The church courts were generally recognized as carrying out specific, and largely utilitarian, tasks. The political and financial pressures were greatly relieved by the diminished power and prestige of the whole apparatus — there was a good deal less interest in intervening in it directly. The main external pressures became themselves legal — writs of prohibition and the like.

3. The barriers to pastoral communication, while still very real, were lowered somewhat by the reduced status of the bishops. More important, the changed approach to law and administration made it possible to introduce pastoral considerations into the apparatus at specific points through articulated administrative or legal decisions.

By the end of the period, the separation of administrative, legal and pastoral aspects had probably gone too far. The whole business of chancellors, officials, visitations, and presentments, was beginning to pass out of the bishop's hands. He must finally have come to see it less as an adjunct of his work as a Christian pastor than as a set of limits within which that work was to be done. In this connection, it is interesting to note the intellectual poverty of the Canons of 1640 as compared with the earlier efforts. It is fairly clear that the Laudians who enacted these can have had no great hope for the church's legal system as a means for accomplishing their purposes.

Actually, though, the system had accomplished a great deal by that time. We tend to underestimate its accomplishments because we tend to leave out of account the magnitude of what it had to overcome. Consider first what the medieval system had become by the sixteenth century, or, to make the point more strongly, what it was in the process of becoming in a Catholic country such as France. Consider further the low pay and prestige of the clergy and the general apathy of the laity, plus the fact that the prelates were charged with maintaining in every parish of England a round of liturgical observances that great numbers of people, including perhaps a majority of the more religiously vigorous and articulate members of the community, did not want.

With all this to contend with, the prelates provided at least as good a ministry as there had been in the Middle Ages (which, to be sure, is not saying a lot), made a conformable or nearly conformable observance the normal thing in virtually the whole country, kept up a steady pressure on lay morals, and accomplished various less important purposes at least as often as not. Anyone who does not see these as substantial accomplishments expects more of an administrative system than any such system can deliver.

On the whole, then, the system was a success. But it was a success in terms of the medieval Erastian synthesis. The goals that it accomplished with fair regularity were the goals that the overall society was content, and had always been content, to assign to the institutional church. Measured by any kind of theological first principles, its work was distinctively spotty. It provided most parishes with a man who would pray for the inhabitants and instruct them in the rudiments of Christanity, but it never achieved a wide distribution of godly ministers who would make whole congregations blush for shame. It shook loose its essential pastoral mission from the inherited legalism, but it never replaced the canons by the laws of God, let alone the Gospel. It wrapped a number of fornicators in white sheets for the edification of their neighbors, but it never became a true nemesis of the ungodly or earnest of the wrath to come. At heart, for all its new vigor, it was still the big, lumbering, sloppy, and somehow beloved, medieval church.

Nowhere is this more apparent than in the operations of Archbishop Laud, who, with the whole apparatus at his command, set out to do something the medieval church had never done — to provide the Almighty, in the person of the institutional church, with His full due from the English nation. This aspect of his program had three parts:

1. To reshape tithe into a radical tenth of the gross national product. This involved setting aside customary commutations (*modi decimandi*) when they no longer reflected true value, improving the collections on new forms of production, and restoring personal tithes on wages, profits, etc. All this fell before the lay courts' insistence that tithe was a customary payment, not a radical tenth, and could be collected only when custom allowed it.

2. To restore impropriated rectories to their sacred function by buying or inveigling them away from their lay owners, or at least to require impropriators to augment vicarages as their medieval predecessors could have been made to do. A limited power to augment was finally accepted by the lay courts, but only on the eve of the Civil War. Nothing was

heard of it after the Restoration.

3. To channel new benefactions into the traditional organization of endowed ministers appointed by bishops or patrons rather than into a body of stipendiary lecturers or preachers appointed by their congregations. The authorities could never stop lectureships, though they tried to discourage them, and make the lecturers conform to the Prayer Book. The whole affair ended in a stalemate.

Now, what Laud had in mind was High Churchmanship conceived in the fullest Gregorian terms. God (i.e., the institutional church) is entitled to a full tenth of the national product. That tenth is sacred, and no layman may lay hands on it. The priest must be endowed or he is a hireling; he must be put in by the bishop or he has not come into the sheepfold by the door. The lay response was just what it had been when the medieval church made the same Gregorian claims. The church and ministry are "established" by lay magnates to do a job. The revenues assigned the church are assigned in order to get a job done. It is only custom that pays the clergy one way rather than another.

Laud (and those historians who see Laud as turning back the clock) entirely misread the medieval situation. The Reformation had done away with the symbolic patterns that disguised the practical failure of the Gregorian program on the points in issue, but in fact the medieval High Church view had been no more successful than the Laudian was:

1. The clergy had been allowed to claim tithe as a radical tenth, but the laity had always insisted that it was a customary payment. The only clash in practice came in the relatively trivial case of *silva cedua*, certain tithes of wood. On this, the honors were about even.

2. The entire revenues of the church had never gone for church purposes. They in fact went to clerics, but many of these clerics spent their time serving laymen in one capacity or another. Probably a larger portion of ecclesiastical revenue supported actual ecclesiastical activities after the Reformation than before.

3. Parish lecturers were actually in precisely the same case as stipendiary chaplains and chantry priests had been. The medieval church authorities had had a modicum of success in keeping these men in order, no success at all in channeling them into the regular ministry. The laity had always insisted on getting the ministrations they wanted and were willing to pay for.

In fine, Laud could not, any more than the medieval church could, accomplish purposes of the kind he had in mind through the ordinary machinery of ecclesiastical government. So he drew on the agencies royal absolutism, mainly the High Commission, for what the agencies of papal absolutism had been too wise to attempt.

Inter arma leges silent. For the legal questions raised by this resort to the *plenitudo potestatis* of the crown, no legal solution could be found. It was the way of the Cross, not the way of administrative adjustment, that ended the brief and strangely moving history of neo-Gregorianism under Laud. The administrative threads picked up at the Restoration were those left by an earlier generation of hard-headed administrators — Parker, Cooper, Whitgift, perhaps Bancroft.

But for this the church had to make its peace with the common lawyers, who were busy putting flesh on a medieval Erastian synthesis of their own.

4. Coke and the Common Law

The common law in the period of the Reformation was in the process of being restated to meet a great many new conditions, not all of them religious. The process was essentially a conservative one, based on meticulous use of medieval precedent. At the same time, many of the problems were new ones, to which the medieval precedents would not yield definite answers without considerable coaxing. Hence, there is a good deal of argument possible (and a good deal of it has in fact taken place) about whether the lawyers and judges in applying these precedents were actually bringing out the deeper significance of their heritage, or whether they were simply lending a spurious continuity to policies developed for entirely contemporary reasons.

In the general political and economic realms of the law, I will forego rendering an opinion on this question (Holdsworth gives a judicious evaluation with which I am inclined to agree).[1] In the realm of church and state, as I indicated in an earlier chapter, I find continuity not only in the precedents but in the ethos with which the precedents were applied. They bespeak, as I said, a view of the Reformation as a continuation of the medieval church-state dialogue on terms more favorable to the state.

There were three ground rules for the conduct of the dialogue in its new form. The first was the continuity of the system. Anything that was the law in the Middle Ages was the law still unless you could point to some statute of Henry or Edward or Elizabeth that had changed it.[2] A proper papal dispensation in Mary's time would hold you a benefice in Elizabeth's. Your rights as a lay impropriator under a patent of Henry VIII depended on the lawfulness of the appropriation in Edward IV's time. The rights of the Elizabethan cathedral chapter of Norwich depended on whether their monastic predecessors had been properly dispensed from their vows.

A corollary to all this was that the crown inherited the powers of the papacy. Not the theoretical *plenitudo potestatis*, but the powers actually exercised in the realm.[3] For instance, if the effect of a royal grant was in issue, the common law

judges would consult their ecclesiastical confrères to see if the pope had made
such grants in the past. This approach was not without its conceptual
difficulties. The Reformation statutes recited that the pope's jurisdiction had
been the result of a usurpation upon the crown. How could legal precedents be
derived from something expressly stigmatized as unlawful? Or why should the
scope of a rightful authority be limited by the extent of a former usurpation?
The answer, as nearly as I can reconstruct it (the judges are not as clear as we
would like on the point) was that "ecclesiastical jurisdiction" was a definite
package, regardless of who was to exercise it, and, as with any other
jurisdictional package, the contents, absent a statute, depended on custom.

From the conception of the jurisdictional package, it followed — and this
was the second ground rule — that church and state had separate and distinct
systems of law.[4] The illegality of a transaction under the canon law did not
prevent its being enforced in the secular courts. An Act of Parliament dealing
with church affairs made no change in the canons on the same subject. If both
gave remedies, you could proceed under either; if both imposed duties, you had
to comply with both.

The preservation of the distinction between the two systems meant the
preservation of the apparatus by which the lay power kept the clerical power in
line. I have already referred to the encounter between Coke and Bancroft on
this point. This was an element of the third ground rule — that the church's
system was subordinate to the state's. The canon law was not to be put into
operation where it was counter to the royal prerogative, to the common law, to
any statute, or to any custom. It was the business of the common law courts to
interpret all four of these limits, and enforce them by writs of prohibition, or
the dread but somewhat shadowy *praemunire*.[5]

This rule looks like more of an innovation than it actually was. In the Middle
Ages, it was a simple derivative from the duality of the two systems. Because
they were separate systems, each went its own way when they differed, and
each preserved its own understanding of the proper place of the other. The
resulting discrepancies were simply lived with, or resolved politically if they
got too bad. But the Reformation was the ultimate political resolution.
Thereafter, the claims which the common law courts had formerly made on
paper could be given effect in actual practice.

Also, the supremacy of the secular law became more visible because it had
more to operate on.[6] Many of the religious changes had been accomplished by
statute. The churchmen would have liked to interpret these statutes and bring
them into a coherent body of ecclesiastical law. But the judges insisted that all
statutes were part of their secular system — a good medieval doctrine, but in a
very new context. Similarly, when it came to custom, the churchmen sought
modifications to meet new needs. So the doctine that custom prevailed over
canon, one that the medieval common law courts had applied with indifferent

success to certain obscure litigations (tithes of wood being the most important), was suddenly brought into the full light of day.

In a few cases, the third rule about subordinating the ecclesiastical law clashed with the second about preserving the duality of the two systems.[7] For instance, when an ecclesiastical judge was pardoned after being convicted in the Star Chamber of taking bribes, it was held that the bishop had to leave him in his judicial office. Or where a statute did away with the canonical proceedings after a successful claim of benefit of clergy in a lay court, it was held that the bishop could not proceed against the offender (in this case, a genuine cleric) to deprive him of his benefice for the same offense. Both of these cases seem to be gratuitous interferences with the work of the ecclesiastical system in achieving its own results in its own way. Certainly, no medieval court would have taken the same position in either.

This brings us to the question of whether the ground rules as I have described them were mere verbal formulations, or whether they were the rules by which the game was really played. Did the principles and precedents actually require the decisions reached, or did the judges simply marshal them behind decisions arrived at for entirely different reasons? The same question has been asked about every creative bench of judges from that day to this, and it is always rash to give it a simple answer.

Before dealing with the question as a general matter, let me try to answer it with regard to two representative cases that gave rise to a good deal of controversy at the time. Consider first the holding that a commutation of tithe (*modus decimandi*) by custom or agreement must be passed on in the lay court rather than the church court.[8] In 1610, King James summoned the common law judges to debate this rule before him against the prelates and church lawyers who wanted the jurisdiction for their own courts. The judges supported their position by drawing on a number of medieval analogies (there was only a little medieval material directly in point), organized pretty much in accordance with the ground rules I have just described.

Hill gives a good deal of attention to the place of this rule about lay jurisdiction over *modus decimandi* cases in the economic controversies preceding the Civil War. But it will not do to say that the judges were simply reworking their precedents to support their position in these controversies of their own time. The Elizabethan and Jacobean arguments over tithe were in fact the same arguments as the medieval ones (to which I have alluded many times) over the nature of tithe. In reworking the medieval material, the judges were implementing the same ideology, and pretty much the same economic and social interests, that had produced the material in the first place.

The medieval common law would enforce any commutation that was supported by a grant or by a custom of sufficient duration, whereas the canonical rule would allow it only if it afforded an adequate substitute for the divinely ordained mathematical tenth. The problem did not come up very often in the Middle Ages, because the usual commutation was a fair enough substitute for the tenth until the inflation of the sixteenth and seventeenth centuries threw it out of line. But judging by the analogous case of tithes of wood, I have no doubt that if a commutation was inadequate by canonical standards the church courts would have disregarded it and tried to collect the full tenth, while the lay courts would have issued prohibitions to protect the commutation. This means that the existence and validity of the commutation would have been tried in the lay court — the principle on which the judges were insisting in 1610.

So the prelates in arguing the other side must have been asserting either that their version of the medieval substantive law should prevail over the common law version, or that they should be allowed to administer the common law version in their own courts. I am not certain which of these was their position, but it is quite clear that neither had any basis in medieval precedent, and that both were quite inconsistent with the ground rules as I have described them.

Next, let us look at Coke's holding that medieval ecclesiastical authorities had no power to imprison people — one of the premises of his judgment that the Jacobean High Commission had no such power.[9] As we saw in the last volume, imprisonment was not much used in the canonical system, although the Decretals did provide for it. It was regularly used in England only in the case of clerical felons handed over by the lay courts. On the other hand, it was episcopal process, not lay process, that held these men in prison once they were handed over, so it is hard to say that a bishop was inherently incapable of holding a cleric in prison by his own writ. I should suppose that a medieval bishop if asked would have said he could imprison one of his clergy whenever he saw fit, and that no one would have argued with him. Granted, an Act of Parliament in 1485 gave him specific authority to do this in cases of incontinence, thereby indicating, as Coke pointed out, that he did not have any such authority absent a statue. I suspect, though, that this statute was enacted to resolve a newly raised doubt, or to encourage the bishops to take a firmer line, rather than to effect a change in the law.

Be that as it may, I doubt if any medieval bishop thought he could imprison a layman without a statutory authority (which he had in the case of Lollards under an act of 1400).[10] I find nothing in the canons authorizing him to do so. Maitland analyzes at someulength the story of a young peasant and an old woman who were shut up for life on bread and water by order of an ecclesiastical council in 1222 for claiming to be Christ and the Virgin Mary respectively — but this is a frail reed on which to rest the powers of King James's High Commission. By 1300 at the latest, it would have been politically unthinkable for bishops to put laypeople in jail. If one of them had done so, the king's courts would surely have let the victim out, and possibly sent the bishop to take his place.

So, if we accept the underlying principles that the ecclesiastical jurisdiction was to be mistrusted in the king's hands in the same way as in the pope's, and that restraints once imposed in the king's name were now restraints on the king, we will have to agree with Coke's holding as regards imprisoning laymen (and note that the cases before him involved laymen), though we might take issue with him when it comes to imprisoning clergy-

At this point, let us return to the general question. Were the judges applying contemporary social biases, or were they really applying traditional law? It seems to me that in most cases they were doing both. They were heirs to the medieval Erastian tradition, representatives of the ordinary Englishman to whom I have alluded from time to time. Their concern was with preserving the overall harmony of a Christian commonwealth; with sustaining the traditional rights of the Christian laity, and holding the churchmen within the place assigned them; with upholding the contingent utilitarian arrangements made by their ancestors against any claim to alter them by divine right. If they were implementing social biases, they were the same biases they had been implementing for three hundred years.[11] They did not have to distort their history to find precedent for what they were doing. All their innovations were in matters of detail, and served to maintain traditional principles against more sweeping innovations by someone else. A drastic upward revision of church taxation, or a promiscuous imprisonment of laymen for church offenses, would have changed the face of English Christianity far more than a few new writs of prohibition did.

So the common law side of the settlement as we review it here was the work of a conservative and Erastian bench. It was a change in the forces they had to deal with, rather than a change in their approach, that developed a somewhat different body of law.

I. Control of Ecclesiastial Courts

A. Procedures.

The writ of prohibition, chief weapon of the lay courts against ecclesiastical encroachments, was one of many procedural forms that were updated during the sixteenth and seventeenth centuries.[12] We saw that in the Middle Ages this writ preserved something of its original character as a device for punishing contempts of the royal authority rather than for determining debatable questions of jurisdiction. It was a little more rough-hewn and a little more vindictive than it should have been. The person invoking it could never be sure of getting his whole story before the judges before they issued a writ of consultation dissolving the prohibition and allowing the proceeding against him to go forward in the church courts. On the other hand, the person trying to litigate in the church courts could never be sure that the lay judges would make a binding determination of his right to do so before they exposed him to the danger of a highly punitive proceeding in attachment.

By the 1590s, perhaps earlier, the courts had largely succeeded in doing away with these uncertainties.[13] In the first place, they developed an informal adversary hearing to determine whether a consultation should issue. At this hearing, they looked not so much at the original pleading (the "libel") from the ecclesiastical court as at the recital of facts (the "surmise") on which the writ of prohibition had been issued. If this was sufficiently implausible, or was bad in law, the consultation would be issued. The person claiming the prohibition could be heard on an order to show cause why the consultation should not issue; the person seeking the consultation (i.e., resisting the prohibition) could present his arguments as an *amicus curiae*.

If either party was unhappy with the result of this informal process, he was entitled (though perhaps the court had some discretion in the matter) to have the issues determined in a full-dress formal proceeding. This took the form of a fictitious attachment. The plaintiff would file a pleading setting forth the surmise on which the prohibition had issued, and adding that the defendant after the issue of that prohibition had gone on litigating in violation of it. The defendant would answer with a "protestation" that he had not litigated in violation of the writ (as indeed he had not), and then "to have a consultation" would proceed to demur or plead to the original surmise. The fictitious issue of whether the defendant had violated the original prohibition would them be left hanging, and the real issued raised by the defendant's seeking a consultation would be determined as in any other case. If the result was in the plaintiff's favor, the defendant would have to stop litigating in the church court, or else be subject to a real attachment; if the defendant won, he could safely go on with his church proceeding.

In the tithe cases that provided much of the prohibition litigation of the period, this improved process was helped along by a statute of Edward VI which provided that a plaintiff must prove his surmise within six months of the time the suit against him was suspended. Otherwise, a consultation was to issue automatically, and the defendant was to recover double costs.[14] This was part of a general legislative package to improve the procedures for collecting tithe — no doubt for the benefit of the new class of lay impropriators.

The shift of emphasis from the libel to the surmise gave the common law courts more flexibility in deciding at what stage of the ecclesiastical proceeding they would intervene, and what the scope of their intervention would be. The traditional classes of cases ("debt or lay chattels not touching matrimony or testament" etc.) were prohibited at the outset. So were cases instituted in violation of the statute of Henry VIII concerning citations.[15] Other cases did not become prohibitable until a particular issue arose that the lay court wished to reserve to itself. Still others became prohibitable when the church court made a determination that the lay court considered erroneous.

These differences were given effect by controlling the surmise and the subsequent pleadings. Let us say we have a case (e.g., a suit for tithes) which is unquestionably within the jurisdiction of the church court, and a defense (e.g., a *modus decimandi*) which the lay court claims exclusive power to try. The defendant (in the ecclesiastical proceeding, plaintiff in the lay court) will state the grounds of his defense in his surmise, and will then add that he raised that defense in the church court and the church court refused to hear it. The latter allegation will be treated as "non-traversable", i.e., fictitious. The opposite party (plaintiff in the church court, defendant here) will not be allowed to deny that the church court refused the tendered defense, but will be required to address himself to the defense itself (e.g., by denying the existence or legal sufficiency of the *modus*). The court will then pass on the defense, issue a consultation if it is not made out, or let the prohibition stand if it is.[16]

Now let us suppose another case where the defense is one (e.g., the person claiming tithes is not the rightful owner of them) that the lay court is willing to have the church court determine in the first instance. In this case, a surmise that the church court refused to hear the defense will not be fictitious. A consultation will issue unless it is shown either that the church court has in fact refused to hear the defense, or that it has heard the defense and made an erroneous decision.[17]

We should not be too hard, incidentally, on the free use of legal fictions in these new procedural forms. Such fictions, and others far more implausible, played a great and on the whole honorable part in the updating of common law procedure during this period. While the device is not very rational in form, in substance it stems from a desire to rationalize the law. That is, we allow a fictitious allegation of fact situation A to be made in fact situation B because we are persuaded that logically the two situations should be dealt with in the same way. So it was with the fictions introduced into the prohibition proceeding: their net effect was to give the courts more scope for dealing with cases according to the actual facts.

By the beginning of the seventeenth century, the common law courts had in the prohibition procedure a device capable of affording a rational program of review over a set of tribunals with important if limited functions in the overall administration of the state — say, the kind of review the federal courts in the United States today exercise over a respected administrative agency. A case could be kept out of a tribunal it did not belong in. A particular issue within a case could be tried by the tribunal best equipped to try it.[18] Erroneous decisions or illegal exercises of power could be set aside. All that was lacking was a sympathetic attitude on the part of the common law judges. The use of the updated procedure was still dominated by the medieval ambivalence toward ecclesiastical jurisdiction as such.

B. Subject-Matter.

1. In General – Only in a few select areas do the post-Reformation law reports show a substantial reworking of the medieval material on the boundaries between lay and ecclesiastical jurisdiction. Certain new emphases, however, were felt all along the line.

In the first place, the authority of the lay courts over matters of custom and statute was abstracted from the particular situations in which it had developed, and made into a general principle.[19] As a result, whenever there was a custom or a statute in the picture, someone was apt to argue that the whole case should be taken away from the church court and given to the lay. The judges were always a little vague about whether to accept such an argument or not. They declined an invitation to pass on everyone's excuse for not going to church (the statute said to go unless you had one). But they seem to have tried to take over all suits for mortuaries in the diocese of Chester because a statute said that the customary mortuaries should continue to be paid there.

Another change, a little harder to pin down, was that the common law courts developed a tendency to pass on disputed questions of canon law, at least where the rights of the laity were affected. Coke gives us, for instance, *Jeffrey's Case*[20]— not a case he decided, but one from his days at the bar, in which he appeared on behalf of the churchmen involved. It was a prohibition brought against an ecclesiastical suit to recover a church rate. Jeffrey claimed he was not liable for the rate because he did not live in the parish. The judges consulted their ecclesiastical opposite numbers and found that the canon law made everyone liable for church rates who owned land in the parish, whether he lived there or not. So the judges issued a consultation as to the land Jeffrey owned, and let the prohibition stand as to land he merely leased.

I have not found any medieval lay court going into nuances of church law in this way. Indeed, the whole procedure seems a bit pointless, since the decision was made on the advice of the same people who would have heard the case on a proper canonical appeal if the prohibition had not intervened. I suspect that cases of this kind arose partly from a lack of technical sophistication (the difference between going outside your jurisdiction and making a mistake inside it has never been as simple as it looks), and partly from a feeling that churchmen could not be trusted to apply their own law impartially when their confrères were litigating with laymen. It is probably just as well that the rationale was never articulated; as a result, this line of cases did not become permanently entrenched in the law. But in the period we are now considering it must have had a certain depressing effect on the work of the church courts in dealing with the legal questions before them.

Another tendency that did the church courts no good was that of the lay judges to expand the scope of the remedies they offered. Trespass on the case, the all-purpose writ that was in the process of modernizing the law of torts and creating a law of contracts, picked up on the way such matters as concurrent jurisdiction over actions for dilapidations. It also made great inroads, as we shall see, into the traditional power of the church to punish defamation. The growing use of trespass actions to try the title to real estate was taken up on occasion by clerics litigating over which of them was the incumbent of a benefice. The new techniques of the Chancery court for equitable administration of funds and assets nibbled at the edges of the church's probate jurisdiction. None of these exercises of lay jurisdiction was exactly unknown in the Middle Ages, but all were pursued with a new élan in this period of rapid development of the law.[21] Even where the church courts were not actually ousted of jurisdiction, we may suppose they were hard put to keep up their end.

2. *Tithe* – Tithe became a good deal more litigious in the post-Reformation period than it had been before. Some of the stepped-up tempo was due to the unsettlement of ecclesiastical property; more of it to changes in the course of agriculture and the value of money.[22] Tithing in most parishes was once a simple matter of counting off every tenth sheaf of a staple crop and letting the church courts decide who was to carry them away, or dividing up the year's calves and lambs with the vicar, splitting the difference in some customary way when there was not an even multiple of ten. Now, however, there were new crops such as potatoes and tobacco. There was land put to new uses — pasture land turned to cultivation, or cultivated fields enclosed for pasture. There were cash commutations, as we have seen, that became totally inadequate with the rise in prices. There were people who took over monastic land free from tithe by papal dispensation, and looked to the lay courts to protect what the pope had granted.

Generally, the vicissitudes of the times had not affected the principle that tithe was to be sued for in the first instance in the ecclesiastical court. The lay court's part was to intervene with writs of prohibition at suitable points.[23] We have already seen how this was done where tithe was claimed under the general law, and the tithepayer raised a *modus decimandi* in his defense. The same thing was done where a *modus* was sued on, and the tithepayer denied its existence or legal effect. Claims that a particular crop or income was not titheable were also heard in prohibition proceedings. These became very detailed as the economy grew; the treatises devote pages and pages to them. Where it was claimed that certain lands were discharged from tithe, say under the act of Henry VIII preserving monastic discharges in lay hands, or under the act of Edward VI giving a seven year exemption to lands newly brought under cultivation, a prohibition proceeding was again in order to determine the claim.

The question of who was entitled to a particular set of tithes appeared in new contexts in the post-Reformation case law. There were two ways, it may be recalled, in which the question might come up in a medieval lay proceeding. One was in a writ of right of advowson, where the tithes amounted to more than one quarter the value of a benefice, and the patron chose to stop an ecclesiastical proceeding with a writ called *indicavit*, and do the necessary litigating himself. The other was in an action of trespass *de bonis asportatis*, where the defendant had carried away the produce he claimed as tithe. On a showing that the produce was in fact tithe, the lay court would decline jurisdiction unless the right turned on some special question (e.g., parish boundaries) on which it claimed competence.

The writ of right of advowson seems to have disappeared after the Reformation, though it would no doubt have been available if anyone had wanted to invoke it. The trespass proceeding continued to crop up from time to time. When it did, it was dealt with in the traditional way: jurisdiction was declined in favor of the church court unless parish boundaries or the like were in question.[24] This was done even when a custom was invoked by one of the parties; evidently the general principle about trying custom in the lay court could not prevail over the wealth of medieval precedent in cases of this kind. Also, where both litigants were churchmen, it was hard to see why the church courts should not deal with the matter in their own way.

Where tithe was claimed by a lay impropriator, the question was different. An act of Henry VIII, just after the Dissolution, provided that rectories and rights belonging to them, when they came into lay hands, should be litigated over like other real estate.[25] Sometimes disputes involving lay impropriators depended on questions of ecclesiastical law (e.g., whether the tithes of hops growing in X field belonged to the impropriator or to the vicar), but often they depended on straight questions of secular land law (e.g., whether A's grant of the impropriate rectory to B created a fee tail in B). I should suppose that at least in the latter case the lay court would retain jurisdiction of a trespass proceeding involving the question, but I have no authority to offer directly in point. The nearest thing to it is a 1602 case between an impropriator and a would-be vicar involving the existence of the vicarage (it had been in abeyance for 160 years). The court in fact decided the question (in the vicar's favor, I am glad to say), but the jurisdictional point was not raised.[26]

The kind of proceeding in which the right to a given tithe was most frequently drawn into question was not trespass, but prohibition. For this, there was no medieval precedent as far as I can see. A medieval parishioner simply counted off his tithes from the nine parts and let the churchmen fight over them any way they cared to. Who won the fight was no concern of his. Consequently, when he was sued for not counting off and setting out tithes as he was supposed to do, he had no standing to contend that the person suing him was not the person entittled to the tithes. There is a case in the Queen's Bench in 1584 denying a tithepayer a prohibition on just this ground.[27] But a number of other cases, not much later than this one, allow the tithepayer some sort of standing to contest his opponent's title, or allow a rival claimant who has intervened in the ecclesiastical proceeding to present some of his contentions to the lay court on prohibition.

It is hard to say just how far this development went. The cases are complicated, and, I suspect, not altogether consistent. The general idea, as far as I can make it out, was not that the lay court would actually try questions of who was entitled to tithe, but that it would make the church courts try them instead of leaving them up in the air. The stated purpose of allowing the prohibition was to protect the tithepayer against the risk of double liability.[28]

Further complications set in when the right to tithe depended on some question like custom, statute, or parish boundaries that was generally triable in the lay court. There were all kinds of different holdings in cases of this kind.[29] For instance, the lay courts were willing to try in a prohibition proceeding the contention that the man claiming tithe had forfeited his benefice under the statute of 13 Elizabeth for not declaring his assent to the Thirty-Nine Articles, but not the contention that he had forfeited it under the act of 31 Elizabeth for simony. The difference seems to have been simply a matter of policy — they thought the church courts understood simony better (or cared about it more?) than they did. Other matters they were not willing to have tried in a tithe proceeding at all. Where you had made a personal composition with the parson (I will leave to a footnote the difference between this and a *modus decimandi*),[30] you had to pay the tithe and sue him at law for breach of the composition. Where he was improperly presented to his benefice, you had to go on paying him tithe until he was put out in some other way.

If the right to tithe turned on who owned an impropriated rectory, the church courts would try the question in the first instance but a prohibition would issue if they decided it wrong.[31] If the issue was simply between two churchmen — whether the tithes of this field belonged to the parson or the vicar, or whether they belonged to the parson of A or the parson of B, the lay courts would interfere only if something like parish boundaries was involved, or if the church court refused to hear the contention at all. As in the trespass cases, the lay jurisdiction over matters of custom gave way before the traditional right of the church to settle tithe disputes between its own people.[32]

For an exercise in applying these doctrines, try this case: Lady Gresham, a lay impropriator, sues one Botham in the spiritual court for tithes of a certain field. He pleads an immemorial custom by which he pays fourpence an acre to the vicar in lieu of tithes, and brings prohibition in the usual form for a *modus decimandi*. What result?

Answer: The court awards a consultation without hearing the merits. This is not a *modus decimandi* case, it is a parson-versus-vicar case. Botham must plead in the spiritual court that the tithes of the field in question belong to the vicar rather than to Lady Gresham. Then if the vicar sues him he can set up the *modus* in the usual way.[33]

In addition to all these complicated proceedings under traditional rules of law, there were two special proceedings set up by an act of Edward VI.[34] They were available (under separate sections, worded a little bit differently) if a man carried his crop off without setting out the tithe, or if he set out the tithe and then carried it off with the rest of the crop. One was a suit for treble damages before a competent judge, which the courts interpreted to mean a lay judge. The other was for double damages and costs before an ecclesiastical judge. Coke rationalized the difference between the double damage proceeding and the treble damage proceeding by saying that in the former, because it was in the church court, you could recover the tithes themselves in addition to the damages. If you sued for treble damages in the church court a prohibition would issue. The treble damage proceeding was invoked from time to time in an ordinary common law action of debt. It was the only way in which tithe proceedings could be brought in the first instance in a lay court.[35]

3. Correction of Morals and Redress of Wrongs – One of the most important changes, I suspect, from the medieval situation of the church courts was a fuller enforcement of the rule against their rendering money judgments. This rule, as we saw in an earlier chapter, had existed on paper since *Circumspecte Agatis* at least, but was somewhat selectively applied. The actions to collect debts on a theory of broken faith *(fidei laesio)*, which formed a staple item of business for the medieval ecclesiastical courts, although the lay courts stood ready to prohibit them when asked, disappear entirely at the Reformation. Nor is there any indication that the defamation actions, which abounded in the post-Reformation church courts, got a successful plaintiff anything but a public apology and costs.

It was in this area of defamation that most of the difficulties over ecclesiastical correction of wrongdoers occurred. In addition to forbidding suits for money damages in the church courts, the lay judges had adopted by the 1580s an extremely elaborate set of rules for what kinds of defamation they themselves could hear and the church courts could not.[36] They began by saying that the accusation of a temporal crime could not be the subject of a church defamation proceeding. They followed this with a determination that if a slander was cognizable in the temporal courts it could not be cognizable in the church courts. This principle they applied to more and more cases, as they expanded the lay remedy to cover any case in which the slander had led to a temporal loss. Thus, in 1593, they held that a woman who had lost a valuable marriage through a slander on her chastity had a lay remedy in an action of trespass on the case, rather than an ecclesiastical remedy in an action for defamation. In 1609, they held that a physician could not proceed in a church court for a slander on his professional skill.

By the end of Elizabeth's reign, they had pretty well worked around to a rule that you could not proceed in the church courts for defamation unless you had been accused of an offense that was itself cognizable in those courts. If someone said you were a witch, a bawd, or the parent of a bastard, you could sue; but if he said you were

> a beastly quean, a drunken quean, a copper-nose quean, she was one cause why B left his wife, and she has misspent £ 500

you were out of luck. If he said you had perjured yourself in an ecclesiastical court, you could sue, but if he said you had perjured yourself in a lay court you could not.

There were a number of refinements. You could sue someone who said you were a cuckold, even though the ecclesiastical offense he was charging was your wife's. You could sue someone who said you had begotten a bastard even though some fathers of bastards were punishable by the justices of the peace. Coke explained that the justices had jurisdiction only where the bastard had become a public charge. Presumably, if someone said your bastard children were supported by the parish poor rates you had no redress.

The medieval genesis of all this lore is instructive; particuarly so as it would be hard to find any kind of post-Reformation social policy behind it. The Elizabethans were a pretty sensitive lot in matters of this kind, and giving them a way to exact public apologies was surely conducive to the general good order of the realm. The medieval rule, it may be recalled, was simply that a man's testimony or his pleadings in a lay court could not be the basis for a spiritual defamation proceeding — a fairly obvious principle for the protection of the lay jurisdiction. The first real expansion of this principle, a case on which Coke relied heavily, was *Anonymous* v. *Abbot of St. Albans* (1482).[37] According to the plaintiff's story in that case, the abbot on a suitable pretext had taken his (the plaintiff's) wife into a room in the abbey, where he (the abbot) had solicited her chastity, and locked her up when she refused him. The plaintiff had been going around telling people that he was planning to sue the abbot for false imprisonment. The abbot then brought defamation proceedings, and the plaintiff had a prohibition.

What I get out of the court's decision is that the prohibition was issued to protect the projected false imprisonment action. So the case stands for the proposition that a person who *plans to sue* in a lay court is entitled to the same protection as a person who *has sued* already. It was left to the Elizabethans to extend the same protection to a person who *can sue* (or can launch a criminal prosecution) even if he is not planning to. Whether these extensions of the original medieval doctrine are good or bad, I am not sure you have to go beyond the doctrine itself to explain them. There seems to be a certain internal logic at work in this course of decisions, independent of whatever economic, social, or political factors may be adduced.

These defamation proceedings seem to have been the one major class of cases in which the post-Reformation church courts persistently followed a different line from the lay. A substantial portion of the defamation proceedings, both those promoted by the victim and those turned up at parish visitations, were prohibitable under the rules I have just described.[38] The church courts had a pretty firm grip on cases of this kind long before the 1580s, when the prohibitions began coming; and even when the prohibition was standard it must have taken a good deal of money and a good deal of self-righteousness to seek one, when it was so much cheaper to apologize at the behest of the church court.

Talking about the minister or churchwardens in connection with their jobs was in a class by itself. The church courts tended to lump verbal and physical abuse into a single category — reasonably enough, because most of the speech involved was abusive rather than defamatory in the usual sense.[39] Calling a churchwarden prating Jack, or saying that the minister is fitter to stand in a swine sty than in a pulpit is not exactly accusing anyone of anything in particular, though it falls short of the sobriety and reverence we would like to see maintained. It is less objectionable than belting people or throwing rotten eggs at them, but it is really the same kind of thing.

If this kind of behavior took place in a church or churchyard, the ecclesiastical jurisdiction was expressly supported by a statute of Edward VI, and the lay courts made no trouble over it.[40] Outside the sacred precincts, however, the only statutory basis for a church proceeding was *Circumspecte Agatis* and the *Articuli Cleri* of 1317, which the lay courts interpreted as narrowly as they could.[41] These statutes applied only where one laid violent hands on a cleric. In 1599 the Queen's Bench held that this meant an actual battery. An assault (an offer or attempt of physical violence without an actual touching) would not do; still less would mere words do. A year later they held that even in a battery case if the defendant alleged an excuse (he said he was defending his servant who had been set upon by the minister) he was entitled to bring a prohibition proceeding to have the excuse tried in the lay court. These ungenerous interpretations of an old rule are probably attributable to the Gregorian origin of the rule itself. For anyone imbued with the spirit of the medieval laity, as the common law judges were, this protection of the clergy in their own courts could not be looked at without reopening old wounds. I suspect that here, as in the defamation cases, the churchmen went their own way when they were allowed to: in many of the verbal abuse cases tried in the church courts there is nothing to show that the words complained of were uttered in a church or churchyard.

In matters like marriage, church attendance, clerical discipline and the like, the lay courts were more accommodating.[42] They turned down a number of invitations to assume exclusive jurisdiction to apply the various statutes in these fields, and in general recognized that the church had important public policies to enforce and needed sufficient leeway to enforce them. The only systematically baneful interference was in the case of pardons, and the analogous case of the clerical felon who had been let off through benefit of clergy; I have already referred to these. The idea seems to have been that, now that the sovereign was recognized as head of the church, ecclesiastical offenses were offenses against the sovereign, and could not be prosecuted when offenses against the sovereign had been pardoned or otherwise disposed of.[43] By the same token, as the condonation was an exercise of royal power (and generally embodied in a statute) it was for the royal courts to say what it meant. So if a cleric subject to a disciplinary proceeding claimed the benefit of a pardon or of a previous conviction in a lay court, a prohibition lay to determine his claim.

As I have said, these holdings seem a bit gratuitous. Granted the king has the power to drop proceedings for the correction of sinners, it does not follow that he intends to do so whenever he pardons secular offenders. Still less does it follow that he intends to leave a parish burdened with every scandalous minister he decides for some reason not to imprison or hang. The trouble was that people in this period, like the medieval churchmen before them, failed to sort out the differences between punishment of an offender against society, correction of a sinner *pro salute animae,* and administrative removal of an unfit minister.[44] Not until 1828 were the differences adequately recognized in the courts.

C. Due Process and Distribution of Functions.

For the power of common law judges to protect the laity against unfair proceedings in the church courts, there was a broad, but not too well articulated, range of medieval precedent. The various traumas of the sixteenth century provided new scope for this protection, and the refinements of ecclesiastical procedure under the auspices of the High Commission provided new need for it. The powers of the lay courts were exercised often through writs of prohibition or habeas corpus, sometimes through collateral attack on ecclesiastical judgments (for instance, where a marriage was improperly annulled, the issue of a later marriage might be held illegitimate), in flagrant cases by setting the justices of the peace on the offender.[45]

The cases that came up most frequently were those in which the canon law, with its Continental tradition, sanctioned a procedure which the common law regarded as unfair. The church courts in a proceeding *ex officio* would swear a man generally to answer whatever was put to him, then would ask him whether he had done such-and-such, and even what he had had in mind when he did it.

This was pretty well routine canonical process, but I do not believe the medieval churchmen made a habit of it except in doctrinal cases. It was certainly the heresy prosecutions of the fifteenth and early sixteenth centuries that made for most of the odium attached to the whole procedure. Many laymen, including St. Germain, felt that people were examined on the vaguest kind of suspicion, trapped into heretical statements, then prosecuted for heresy on the basis of those statements.[46]

The statute under which the Royal Commissioners in Ecclesiastical Causes (the High Commission) sat specifically forbade them to punish anything as heresy that was not denounced by the first four general councils or by the plain words of scripture. Coke said that while the ordinaries were not bound by this they would do well to limit themselves in the same way — as in fact they did in one or two heresy proceedings that came before them.[47] But the old inquisitorial process was still available, and still used, to ferret out recusants and liturgical violators for the several punishments the laws provided. It was used for other purposes as well. In addition to recusancy (popish or sectary) and liturgical violations, the chancellor of the Norwich diocese, writing to his bishop in 1603, listed pluralism and nonresidence, unlawful marriages, profaning of churches, bribery and extortion by apparitors, and evil and corrupt keeping of church registers as offenses that could not be effectively dealt with except by proceeding in this way.[48] Still, it was hard to think of the process without thinking of the fires of Smithfield.

From the beginning of Elizabeth's reign, the common law judges were holding when asked that this process could not be used to compel a person to expose himself to a temporal penalty.[49] It was finally established that you could accuse him *pro salute animae,* and put him to penance on the basis of his sworn answer, but you could not affect his property, his status, or even his tenure of his benefice. Coke as chief justice of the Common Pleas, and Popham as chief justice of the King's Bench made two further points in a response to the Council in 1607. One was that you could not swear a person to answer accusations against him before he had seen what the accusations were and whether they were lawful. The other was that you could not require him to divulge his interior thoughts or opinions. I do not find the first of these doctrines embodied in an actual case. The second was used in 1609 to stop a defamation proceeding where the accused was asked what he meant by drawing a horn opposite the complaining witness's name.

Here again, the church courts did not give up following their own procedures because the lay courts said to. The High Commission in particular pursued its inquisitorial ways as best it could until the Long Parliament put an end to it. My impression is that the occasional interventions of the lay courts did not seriously affect the work of the commission during Elizabeth's reign, and that the honors were about even during the great confrontations under James, and until the brief period before the dénouement when the Laudians had established a more compliant bench of common law judges.[50]

Venue in the church courts provided another important procedural bone of contention.[51] I have pointed out that Henry VIII was responding to a long-standing medieval grievance when he passed a statute forbidding anyone to be cited into an ecclesiastical court outside the diocese in which he lived. It was with regard to that statute that the lay courts first laid down the rule that they had exclusive jurisdiction over the application of statutes. The churchmen could not be trusted to administer a restraint on one of their most inveterate abuses. This statute and the exceptions for which it provided were regularly (and, to my mind, fairly) interpreted by the lay courts from the beginning.

The judges added a more general control of venue, which they ultimately rationalized on the theory that there was a trespass on the royal prerogative, to be redressed in the common law courts, whenever any court exceeded its allotted jurisdiction. The rationale did not come till 1622, but as early as 1578 the judges allowed a collateral attack on an order of a diocesan court granting administration of an estate that should have been administered by the metropolitan.

By the end of Elizabeth's reign, this concern with having suits brought in the right ecclesiastical court was leading the common law judges to issue prohibitions to the High Commission when they thought a case was not of sufficient moment to be within the contemplation of the statute by which that body sat. Suits affecting private rights (tithes, pensions, and the like — *meum* and *tuum* as Coke put it), matrimonial cases, defamation, and run of the mill offenses (drunkenness, fornication, Sabbath-breaking, etc.) were all to be left to the regular tribunals.[52]

For their position on private litigation, the judges had fairly good authority — the statute in fact referred only to offenses. The limitation to major offenses was a little harder to support. Coke explained it mainly on general policy grounds:

> as necessity did cause this commission, so it should be exercised but upon necessity, for it was never intended that it should be a continual standing commission, for that should prejudice all the bishops of England in their ecclesiastical jurisdiction, and be grievous to the subject to be drawn up from all the remote parts of the realm, where before their own diocesan they might receive justice at their own doors.

On the whole, these arguments were specious. The bishops, many of whom sat on the commission anyhow, were the last people to complain about having their disciplinary powers supplemented by the more formidable procedures of this body. As for drawing people out of the remote parts of the realm, the government was quite flexible in appointing branch commissions to sit in those

romote parts. It would have appointed more of them if the commission had
been subjected to the act of Henry VIII about citing people out of their home
diocese.

There were also the plain words of the statute to be gotten around. They set
no limits on the kinds of offense with which the commission might deal.
Coke's main argument here was *cessante ratione cessat ipsa lex* — that the
commission should deal only with the kinds of situation that led Parliament to
set it up. He supplemented this argument with a case showing that a statutory
grant of power to the crown should not be interpreted as taking away the rights
of any subject — in this case the rights of the bishops to hear the kinds of cases
they had been hearing in the past.

The extent of the commission's jurisdiction and the scope of its inquisitorial
powers were two of the three fronts on which the common law courts attacked
the commission during King James's reign. The third was its power to
imprison; I have already dealt with one aspect of this subject. The courts held,
with good reason in view of the language of the statute, that the commission
could not imprison anyone who could not have been imprisoned by an
ecclesiastical judge before the Reformation. They added, with the historical
justification I have described, that an ecclesiastical judge before the
Reformation could imprison only for heresy under a statue of Henry IV or for
clerical incontinence under one of Henry VII.

As with the *ex officio* oath, the commission did not acquiesce in the limits set
by the common law courts. My impression is that power to imprison was freely
exercised except in a couple of celebrated cases where it was challenged
(mostly in habeas corpus proceedings, though in one case a man killed the
pursuivant sent by the commissioners to arrest him, and was let off on grounds
of self defense).[53] Whether the commissioners stopped hearing petty cases in
James's reign we cannot really say, but they were certainly at it again by the
1630s. It was only at the Restoration that the common law view of
ecclesiastical process, as formulated by Coke, became fully established.

I have no wish to add to the literature on the political battles over the High
Commission. But it is worthwhile noting from the standpoint of the common
lawyers what all the excitement was about. As early as 1382, the Commons,
repealing a statute inadvertently put through without their consent, stated that

> it was not their intention to oblige themselves or their successors to the
> prelates or to be subject to their jurisdiction any further than their ancestors
> had been in times past.[54]

We can see much of the work of the seventeenth century judges as a gloss upon
that sentiment. The trouble with the High Commission was not that it cut in on
the bishops or made people travel about the country, but that it corrected
manners and morals with such ruthless efficiency. It could send a pursuivant to

arrest you and haul you in, could examine you under oath about anything you had ever done wrong, could impose a fat fine and keep you in jail till you paid it, could even make you post bond to sin no more.[55] This kind of power was beyond the wildest dreams of medieval churchmen. The common law judges, as lay and conservative spokesmen, had good reason not to put up with it in their time.

D. Recognition and Enforcement.

The traditional ambivalence of the lay judges persisted regarding the place of their ecclesiastical colleagues in the general administration of the law. They recognized that a judge of a church court was properly included within a statute against bribing judges, but they were not ready to grant him inherent judicial powers to protect himself against contempt, or against tampering with his records.[56] They could not make up their minds about whether he could give costs in a suit which he had no jurisidiction to determine. If he was holding a proper court, he ought to be allowed to give costs to a defendant who prevailed on a jurisdictional point, just as to one who prevailed on some other point. The common law judges seem not to have been quite sure he was holding a proper court.

Their ambivalence was particularly apparent in cases where they had to consider the effect of a judgment made final in a church court, but called into question in a lay. It seems that some, but not all, of the grounds on which a case could have been prohibited at earlier stages were still open after a judgment had come down.[57] Lack of jurisdiction over the subject-matter probably was. Improper venue (e.g., citation outside the home diocese in violation of the act of Henry VIII) was not. Improper handling of a question of secular law that came up incidentally in the course of the proceedings may or may not have been. There was a simony case from 1601 where a deprived incumbent tried to get the lay court to construe a general pardon as applicable to his case. In one place in the report the court examined the pardon and said it did not apply; farther on, though, it said it could not go beyond the ecclesiastical judgment.

On the question whether a judgment affecting the tenure of a benefice could be collaterally attacked, the cases were all over the lot.[58] There was one, for instance, involving a lease given by a dean of Wells who was deprived by his bishop for pluralism in King Edward's time; the deprivation was reversed under Mary, and the reversal reversed under Elizabeth. The court discussed a bit whether a bishop could deprive a dean, then left to the jury the question of whether this one was deprived when he gave the lease. But in another lease case in King Charles's, time, the court said it could not look behind a sentence of deprivation at all. A case from 1588 said a man wrongfully deprived could not attack the deprivation in a trespass suit brought by his successor. But one from 1609 and another from 1610 suggested that he could test his rights by suing parishioners for tithes.

Similarly, if a man was accused of forging a will, the courts were not quite sure how much weight to give the ordinary's judgment admitting the will to probate. Or if a bishop certified something or other in response to a question from a lay court, they were not quite sure whether you could claim that he had made a mistake. And if you had a marriage annulled in the church courts and married again, you could not be sure whether the lay courts would listen to a claim that your children were bastards because the first marriage was not properly annulled when you entered the second.[59]

An ecclesiastical judgment fared better on direct enforcement than it did on collateral attack. There were three processes, all of them ancient, whereby an ecclesiastical judgment as such would be enforced by the lay courts. One was the suspension of a lay proceeding on showing that the plaintiff was excommunicated. One was the writ *de vi laica amovenda,* whereby the sheriff could be ordered to remove any lay force resisting the execution of an ecclesiastical judgment — usually one for possession of a benefice. One was the writ *de excommunicato capiendo,* whereby the sheriff could be ordered to seize an excommunicate and imprison him until he submitted to the judgment of the church.

The first of these was little affected by the Reformation. There was some debate over whether newly created church courts should be added to the list of those entitled to certify an excommunication so as to stop a lay proceeding; it was decided that they should.[60] Coke asserted that the certificate filed for the purpose should recite the ground of the excommunication, but there is no indication that he claimed to review the validity of that ground any more than his predecessors had done.

The two cases I have found on the *vi laica* writ show a little more sophistication in its use.[61] The medieval presupposition was that when the lay force was put out of the picture the ecclesiastical processes could be executed by the archdeacon or rural dean by his own authority. Thus, the sheriff's intervention was not supposed to affect the actual possession of the subject-matter at all. But the post-Reformation cases show a recognition that chasing A out was tantamount to putting B in. So it was decided that a writ of restitution could be sought out of Chancery to put A back in if he ought not to have been chased out. Chancery was also prepared to intervene at other points in the process by issuing appropriate injunctions to supplement the work of the sheriff. Suppose, for instance the sheriff put X's lay force out of a church so the archdeacon could go through the act of inducting Y, but X was still in possession of the parsonage. It seems the chancellor would order him to get out.

With the availability of injunctions and writs of restitution, the Chancery was doing something more than dissolving the lay force and letting ecclesiastical processes take their course. It was actually determining who should possess the property in question. Here it seems the lay judges took reasonable care to follow the decisions of the church courts. Where a man was deprived of a benefice, for instance, they would put his successor in possession, and leave him there unless the deprivation was canonically reversed.[62]

The process on the writ *de excommunicato capiendo* was modified by a statute of 1563.[63] The medieval writ had not been "returnable" — that is, the sheriff did not have to report to anyone whether he had executed it or not. So if he felt he had better things to do than catch excommunicates, the processes of the church would go unenforced. The 1563 act made the writ returnable into the Queen's Bench. You would take it there for enrollment after you had been issued it by the Chancery. It would then be delivered to the sheriff in open court, and he would have to report in the following term either that he had jailed the excommunicate or that he could not find him in the county.

In most of the usual disciplinary cases (doctrinal or sexual deviation, and one or two others), if the excommunicate could not be found, the statute provided a process called *capias*, whereby he could be proclaimed in the county court, and subjected to substantial cash forfeitures until he turned himself in. In cases between parties (tithes, defamations, marriage and will cases, etc.), however, it was presumably left to the injured party to go and find his adversary and tell the sheriff.

The statute, according to its preamble, was intended to improve the enforcement of ecclesiastical process, but actually it cut both ways. While you were better protected against a negligent sheriff, it was made harder for you to work with a willing one. If you did not enroll your writ in the Queen's Bench (and pay a fee no doubt for doing so), it was void, and the excommunicate would be let out on habeas corpus if the sheriff arrested him. Thus the whole process added to the cost which was the main barrier to using the writ in disciplinary cases. If the cash forfeitures provided for in the statute had gone to the ecclesiastical courts, it might still have been worthwhile to proceed, but the statute was clear that these went to the Exchequer.

Coke thought that before the sheriff took in the excommunicate the court ought to determine whether the excommunication was lawful by the secular law.[64] He even asserted (in this he was clearly wrong) that at common law the writ *de excommunicato capiendo* could not be issued unless the bishop signified the cause of the excommunication so specifically that such a determination could be made. What he proposed might have been a good idea — though it would have added to the cumbersomness of the process and so to the weakness of ecclesiastical sanctions — but I have found no case of its being done in his time. Eventually, the 1563 Act (not the common law) was interpreted to require the determination Coke envisaged, but this was not until 1700.

II. Secular Interests

Needless to say, the common lawyers followed in the footsteps of their medieval predecessors in guarding the ecclesiastical interests of their secular constituents. Many of the old sources of litigation had disappeared, though. If the justices of the peace wanted to deal with the extortionate use of church process, no one was so enamoured of clerical prerogatives as to argue with them. Sanctuary was no more. Benefit of clergy was a mitigation of the criminal law in which the church played no part after 1576. The mortmain laws were still in force, but nobody was much interested in evading them.[65] Of the old standbys there remainned only patronage rights, no longer valuable for supporting bureaucratic establishments, but still important for servants and poor relations, and newly important to gain pulpit support for your particular nuances of political or religious opinion; often too, alas, valued as a source of clandestine lucre. New to the scene, on the other hand, and fruitful in lawsuits, were the tithe rights (to be free of them or to collect them) inherited from the suppressed religious houses, and a miscellany of other rights bought, leased, or confiscated from their ecclesiastical owners.

A. Patronage.

For someone who enjoys unravelling legal technicalities, the law of patronage has a fatal fascination. Such a person could, if he chose, draw out of the reports from this period almost (not quite) as convoluted a narrative as the medieval reports afford. But in all but a few respects it would be the same story; I have no good excuse for telling it a second time. I will limit myself to three main trends that seem to me new in this period. Except for these, we can say with tolerable safety that the law remained as I described it in the first chapter of this volume — subject (like all land law) to a good deal of procedural simplification.[66]

The three trends I want to take up have in common that they involve more protection for the patron's interest in presenting the cleric of his choice, as against the church's interest in keeping benefices filled with qualified men. One might attribute this increased tenderness for the patron to a political alliance between the common lawyers and the landed gentry, except that the same alliance seems to have existed in the earlier period when the law was different. What changed was not the attitude of the courts toward the landed gentry, but their attitude toward the law. For the medieval lawyers, common and canon law were coordinate parts of the whole system. Each was expected to protect the interests committed to it with the means at its disposal. After the Reformation, this understanding of the relation between the two systems was tacitly altered. The common lawyers came to regard the canon law as an inferior, not a coordinate branch — a presumptuous servant, so to speak, rather than an encroaching neighbor.[67] The new way of thinking tended naturally (without any articulated change in policy) to put the interests protected by the higher system in a better position, those protected by the lower in a worse.

Here, in any event, are the three trends:

1. *Lapse,* the situation in which the authorities could fill a benefice which the patron neglected to fill, was a good deal more litigated over than it used to be. This was partly because there were a number of statutory provisions (pluralism, simony, failure to subscribe the Articles, failure to pay first fruits and tenths) making benefices ipso facto void, and therefore subject to lapse, even though there was someone ostensibly in possession. It was partly also becauses lapses were more apt to be detected: visitations were more frequent in which the bishop could learn of a vacant benefice. Also, the crown, rather than the papacy, got to fill the benefice if the bishop and the metropolitan failed: a cleric who learned of a vacant benefice and wanted it for himself could have it by going to Westminister instead of to Rome.

Most of the trouble came when the patron complained that the benefice had been filled for lapse before he knew it was vacant. He would claim he was entitled to notice of the vacancy. Whether he was right or not depended on why the benefice was vacant.[68] If the last incumbent was dead, the patron was not entitled to notice — he was in as good a position as the bishop to find out. But if the incumbent was canonically deprived or had resigned, the vacancy had come officially before the bishop, and the bishop had to give official notice of it.

Where the canons made the benefice ipso facto void (where the incumbent was a layman, for instance) the voidance still had to be established in a judicial proceeding before the patron was affected, and then he had to be given notice of the result.[69] But where the ipso facto voidance was by statute, rather than by canon, the patron was not entitled to notice unless the statute so provided.[70] The one on first fruits and tenths did not so provide. Nor did Henry VIII's act on pluralism. It followed that if the ostensible incumbent was not within one of the exempted classes (royal chaplains etc), and the benefice was worth more than £ 8 in the King's Books, the bishop could fill the benefice without telling the patron. But in other cases of pluralism the benefice was only canonically void, so the bishop had to bring a proceeding, tell the patron, and wait six months.

On the other hand, the act of 13 Elizabeth, creating a voidance for not subscribing the Articles, provided expressly that the patron should not be prejudiced until six months after he had been given notice.[71] The patron could take advantage of the failure by making a new presentment whenever he chose, but he did not have to do so until official notice was given him. This had to be personal and official notice from the bishop; it made no difference if the patron already knew in some other way.

Simony was in a class by itself.[72] If the patron was a party to the corrupt transaction, his rights were forfeit to the crown, so the problem of giving him a chance to present did not arise. But if he was innocent (say you had given his brother something to put in a good word for you), he was entitled to make a new presentment, and the statute provided for notifying him before his rights were lost to the crown.

2. *The protection of the incumbent* in patronage cases was somewhat eroded.[73] For one thing, if he had been put in for lapse, he could be put out again if the lapse was not properly invoked under the rules just described. Thus, the various Elizabethan statutues that provided for automatic deprivation, but protected the patron, created the possibility of a whole new class of insecure incumbents.

The various standing problems that had plagued medieval incumbents were resolved by a close reading of the 1350 statute on the subject. The results were better for the incumbent than the worst medieval cases, but worse than the better ones. He was no longer in danger of being put out of court for not claiming the advowson himself. On the other hand, he no longer had a chance of being allowed to rely on his canonical incumbency. He could save himself only by showing that his patron had a good title. The ordinary, to whom the medieval cases had given some standing to litigate patronage claims for the protection of the incumbent, was now given no standing beyond what the statute gave him in cases of lapse. An incumbent whose patron did not choose to protect him was on his own.

The royal presentee, who was in a particularly good position in the Middle Ages, seems to have been in a particularly bad one now. The courts, in their general consideration of the royal prerogative, had developed (I do not know just when) a doctrine that a crown grant based on misinformation was ineffective — the queen was "deceived in her grant", the Elizabethans said. Accordingly, where the queen had no right to present to a benefice, her presentment to it was void, and the ensuing institution of the incumbent equally so. Thus, her presentee could be put out any time as an intruder. By contrast, if a subject presented to a benefice when he had no right to, the institution of his cleric would constitute a successful usurpation of the advowson, which could not be redressed without an action of *quare impedit;* even then, the usurper's presentee might be entitled to keep the benefice.

Here is *Green's Case,* from 1602, which raises several of the above points, and will serve to show what an actual case might look like.[74] It seems that the patron of a certain benefice presented X in 1574. Then in 1583 he brought suit in the ecclesiastical court to have X deprived for not subscribing the Articles as required by the 1571 statute. Note, by the way, that he did not have to do this; he could simply have presented a new incumbent, ince the statute made the benefice ipso facto void. At any rate, the suit proceeded to a sentence of deprivation, but a few days before the sentence came down the patron died. Thereafter, the queen presented A on the basis of a supposed lapse, and A was duly instituted and inducted. He continued in possession till 1597. X, meanwhile, had died in 1594 or so. In 1597, the current patron (successor to the one who died in 1583) presented B, who was also instituted and inducted. B now sues A for trespass.

B. wins. While the 1571 statute makes the benefice void, the voidance cannot prejudice the patron until six months after he is given official notice of it. As the patron was never officially notified of this voidance, the queen cannot claim a lapse on account of it. Therefore, she was deceived in her presentment of A in 1583, so that presentment, and A's institution on the basis of it are void. If the queen had presented A again a proper time after X died in 1594, it would be a different story, since the patron is not entitled to notice of a vacancy due to death. But even after a lapse occurs, the patron can still make a presentment until the authorities have actually filled the benefice. So the 1597 presentment was perfectly good, and B was perfectly entitled to the benefice.

These incumbent cases illustrate, it seems to me, the point I was making about the changed relation between the two systems. The medieval judges were not irresistably impressed by a canonical incumbency, but they set more store by it than the Elizabethan or the Jacobean judges did. They understood that the bishop was supposed to see that the services were kept up, and that the incumbent was supposed to keep them up. By contrast, Sir Henry Hobart, Chief Justice of the Common Pleas, writing on the subject in 1620, seems to regard the incumbent as a kind of leaseholder *manqué* of the patron, and treats the ordinary as if he has no concern except to see that the patron gets what he deserves:

> I have been the larger in this discourse, because I see the inheritances of advowsons so incumbered by wilful usurpations, and disturbances of pretended patrons, Ordinaries and clerks. . . that it is almost impossible, if a true patron be put to his action, but he will be tried.[75]

3. The right of the bishop to reject an unfit presentee was also eroded for the benefit of the patron. Under the medieval cases, as we have seen, the question of unfitness could be raised in a lay proceeding, and sent to the metropolitan (or sometimes even to a jury) for trial. But I do not find that the lay courts took an independent line on what standards of fitness should be applied, or ever held a canonical disqualification to be insufficient under the secular law. Nor did they attempt to pass judgment on the bishop's manner of examining presentees or of notifying the patron when he rejected one.

All these things they began doing in Elizabeth's reign.[76] By the 1590s they had established a whole set of rules. Only a serious doctrinal or moral deviation was ground for rejection; a mere violation of the canons (*malum prohibitum* as opposed to *malum in se*) would not do. In 1567, the judges held that a man could not be rejected as a "haunter of taverns and illegal games." In 1586, they were in doubt as to whether a man who spoke no Welsh might be held unfit for a benefice in Wales. If the bishop did have a sufficient ground for rejection, he had to plead it specifically enough so the court could pass on it. In 1591, "inveterate schismatic" was held too vague.

The courts did not try to tell the bishop how to examine a presentee, but they did hold that he could not unilaterally set an examination and reject the presentee out of hand if he failed to show up. Finally, they held that the bishop could not declare a lapse after rejecting a presentee unless he had given timely and personal notice to the patron so the patron could try again before the six months ran out.

Coke rationalized all this learning by saying that the original statutory protection for the bishop's determination of fitness (in the *Articuli Cleri* of 1315) applied only to "reasonable" determinations.[77] Hence, the reasonableness of the bishop's refusal had to be open to question in a lay proceeding. The result was once again to give the lay courts a general power of supervision over a canonical process.

B. Tithes and Impropriations.

Despite a number of accusations both then and now, I do not find that the common law courts exercised their miscellaneous powers over tithe litigation with any general hostility to the institution of tithe. Take, for instance, the question of what is tithable, on which they are supposed to have changed the law for the benefit of tithepayers. What they really changed was not "the law" but the balance of power between their version of the law and the very different version put out by the churchmen.[78] On tithability of minerals, where Coke's doctrine is said to have "flatly contradicted medieval practice," the medieval practice it contradicted was considered a usurpation on the part of the churchmen, and was complained of in Parliament as early as 1376. Now that they had the power, the common lawyers naturally resolved these old conflicts in favor of the positions their predecessors had taken. But when it came to new forms of production, it seems to me that they went impartially enough about the difficult task of bringing traditional principles to bear. In fact, they decided for tithability as often as not. And they held most new crops to be "small tithes" collectible by vicars, rather than "great tithes" collectible by lay impropriators.

Even the *modus decimandi* cases were not always decided against the claims of the church.[79] While the judges rejected, as the laity had always done, the view that the *modus* had to be a fair substitute for the mathematical tenth, they did insist that it had to be a definite payment, and one to the person entitled to the tithe. They rejected a custom of paying the produce of every tenth strip in a field instead of a tenth of the produce of the whole field (the parishioners had neglected the cultivation of the tithe strips in order to spite the vicar). Ditto a custom of paying a specified sum to the parish clerk in lieu of tithe to the vicar.

Also, they were quite strict with customs of not paying tithe at all.[80] At common law, they held no such custom was good unless it ran in favor of a churchman. In the absence of a statute, tithe-free land still became tithable if it passed into lay hands, whether by sale or by lease. Even glebe, which traditionally never paid tithe, was tithable in the hands of a lessee. In one case (1579) a parson leased his glebe "free from all exactions," and still collected tithe from his lessee — tithe was not an "exaction" but a personal obligation.

The statute of Henry VIII dissolving the greater monasteries (1539) made an exception to the principle that only churchmen could be free of tithes. It provided that any discharge of monastic lands would be preserved when these lands came into lay hands by reason of the dissolution. This was a simple enough provision, but it raised some difficult legal problems. These the courts resolved fairly enough, and on the whole in favor of collecting the tithes.[81] The statute applied only to the greater monasteries; lands taken from the lesser houses in 1535 could not be exempted under it. Discharges by papal authority were limited by the canons of the Fourth Lateran Council, and by medieval statutes restricting the use of papal bulls. Where the monastery that owned the land was also the appropriator of the rectory to which the tithes were due, and thus avoided tithes through "unity of possession", the new owner of the land did not escape payment to the new owner of the rectory unless the unity had been "perpetual." That is, if it could be shown that the monastery either acquired the land or appropriated the rectory after 1189, the tithe had to be paid.

There was one other statutory ground of exemption. In order to encourage agricultural development, it had been provided under Edward VI that land newly brought into production should be exempted from tithe for seven years.[82] The courts applied this (rightly, it seems to me, in view of its purpose) to former pasture land, even if it had paid tithes of lambs and wool before being cultivated. But they did not apply it to the land that had merely been suffered to lie fallow, or to go to weeds and gorse through bad husbandry. They insisted that the new cultivation must be brought about through capital expenditure or extra work. In short, the statute was interpreted as a reward to useful enterprise, which was what it was for, and not at all as a pretext to get people out of paying tithe.

The courts took a fairly moderate stand on the highly controversial subject of urban tithes.[83] Since nothing was grown in a city, provision was made during the Middle Ages for paying a percentage of the rental value of each house in lieu of tithe. In London, this arrangement had been given its final form in Henry VIII's time in arbitration proceedings (confirmed by statute) between the city fathers and the clergy. In other places, the percentage payments were merely a custom. Hill tells us that city people were particularly disaffected toward any kind of tithe payment, because they were of the incipient capitalist class, imbued with ideas of free enterprise and private property, as well as being for the most part puritans. They wanted to hang onto their money and spend it on stipendiary ministers of their own choosing.

The clergy, especially in London, were interested in taking a new look from time to time at the valuations on which the prescribed percentages were being paid, and at transferring the collection process from the lay courts to their own. The common lawyers were evidently willing enough to have the percentages paid on true value, but not to increase the jurisdiction of the church courts. In London, King Henry's arbitrators had provided for all cases to be heard by the Lord Mayor's court, with an appeal to the chancellor; a proceeding anywhere else was held prohibitable. In places not covered by the award, the customary percentages were treated like any *modus decimandi:* proceedings could be begun in the church courts, but the existence and application of the custom would be tried in the lay court under the procedures I have already described.

But Coke turned down what seems to me an extremely plausible argument for virtually abolishing these payments. In *Dr. Graunt's Case* (1614),[84] the householder argued that a custom of tithing on a house could not be upheld because a house was not properly a subject of tithe. In other words, a *modus decimandi* is a way of tithing, so it ought to be related in some way to something tithable. This argument is not completely unanswerable, but it is no worse that the arguments that prevail in many a case. Certainly a judge strongly committed to the cause of citizens' not paying tithe could have accepted the argument without sacrificing his professional integrity.

Coke rejected it on two grounds. First, the custom might have been started before the parish was all built up, i.e., the parishioners might have had both houses and agricultural land, and agreed to pay on the one instead of the other. This is hard to take seriously. The other ground was probably the real one:

> . . .every ancient city and borough has for the most part such custom, *de modo decimandi,* for their house, for the maintenance of their parson.

In other words, accepting the argument would mean the end of most urban tithes (except in London, where the arrangement had been made statutory), and leave the ministry dependent on the voluntary offerings of the faithful. Coke was not that much committed to free enterprise.

While the judges were more sympathetic to lay impropriators than their predecessors had been to the monasteries, there is no indication that they made any difficulty about regular proceedings to subject impropriators to their canonical duties, such as paying ancient pensions, or repairing the chancels of their churches. Most of the agitation on these matters came because the regular church processes were inadequate to coerce lay magnates. The prelates wanted to use the extra powers of the High Commission, and so ran afoul of the rule that that body was not to be used for litigation between parties. The prohibitions were duly issued and duly complained of.[85]

Another bone of contention was vicarages. By general medieval canonical rule, supported by statutes of Richard II and Henry IV, a religious body that appropriated a rectory had to endow a vicarage with sufficient sources of revenue to afford the incumbent a *congrua sustentatio*. But in the fifteenth century the pope took to giving licenses to avoid this obligation, or to appropriate a vicarage to the house that had already appropriated the rectory. The lay impropriator at the Dissolution would take over the entire revenue of a parish thus dealt with, subject only to the requirement of hiring a curate to do the work.

The churchmen sniped at this state of affairs when they could. In the case of *Britton* v. *Wade* (1619),[86] they tried to re-establish a vicarage (by getting the crown to present to it as for a lapse) that had been endowed in the thirteenth century and appropriated by papal license in Henry VI's time. But the court held, after interminable arguments, that the pope had authority in those days to grant such a license, that the statutes of Richard II and Henry IV requiring vicarages did not apply to appropriations already in effect, and that in any event the statutes of Henry VIII dissolving the monasteries gave de facto as well as de jure appropriations to the king.

Another attack on impropriators was made by Laud. He tried in a number of ways to separate these men from their ecclesiastical revenues, which he and his followers considered it sacrilegious for them to have. His one strictly judicial attempt was to revive the ancient right of the bishop to augment the vicarage at the expense of the appropriator when the endowments turned out not to be enough for the vicar to live on. Laud's first step in this campaign was to attack not a lay impropriator but a church corporation, the Choristers of Salisbury Cathedral, who had a certain rectory appropriated from before the Reformation. To his great joy (and probably surprise), in the case of *Hitchcock* v. *Thornborough* (1634),[87] the common law courts refused a prohibition and let his augmentation proceeding go through.

Hill says that *Hitchcock* shows the more compliant temper of the Caroline bench, some years removed from Coke's influence and subjected to Laud's. He shows that Laud was planning to use the precedent to take on lay impropriators, and would have done so had not the unfortunate events of the 1640s intervened. I suspect, though, that Laud would have been disappointed, that even the Ship Money judges would not have given him what he asked. Conversely, it does not seem to me that *Hitchcock* said anything Coke himself would not have said if anyone had asked him.

The point of the case is that the rectory in question had never been in lay hands, and therefore had never been subject to the Henrician statute making impropriated rectories into lay hereditaments.[88] The impropriator was subject to his pre-Reformation obligations because nothing had happened to change those obligations. In the case of lay impropriators, on the other hand, the courts were faced with the conceptually exacting task of making ecclesiastical positions into lay hereditaments. Their response was as much technical as political. The view toward which they eventually worked was that fixed or measureable obligations (pensions, repairs) were carried over, whereas forms of subjection to the discretion of the bishop (augmentations) were inconsistent with the nature of a lay property right. Politics quite aside, this seems to me as professionally satisfactory as any other distinction they were likely to be offered.

C. Offices.

The office of churchwarden, on which the prelates had pinned so much of their hope for a revival of discipline, required a good deal of juridicial clarification. The common law courts, impressed no doubt with the traditional function of the churchwardens in representing the parish laity in their various economic concerns, made them a lay office, and gave them some of the attributes of a corporation.[89] The churchmen, on the other hand, who had regarded them in the Middle Ages simply as the people who showed up when the parishioners were sent for, began to treat them now as the agents of God and the bishop for improving their neighbors. Actually, the clash between the two conceptions was not as sharp as one might have expected.

The canons, as we saw, provided for the minister to appoint one churchwarden and the parishioners to elect the other. The lay courts were content to let this rule take its course unless they were shown a custom of making the choice in some other way. They even maintained the balance of power by not allowing one churchwarden to bind the parish without his colleague. Where there was a custom, though (usually it was one of the parishioners electing both churchwardens), they were strict about its prevailing over the canon. They would issue a writ of mandamus to have the men chosen in the customary way sworn in, and a writ of prohibition to stop the swearing in of anyone else.[90]

I do not find any lay interference with proceedings in the church courts to correct churchwardens who failed to do their job of reporting offenders and keeping up the fabric and furniture of the church. It does seem, though, that they were not to be held answerable in the church courts for mishandling parish property or funds. Their annual account was rendered before the minister and parishioners, and could not be reopened by higher church authorities.[91] Where the minister and parishioners were to litigate if they themselves were dissatisfied with the account was left up in the air by the cases.

Oddly enough, the office of parish clerk was more fully laicized than that of churchwarden. This office involved cleaning up the church, ringing the bells, laying out cloths and vessels for the services, and saying or singing responses after the priest. It had no fixed emoluments except by parochial custom. The vagaries of economic history had left it lucrative in a few places, but generally it was as petty as it was menial.[92] The ancestor of the parish clerk was the *aquaebajulus* (holy water carrier) of medieval documents, servant or apprentice to the mass-priest. He had received first tonsure and perhaps minor orders, and perched precariously under the umbrella of protection afforded by law to the clerical state. Generally, I suppose no one cared if the priest appointed him, but if the parishioners had enough money invested in him they probably demanded a say. A medieval canon provided that the priest should appoint him regardless of what the parishioners demanded, and that he could sue for customary offerings in the church courts.

The new liturgy did away with first tonsure and minor orders, and thereby made the parish clerk canonically a layman. But as his job was concerned entirely with the services of the church, the prelates still expected to control him. The Canons of 1604 repeated the medieval rules both as to appointment and as to payment. But the common law judges insited that the clerkship was purely a lay office.[93] Not only did they hold that a custom of election would be enforced against the canon; they at least hinted that election would be required in all cases unless a custom of appointment could be shown. For good measure, they added that the spiritual courts could not deprive the clerk of his office, even if he performed the services all wrong. By the same token, it seems they would not let him sue in the spiritual court for his wages.

A number of offices in the gift of churchmen were affected by the lay courts' insistence that they were property. The consequences of this doctrine were particularly serious in the case of ecclesiastical judgeships; it became a good deal harder than it should have been to get rid of a corrupt or incompetent judge. This was for the most part a post-Reformation problem. In the old days, the men who worked for a prelate got most of their compensation through being presented to benefices. As they had security of tenure in their benefices, they did not need security of tenure in their bureaucratic functions. But when these functions were turned over to laymen who held no benefices, it became necessary to give them security in their jobs. Life grants of offices became customary. Coke was probably right in saying that good men could not otherwise be attracted to fill them.[94]

It is not clear to me just what the reasoning process was that made the office a piece of property as soon as it was granted for life. Nowadays, we think of property as something more concrete. A person who has tenure in a position (say a professor of law) thinks of his right as cotractual. But the conception of an office as property goes back a long way.[95] In 1334 an assize of novel disseisin was entertained for the mastership of a hospital. The office of registrar of the admiralty court was dealt with in the same way in Queen Mary's time. But why the job was real estate rather than something else was never discussed; presumably the judges considered it too plain for question. My own explanation is that where a modern man thinks of his "property" as a piece of the physical world which he is free to subject in some way to his will, a medieval man thought of it more as the right to draw revenues from a specific source. So an office, with the right to collect specified fees, was not all that different from a manor, with the right to collect specified rents. In some ways, to be sure, the seventeenth-century courts were beginning to move from medieval to modern conceptions, but their view of property was still a conservative one.

Their conception of a property right made it, as I say, hard for a prelate to get rid of an official he could not work with. While the lay judges did not entirely do away with an ecclesiastical proceeding for deprivation, they allowed it to be harassed with prohibitions while it was going on, and reviewed in real property actions after it was over. They admitted that a man might be fired for not doing his job or not doing it competently, but they split over whether he might send a deputy instead of doing it himself.[96] So a bishop, for instance, could not be sure of having his consistory court actually run by the man he had chosen to run it.

This was bad enough when the bishop was stuck with a negligent or incompetent man he had himself made the mistake of appointing. But often he had to deal with men appointed by his predecessors. In one case, the predecessor had not only granted the office to one man, he had granted the succession to an eleven-year-old boy, with express permission to appoint a deputy in case he was still too young when the first man resigned or died.

A great deal of litigation came up over whether the grant of an office, being a grant of property, fell within the various statutes governing alienations of ecclesiastical property. Coke laid down in a case in 1614 that if the office was both ancient and necessary, and was granted with no more than the usual fees, it did not come within the statute of 1 Elizabeth forbidding certain alienations, because the grant of it did not diminish the grantor's revenues. Since the office was ancient, he did not diminish his ancient revenues by granting it; since it was necessary, he could not practicably augment his revenues by leaving it ungranted.[97] Coke added however that a bishop could not bind his successor unless his grant was confirmed by the dean and chapter of his cathedral (evidently because the statute of Henry VIII limiting the common law requirement of confirmation applied only to land), and that a grant for more than a single life would not bind the successor (because a longer grant was not "necessary").

I do not suppose that in dealing with ecclesiastical offices the lay courts set out to frustrate ecclesiastical efficiency. Certainly neither they nor their constituents had any stake in having the work of the church done by corrupt or incompetent men. But once they had decided that an office was real property, they had a great conceptual weight bearing down on them. Their traditional work of protecting property was not easy to square with the administrative needs of the church. In some cases they tried, but the general tendency was still for an interest protected by the common law to prevail over one protected by the canons.

III Religious Policies

As in the Middle Ages, there were cases where the interests of lay piety or public order could not adequately be served by leaving religious matters to churchmen. Even Elizabeth, committed as she was to accomplishing her ecclesiastical ends with her ecclesiastical powers, found it necessary, or at least politic, to let Parliament, the common law courts, or the justices of the peace take a hand on occasion. We have seen how the regular processes of parish poor relief were almost completely secularized in her reign. Otherwise, it was the traditional concerns that elicited most of the attention: controlling the alienation of church endowments, enforcing pious or charitable benefactions, helping to coerce the heterodox. A certain amount was done too with sexual morals, a matter on which the medieval temporal law had been not completely silent, but nearly so.

A. Alienations and Leases.

The problem of alienation was of course an old one, but the forms that it took after the Reformation were rather new. The private person complaining that lands which he or his ancestor had given for religious purposes had been given away by the grantees was no longer a significant factor in the situation. Most grants of the kind he was interested in had perished under Henry VIII or Edward VI. New benefactions, as we shall see, were generally in the hands of trustees, who had nothing to gain from selling them for cash.

So it was now the public sector in the church — bishops, cathedral chapters, colleges, parsons — that had to be kept from impoverishment. These were men who in popish times could take care of themselves, but now they were under more pressure, and had less to spare. Their temptations and their ways of succumbing (mostly long leases) I covered in the last chapter. Here I will take up the secular laws on the subject. These were complicated, and required a good deal of interpreting. How far they did the job is problematical, as we have seen.

At common law, a corporation aggregate (one with a body of members — a college or cathedral chapter usually) could freely sell off its property, so long as a proper vote was taken. A corporation sole (one-man corporation, a bishop, a dean, a prebendary, an archdeacon, a parson or vicar, etc.), on the other hand, could not alienate property beyond the time of the current incumbent without suitable confirmation. The incumbent would be bound for his own time by his own deed, but to bind his successor a bishop had to have confirmation from the dean and chapter of his cathedral, a parson or vicar from his patron and his ordinary, other incumbents from various sources.

A statute of Henry VIII (1540)[98] exempted certain ecclesiastical leases from the common law rule (along with leases by a husband of his wife's land, leases by a tenant in tail, and what have you). It provided that a lease would be binding on a successor without confirmation if it ran for not more than three lives (lives, as I said in the last chapter, of persons all living when the lease was made) or 21 years, if it was of lands customarily leased, with the customary rental reserved (note that word "reserved"; leases of certain types of property, for instance a fair, were outside the statute because you collected the rent personally from the lessee rather than "reserving" it out of the property),[99] and if it was in the lessor's possession when the lease was made (or out of possession under a former lease with not more than a year to run). Leases by parsons and vicars were specifically excluded from all this: they still had to get confirmation from patron and ordinary to bind their successors. Note that Henry's statute did not forbid or invalidate anything. It merely validated leases that met the conditions, leaving all others to stand or fall by the common law.

Two statutes were made in Elizabeth's reign, imposing more or less the same conditions *for validity*.[100] One (1559) applied to bishops, but exempted sales or leases to the crown (a favor which James gave up in 1603). The other (1571) applied to all other churchmen or church corporations — including parsons and vicars. This one did not exempt sales or leases to the crown. These statutes provided that a lease for more than three lives or 21 years (or any grant of an interest greater than a term of years), or a lease on which the customary rent was not reserved (again the word "reserved" was used) would be absolutely void. The courts interpreted this to mean void against the successor of the man who made it; the original lessor, for his own time, was still bound by his own act. Note that Elizabeth's statutes, in contrast to Henry's, were strictly *invalidating*. Compliance with them would not save a lease that was void for some other reason.

While Elizabeth's statutes adopted Henry's criterion of three lives or 21 years, they differed from Henry's in a number of details. Henry's applied only to "lands, tenements or hereditaments" whereas Elizabeth's had a more comprehensive scope. Henry's required that the land be customarily leased; Elizabeth's did not (unless the requirement that the customary rent be reserved can be interpreted to require that there be a customary rent — I have found no cases on the question). Henry's made no exception for leases to the crown, as Elizabeth's did until 1603 if the lessor was a bishop. Finally, Henry's act required that the property leased be in possession or subject to a lease with no more than a year to run. Elizabeth's statutes made no such requirement. An amending act of 1576 voided leases made where an existing lease had more than three years to run;[101] this, however, applied only to the 1571 act, so it did not cover leases by bishops.

Now, let us see where we have gotten so far. We will have to defer consideration of parsons and vicars for a moment, because we must look at yet another statute before we can make sense of their case. But we can handle most other cases by putting together the statutes just covered.

First, note that all our problems involve the successor of the man who actually made the lease. The man himself was bound by his own act, and no statute protected him. In fact, the successor might also be bound if he started accepting rent under the lease.[102]

Next, the only problem about a lease or conveyance by a bishop to the crown before 1603 was whether it had to be confirmed by the dean and chapter. All such transactions were exempted from Elizabeth's statutes. But if they were not within Henry's statute they would still not be binding unless they were confirmed.

Aside from these gifts by bishops to the crown, no grant of the freehold (fee simple, fee tail, etc.) in church lands, and no lease for longer than three lives or 21 years (e.g., four lives, thirty years) could be made under any circumstances. Elizabeth's statutes forbade them across the board.

A straightforward land lease for no more than the statutory period, and subject to the customary rent, was good under Elizabeth's statutes, and was good without confirmation under Henry's. If the thing leased, though, was not a "land, tenement, or hereditament, " Henry's statute did not apply, and the lease, though good under Elizabeth's statutes, would have to be confirmed in accordance with the rules of the common law (unless of course the lessor was a corporation aggregate). This is why all grants of offices had to be confirmed — as we saw in an earlier section. A few things, because no rent could be "reserved" on them, could not be leased at all.[103]

The most difficult problems arose when a lease was made while someone was in possession under another lease. If the lessor was not a bishop, and the old lease had more than three years to run, the new lease was invalid under the 1576 act. If the old lease had between one and three years to run, the new one would be valid if confirmed (or if made by a corporation aggregate): neither the 1576 act nor Henry's statute applied. If the old lease had less than a year to run, the new one was good without confirmation: it was exempted from the 1576 act, and covered by Henry's.

If the lessor was a bishop, the 1576 act did not apply. Arguably, therefore, the new lease would be all right however long the old one had to run (though it would have to be confirmed if the old one had more than a year left). Some judges did not like this result, and tried to interpret the 1559 act to prevent it. Coke, for instance, argued that rent could not be "reserved" under one lease while the land was possessed under a different one — the right to distrain physically for the rent being of the essence of reservation. I have found two cases, one going each way, so I cannot say how this argument came out.[104]

So much for the higher clergy. Parsons and vicars, as we have seen, were entirely omitted from Henry's act, although they were included within Elizabeth's second one (1571). Thus, a lease by a parson or vicar, even if it ran no longer than the statutory period of three lives or twenty-one years, and complied with all the other requirements of the 1571 act, would not bind a successor incumbent unless it was confirmed by the patron of the benefice and by the ordinary. Even with the necessary confirmations, the lease had a possible infirmity. There was a statute, also from 1571, for encouraging the clergy to reside. It provided that a lease of revenues belonging to a benefice with cure would be valid only so long as the lessor resided and served the cure.[105] In the case of *Mott* v. *Hales* (1588), a majority of the court seems to have held that a lease became void under this statute when the lessor died. Since the statute seems to envisage invalidating the lease as a punishment for the misconduct of the lessor, the result seems incongruous, although it is true enough that a dead man can neither reside nor serve a cure. In any event, until the *Mott* case was overruled in 1673, it must have cast doubt on whether an incumbent, even with the necessary confirmation, could make a lease good beyond his own time.

What is discouraging about all this learning is its irrationality. It was an intelligible (though hardly inspired) policy decison to permit ecclesiastical leases, subject to a time limit and the requirement of a reasonable rent. But all the distinctions between one kind of lease and another seem to rest on no sensible policy ground.

It does not seem to me that the courts were to blame. They applied the underlying policies when they could. Where the statutes permitted, they tried to uphold leases for reasonable times and steady rents, and to put down others. The court of Chancery helped by saying that where its aid was required (for instance, where the lease had been inadvertently worded in such a way as not to be valid at law) it would intervene to save a lease only if the terms were fair.[106] But most of the time the judges saw their decisions as required by the very words of the different statutes involved. Perhaps they set more store by the literal wording of a statute than some modern judges (most American and a few British) would do. But I do not think one can get out of their decisions a bias either for or against church leases.

We have here a fairly common legal phenomenon — judges trying to cope with a set of badly drafted statutes. The 1559 legislators (to be sure, they were busy with other things) should either have revised Henry's act or repeated its terminology in their own. Similarly, the 1571 act should either have repeated or changed the 1559 one (I gather the omission of leases to the crown was inadverent). Then the 1576 act should have applied to both of the previous ones instead of just one. Also, it should have picked up the one year period of

Henry's act or else changed that. Finally, the statute on leases by nonresidents should have provided that a lease was valid only so long as the lessor *or his successor* resided and served the cure. This should have been followed with a clause saving the applicability of the other 1571 act. If all this had been done, there would have been a rational statutory program for church leases. But the judges were not prepared (and I suppose they were right) to make an across-the-board revision of the statutes to do what the legislature should have done.

B. *Charities, Schools, etc.*

I have already described how systematic poor relief became secularized under the Tudors, and provision for it shifted from a charity to a tax. Particular charities, such as schools, hospitals and parish lectureships, underwent a more subtle transition. Keeping these up had always been a concurrent interest of church and state, as we saw in an earlier chapter. Now, though, the state was crowding out the church by doing a better job. This development was part of a general reshaping of equity jurisprudence in the period. The story has been told often enough, but some parts of it are still obscure.

The problem, then as now, was for the would-be philanthropist to find a suitable legal form for giving effect to his intentions. It is all very well to give your property for some religious or charitable purpose, but there have to be real people deputed to hold the land, assemble the personal property, collect the money, and do the good deeds you have in mind. In the sixteenth century, the easiest way to make a permanent provision for such people was through an existing corporation. Men came and went, but there would always be a Dean and Chapter of Lincoln. If you gave them property, you could expect them as responsible people to use it for the purposes you prescribed, and you could expect both lay and ecclesiastical authority to intervene if they did not. You could freely give or leave them property for specific purposes, and with a mortmain license (a bit expensive, but otherwise not hard to get) you could give them land. You could not directly leave them land in your will, but you might accomplish the same result by indirection.

A great many benefactions of this kind perished under Henry or Edward, either because the corporations to which they were given were monastic or because the purposes they served were done away with. But there was a good deal of property given to cathedrals, municipal corporations and guilds for schools, relief of the poor, or permitted forms of religious worship (property given for prayers or "divine worship" *simpliciter* was not subject to confiscation).[107] There were many more such donations after the Reformation. For instance, lectureships in the hands of municipal corporations and guilds played a prominent part in the seventeenth-century controversies.

Many pre-Reformation donors, however, had preferred to set up their own corporations. The founder of such a corporation could write his own statutes, and provide elaborately for the manner of carrying on the prescribed works and for the rendering of spiritual benefits to himself and his heirs. Colleges of chantry priests or of teachers and students, and "hospitals" composed of dispensers and recipients of indoor relief, were often set up in this way. Also, men often banded themselves together into self-perpetuating guilds for religious purposes such as buying candles for a given shrine, or finding a priest to celebrate an annual mass. My impression is that the church recognized these arrangements without imposing any particular formalities on them. The state required a mortmain license if the foundation was to have land. Evidently, the mortmain license also served to confer whatever corporate status was required to hold the land — the difference between a corporation and an unincorporated association was not as sharp as it became in later centuries.[108]

Many of these foundations also were confiscated in Edward's time. Those, however, that were primarily ordered to education or poor relief were preserved, and there were a good many. A good many more were founded after the Reformation. A statute of 1597 provided that hospitals of this kind for the relief of the poor (not for education or religious worship) might be freely founded by a deed enrolled in Chancery, without the necessity of a license, as long as the lands provided were worth from £ 10 to £ 200 a year.[109]

For smaller or less elaborate charities than these, there were always the parish churchwardens.[110] I gather that if anyone left money or goods for charitable purposes in a specific parish without leaving it to anyone in particular, the churchwardens — assisted, and if need be prodded, by the parish visitors — would collect the legacy and administer it. But the common law courts would not allow them to hold land — they were a corporation for some purposes but not for this one. You could leave them a rent issuing out of a piece of land (I think, but am not sure, that they would have to use the church courts to collect it from the occupier), but not the land itself.

A number of charitable purposes could be effected by the executors of a will.[111] If you left property for religious services or for poor relief, they had a good deal of discretion in using it to accomplish your purposes. There was evidently no fixed limit to how long they could go on administering your estate in the manner you provided, but of course they themselves were mortal. If you had provided for a perpetual charity, they would have to make arrangements for carrying it on. This they could do through any device you could have chosen in your lifetime. I gather it was not necessary for you to make specific provisions in your will.

A more modern device, rapidly becoming popular, was the trust. You could give (or after the Statute of Wills, 1540, leave) lands to someone (the "trustee") in trust to use them or the profits from them for a given charitable purpose. He and his heirs could either hold the lands and carry out the trust or else take out a mortmain license and form a corporation to take over. If the trustee neglected his duty, the royal Chancery would intervene (I am not sure at whose behest; I suspect that of someone entitled to benefit by the terms of the charity). Also, you could fortify your gift or devise with a condition that the charitable trust be performed; then your heir could take the land if the trustee did not perform.[112]

The trustee could not keep any of the profits for himself. In the *Thetford School* case (1609),[113] lands worth £ 35 a year had been devised to maintain a combination school and almshouse. Specific annual sums totalling £ 35 were provided for the master, the scholars, a preacher, and the poor people. The annual income over the years had risen to £ 100. The trustees proposed to spend £ 35 of this making the specified payments, and keep the other £ 65 for themselves. But the court said the increase had to be spent on augmenting the original sums.

Religious and charitable trusts ended up not being subject to the mortmain laws.[114] The original law covered only grants to corporations, or trusts which some corporation had the right to enforce. An act of Henry VIII (1532), reciting that trusts for unincorporated associations or for religious purposes were open to the same objections as grants in mortmain, made such trusts void. But in the 1590s the judges decided that this applied only to trusts for "superstitious" purposes; it did not affect trusts for education, poor relief or lawful forms of worship. It was argued at the time that reading Protestant theology into King Henry's statutes was anachronistic — a view I am inclined to agree with despite the reasoning of the court. But rightly or wrongly that is how the statute was limited. Its role in later centuries was in defining what charitable purposes were legitimate, rather than how legitimate purposes were to be given effect.

An act of 1597 (re-enacted with slight revisions in 1601, usually referred to by the latter date) produced great and sometimes unexpected changes in the uses of all these forms.[115] It empowered the lord chancellor to nominate commissioners in every diocese for the enforcement of local charities. The bishop (unless the see was vacant) and his chancellor had to be included in the commission or it was void, but they did not have to be included in the quorum. These commissioners could make inquiries by examining evidence, or by summoning special juries in the medieval manner. If they found any property, real or personal, that had been willed or granted for charitable purposes, they were to enforce the charity according to the intentions of the donor. To this end, they could make any kind of administrative arrangement they considered necessary. They could also impose restitution on anyone who had misappropriated the proceeds in the past. The only appeal from their decisions was to the lord chancellor in person (not to the Court of Chancery as such). The act did not apply to any charity for which outside visitors had been provided by the terms of its foundation. This cut out Oxford and Cambridge colleges, and most other major medieval corporate foundations. Otherwise, the commissioners were expected to make a clean sweep.

How clean a sweep they made is of course impossible to say. They were certainly active enough in the period from 1597 to the Civil War. They did most of their work by imposing trusts.[116] Where the property was in the hands of a church or municipal corporation, they would often make that corporation trustee to carry out the donor's instructions. In other cases, they would actually appoint trustees. It seems they could not set up a corporation where none existed before; nor could they empower churchwardens to hold land. But they could give land to an existing corporation without a mortmain license.

They could also validate gifts that would otherwise have failed on some technicality or other. For instance, if a tenant in tail made a gift to charity without going through the judicial rigmarole of a common recovery in order to bar the entail, the commissioners could still enforce his gift. Or a charitable devise to a corporation, ineffective under the Statute of Wills, could be given effect by the commissioners. Most important of all, a trust that would formerly have failed for lack of a definite trustee with capacity to take the property could now be made good. Thus, where a testator directed the parson, churchwardens and four honest men of a certain parish to sell his land and devote the proceeds to charity, the commissioners had his instructions carried out. Without them, the devise would have failed: the parson could not have taken the land without a mortmain license, the churchwardens could not have taken it at all, and the four honest men could not have been designated.

The statute had a great list of different kinds of charities in its preamble. This seems to have given some guidance to the judiciary in deciding what was a charitable purpose, although the list was never considered exhaustive. It was extended by the courts to cover gifts for religious purposes — all the objects listed in the preamble were secular. In this way, the preaching minister (lecturer) appointed by trustees became an important figure on the ecclesiastical scene.[117]

In enforcing religious benefactions, the judiciary put this 1597-1601 act together with Henry VIII's 1532 extension of the mortmain laws and Edward VI's 1547 act confiscating chantries. The last of these applied only to gifts made before it was enacted. But it was held that the same criteria that governed confiscation under Edward's act would govern future illegality under Henry's. So was born the doctrine, already referred to, that trusts for "superstitious" (i.e., illegal religious) purposes were void. But if the purpose was not superstitious, a religious trust was not only valid, it was protected under the 1597-1601 act. So gifts for permitted religious purposes were fully enforceable through the new machinery, and gifts for other religious purposes were void.[118]

All this doctrine and all this machinery rests on one fact that was neither more nor less true after the Reformation than before. The religious impulses of a Christian people cannot be confined within the channels prescribed by ecclesiastical authority. People founded schools, hospitals and almshouses precisely to their taste just as they had always done, with only limited ecclesiastical control. Their parish and municipal lecturers looked like something new theologically, but juridically they were friars and chantry-priests all over again. Like their predecessors, they cut in on the revenues and influence of the parish priest, they were hard to keep in order in their spare time, and they were hard to check for the purity of their doctrine.

As in earlier times, the prelates were obliged to compromise between their interest in an orderly deployment of a regular ministry and the interest of the laity in having the ministrations they wanted and were able to afford. The controls which the church preserved in this period were these:

1. The bishop and his chancellor were entitled to seats on the statutory charity commission for the diocese. This would presumably give them a chance to initiate action, though not to block it. It might also give them some influence on the way charities in the diocese were administered. How they used these opportunities, if at all, does not appear.

2. Many charities had the bishop or some other prelate as visitor. It was laid down however that in this capacity he acted under the terms of the (lay) foundation, and not in right of his office.[119]

3. However a school was founded, the masters had to be licensed by the bishop, and were subject to a few other canonical rules. My impression is that no large-scale educational effort could be mounted in this period without complying.[120]

4. All ministers were subject to the various canonical rules described in the last chapter. The bishop could not exactly control who ministered, but he could often exclude a man who violated a definite rule of law.

5. Finally, a vague feeling that a bishop was entitled to run his diocese seems to have led people to seek his cooperation or approval for arrangements they planned even where it would be hard to find a legal duty for them to do so.

But the one thing the bishop could not do — not even Laud could — was channel the available funds into the regular ministry or into other works he considered more suitable. It was always the work of the lay courts to apply lay funds.

C. Benefices and Services.

Absent a statute, the concern of the lay courts with services was limited to peripheral matters involving private rights.[121] They would enforce your right (if you had one) to have the vicar hold private services for you and your family, but not to have him hold public services in your chapel. They would decide whether a woman had to wear a veil to be churched (yes, if it was the custom), or whether a householder could have a prescriptive duty to set up food and drink for the parish rogation procession (no). They would protect an heir's right in the monuments set up in church in memory of his ancestor.

They intervened in the growing body of pew litigation only to protect immemorial prescription.[122] If a pew had always been annexed to a house, and if the occupants of that house had always made the repairs to it, the lay courts would issue prohibitions to prevent the church authorities from interfering with it, and would entertain actions on the case against anyone else who interfered with it. The right had to be ancient: a person newly established in the parish was "within the sole order and disposition of the Ordinary for his pew and seat in the church." The pew had to be annexed to a house: it could not be held in gross, nor could it be annexed to vacant land. Generally, it was only aisle seats that met these qualifications. Many aisles had been built by local squires for their own convenience (or for their own prestige), and the courts were fairly ready to treat them as private property. The main body of the church, on the other hand, was normally at the disposition of the churchwardens under the supervision of the ordinary, so that they could arrange for everyone to hear services. If you had a right to a seat there, it was canonical right with which the church courts could freely deal. By the mid-eighteenth century, it was established that even in the main body of the church immemorial possession plus repairs could annex a pew to a house and earn it the protection of the lay courts — but that point remained debatable for most of the seventeenth century.

Sometimes the employment of chaplains and curates created common law rights. A stipend assigned by the bishop was collectible in the bishop's courts, but an agreed-on wage was to be sued for like any debt.[123]

I have already shown how an act of Henry VIII gave the sanction of temporal law to the traditional lay concern with controlling pluralism and nonresidence. Like all statutes, this was applied by the lay, not the spiritual, courts. On these matters, the two systems went their separate ways. The fact that your plurality or nonresidence was permissible under the statute would not save you if it was forbidden under the canons, and vice versa.[124]

The provisions on nonresidence provided a forfeiture which a private informer could sue to collect. There were not a lot of such suits, but there was one to which Coke appended a bit of a treatise on such matters as whether you could live somewhere else in the parish instead of the parsonage (no; you had to keep up the parsonage for your successors), or whether being in prison was an excuse (yes; the law does not require the impossible).[125]

The provisions on pluralism gave rise to a brisker business. Where they were violated, the first of the two benefices involved was automatically void, and various litigations were based on the voidance.[126] There were trespass or ejectment cases brought by rival incumbents, cases of parishioners refusing tithes, *quare impedit* cases claiming lapses. A miscellany of interpretation questions came up: if you were exempted from the act, could you hold three benefices? No, only two. If you neglected to subscribe the Articles on taking your second benefice, did you lose your first? No, you were never the legal incumbent of the second. If a magnate entitled to four pluralist chaplains had five chaplains, which four could be pluralists? The first four appointed, not the first four to take pluralities. Suppose you became a pluralist first and a chaplain second? Too bad. Again, this is pretty straightforward legal work. Pluralism was a good deal of a political football in the period, but it would be hard to relate these decisions to any of the interests involved.

Simony, which had previously been of purely ecclesiastical concern, was made the subject of a statute, and therefore of lay jurisdiction, in 1589.[127] I have already taken up the main provisions of this statute, and some of the problems that arose in applying it. Like the provisions on pluralism and nonresidence, it operated alongside the canons on the same subject, without displacing them. It went beyond the canons, as we have seen, in punishing a guilty patron by taking away his right to present for that turn, and in reaching transactions where the presentee was not personally involved.

One thing the statute did not do until much later was invalidate simoniacal contracts. If I agreed, for instance, to pay you £ 100 for presenting me to a certain benefice, the statute was clear about not letting me have the benefice, but it said nothing about not letting you collect the £ 100. There was, to be sure, a general rule against enforcing a contract made to promote an illegal object, but Coke and his contemporaries seem to have applied this rule only when the illegal object was *malum in se*. Despite the scriptural denunciation of Simon Magus, they evidently considered simony *malum prohibitum*.[128]

Even if they had called it *malum in se,* they would not have helped me in the usual case where my undertaking to pay the £ 100 was embodied in a sealed instrument (bond) that made no mention of the presentment. Not until 1767 was it established that illegality not apparent on the face of the instrument could be a defense to recovery on a promise under seal.[129]

On a simple contract, I might escape through failure of consideration.[130] The consideration for my promise to pay you the £ 100 was your presenting me to the benefice. Since the statute made the presentment "utterly void, frustrate, and of none effect in law," you never effectively rendered the consideration. But this line of reasoning too was of no help if my promise to pay the money was under seal. Consideration was not necessary to make a sealed instrument effective, so failure of consideration was no defense to it.

The courts developed in the next century or so a more sophisticated approach to illegality and a less reverential approach to sealed instruments. But this formative period left as its legacy the institution of the resignation bond, which was to trouble ecclesiastical independence for the next two centuries. This was a bond executed by a presentee in favor of his patron for a large sum of money which he was to forfeit if he did not resign the benefice when the patron told him to. Through the enforcement of such a bond, of course, his canonical life tenure of the benefice was reduced to tenure during the pleasure of his patron.

The courts established, beginning in 1611, that the validity of a resignation bond depended on the use the patron made of it.[131] If he used it to insure the minister's good behavior — intending to make him resign if he failed to reside, accepted another benefice, took to drink, etc. — it was legal. It was legal also if he used it to hold the benefice for a relative — making the minister resign, say, when the patron's youngest son grew up, took orders, and was ready to be presented to the benefice. On the other hand, if the patron held the bond over the minister's head as a means of extorting money or favorable leases, he was guilty of simony.

But what should have been considered simony (and was finally held to be in 1826) was the exaction of the bond in the first place. Regardless of how the bond was subsequently used, it was something of value to the patron, and it was given him by the presentee in order to be presented. The courts in the early resignation bond cases did not consider this line of argument at all. The reason they did not, it seems to me, was that simony (or any other illegality for that matter) in the making was not at that time a defense to liability on a sealed instrument.[132]

The treatment of resignation bonds by the courts lends itself particularly well to an economic interpretation. The two uses of the bonds that were expressly held legitimate were of especial importance to the lay patrons of the time. Making the minister behave better than the decrepit canons could make him was of great concern to a godly patron, while placing relatives was of equal concern to a worldly one. Even so, I think there is a good deal of evidence to support a view that the main concern of the judges was not with patrons but with sealed instruments.

D. Conformity, Morals, and Good Order.

Most offenses against the settlement were theoretically secular as well as ecclesiastical. There were statutes that forbade using a form of service other than that in the Prayer Book, reviling the established services or the Sacrament, harboring Jesuits, seminary priests, or nonconformist schoolmasters, hearing or saying mass, executing papal process, staying away from church on Sunday, and what have you. Some of the offenses thus created were made treason or felony.[133] Some, in order to impart a medieval flavor to the proceedings against the pope, were made subject to *praemunire*. Many were visited with a sliding scale of financial penalties, often collectible by informers.

Most of this formidable apparatus existed merely on paper, however. In practice, the government was generally content to leave enforcement of the settlement to the concurrent jurisdiction of the regular ecclesiastical courts, or of the High Commission. When they wanted to deal severely with a religious dissident, they preferred to find or to trump up a secular charge like plotting to murder the queen or blow up the Houses of Parliament. Lambarde includes the whole set of religious offenses in his model inquiries for justices of the peace to use at their quarter sessions, but I do not find that they actually did anything about these offenses beyond suppressing an unlicensed schoolmaster or two, and collecting weekly or monthly fines for not going to church.[134]

I have trouble seeing why there was not enough venality in the country to produce a vigorous enforcement of those statutes that imposed money penalties collectible in part by anyone who cared to sue.[135] In some cases, the game may not have been worth the candle. Half of a forty-shilling penalty for keeping popish books would no doubt be more than used up in court fees by the time you had proved your case. But one-third of the 100-mark penalty for hearing mass, of the £ 20 a month for not attending church (this was in addition to the 12d. a week collectible by the churchwardens or the justices of the peace), or of the £ 100 for not having your child baptized in church, all seem worth litigating for. On the other hand, the informer was not a popular man, and courts or juries may have made more trouble for him than the records show. In any event, it appears that informer actions were more common in the commercial field than in the religious, that the government often intervened to stop them, that they were often brought not for lucre but for spite, and that they never made a real dent in violations of any statute they were intended to enforce.

One statute, though, that received a certain amount of enforcement for private gain was that of 1571 on subscribing the Thirty-nine Articles. This, it will be recalled, voided the benefice of any cleric who failed to comply. Without waiting for any formal deprivation, the patron could present a successor, the parishioner could withhold his tithes, anyone could put the offender's lessees out of their leaseholds. All these opportunities occasionally inspired people to take advantage of them, so that the statute made fairly frequent appearances in the courts.

In moral or religious areas not involving the settlement, there were three statutory felonies, a batch of misdemeanors, and a few matters that had no specific statutory basis, but evoked the general interest of the justices of the peace in keeping order. Most of these came in with the Stuarts, though some were earlier. The felonies were sodomy, bigamy and witchcraft; why these and no others I cannot say.[136] Sodomy was first made a felony in 1534, though Coke says people were hanged for it in the Middle Ages. The bigamy statute was new in the first year of King James; the witchcraft one was remodelled that year out of precedents going back to Henry VIII's time. The statutory crime of sodomy was about what you would expect, but the bigamy and witchcraft statutes did not either of them cover as much ground as the moral and canonical principle it implemented. If you committed bigamy, for instance, after a judicial separation from your first wife, or after she had been out of the country seven years (even if you knew where she was), your offense was purely ecclesiastical; the statute did not apply.

The witchcraft statute drew a set of distinctions that bespeak a mixture of religious and social concern. You could hang for a first offense only if you dug up corpses for your purposes, or if it appeared that you had killed or injured someone with your art or that an evil spirit had actually shown up at your bidding. If you succeeded in damaging people's goods, or if you tried (whether or not you succeeded) to inflict bodily harm, to find hidden treasure or lost property, or to provoke any person to unlawful love, it was a year in jail for the first offense, hanging for the second. If you tried only to cure sick people or animals, or to provoke someone to lawful love, you were left to the processes of the church. I do not find that this act was much enforced. Holdsworth and Maitland suggest that as there are no genuine witches you cannot convict anyone of being one without false testimony or confessions under torture. But half the things made criminal by this act involved a mere offer or attempt to exercise supernatural powers, and could be committed even if there were no such powers to exercise. Anyhow, there must have been a lot more people calling spirits from the vasty deep (whether they came or not) than were prosecuted under this act.

Turning from felonies to misdemeanors and private wrongs, we find on the whole a livelier body of law.[137] The justices of the peace, and to some extent the higher courts, were expanding their jurisidiction, or having it expanded by Parliament, to cover a number of matters which the medieval authorities had been content to leave to the church. I have already tried to show how the laws affecting usury, poor relief, and defamation were modified in this way. There are a number of other examples. Drawing or using a weapon on church premises was made a secular offense in 1552, disrupting services in 1554, perjury (insofar as it affected testimony before lay tribunals) in 1563, bastardy in 1576, eating and selling flesh meat on fishdays (still basically an ecclesiastical offense, though fishdays were now supposed to serve economic rather than devotional purposes) in 1548 and 1585 respectively, drunkenness in 1607, swearing in 1624.[138] The church retained a concurrent jurisdiction over all these offenses except perjury.

On the whole, we should not think of these extensions of lay jurisdiction as putting the state into the business of policing morals. They all supported economic, social, or administrative policies quite distinct from advancing Christian charity or moving sinners to repent. Usury and poor relief involved the financial and labor resources of a changing economy. Defamation was redressed in order to restore out-of-pocket losses, or to prevent potential disorders. Perjury was punished to protect the integrity of the increasingly complicated processes of lay administration.

Similarly, the new concern of the lay authorities with sexual offenses was pretty well limited to protecting the parish poor rates. The 1576 bastardy statute contained appropriate language about violation of divine and human laws, but what it actually provided for was relieving the parish by making the erring parents support their child. The justices of the peace in applying it tended to prefix their support orders with bits of moralizing about the detestable sin of fornication, and to supplement them with whippings (especially for the mother). But they did not actually do anything about this detestable sin unless a bastard resulted, and a poor bastard at that.

Sabbath-breaking often brought out a puritanical streak in the justices, although they had no general statutory power to deal with it. In one case, for instance, they whipped the parents of a bastard extra hard for engendering it on the way home from a Sunday dance. They had a fiddle played at the whipping to drive the lesson home. Other justices dredged up, for use on Sundays only, a set of medieval and Henrician statutes against football and other games (the original purpose of which was to discourage frivolous amusements so people would practice archery and make themselves fit to fight the French).[139] Most justices used their powers over alehouses to deal with any that stayed open in service time, and their general commission to conserve the peace to punish any Sunday merrymakers that were boisterous enough to disrupt the public tranquillity.

But despite their professed zeal for the Lord's Day, they give the impression that public order, not private morality, was their main concern. Their cases involved games and dances, usually noisy ones. I do not find them punishing Sunday labor, as the church courts did. Even the standard fines for not coming to church were more apt to engage the justices' attention if a man raised a tumult or drew a crowd than if he simply went fishing or stayed in bed.

In other areas of ecclesiastical concern also, the justices, whatever their statutory powers, would probably leave you to the archdeacon unless you went into business or made a disturbance. For instance, they enforced the 1585 statute against people who sold meat on fishdays, rather than the 1549 one against people who ate it. They were pretty faithful about enforcing King James's measures against innkeepers who let people get drunk on the premises, but the companion measures against the drunks themselves were apt to be overlooked if a man staggered home quietly and slept it off. It is drunkenness with something added — brawling, staying away from church, or even theft — that figures most usually in the reports. By the same token, the statute against using weapons in church seems to have been enforced in all kinds of cases, but that against disturbing services only where the disturbance became general or violent. Similarly, where scandal, or other things the church courts would deal with as breaches of charity, came before the justices, one can usually sense a general row, actual or potential, in the background.

The justices showed rather more restraint in these matters than their constituents did. Parish constables covered a good deal more ground in their presentments than the justices did in their indictments and orders. Still more ground was covered by the "articles" submitted from time to time by irate citizens. These would list all manner of grievances agains a particular person, which the justices would have to sift for whatever offenses they might find worth their attention. Matters thus put before the justices and not acted on included nonresidence and railing on the part of the clergy, incontinence by clergy and laity alike, defamation and harsh words of all kinds, and sometimes just general orneriness. It seems that if a man's neighbors were exasperated enough they preferred the efficient processes and corporal punishments of the justices to the citations and white sheets of the ecclesiastical courts. But the justices were generally not to be diverted from their assigned function of maintaining the economic and social order and the king's peace. The suppression of vice they continued to leave to the church.

IV Conclusion

For the common lawyers, as I have said, the Reformation settlement was a continuation of the medieval church-state dialogue on terms more favorable to the state. You can see this dialogue, as Pollock and Maitland do, as "a brisk border warfare between two sets of officials." But I have tried to show in these volumes how it reflected something deeper — a tension, basic to Christianity, between two ways of looking at the institutional church. These I have labelled High Churchmanship and Erastianism. In this terminology, the medieval churchmen took a High Church view, inherited from the Gregorian reform. They saw their rights and institutions as embodying a transcendent divine presence in the affairs of men. The laity kept up the Erastian end of the dialectic. For them, the church was but one of the institutional forms through which a Christian society pursued its ends.

Hence the more concrete differences between the two systems. The laymen were utilitarians: they saw the church as set up to do a job, whereas the churchmen were transcendental: they saw it as embodying the presence of God. The laymen were historical: they took their rules from custom and precedent, whereas the churchmen were ideological: they took theirs from first principles. The laymen were above all technical: their talk was of jurisdictions, writs and processes, whereas the churchmen were romantic: theirs was of the higher reaches of truth and justice.

The common lawyers, with this Erastian tradition, were able to play a conservative part after the Reformation. They could still see the church as set up to do a job, and, barring prayers for the dead, pretty much the same job. They still took their rules, and, as far as possible, their statutes, from custom and precedent. Their talk was still of jurisdictions, writs, and processes. Their social or political aim, if they had one, was to bring the old Erastian synthesis up to date.

In fact, there was nothing in the religious or economic changes of the period that the old synthesis could not absorb. The patronage system was intact, and its basic objective of putting a minimally qualified man into every parish was acceptable to the great mass of the people. If no one was very happy with the existing means of financing the clergy, no one was for putting them on the dole, either. Treating endowments for good or ill like any other form of property (a principle expressed by the Commons in 1406)[140] was probably everyone's second choice, and most people's first. If there was a rising middle class intent on hiring their own clergy to offer their own kind of worship, there was still nothing new about hired clergy as such.

So the new tasks imposed on the common law were in great part technical: slipping the monarch into the pope's shoes; modifying prohibition procedures for a more sensitive control over the church courts; preventing the uncontrolled diversion of church endowments; supporting approved forms of private charity; implementing the transformation of appropriated rectories into lay hereditaments, the establishment of property rights in church offices, the secularization of peripheral functions like poor relief; maintaining ecclesiastical efficiency in certain areas (e.g., pluralism, simony) where the canons were considered inadequate; keeping order while all this was going on.

Those who cast the common lawyers in an avant-garde role do so, it seems to me, because they erroneously cast the Laudians in a reactionary one.[141] It was Laud, not Coke, who wanted

To grasp this sorry scheme of things entire,
. . .shatter it to bits, and then
Remould it nearer to the heart's desire.

Laud was a High Churchman and an ideologue. He was not trying to restore the past, because the past had never conformed to his principles. His opponents knew this, even if he did not.

In any event, it was not a restoration he claimed. He wanted impropriations back not because they had once been ecclesiastical (he made no claim to the former temporal holdings of monasteries), but because they were inherently so. He wanted fixed and comfortable incomes for the clergy not because they had had them in the past (nothing in the data convinces me that the state of a seventeenth-century curate was as abject as that of a medieval one), but because they ought to be free of human respect. He tried to make tithe a full tenth of the gross national product not because it had once been so, but because God wanted it so.

The common lawyers in opposing Laud (or rather in opposing his forerunners; the game was about over by the time Laud came in) did not raise countervailing ideological arguments, as the puritans did. They simply talked about something else — property, contract, custom, above all, law — just as their predecessors had done when faced with the Gregorian claims. Only in very transitory political situations did they make common cause with the puritans. Had they faced (if we can stretch our imaginations so far) a puritan Charles and a puritan Laud, they would have mounted a very similar resistance. The people who said a bishop could not reject a presentee to a benefice for being a haunter of taverns and illegal games would not have given much support to putting a preaching minister in every parish. And considering how they treated church proceedings, they would scarcely have put up with the godly discipline.

Again, *inter arma leges silent*. The updated Erastian synthesis of the common lawyers was menaced by ideologies right and left. Had one succeeded in triumphing over the other, the whole delicate balance would have been overthrown. As it was, though, when it came to a trial of arms, the two ideologies cancelled each other out, and it was for the heirs of Coke to pick up the pieces.

Things would not have fallen out quite as they did, though, if the restored common lawyers had not found a restored church they could work with. Fortunately for the Restoration settlement, there was much in the earlier experience that left the churchmen open to an Erastian line. I showed in the last chapter how much they drew on precedent in formulating their administrative devices. Also, many of them, if they had ideological preferences, had them for some system other than the one in effect. They were prepared to accept the church as doing a job under conditions laid down by positive law. Note in this connection that the phrase "the Church of England as by law established," epitome of the Erastian view of things, comes not from a common law source but from Bancroft's Canons of 1604.

Laud and his followers, as we have seen, had little to do with the administrative structure set up by these people. They did their work through the *plenitudo potestatis* of the crown and its chosen instrument, the High Commission. With Laud and the presbyterians alike out of the picture, the old system more or less automatically came back together. When it did so, it claimed to exist not because anyone thought it ought to, but because the Interregnum acts abolishing it were no laws.

Once back in operation on these terms, the prelates were willing to collect their old tithes by old custom instead of by divine right, and to accept new powers by Act of Parliament on utilitarian grounds. With the prelates relying on custom and utility instead of divine right, the common lawyers became more receptive to the concerns of the church. Arguments based on custom and utility they could understand.

So there developed after the Restoration an Erastian synthesis acceptable alike to church and state. Both sets of officials saw themselves as harmoniously administering the salutary (if contingent) arrangements of their forefathers for the common purposes of a Christian society, under the overall supervision of common and statute law. The arrangment was beautiful; it was orderly; it was even medieval. The question is, was it Christian? If you believe, as I do, that the High-Church-Erastian dialectic is inherent in Christianity, you cannot but have misgivings about an arrangement so devoid of High Church elements as this (not that there was no High Church thinking, but it had no adequate institutional expression). The lack was not soon felt, but it finally was.

Citations

Acts of Parliament and post-medieval cases are cited in accordance with the forms generally used in legal writing. Year Book cases that appear in modern editions are cited to those editions only. Other Year Book cases are cited to the Sergeant Maynard edition by term, regnal year, and page, followed by a citation to the entry in Fitzherbert's *Graunde Abridgement,*, if there is such an entry.

The Anglican canons of 1571, 1585, and 1597, which are not numbered, are cited by year and page, the page reference being to Cardwell's *Synodalia*. The canons of 1575, 1604, and 1640, which also appear in Cardwell's *Synodalia,* are cited by canon number only. I have characterized the provisions adopted by Convocation in 1575 as canons because of their provenance, although they were referred to at the time as articles. See Cardwell, *Doc. Ann.,* 132-36n. Marchant, 129n, sets forth the reasons for assigning the great Jacobean compilation to 1603 instead of 1604. In my opinion, those reasons do not outweigh the fact that they were officially promulgated in 1604. Kemp, 159.

Visitation articles and injunctions have been cited by the name of the bishop issuing them, the year, the number (#), and the source from which I took them. Some other canonical material has been given similar treatment.

The translation of regnal years into calendar years can be done with complete accuracy only by determining exactly when during a given regnal year the event to be dated took place. For most of my material, this degree of accuracy has not seemed worth the trouble to attain it. Accordingly, where my sources have not provided me with a calendar year, I have contented myself with assigning all of any given regnal year to the calendar year in which it began.

Abbreviated citations, besides those dealt with above, are:

Ames	*Year Books of Richard II,* ed. Deiser, Plucknett, and Thornley (Ames Foundation, Cambridge, Mass., 1914-) (volumes cited by regnal year).
Bodl.	= Material in the Bodleian Library, cited by call numbers.
Brinkworth	*Acts of the Archdeacon's Court of Oxford, 1584,* ed. Brinkworth (Oxfordshire Record Soc., xxiii, xxiv, 1942-46).

Burn	R. Burn, *Ecclesiastical Law* (2 vols., London, 1763).
c.	canon, or, in statutory material, chapter.
Cal. Close Rolls	*Calendar of the Close Rolls* (H.M.S.O.)
Cal. Papal Reg.	*Calendar of Entries in the Papal Registers relating to Great Britain and Ireland* (H.M.S.O.)
Cal. Pat. Rolls	*Calendar of the Patent Rolls* (H.M.S.O.)
Cardwell, *Doc. Ann.*	*Documentary Annals of the Reformed Church of England,* ed. E. Cardwell (2 vols., Oxford, 1844).
Cardwell, *Synodalia*	*Synodalia,* ed. E. Cardwell (2 vols., Oxford, 1842).
Churchill	I.S. Churchill, *Caterbury Administration,* (2 vols., London, 1933).
Co. Inst.	Coke's *Institutes,* cited by number and original pagination.
C.S.P.D.	*Calendar of State Papers, Domestic series* (H.M.S.O.)
C.Y.S.	= Canterbury and York Society
Dedham Classis	*The Presbyterian Movement in the Reign of Queen Elizabeth as Illustrated by the Minute Book of the Dedham Classis 1582-1589,* ed. Usher (Camden, 3d ser., viii, 1905).
D.N.B.	*Dictionary of National Biography,* cited by person.
Doctor and Student	C. St. Germain, *A Dialogue between a Doctor of Divinity and a Student of the Laws of England* various editions, cited by Dialogue number and chapter.
Duke	G. Duke, *The Law of Charitable Uses* (London, 1676).
Edw. VI Inj.	"The Royal Injunctions of Edward VI, 1547," F. ii, 114-30.
F.	*Visitation Articles and Injunctions,* ed. W.J. Frere (3 vols., 1908-1910). Where no volume number appears, citations are to vol. iii.
F.G.A.	A. Fitzherbert, *La Graunde Abridgement,* various sixteenth-century editions, cited by title and number.
F.N.B.	A. Fitzherbert, *New Natura Brevium* (9th ed., Dublin, 1793).
Foster	*The State of the Church,* ed. C.W. Foster (L.R.S., xxiii, 1923).
Gabel	L.C. Gabel, *Benefit of Clergy in England in the Later Middle Ages* (Northampton, Mass., 1928).
Grindal, *Remains*	E. Grindal, *Remains* (Parker Soc., 1843).

Harison	*The Registrum Vagum of Anthony Harison,* ed. Barton (2 vols., Norfolk Record Soc. xxxii, xxxiii, 1963-64).
Hart, *Country Clergy*	A.T. Hart, *The Country Clergy 1558-1660* (London, 1958).
Hart, *The Man in the Pew*	A.T. Hart, *The Man in the Pew 1558-1660* (London, 1966).
Hill	C. Hill, *Economic Problems of the Church from Archbishop Whitgift to the Long Parliament* (Oxford, 1956).
Holdsworth	W.S. Holdsworth, *A History of English Law* (various editions).
Hughes	P. Hughes, *The Reformation in England* (3 vols., London, 1954-56).
Johnson	*A Collection of the Laws and Canons of the Church of England,* ed. J. Johnson (new ed., London, 1850-51, vol. ii).
K.	*Elizabethan Episcopal Administration,* ed. W.P.M. Kennedy (3 vols., London, 1924).
Kemp	E.W. Kemp, *Counsel and Consent* (London, 1961).
Knowles, R.O.	M.D. Knowles, *Religious Orders in England* (3 vols., Cambridge, 1956-59).
Lambarde	W. Lambarde, *Eirenarcha or the Office of the Justice of Peace* (London, 1581).
Lib. Ass.	*Liber Assisarum,* ed. Maynard (London, 1679), cited with regnal year of Edward III preceding, page following.
L.R.S.	= Lincoln Record Society
Mansi	*Sacrorum Concilium Nova et Amplissima Collectio,* ed. G.D. Mansi et al. (facsimile ed., Paris, 1903).
Marchant	R.A. Marchant, *The Church under the Law* (Cambridge, 1969).
Parker, Advts., 1566	"Archbishop Parker's Advertisements, 1566.," F. 171-80.
Peters	R. Peters, *Oculus Episcopi: Administration in the Archdeaconry of St. Albans 1580-1625* (Manchester, 1963).
Pollock and Maitland	F. Pollock and F.W. Maitland, *The History of English Law before the Time of Edward I* (2d ed., 2 vols., Cambridge, 1898).

Powicke and Cheney	*Councils and Synods, with other Documents Relating to the English Church*, ed. F.M. Powicke and C.R. Cheney (ii, 2 parts, Oxford, 1964).
Purvis	*Tudor Parish Documents of the Diocese of York,* ed. J.S. Purvis (Cambridge, 1948).
Q. Inj.	"The Royal Injunctions of Queen Elizabeth, 1559," F. 8-29.
Redman's Visitation	*Bishop Redman's Visitation, 1597,* ed., J.F. Williams (Norfolk Record Soc., xviii, 1947).
Reg. Antiq.	*The Registrum Antiquissimum of the Cathedral Church of Lincoln,* ed. Foster and Major (8 vols., L.R.S. xxvii-xxix, xxxii, xxxiv, xli, xlvi, li, 1931-58), cited by document number.
Reg. Chichele	*The Register of Henry Chichele, Archbishop of Canterbury, 1414-1443,* ed. Jacob (4 vols., C.Y.S. xlv, xlii, xlvi, xlvii, 1937-47).
Reg. Cooper	*Lincoln Episcopal Records in the Time of Thomas Cooper,* ed. Foster (L.R.S. ii, 1912).
Reg. Parker	*Registrum Matthei Parker, diocesis Cantuariensis, A.D. 1559-1575,* ed. Thompson and Frere (3 vols., C.Y.S. xxxv, xxvi, xxxix, 1928-33).
Reg. Pilkington	*The Registers of Cuthbert Tunstall, Bishop of Durham, 1530-59, and James Pilkington, Bishop of Durham, 1561-76,* ed. G. Hinde (Surtees Soc. clxi, Durham, 1952).
Reg. Pontissara	*Registrum Johannis de Pontissara, episcopi Wyntonensis, A.D. MCCLXXXI-MCCCIV,* ed. Deedes (2 vols., C.Y.S. xix, xxx, 1915-24).
Reg. Sudbury, London	*Registrum Simonis de Sudbiria, diocesis Londoniensis, A.D. 1362-1375,* ed. Fowler (2 vols., C.Y.S. xxxiv, xxxviii, 1927-38).
Reg. Sutton	*The* rolls and *Register of Bishop Oliver Sutton,* 1280-1299, ed. Hill (4 vols., L.R.S. xxxix, xlii, xliii, xlviii, 1948-54).
Reg. T. Cantilupe	*Registrum Thome de Cantilupo, episcopi Herefordensis, A.D. MCCLXXV-MCCLXXXII,* ed. Griffiths and Capes (C.Y.S. ii, 1907).
Reg. Trillek	*Registrum Johannis de Trillek, episcopi Herefordensis, A.D. MCCCXLIV-MCCCLXI,* ed. Parry (C.Y.S. viii, 1912).

Reg. Winchelsea	*Registrum Roberti Winchelsey, Cantuariensis archiepiscopi, A.D. 1294-1313,* ed. Graham (2 vols. C.Y.S. li-lii, 1952-56).
Rot. Parl.	*Rotuli Parliamentorum* . . . (6 vols., London, 1783).
R.S.	= Rolls Series. Year Books in this series are cited by regnal year, volume number and page.
S.S.	= Selden Society
Strype	J. Strype, *Annals of the Reformation* . . . (4 vols, vols. 1-3 in 2 parts each, Oxford, 1824).
Strype, *Whitgift*	J. Strype, *The Life and Acts of John Whitgift, D.D.* . . ., (3 vols., Oxford, 1822).
Tate	W.E. Tate, *The Parish Chest* (Cambridge, 1960).
V.C.H.	=Victoria Country History (followed by abbreviation of county).
Vol. I	R.E. Rodes, *Ecclesiastical Administration in Medieval England* (Notre Dame, 1977).
Wakefield Rolls	*Court Rolls of the Manor of Wakefield,* ed. Baildon, Lister and Walker (5 vols., Y.A.A. xxix, xxxvi, lvii, lxxvii, cix, 1901-45).
West Riding Sessions	*West Riding Sessions Records, 1611-42,* ed. Lister (Y.A.A., liv, 1915).
Whitgift, 1584	Whitgift, "Articles touching preachers and other orders for the church," Cardwell, *Doc. Ann.,* 466-71 (1584). Cited by article number.
Wilkins	*Concilia Magnae Britanniae,* ed. D. Wilkins (4 vols., 1737).
Winchester Cons. Ct.	*Winchester Consistory Court Depositions, 1561-1602,* ed. A.J. Willis (Hampshire Record Soc., 1960).
Woodcock	B. Woodcock, *Medieval Ecclesiastical Courts in the Diocese of Canterbury,* (Oxford, 1952).
Wood-Legh	S. Wood-Legh, *Church Life in England under Edward III* (Cambridge, 1934).
Y.A.A.	=Yorkshire Archaeological Association Record Series.
Y.B.	Year Books, ed. Maynard (11 parts, 1678-79). Cited by term, regnal year, and page.

Notes

1: The King's Crown and Dignity

1. *Rot. Parl.*, iii, 466a (1400-1).
2. The subscription to Magna Carta is from the preamble, 1225, reissued 1297. Cf. Henry V's statement opening the Parliament of 1414, *Rot. Parl.*, iv, 15a. The excommunication first appears in the statutes as 38 Hen. 3 (1253), and is reiterated at regular intervals thereafter. See *Rot. Parl.*, iv, 421a (1433) for a request by the Commons that a general excommunication be fulminated against secular wrongdoers so that those who fear no human justice may fear divine. The reference to the realm and its holy church is in id. ii, 154a (1344). For other examples of parliamentary piety, see id., iii, 540b (1403-4); 541a (1403-4); iv, 9a (1413); vi, 158b (1472-75); 188a (1477), where the Commons explore the temporal and spiritual dimensions of, respectively, failure to pay tithe, usury, money penances for adulterers, putting weirs in rivers (a violation of Magna Carta, and therefore ground for excommunication), and "Dise, Coyte, Foteball & such like Pleys." At times, to be sure, the approach became rather blatantly hypocritical. See id. iii, 421a (1399), the articles of impeachment against Richard II, and vi, 195a (1477), the death warrant of the Duke of Clarence.
3. *Rot. Parl.*, iv, 158a (1421), a preamble to a petition by the physicians against unlicensed practitioners.
4. *Rot. Parl.*, i, 219a, quoted in the preamble to the Statute of Provisors, 25 Edw. 3, St. 6, (1350).
5. *Rot. Parl.*, iii, 583a (1406).
6. For examples of clerical rhetoric, see *Rot. Parl.*, 294b (1351-52), an appeal to the memory of St. Thomas Becket, and id., iii, 177a (1383-84), the bishop of Durham's use of St. Cuthbert's body. For complaints of clerical evasion, see id., ii, 356a (1376); iii, 65a (1379). As to the government's reliance on precedent and positive law, see the royal responses to clerical petitions id., ii, 129a-130b (1341); 244a-245b (1351-52).
7. *Rot. Parl.*, ii, 373b (1376-77); cf. id., iii, 83a-b (1379-80).
8. For instance, treating prayers as feudal dues raised the problem of transferring the right to be prayed for, *Abbot of Hartland* v. *Beaupel*, S.S., xx, 164 (1310), lxiii, 281 (1311), xlv, 105 (1316); and the problem of making up arrearages, *Anon.* R.S. 33-35 Edw. 1, 262 (1306); *Anon* v. *Prior of Salisbury*, id. 489 (1307). Analogizing successive incumbents of a church office to successive heirs to a piece of land raised the problem of determining degrees of descent for writs of entry, *Adam* v. *Abbot of C.*, R.S. 20-21 Edw. 1, 412 (1292); the problem of dealing with rights and liabilities not involving land, *Codeston* v. *Prior of Tunbridge*, S.S., xvii, 65 (1308) (lord cannot take heriot on death of prior, since prior is religious and owns nothing); *Anon* v. *Abbot of St. Augustine's,*

Y.B., P.5 H. 7, 25, F.G.A., "Abbe," no. 6 (1489) (attempt to charge abbot with debt he contracted as prior of another house — no decision reported); and the problem of a hiatus in succession between the death or resignation of one incumbent and the appointment of another, *Campo Arnulphi* v. *Abbot of Tavistock,* Y.B., T. 7 E. 3, 35, F.G.A., "Abbe," no. 16, (1333) (abbot attempts, unsuccessfully, to avoid deed made by prior during vacancy of abbacy, claiming prior was not his predecessor). The analogy of successive guardians of the same ward may have served better. Holdsworth, iii, 471. On the state of medieval English corporate doctrine generally, see Pollock and Maitland, i, 486-511.

9. The two causes célèbres were that of the bishop of Worcester, who attempted to excommunicate the sheriff for usurping the bishop's right to hold certain secular pleas, *Cal Pat. Rolls, 1247-58,* 65, 68; *Cal. Papal Reg.,* i 265, 270 (1250), and that of the archbishop of York, who excommunicated his suffragan of Durham for putting a couple of archiepiscopal messengers in his secular jail, *Rot. Parl.,* i, 102a (1293). Evidently if the bishop of Durham had put the messengers in his ecclesiastical jail the archbishop would have been safe in excommunicating him, but by using his secular jail he acted as count palatine rather than as bishop. Clerical privileges respecting homage and blood judgments are established in the eleventh and twelfth of the Constitutions of Clarendon, 1164, Wilkins, i, 436. In connection with blood judgments, see *Rot. Parl.,* ii, 64b-65a (1331), where the prelates withdraw from a parliamentary discussion of criminal justice, and fulminate excommunications of wrongdoers while their secular colleagues are preparing more sanguinary measures.

10. *English Historical Documents,* ii, ed. Douglas and Greenway (Oxford, 1968), 609-626.

11. See the case of bishop Orleton of Hereford, *Rot. Parl.,* ii, 427a (1329), that of bishop Wykeham of Winchester, id., 373b (1376-77), *D.N.B.,* Wykeham, and that of the three bishops in *Rot. Parl,* vi, 250a (1483). The beheading of Archbishop Scrope by Henry IV in 1405 was an exception, but nothing much in the way of legal justification was offered for it. Translations to nominal sees were effected in the case of Thomas Rushook, bishop of Chichester, *Rot. Parl.,* iii, 274a (1389), that of Alexander Neville of York, id. 236b (1387-88), and that of Thomas Arundel, archbishop of Canterbury, id., 351b (1397). A number of licenses to accept papal provisions were issued in connection with Arundel's translation and replacement by Roger Walden, *Cal. Pat. Rolls 1396-99,* 291-2 (1398); these may have been a quid pro quo for the pope. On the accession of Henry IV, Arundel's translation was treated as a nullity, *Rot. Parl.,* iii, 434b (1399), as well as a ground of impeachment against Richard II, id., 421a. See *D.N.B.* entries for all these bishops, including Walden, for further details.

12. *Rot. Parl.,* ii, 245a (1351-52); 25 Edw. 3 St. 3, c. 6 (1350). The petition seems preliminary to the statute, despite carrying a later date.

13. For rationales, see W.E.L. Smith, *Episcopal Appointments in the Reign of Edward II* (chicago, 1938), 1, 4; *Rot. Parl,* iv, 424b (1433). For early examples of royal participation in the election process, see Wilkins, i, 404 (1122), 412 (1136); 488 (1184); 494-95 (1191-93). The case of the chapter anticipating the messenger is *R.* v. *Prior and Convent of Holy Trinity Dublin, Rot. Parl.,* i, 152b (1302). The attempt to use the *congé d'élire* to influence the outcome is in *Cal. Pat. Rolls, 1396-99,* 282 (1398).

14. *Rot. Parl.,* i, 13a (temp. Edw. I) (king intervenes with bishop on behalf of farmer of rectory because rector is king's chaplain); *Cal. Close Rolls 1296-1302,* 210, 215 (1298) (intervention on behalf of king's clerics occupying church of Axminster); *Cal. Close Rolls 1346-49,* 519, (1348) (intervention between archbishop and royal cleric occupying cathedral prebend). On discipline and residence of the king's clerics generally, see Art. Cler., 9 Edw. 2, St. 1, c. 8 (1315); *Reg. T. Cantilupe,* 126, 169,

xxvi. But see *R. v. Pickering*, S.S., lvii, 136 (K.B. 1293), where the king uses a papal dispensation to keep his clerics nonresident.

15. See *Cotes' Petition, Rot. Parl.*, ii, 45a (1330); id., iii, 116b (1381); cf. id., ii, 304a (1373) (petition that great offices of state be reserved to laymen); id., iv, 382b, 406b, 451b (1430-33) (petitions that writs of prohibition and attachment in cases involving tithes of wood be issued out of King's Bench or Common Pleas when they are refused in Chancery — denied). The cases referred to in text are, respectively, *Crosseby v. Risheton, Rot. Parl.*, ii, 17a (1328); id. 41b (1330); and *R. v. Boqueinte*, S.S. lvii, 147 (1293); Instructive on the use of benefices is *Haliwell's Petition, Rot. Parl.*, i, 418b (1324-25), where a Chancery clerk seeks a benefice on the ground he is too sick to work any longer.

16. *E.g., Cal. Pat. Rolls, 1396-99*, 283, 347 (1398); id. *1446-52*, 108 (1448). The first two grants referred to are temporary until a benefice can be provided.

17. The same principle applied where the advowson was in the king's hands due to outlawry of the owner, *Reg. Trillek*, 313, or because it belonged to an alien priory. *Cal Pat. Rolls, 1396-99*, 284 (1398). It applied also where the benefice had fallen vacant before the advowson came into the king's hands, but had not yet been filled. *R. v. Archbishop of York*, S.S., xlv, 79 (1316). It was sometimes unsuccessfully contended that the rule did not apply to vicarages because they were merely spiritual. E.g., *R. v. Prior of Pontefract*, F.G.A., "Quare Impedit", no. 178 (1325). On filling old vacancies, see *R. v. Marshal and Swain*, S.S., xliii, 38 (1313); *Reg Sudbury, London*, 26-30 (presentment in 1368; vacancy ended 1362); *Cal. Pat. Rolls, 1348-50*, 125 (1348) (presentment in 1345 based on vacancy temp. Edw. I). But this rule did not apply if the king's original possession was improper. Id., 33 (1348); *R. v. Abbot of Reading*, Y.B., M. 39 E. 3, 21, F.G.A., "Presentment al Esglise", no. 3, (1365). The 1350 limitation was adoped in 25 Edw. 3 St. 3, c.1 (repealing a three year limitation enacted 14 Edw. 3 St. 4, c. 2). In *R. v. Bishop of Coventry and Lichfield*, Y.B., M. 11 H. 4, 7, F.G.A. "Quare Impedit", no. 118, (1409), the court enforced this statute against a contention that it had never been enforced before. Cf. *Helewell's Petition, Rot. Parl*, ii, 177b (1347) for evidence of failure to enforce the earlier statute. The revocation of presentments when the king has been misinformed will be taken up below.

18. *Cal. Close Rolls, 1296-1302*, 205 (1298); id. *1346-49*, 5ll, 555 (1348); id. *1396-99*, 279 (1398). Cf. *Cal. Pat. Rolls, 1396-99*, 318 (1398), where the king takes advantage of a similar right of the archbishop of York when the archbishopric is vacant. Enforcement in the king's courts of the duty to grant such a pension is referred to in *Abbess of Dunstowe's Petition, Rot. Parl.*, i, 381 (1320). A bond conditioned on compliance appears in *Reg. Trillek*, 50. On extinguishing the pension, see *Anon.*, F.G.A, "Annuitie," no. 2 (1424) (tender and refusal); *R. v. T.F.*, Y.B., T. 7 H. 4, 16 (1405) (marriage of cleric extinguishes pension, presumably by making him ineligible for benefice). In *Anon.*, F.G.A., "Annuitie," no. 46 (1324), a benefice worth 100 marks was required to extinguish a £20 pension, and in *Anon.*, id. no. 49 (1325), a ten mark benefice was required to extinguish a £2 pension. The cleric had the burden of proof on whether the benefice offered him was too small. *Syndon v. Abbot of Malmesbury*, R.S., 20 Edw. 3, ii, 406 (1346).

19. F.N.B., 525-30, S. Wood, *English Monasteries and their Patrons in the Thirteenth Century* (Oxford, 1955), 107. There is language attributing the right to prerogative in *R. v. Prior of St. Bartholomew*, Y.B., H. 14 H. 6, 11, F.G.A., "Corodie" no. 1, (1435) and in some material referred to in F.N.B., 525. But the patronal origin seems clear from *R. v. Abbot of Colchester*, F.G.A., "Corodie," no. 5 (1339). In this case, as in *Cal. Pat. Rolls, 1340-43*, 293 (1341), the abbot made the necessary showing to escape liability. It appears that if the king was founder, the house

would be liable even if it held no land of him except in almoin. *R.* v. *Prior of M.,* F.G.A., "Corodie," no. 4 (1340). Conversely, if the house held land of the king, it would be liable even if he was not the founder. *R.* v. *Abbot of St. Oswald's,* Y.B., M. 24 E. 3, 33, F.G.A."Corodie," no. 6 (1350). Where the king held patronage rights in the right of someone else (e.g., a minor), it is not clear whether he could impose a corrody. Compare *Cal. Close Rolls, 1396-99,* 392 (1398) with F.N.B., 526n. Occasionally, the king granted away his rights. *Cal. Pat. Rolls, 1447-54,* 180 (1448). For cases where the king agreed that compliance would not set a precedent, see *Cal. Pat. Rolls, 1345-8,* 51, 201 (1348); *Cal Close Rolls, 1346-9,* 587 (1348); *Petition of Prior and Convent of St. Swithin, Rot. Parl.,* ii, 198a (1347). For examples around the turn of the fourteenth century of royal servants who had trouble getting placed, see *Cal. Close Rolls, 1298-1302,* 206, 479, 491 (John de Hibernia); 401, 405, 479 (Roger de Cestria); 402, 405, 406, 483 (Gilbert le Braconer); 402, 406 (John de Yatinden); 404, 570 (Stephen Mewe or Meu).

20. *Cal. Close Rolls, 1298-1302,* 206, 207, 211 (1298); id., *1346-49,* 500, 554 (1348); id., *1396-99,* 286 (1398); F.N.B., 95. The first of the 1348 cases is the one involving the negligent predecessor. Later on, there is talk of corrodies in specific cash amounts. *Petition of Abbot and Convent of Malmesbury, Rot. Parl.,* vi., 388b (1487). Occasionally, the king would transfer a corrody at the request of the holder. *Cal. Close Rolls, 1346-49,* 554 (1348); id., *1446-52,* 57 (1448). One man somehow came by two, and had one transferred to his brother. Id., *1396-99,* 407 (1398). One Dionysia F. had her corrody in Oseney Abbey transferred to herself and William G. jointly, perhaps as a dowry. Id., 290 (1398).

21. *Cal. Close Rolls, 1346-49,* 554 (1348); id., 420 (1347); *Rot. Parl.,* i, 58a; id. 156b (1302), respectively. The Duke of Bedford's proposal is in *Rot. Parl.,* iv, 424b (1433).

22. For examples of religious houses not subject to custody, see *Rot. Parl.,* i, 80b, 89b (1292) (Chester); *Cal. Close Rolls, 1346-49,* 439 (1348) (Quarr); id., 441 (1348). On Rochester, see Churchill, i, 279-87. Included among the temporalities were a few odd rights, such as that of the archbishop of York to impose a clerical pension on a new abbot of St. Mary's. *Cal. Pat. Rolls, 1396-99,* 318 (1398). On royal custodians taking spiritual revenues, see, e.g., *Reg. Pontissara,* 774-75; *Rot. Parl.,* i. 425a (1324-25); id., ii, 439a (temp. Edw. III).

23. *Rot Parl.,* i, 372b (1320); id., iii, 22a (1377). See *Vetus Liber Archidiaconi Eliensis,* ed. Feltoc and Minns (Cambridge Antiq. Soc., 1917) pp. xxiv-xxv on the bishop's right to correct the archdeacon's official while the archdeaconry is in the king's hands.

24. See *Abbot of Burton-on-Trent* v. *Escheators, Rot. Parl.,* i, 195b (1306), where two sets of escheators entered the abbey lands, and *Abbot of Bardney's Petition,* id., 323a (1314-15), where the abbot has trouble getting rid of the escheators when his deprivation is reversed in Rome.

25. For correspondence related to this measure, see *Reg Trillek,* 260, 284, 337 (1346-52).

26. Knowles, R.O., i, 273. On commutation and its effects, see *Rot. Parl.,* ii, 390a, 397b (temp. Edw. III); *Cal. Pat. Rolls, 1348-50,* 103 (1348); id., *1396-99,* 290, 406 (1398); id. *1446-52,* 209 (1448); id. *R.* v. *Abbot of Reading,* Y.B., M. 39 E. 3, 21, F.G.A., "Presentment al Esglise," no. 3,(1365).

27. *Cal. Pat. Rolls 1446-52,* 279 (1448).

28. E.g., *Cal. Close Rolls, 1346-9,* 474 (1348); *Cal. Pat. Rolls, 1396-9,* 405

(1398), involving nominal priories, and *Rot. Parl.*, ii, 302a (1369); id., 342a (1376); id.
iii, 213b (1385), involving conventual priories. As for rents, Steventon Priory, valued in
1294 at £99 11s. 9d. temporalities, and tithes averaging £20, was farmed at not less
than £70. *Cal. Close Rolls, 1346-49,* 445 (1348). These rents, to the extent they
exceeded the payments formerly made to the motherhouses, were remitted in 1401. *Rot.
Parl.*, iii, 469a. Escape from alien status was generally accomplished either by a papal
exemption from the authority of the motherhouse, *Petition of Prior of Montagu, Rot.
Parl.*, iv, 27a (1414); *Cal. Pat. Rolls, 1446-52,* 279 (1449), or by a transfer of the
latter's rights to an English house, id., *1396-9,* 348, 352, 374 (1398); *Cal. Close Rolls,
1447-54,* 64 (1448); *Rot. Parl.*, iv, 13a (1413). Evidently, either of these steps required
a royal license.

29. *Reg. Sutton,* xix-xx; *Reg. Winchelsea,* x-xvi.

30. *Reg. Chichele,* iii, 97. For examples of the various maneuvers described in text,
see id., i, cxxv (prorogation); *Reg. Trillek,* viii-ix; 18 Edw. 3, St. 3, c. 1 (1344); *Rot.
Parl.*, v, 152b (1449) (concession); id., iii, 90a (1380), 168a (1383) (conditional
grants).

31. *Rot. Parl.*, 128b (1381-82); *Prior of St. Catherine's* v. *Rector of Springthorpe,*
S.S., lviii, 106 (K.B. 1301).

32. This, and the following two paragraphs, where not otherwise documented, are
based on Kemp., 120-34.

33. E.g., *Cal. Close Rolls, 1346-49,* 427 (1348); *Cal. Pat. Rolls, 1446-52,* 157
(1448); *Rot. Parl.*, ii, 86a (1334).

34. *Rot. Parl.*, vi, 418a.

35. *Rot. Parl.*, ii, 163b (1346), iii, 24b (1377), 651a (1411); id., ii, 130b (1341);
419b (temp. Edw. III); *Cal Close Rolls 1346-9,* 434 (1348).

36. The Statute of Westminster II, 13 Edw. 1, St. 1, c. 24 (1285) extended the lay
jurisdiction to this hypothetical case also. Cf. *Anon.*, Y.B., M. 19 H. 6, 7, F.G.A.,
"Jurisdiction," no. 7 (1440).

37. Art. Cler., 9 Edw. 2, St. 1, c. 1 (1315). Some versions of *Circumspecte Agatis,*
13 Edw. 1, St. 4 (1285) contain similar language. But a case dated 1228 seems to permit
the church suit. *Anon.*, F.G.A., "Prohibicion," no. 20.

38. *Anon.*, F.G.A., "Attachement sur Prohibicion," no. 8 (1363); *Anon.*, F.G.A.,
"Prohibicion" no. 21 (1235).

39. Note, 22 Lib. Ass., 70 (1347).

40. Pollock and Maitland, ii, 185-98; Woodcock, 89-92; Helmholz, "Assumpsit and
Fidei Laesio," *L. Q. Rev.*, xci (1975), 406; Note, 22 Lib. Ass., 70, F.G.A.,
"Prohibicion," no. 2 (1347); Note, Y.B., P. 38 H. 6, 29, F.G.A., "Prohibicion," no.
6 (1459). In 1410, the Commons sought unsuccessfully to impose a criminal penalty for
holding these suits. *Rot. Parl.*, iii, 645b.

41. *Rot. Parl.*, i, 207a, 219a-220b (1306); 38 Edw. 3, St. 1, c. 4 (1363); see *Dean of
Windsor* v. *Vicar of Saltash,* Y.B., M. 2 H. 4, 9, F.G.A., "Consultacion,"
no. 3 (1400).

42. *Anon.*, Y.B., T. 11 H. 4, 88, F.G.A., "Attachment sur Prohibicion," no. 4,
"Prohibicion," no. 12 (1409); Note, F.G.A., "Consultacion," no. 2 (1481).

43. *Anon.*, Y.B., M. 8 E. 4, 13, F.G.A., "Prohibicion," no. 9 (1468); F.N.B., 97
G, 102 K; see the discussion in *The Case De Modo Decimandi,* 13 Co. Rep. 36, 77
Eng. Rep. 1448 (1610). On other questions of tithability, see note 81 *infra.*

44. *Circumspecte Agatis,* 13 Ed w., 1, St. 4 (1285); Art. Cler., 9 Edw. 2, St. 1 c. 2
(1315). On the writ of *indicavit,* see F.N.B. 105; Burn, ii, 615. If your suit was stopped
by an *indicavit,* your patron could bring a writ of right of advowson concerning the
tithes in issue, and you could resume your church suit if he won. Statute of Westminster
II, 13 Edw. 1, St. 1, c. 5 (1285). For more discussion of these matters, see *William* v.

John, Y.B., T. 8 E. 3, 49, F.G.A., "Attachment sur Prohibicion," no. 11 (1334);
Anon., Y.B., H. 38 H. 6, 19, F.G.A., "Consultacion," no. 1, "Indicavit," no. 2
(1459); *Boteraux* v. *Official and Commissaries of the Bishop of Exeter,* Y.B., P. 31 H.
6, 13, F.G.A., "Indicavit," no. 1 (1452). The last of these raises the question whether
a vicarage is to be valued separately from its rectory in applying the one-fourth rule.

45. On the collection process generally, Burn, ii, 439-41, can be applied to the
period under consideration with only minor changes. *Abbot of T.* v. *Parson of C.,*
F.G.A., "Jurisdiction," no. 58 (1439) is a typical example of a trespass case in which
the lay court denied jurisdiction. Cases where the court took jurisdiction because the
right to tithe turned on a matter of secular law include *Anon,* Y.B., H., 5 H. 5, 10,
F.G.A., "Jurisdiction," no. 39 (1417) (parish boundary); *Parson of Stoutle* v. *Parson
of Saltmarsh,* Y.B., T. 50 E. 3, 20, F.G.A., id. no. 15 (1376) (same); *Provost of C* v.
Anon., 22 Lib. Ass., 75, F.G.A., "Jurisdiction," no. 31 (1348) (royal grant). My
guess, based on the material cited *supra,* note 44, is that the lay court would not accept
jurisdiction of a trespass case merely on the ground that the tithes in issue amounted to
more than one-fourth of the value of the benefice. Note that even if the right to tithe was
in issue, the court would entertain jurisdiction if the actual grain had been converted
back into lay chattel by a sale. *J.* v. *Constable* Y.B., P. 42 E. 3, 12, F.G.A.,
"Jurisdiction," no. 47 (1368). Cases where the right to tithe was not in issue include:
Parson of Chesterton v. *Prior of Huntingdon,* S.S., xx, 40 (1310) (location of incident);
Prior of J. v. *Strade,* Y.B., M. 39 H. 6, 20, F.G.A., "Quare Impedit," no. 96 (1460)
(who is parson of church to which tithes belong).

46. 1 Ric. 2, c. 14 (1377); see the clergy's request, *Rot. Parl.,* iii, 358b (1376). For
an example of the earlier practice, see *Abbot of S.* v. *Parson of E.,* S.S., xvii, 36
(1308). On applying the statute to the churchman's servant, see *Abbot of Chichester* v.
Anon., Ames, 13 Ric. 2, 32 (1389); *Anon.,* Y.B., M., 31 H. 6, 11, F.G.A.,
"Jurisdiction," no. 10 (1452); but see *Abbot of Osney* v. *Anon.,* Y.B., M., 1 H. 6, 5,
F.G.A., id. no. 1 (1422).

47. *R.* v. *Prior of Fortham,* Y.B., M. 44 E. 3, 31, F.G.A., "Attachment sur
Prohibicion," no. 6 (1370); *Anon.,* Ames, 12 Ric 2, 63-4 (1388); *Abbot of Sawtry* v.
Netherstrete, Ames, 13 Ric. 2, v, 84 (1389).

48. *Anon.,* Y.B., M. 10 H. 4, 1, F.G.A., "Attachment sur Prohibicion," no. 12,
"Premunire Facias," no. 13 (1408); *Adam* v. *Parson of C.,* R.S. 21-2 Edw. 1, i, 588
(1294).

49. *Anabilia, Recluse of Donecastre* v. *Abbot of Roche,* Y.A.A., xvii, 184 (1289)

50. 13 Edw. 1, St. 1, c. 25(3) (1285).

51. On the ambiguous status of pensions, compare Note, Y.B., H. 20 H. 6, 7,
F.G.A., "Collusion" no. 23 (1441) (pension not subject to Mortmain Act, as not charge
on land) with *Prior of Hospital* v. *Abbot of St. Edmund,* R.S., 20 Edw. 3, ii, 90 (1346),
where seisin is talked about and an analogy drawn to rent-charge. On lay jurisdiction,
patronage rights and the requirement of a lay contract, see *Ry* v. *Dean and Chapter of
Lincoln, Rot. Parl.,* ii, 193b (1347); *Prior of Bermondsey* v. *Parson of Fyfield,* R.S., 16
Edw. 3, ii, 550 (1342). The churchmen's requests of 1376-77 appear in *Rot. Parl.,* ii,
358a, 373a, iii, 26b. The provision of *Circumspecte Agatis* referred to in text is 13 Edw.
1, St. 4 (6) (1285), and the case where the prelates are said to have made *Circumspecte
Agatis* themselves is *Bishop of Winchester* v. *Archdeacon of Surrey,* R.S., 19 Edw. 3,
289 (1345). Considerations somewhat similar to those involved in the pension cases
come up in *Bishop of Norwich's Executors* v. *Wath,* R.S., 19 Edw. 3, 95 (1346), where
an action to recover first fruits is held to be outside the lay jurisdiction.

52. Respectively, *Berewyk* v. *Brembre,* S.S., xxvi, 9 (1311); *Clopton* v. *Pewer,*
Y.B., T. 39 E. 3, 15, F.G.A., "Dowere," no. 35 (1365). An exception might be made,

though, if the question was too esoteric for a lay jury. *Bradford* v. *Abbess of Winchester*, 38 Lib. Ass., 29 (1364).

53. Cases where alleged bastard is not a party: *Anon.*, S.S., lxi, 149 (1317); *Asshewell* v. *Stanes*, S.S. xvii, 95 (1308-9); *Anon.*, R.S., 20-21 Edw. 1, 190 (1292); *Pontyngdon* v. *Courtenay*, *Rot. Parl.*, iii, 489b (1402). Assize cases: *Anon.*, 38 Lib. Ass., 24, F.G.A., "Trial," no. 82 (1364); *De Hodie* v. *Delto*, 38 Lib. Ass. 30, F.G.A., "Trial", no. 83 (1364). Two curiously identical cases from the same year, 1365, suggest that a bastard might make the best tenant from the seigneural point of view; for if he died without issue, the land escheated without the necessity of considering the possible claims of other heirs. *John Osborn's Assize*, Y.B., M. 39 E. 3, 29 (1365); *J. de B.* v. *Prioress of N.*, 39 Lib. Ass., 7 (1365).

54. Annulment: Pollock and Maitland, ii, 376-77; *Anon.*, F.G.A., "Bastardy," no. 21 (1301); *Bliont* v. *Anon.*, S.S., lxi, 262 (1317); Cf. *Anon.*, 39 Lib. Ass., 10, F.G.A., "Bastardy," no. 18 (1365), where lay court refuses to recognize annulment because of inadequate procedure in church court. Marriage after child born: *Soard* v. *Anon.*, Y.B., T., 11 H. 4, 84 F.G.A., "Bastardy," no. 6 (1409); *Bingham* v. *Bingham*, 11 Lib. Ass., 20, F.G.A., "Bastardy," no. 12; W.C. Bolland, *Chief Justice Sir William Bereford*, 22-3 (Cambridge, 1924). Adultery: *John T.* v. *Robert*, Y.B., M., 39 E. 3, 31, F.G.A., "Trial" no. 41 (1365). In this and the previous case, it was noted that once the bishop responded to the court's inquiry it was too late to complain that his decision violated secular law. *Anon.*, Y.B., 39 E. 3, 14, F.G.A., "Bastardy," no. 8 (1365); *Coates* v. *Bingham*, Y.B., P. 17 E., 3, 28, F.G.A., "Certificate," no. 4 (1343).

55. The bishop's judgment could evidently be avoided in a later suit by an express allegation that the person in question was born before the marriage of his parents, see cases cited *supra* note 54, but not by a general allegation of bastardy. Note. F.G.A., "Trial," no. 23 (1330). On collusive suits, see *Rot. Parl.*, ii, 171a (1347). 9 Hen. 6, c. 11 (1430), besides making special provision for a particularly notorious case involving the inheritance of the earl of Kent, required for the future that public proclamation be made at the suit of any party before a question of bastardy was sent to the ordinary, so other interested parties could appear. Since this applied only when a party to the original proceeding requested it, it is hard to see how it helped where the original proceeding was collusive.

56. Forbidding ecclesiastical appeal: *Succession of William of Monte Canis*, *Rot. Parl.*, i, 16b, 38b, 84a (1290). Forbidding independent ecclesiastical proceeding: Burn, i, 92; cf. *Corbet* v. *Corbet*, F.G.A., "Consultacion," no. 5 (1483) (widow brings prohibition against jactitation suit by brother-in-law); *Ludgate's Case*, *Rot Parl.*, i, 49b (1290) (man attempts to defend legitimacy of son).

57. *Anon.*, F.G.A., "Prohibicion," no. 13 (1218); *Anon.*, S.S., xvii 39 (1308) (where a local custom gives decedent's children rights in his chattels, lay courts will enforce those rights against the executors); *Thyke* v. *Fraunceys*, S.S., lxiii, 240 (1311) (suit by married woman's executor).

58. 13 Edw. 1, St. 1, c. 19 (1285); 31 Edw. 3, St. 1, c. 11 (1357); *Anon.*, F.G.A., "Prohibicion," no. 17 (1220); *Anon.*, id. no. 28 (1220). The modern rule is that probate courts and courts of general jurisdiction have concurrent jurisdiction over these cases.

59. The statute denying dower to the adulteress is 13 Edw. 1, St. 1, c. 34 (4) (1285). See *Paynel's Petition*, *Rot. Parl.*, i, 146a (1302). On manor court practice, see *Select Pleas in Manorial Courts*, ed. Maitland (S.S. ii, 1889), 12, 97, 98; *Wakefield Rolls*, iii, 10, 95, 108, 113, 122; iv, 33, 53, 185; v, p. vi. On the Star Chamber, see *Dyon* v. *Sotheby*, *Yorkshire Star Chamber Proceedings* (4 vols, Y.A.A. lxi, lxv, li, lxx (1909-27), i, 118; *Delaryvar* v. *Barton*, id., ii, 67 (c. 1521); *Rooke* v. *Rooke*, id., iv, 36 (1523-24); Leadem, "Introduction" *Select Cases in the Star Chamber*, S.S., xvi,

pp. cx-cxiv.

60. *Anon.*, Y.B., 1 H. 7, 6 (1485).

61. Art. Cler., 9 Edw. 2, St. 1, c. 3, 4, (1315); *Anon.*, Y.B., T. 11 H. 4, 88, F.G.A., "Attachement sur Prohibicion," no. 4 (1409); *Anon.*, Y.B., M. 7 H. 4, 1, F.G.A., "Prohibicion," no. 10 (1405).

non., Y.B., M. 7 H. 4, 1, F.G.A., "Prohibicion," no. 10 (1405).

62. I Edw. 3, St. 2, c. 11 (1327). For a prohibition founded on this principle, complete with rhetoric, see *Reg. Trillek*, 323-4 (1349).

63. 11 Hen. 7, c. 8. The Commons tried to get the government to act earlier. *Rot. Parl.*, iii, 541a (1403-4) (petition against alien brokers); cf. *Clernans* v. *Appleby*, id., i, 46b (1290) (individual suit against usurer, referred to church courts). For the London custom, see id., iii, 142b (1382). For the case of the dead usurer, see id., ii, 129a-130b (1341); 15 Edw. 3, St. 1, c. 5 (1341).

64. On coerced marriage, see Leadem, *supra*, note 59. On coerced resignation, see *Draiton* v. *Veer, Rot. Parl.*, i, 376a (1320); *Stokes' Case*, id., iii, 444b (1399).

65. Art. Cler., 9 Edw. 2, St. 1, c. 6 (1315).

66. *Shiraks* v. *Archbishop of York*, Y.B., M., 8 E. 3, 69, F.G.A., "Excommengement," no. 2 (1335); *Draiton* v. *Veer, Rot. Parl.* i, 376a (1320), 2 Hen. 5, St. 1, c. 3 (1414); *Peckham* v. *Winterburne*, Y.B., M., 4 E. 4, 37, F.G.A., "Prohibicion," no. 8 (1464).

67. *Friars Preachers of London* v. *Abbot and Convent of Hyde, Rot. Parl.*, ii, 186b (1347); cf. *Paunton* v. *Bishop of Ely*, S.S., lxiii, 123 (1311), a *quare impedit* proceeding where the bishop is treated as a disturber on account of the delays he imposes in his own court.

68. The diocesan official: *Warkwickshire and Coventry Sessions of the Peace, 1377-97*, ed. Kimball (Dugdale Soc. xvi, 1939), 96-7. The dean: *Some Sessions of the Peace in Lincolnshire, 1381-96*, ed. Kimball (L.R.S. xlix, 1955), p. xlviii. The same dean frightened another man away from his home, to his lord's damages of £10. The man who cited his opponent in three places: *Butiller* v. *le Wronge*, S.S., lxiii, 121 (1311). The multiple citations seem to have been treated as a separate wrong from usurping the royal jurisdiction over trespass cases. For a complaint about blank citations, see *Rot. Parl.*, ii, 319a (1373). See also Vol. I, 138.

69. *Whytine* v. *Vicar of Blyth*, S.S., lviii, 95 (K.B. 1300) (conspiracy). On the general availability of remedies, see the royal responses in *Rot. Parl.*, i, 60b (1290); ii, 142b (1343). On the commissions of the peace, see 18 Edw. 3, St. 3, c. 6 (1344); 25 Edw. 3, St. 3, c. 9 (1350); 31 Edw. 3, St. 1, c. 4 (1357); *Rot. Parl.*, iii, 83a (1379-80); note 68 *supra*.

70. 3 Hen. 5, St. 2, c. 8; *Rot. Parl.*, ii, 171a (1347), 313a (1372), iv, 8b (1413). Archbishop Chichele's constitution on the subject, Wilkins, iii, 377 (1415) may have done enough good to prevent the renewal of the 1414 statute. The 1341 complaint of the clergy is in *Rot. Parl.*, ii, 129a-130b, 133a. The royal reply in id., iii, 43b (1378) seems to envisage a secular remedy already existing. To the same effect as to fees for admission of clerics into benefices, see id., ii, 352b (1376). Presumably, if the ordinary refused admission because an excessive fee was not forthcoming, he would be liable to the patron in *quare non admisit*. On citing people at a distance, another source of complaint, see *Rot. Parl.*, iii, 43b (1378), 163b (1383), iv, 8b (1413).

71. General writs: *Reg. Trillek*, 365 (1356); *Cal. Pat. Rolls, 1348-50*, 152 (1348); *Cal. Close Rolls, 1396-99*, 354 (1398). Law itself: *Anon.*, Y.B., M. 21, E. 3, 38, F.G.A., "Attachement sur Prohibicion," no. 13 (1347); Note, F.G.A., id. no. 15 (1385). Chancery writs: *Brevia Placitata*, ed. Turner (S.S. lxvi, 1947), 62, 170; F.N.B., 94E; *Reg. Trillek*, 323-4 (1349); See the clerical complaint in *Rot. Parl.*, ii, 151a (1344).

72. *Rot. Parl.,* iii, 26b.

73. *Parson of Phillingham* v. *Abbot of Blanka Landa, Rot. Parl.,* i, 53b (1290). The routine procedure for the writ of consultation was established by ordinance the same year. id., 32b, 47b. The 1296 statute is 24 Edw. 1. Bracton's discussion of the earlier practice is in *De Legibus,* ed. Thorne (Cambridge, Mass., 1977), iv, 262.

74. An exception was made when a consultation was sought after an *indicavit* on the ground that the tithes in issue in the church court were worth less than one-fourth the value of the benefice. The chancellor would put the question to the bishop, and issue the consultation in accordance with his reply. F.N.B., 119L: *Anon.,* F.G.A., "Prohibicion," no. 1 (1465).

75. In *Lincoln* v. *Herion,* S.S., lxiii, 120 (1311), plaintiff claimed £20 damages for a suit over a £5 debt. In *Butiller* v. *Le Wronge,* S.S., lxiii, 121 (1311) plaintiff recovered £100. On lifting the excommunication, see *Walker* v. *Lavers,* Y.B., T. 7 E. 4, 14, F.G.A., "Excommengement," no. 16 (1467). On the necessity of showing special damages in an attachment, see *Spigurnel* v. *Bishop of Ely,* Y.B., T. 28 E. 3, 18, F.G.A., "Attachement sur Prohibicion," no. 10 (1354). The king may have been entitled to a fine as well. See F.N.B., 95F.

76. On the law itself as a prohibition, see note 71, *supra.* The same argument was rejected in *Anon.,* Y.B., H. 9 H. 6, 61, F.G.A., "Attachement sur Prohibicion," no. 2 (1430). The argument that even though the plaintiff was entitled to proceed in the church court he should have sought a consultation before doing so seems to have prevailed in *Anon.,* F.G.A., id., no. 14 (1359). But *William* v. *John,* Y.B., T. 8 E. 3, 49, F.G.A., id., no. 11 (1334) seems to consider the merits even though a prohibiton was taken out and no consultation issued. The language of *Circumspecte Agatis (In omnibus istis casibus habet judex ecclesiasticus cognoscere regia prohibicione non obstante)* seems to support the latter approach. I do not know what to make of Note, F.G.A., "Prohibicion," no. 22, as it carries a date of 15 H. 3 (1230), but refers anachronistically to suing out a consultation. On the suspicionsness of citations to the reign of Henry III in Fitzherbert, see Bolland, *The Year Books* (Cambridge, 1921), 7-8. Consultations are attacked in *R.* v. *Prior of Fortham,* Y.B., M. 44 E. 3, 31, F.G.A., "Attachement sur Prohibicion," no. 6, "Ley," no. 34 (1370); *Frankley* v. *Heyning,* Y.B., H. 50 E. 3, 10, F.G.A., "Attachement sur Prohibicion," no. 7 (1376); *Anon.,* F.G.A., "Prohibicion," no. 1 (1464). See the clerical complaint in *Rot. Parl.,* ii, 357b (1376), which refers also to the practice of taking out a second prohibition after a consultation is given on the first.

77. On jury verdicts, see Pollock and Maitland, ii, 629-31. As for wager of law, it is not clear when this form of trial was permitted on an attachment. In *Butiller* v. *le Wronge, supra,* note 75, it was denied because of the heinousness of the offense. It was allowed in *Lincoln* v. *Herion, supra* note 75, and in *Clerbeck* v. *Bishop of Lincoln,* S.S. xxvi, 97 (1311). In *R.* v. *Prior of Fortham,* and *Frankley* v. *Heyning, supra,* note 76, defendant offered to wage his law, but thought the better of it. In *Anon.,* Y.B., H. 24 E. 3, 39, F.G.A., "Ley", no. 62 (1350), the commentator is surprised that defendant was allowed to wage his law. In *J. King* v. *Anon.,* R.S., 17-8 Edw. 3, 466, F.G.A., "Ley" no. 77 (1344) Fitzherbert reports that wager of law was permitted, while the Year Book reports the opposite. The suggestion that the court record be consulted appears in *Rot. Parl.,* i, 293a (1314-15). This subject is developed more fully in Helmholz, "The Writ of Prohibition to the Court Christian before 1500," *Mediaeval Studies,* xliii (1981), 297, which appeared too late for me to use it.

78. *Rot. Parl.,* iii, 357b-358b, 373a-b, iv, 27a (1376-77). Cf. *Reg. Pontissara,* 772.

79. The royal courts evidently claimed a general power to have anyone absolved who was excommunicated in violation of the king's rights. Art. Cler., 9 Edw. 2, St. 1, c. 7 (1315). But I find no indication that they used it except as a form of ancillary relief

in an attachment proceeding.

80. The Commons' complaint about poverty is in *Rot. Parl.*, iii, 645b (1410). A request to use ecclesiastical censures against vexatious prohibitions appears in *Reg. Pontissara*, 775; *Rot. Parl.*, iii, 358b, par. 200 (1376). The general canon law forbade any use of lay process to stop ecclesiastical proceedings. Archbishop Pecham attempted to enforce this principle in a set of statutes adopted in 1279, but he was forced to back down. *Rot. Parl.*, i, 224b (1279). But a Chancery clerk ran afoul of the canonical principle in 1328, and had to be rescued by the king. *Crosseby* v. *Risheton, Rot. Parl.*, ii, 17a (1328). And in 1315 a parson was unwilling to be named as plaintiff in an attachment suit. *R.* v. *Bray*, S.S., xli, 197 (1315). The constitution *Accidit novitate perversa* of Archbishop Stratford, Wilkins, ii, 707, Johnson, ii, 397 (1342) contains a sweeping denunciation of vexatious interference with ecclesiastical proceedings, including vexatious use of royal process. It was evidently enforced on occasion despite the lack of permission form the king. Helmholz, "Writs of Prohibition and Ecclesiastical Sanctions in the English Courts Christian," *Minn. L. Rev.*, lx (1976), 1011. The London ordinance referred to in text appears in *Rot Parl.*, i, 282b (1312).

81. *Frankley v. Heyning, supra*, note 76; *Rot. Parl.*, ii, 142b (1343); iii, 43b (1378); 470a (1400-1); iv, 382b (1430). The statute 45 Edw. 3, c. 3 (1371) does nothing much to clear up the situation described in text — it says there is to be a prohibition where tithes of great wood are demanded under the name of *silva cedua*. For other, less serious, tithe complaints, see *Rot. Parl.*, ii, 370a (1376-7) (coal), iii, 474a (1400-1) (agistments), 540b (1403-4) (rocks and slates), 591b (1406) (same). In all cases, the principle is affirmed that tithe is to be taken only if customary, but no remedy other than prohibition is afforded.

82. Pollock and Maitland, ii, 517; *Petition of de Turville*, S.S., lvii, 80 (K.B. 1292); *Crosseby* v. *Risheton, Rot. Parl.*, ii, 17a (1328); *Crochille's Petition, Rot. Parl.*, ii, 178a-b (1347); *Cal. Pat. Rolls, 1348-50*, 70, 153, 169, 239 (1348). For an example of the elusiveness of such persons, follow the affairs of Nicholas Hethe, would-be prebendary of Hunderton: *Reg. Trillek*, 44, 326, 328, 336, 354, 356; *Cal. Pat. Rolls, 1348-50*, 310, 313 (1350); id., *1350-54*, 178, 189, 198, 206 (1351), 207, 224, 277-78 (1352), 418 (1353), id., *1354-58*, 513, 635, (1357).

83. 25 Edw. 3, St. 6 (1350); 27 Edw. 3, St. 1, c. 1 (1353). On the sanctions under the Statute of Provisors, see *Derling* v. *Eymar, Rot Parl.*, iii, 482b (1400-1). The remedies provided in both these statutes were available only in special proceedings. *R.* v. *Kemp*, Y.B., M. 27 H. 6, 5, F.G.A., "Praemunire Facias," no. 3 (1448) (*praemunire* proceeding cannot be begun by bill); Note, F.G.A., id. no. 1 (1424) (relief under Statute of Provisors cannot be given in *quare impedit* proceeding). For an outlawry imposed under the Statute of Praemunire, see *Anon.*, Y.B., H. 43 E. 3, 6 (1369) F.G.A., "Praemunire Facias," no. 7. On the question of whether the principal must be convicted under that statute before the accessories are tried, see *R* v *Anon.*, F.G.A., id. no. 9 (1356); *Anon.*, F.G.A., id. no. 12 (1385).

84. F.G.A., "Attachement sur Prohibicion," no. 12 (1407) is a *praemunire* case.

85. *Anon.*, Y.B., M. 5 E. 4, 6, F.G.A., "Praemunire Facias," no. 5 (1465); *Reg. Chichele*, iii, 283-4 (1439). Cf. Waugh, "The Great Statute of Praemunire," *Eng. Hist. Rev.*, xxxvii, 173 (1922). Yelverton evidently thought it applied also to a suit in Rome that could have been brought in an English church court. Note, F.G.A., "Praemunire Facias" no. 6 (1469).

86. The dispute over whether the Archbishop of York can have a cross borne before him in Canterbury Province: *Rot. Parl.*, ii, 67b (1332). Town and gown disputes: *Cal. Pat. Rolls, 1292-1301*, 382 (1298); *Reg. Trillek*, 346 (1352). Murder of monk: *Cal. Pat. Rolls, 1292-1301*, 216, 260, 317-18 (1296).

87. Pollock and Maitland, ii, 590-1; F.N.B., 151C. Art. Cler., 9 Edw. 2, St. 1, c. 10 (1315); *Reg. Pontissara,* 773-74; *Rot. Parl.,* iii, 27b (1377). As to assisting the suspect, see Note, F.G.A., "Corone," no. 313 (1329). Even before the forty days were up, one might be suspected of being an accessory. *R.* v. *Atte Gate,* S.S. lviii, 155 (1306). On persons already convicted, see Note, F.G.A., "Corone," no. 313 (1329); *Anon.,* Y.B., T. 9 E. 4, 28, F.G.A., id., no. 32 (1469); J.C. Cox, *The Sanctuaries and Sanctuary Seekers of Medieval England* (London, 1911), 51-52. As to civil arrest, see *Reg. Sudbury, London,* 56-58 (1363); *Rot. Parl.,* iii, 345a (1397); but cf. *Whytegift's Petition,* id., i, 476b (temp. Edw. 1-2). On arrest during services, see id., 357b-358b, 373a-b, iii 25a-27b (1376-77); 1 Ric. 2, c. 15 (1377); cf. *Reg. Trillek,* 115 (1347) (question of pollution during forcible removal). On Westminister and other charter sanctuaries, see *Rot. Parl.,* iii, 37a-b, 50b, 51a (1378); 2 Ric. 2, St. 2 c. 3 (1379); *V.C.H. London,* i, 444-45.

88. This section, where not otherwise documented, is based on Vol. I, 138-39 and on Gabel.

89. Note, F.G.A., "Corone", no. 283 (1346); *Widyndon* v. *Bishop of Lincoln, Rot. Parl.,* ii, 73a (1334); id., 284b (1351-52); *R.* v. *Haxey,* id., iii, 341a (1397); *Anon.,* Y.B., M. 19 H. 6, 47, F.G.A., "Corone", no. 8 (1440). There seems to have been a contention, repudiated by the king, that newly established crimes were not clergyable. *Rot. Parl.,* iii, 494a (1402); 4 Hen. 4, c. 2 (1402).

90. *Anon.,* Y.B., T 34 H. 6, 49, F.G.A., "Corone", no. 20 (1455). On whether a person known to be a cleric could be hanged if he failed to claim his privilege at all, see *Lacy's Case,* F.G.A., "Corone", no. 254 (1348). There was a problem of asserting the privilege after a cleric took sanctuary and abjured the realm. Art. Cler., 9 Edw. 2, St. 1, c. 10 (1315); *Anon.,* F.G.A., "Corone", no. 155 (1326).

91. *Rot. Parl.,* iii, 23a (1377), iv. 151b (1449); cf. 4 Hen. 4, c. 3 (1402). On denying purgation after confession in court, see Note, F.G.A., "Corone," no. 128 (1347); *Anon.,* Y.B., H. 27 H. 6, 7, F.G.A., id., no. 16 (1448); *Anon.,* Y.B., M. 13 E. 4, 3, F.G.A., id., no. 38 (1473). On posting bond against purgation, see Gabel, 53; *Reg. Pontissara,* 772, 459-61. Another device used by the lay authorities to keep a cleric from getting off too easily was to arraign him for a series of offenses, one at a time, and keep him in jail until he had been through them all. *Anon.,* F.G.A., "Corone," no. 394 (1314); id., no. 461 (1348). This practice was abolished by 25 Edw. 3, St. 3, c. 5 (1350); *Rot. Parl.,* ii, 244b (1351-2).

92. Liability for escape: *R.* v. *Turnebole,* R.S., 17 Edw. 3, 210 (1343); *Anon.,* Y.B., H 27 H. 6, 7, F.G.A., "Corone," no. 16 (1448). Treatment of lands and goods: *R.* v. *De Bryland,* S.S., lviii, 4 (K.B. 1294); *Osmund's Petition,* S.S., lvii, 169 (K.B. 1293); *Cal. Close Rolls, 1346-49,* 460, 474 (1348).

93. *R.* v. *Godsfield,* S.S., lviii, 168 (K.B. 1307) (ordinary examines in court); *Anon.,* Y.B., T. 34 H. 6, 49, F.G.A., "Corone," no. 20 (1455) (archdeacon brings book); *Anon.,* id., no. 233 (1326) (ordinary penalized for claiming man without dress and tonsure); *Anon.,* Y.B., P. 9 E. 4, 28, F.G.A., id., no. 32 (1469) (ordinary fined for claiming man who could not read). Cases of clerics hanged because the ordinary did not claim them include *Anon.,* id., no. 117 (1338); *Anon.,* R.S., 12-13 E. 3, 68 (1339); *Anon.,* F.G.A., "Corone," no. 250 (1349); *Anon.,* 27, Lib. Ass. 42, F.G.A., id., no. 205 (1353). In all these cases, the cleric had committed some crime against the church — sacrilege or breaking the ordinary's prison — and reference is made to the fact that he has broken the very law whose benefit he seeks.

94. Gabel; *Anon.,* Y.B., T. 34 H. 6, 49, F.G.A., "Corone," no. 20 (1455); *Anon.,* Y.B., P. 9 E. 4, 28, F.G.A., id., no. 32 (1469). Women were also included. F.G.A., "Corone," no. 461. The custom may have come in about this time of always using the

same scriptural passage (the "neck verse") to test literacy, so that the benefit was available to anyone who memorized the verse, even if he could not read. In at least one case, a convicted felon learned to read while in jail awaiting execution, so it cannot have been too hard a feat. See the case from 7 Richard II (1384) referred to in a note in 2 Dyer 205, 73 Eng. Rep. 453, and Art. 11 of the articles of inquiry in 27 Lib. Ass., 44 (1353).

95. C. 16, Lyons 1274, Mansi, xxiv, 91. 4 Edw. I, St. 3, c. 5; (1276) 18 Edw. III, St. 3, c. 2 (1344); *Simonel* v. *Sovingle,* Y.B., M. 11 H. 4, 11, F.G.A., "Corone," no. 85 (1409); *Rot. Parl.,* ii, 333a. For the history of the rule excluding *bigami* from the clerical state, see Vol. I, 36-7.

96. 4 Hen. 7, c. 13. For earlier requests that certain crimes be treated as treason and so excluded, see *John Carpenter's Case, Rot. Parl.,* iv, 447b (1435) (a particularly brutal wife murder); id., v, 333a (1455) (recidivism), 632b (1467-8) (church robbery).

97. *Reg. Trillek,* 291 (1346), 339 (1350), 256-57 (1344-45); *Reg. Pontissara,* 206, 774.

98. Imprisonment: *Cal. Close Rolls, 1296-1302,* 214 (1298); *Rot. Parl.,* ii, 129a-130b (1341); iii, 26a (1377). Outlawry: *Cal. Pat. Rolls, 1348-50,* 106 (1348); id., *1396-99,* 323 (1398). The prelates' tentative proposal appears in *Reg. Pontissara,* 772. The case of the cleric who preferred the bishop's prison to debtor's prison is *Shirbourne* v. *Jenycoght de Gales, Rot. Parl.* v, 106b (1444).

99. *Petition of Thresk, Rot. Parl.,* ii, 183a (1347).

100. Art. Cler., 9 Edw. 2, St. 1, c. 9 (1315); *Rot. Parl.,* 129a-130b (1341).

101. By the Statute of Westminster II, 13 Edw. 1, St. 1, c. 5 (1285), one who succeeded in ousting the rightful patron of a presentment was liable to him for two years' income of the benefice.

102. On posting notice: *R.* v. *Anon.,* Y.B., M. 11 H. 6, 3, F.G.A., "Brief al Evesque," no. 4 (1432). On effectuating a forfeiture: *Earl of Hereford* v. *Dean and Chapter of Hereford,* Y.B., T. 21 E. 3, 27, F.G.A., "Quare Impedit," no. 50 (1347); Cf. *Dacre* v. *Dean and Chapter of Lincoln,* R.S., 16 Edw. 3, 208 (1342). On advowsons appurtenant: F.N.B., 85F.

103. *Raby* v. *Grenevil,* Y.B., P 22 E. 3, 6, F.G.A., "Darrain Presentment," no. 1 (K.B., on writ of error, 1348).

104. On the assize of darrein presentment, see F.N.B., 71-74; Turner and Plucknett, "Introduction," *Brevia Placitata,* ed. Turner (S.S. lxvi, 1947), p. xcvii. On *quare impedit,* F.N.B., 74-85; Burn, i, 30. On the writ of right of advowson, F.N.B., 69-71. On enforcing the judgment after recovering on a writ of right, see F.N.B., 77I, 84A; Note, Y.B., P12 E. 2, 377 (1318); *R.* v. *Anon.,* F.G.A., "Quare Impedit," no. 139 (1371). The statutory provisions mentioned in text are all in 13 Edw. 1, St. 1, c. 5 (1285). On the effect of this statute in ousting an incumbent, see note 114 *infra.* It was the same statute that provided for damages, six months' revenues if you won your presentment, two years' revenues if you were too late. But if your opponent gave way and your presentee was admitted before you started your suit, you could not recover damages for the trouble you had been caused in the interim. *Anon.,* Y.B., M. 12H. 4, 11, F.G.A., "Quare Impedit," no. 121 (1410); but cf. *Prior of Lewes* v. *Fitzwauter,* Ames, 11 Ric. 2, 76 (1387). On the right of the bishop to leave a litigious benefice vacant, and collate after six months, see *Bohm'* v. *Bishop of Lincoln,* Y.B., P. 34 H. 6, 38, F.G.A., "Quare Impedit," no. 89 (1455); *R.* v. *Dant',* Y.B., M. 47 E. 3, 10, F.G.A., id., no. 141 (1373); Note, F.G.A., "Quare non Admisit," no. 12 (1335); *R.* v. *Bishop of Exeter,* Y.B., T. 24 E. 3, 30, F.G.A., id., no. 11 (1350). Note that if the bishop failed to collate after six months, the patron could still present when his right to do so was established. *Earl of Arundel* v. *Bishop of Chester* [read *Exeter?*], Y.B., H. 38

E. 3, 2, F.G.A. "Quare Impedit," no. 124 (1364). Note also that the ordinary could get in trouble if the third party claim that made the benefice litigious was his own. *R. v. Archbishop of York,* R.S., 20 Edw. 3, i, 162 (1346).

105. *Abbot of Burton* v. *Bishop of Ely,* Y.B., P. 2 E. 3, 10, F.G.A. "Collusion" no. 7 (1328).

106. *Anon.,* Y.B., P. 42 E. 3, 8, F.G.A., "Quare Impedit," no. 132 (1368); *Anon., S.S.,* xx, 38 (1310).

107. *Helygan* v. *Bishop of Exeter,* R.S., 12-13 Edw. 3, 270, 283, 286 (1338) *(quare impedit); Grenevil* v. *Bishop of Exeter,* R.S., 17-18 Edw. 3, 94 (1343), R.S. 19 Edw. 3, 229 (1345), Y.B., H. 21 E. 3, 3, F.G.A., "Quare Incumbravit," no. 4 (1347) *(quare incumbravit)* ; *Despenser* v. *Bishop of Norwich,* R.S. 20 Edw. 3, i, 26 (1346) *(quare non admisit).* For examples of the inquiries referred to, see *Reg. Chichele,* i, 178-80 (1420), 186 (1419), 229 (1425).

108. *Frome* v. *Bishop of Salisbury,* S.S., xlv, 114 (1316) and *Bohm'* v. *Bishop of Lincoln,* Y.B., P. 34 H. 6, 38, F.G.A., "Quare Impedit," no. 89 (1455) support the bishop in taking no action, whereas *Boulement* v. *Archbishop of York,* Y.B., 22 H. 6, 28, F.G.A., id. no. 83-84 (1443) indicates that he must make the canonical inquiries and act in accordance with the result. As to his liability for putting the wrong man in, F.N.B., 111H says there can be no *quare incumbravit* unless the bishop had received a writ of *ne admittas* before encumbering the benefice. But *Grenevil, supra,* note 107, and some of the argument in *Paunton* v. *Bishop of Ely,* S.S., lxiii, 123 (1311) seem to indicate that other kinds of notice of an adverse claim will support the action. In any event, the bishop will be liable in *quare impedit* if not in *quare incumbravit.* F.N.B., 111 H.

109. The bishop was allowed to contest the patron's claim despite the contention that he had no standing. *Misterton* v. *Archbishop of York,* S.S., xix, 165 (1328); *Anon.,* Y.B., T. 5 H. 7, 34, F.G.A., "Quare Impedit," no. 107 (1489).

110. *Rot. Parl.,* ii, 244b (1351-52); *R.* v. *Bishop of Lincoln,* R.S., 19 Edw. 3, 164 (1345); *R.* v. *Bishop of Exeter,* id., 214 (1345). The second case raises the question whether it suffices if the bishop puts the person designated by the lay court into physical possession on top of the canonical incumbent, or whether he must also mount a canonical process to oust the latter.

111. *Anon.,* R.S., 33-35 Edw. 1, 166 (1306); 25 Edw. 3, St. 3, c. 8 (1350); *Bayeux* v. *Bishop of Lincoln,* S.S., lxi, 231 (1317) (metropolitan); *Boulement* v. *Archbishop of York, supra,* note 108 (jury). Cf. *R.* v. *Bishop of Norwich,* S.S., xlv, 56 (1315), a *quare non admisit* case where the bishop found himself in a procedural dilemma. He was afraid to plead that his inquest had found the benefice full, as that could be regarded as a failure to plead that it was in fact full. So he pleaded that it was in fact full, whereupon the king's counsel objected that he had failed to plead that he had acted canonically by following the result of an inquest. No decision is recorded.

112. *R.* v. *Anon.,* Y.B., P. 15 H. 7, 6, F.G.A., "Encumbent," no. 14 (1499). *Anon.* v. *Bishop of R.,* Y.B., P. 40 E. 3, 25, F.G.A., "Quare Impedit," no. 128 (1366); *Abbot of Tewkesbury* v. *Bishop of Worcester,* R.S., 33-5 Edw. 1, 44 (1305). If the presentee had died since his rejection, his fitness would be tried by a jury. *Earl of Arundel* v. *Bishop of Chester* [read *Exeter?*], Y.B., H. 39 E. 3, 1 (1365).

113. *R.* v. *Anon.,* F.G.A., "Quare Impedit," no. 29 (1341); *Cal. Close Rolls, 1296-1302,* 224 (1298); *R.* v. *Clifton,* F.G.A., "Quare Impedit," no. 1 (1357). In *Paunton* v. *Bishop of Ely,* S.S., lxiii, 123 (1311), the bishop was accused of deliberately creating a lapse by not processing plaintiff's presentment. *Dandele* v. *Bishop of Llandaff,* Y.B., T. 5 E. 3, 26 F.G.A., "Quare Impedit," no. 36 (1331) holds that the bishop cannot take advantage of a lapse where the adverse claim making the benefice

litigious is his own. Cf. *R.* v. *Archbishop of York,* R.S., 20 Edw. 3, i, 162 (1346).

114. By the Statute of Westminster II, 13 Edw. 1, St. 1, c. 5 (1285), plenarty on the defendant's presentment is not a defense in *quare impedit* or darrein presentment unless the incumbent was in for six months before the writ was brought. *Bayeux* v. *Bishop of Lincoln,* S.S., lxi, 231 (1317) indicates the same rule as to *quare non admisit. Anon.,* F.G.A., "Quare Impedit," no. 169 (1319) (party cannot claim last presentment unless presentee was in six months before suit brought). The six-month requirement evidently did not obtain under prior law. *Broghten's Petition, Rot. Parl.,* i, 5a (1278). The dictum in *Anon.,* Y.B., H. 38 H. 6, 19 F.G.A., "Quare Impedit," no. 93 (1459) that the statute created the right to plead plenarty at all seems to be mistaken. For Coke's treatment of this history, see *Boswel's case,* 6 Co. Rep. 48b, 77 Eng. Rep. 326 (K. B. 1606); 2 Co. Inst. *360. On *quare incumbravit* see F.N.B., 111I. On the time between institution and induction, see *Prior of Bermondsey* v. *R., Rot. Parl.,* i, 116a (1293); *Anon.,* F.G.A., "Quare Impedit," no. 11 (1356); cf. *R.* v. *Bishop of D.,* Y.B., H. 38 E. 3, 3, F.G.A., id., no. 125 (1364) (king may revoke presentment until induction).

115. *R.* v. *Prioress of Schaft'* [Shaftsbury?], Y.B., M. 24 E. 3, 34, F.G.A., "Quare Impedit," no. 14 (1360); *R.* v. *Bishop of Lincoln,* R.S., 19 Edw. 3, 164 (1335); *Rot. Parl.,* iii, 273b (1389), 438b (1399).

116. *R.* v. *Fitzhugh,* R.S., 20 Edw. 3, ii, 45 (1346); *R.* v. *Prior of Durham,* Y.B., T. 18 E. 3, 23, F.G.A., "Encumbent" no. 5 (1344); *Panton* v. *Bourne,* S.S., xxxiii 170 (1312). The statute referred to in text is 25 Edw. 3, St. 3, c. 7 (1350). For different interpretations of its effect, see *Prior of Durham* v. *Vernon,* Y.B., M. 39 E. 3, 30, F.G.A., "Encumbent," no. 1 (1365); *Anon.,* F.G.A., id., no. 11 (1409); *Anon.,* Y.B., H. 9 H. 6, 56, F.G.A., id., no. 12 (1430); *Anon.,* Y.B., M. 8 H. 5, 9, F.G.A., id., no. 15 (1420). Since the statute refers to denying the king's right to present, there is also a question whether the incumbent, if allowed to plead at all, can plead plenarty. Note, F.G.A., id., no. 4 (1379) (no); *Anon.,* Y.B., M. 22 H. 6, 14, F.G.A., id., no. 13 (1443) (yes). See Coke's discussion of these matters in *Hall* v. *Bishop of Bath and Wells,* 7 Co. Rep. 25b, 77 Eng. Rep. 449 (1589).

117. On the power of the bishop, if a party, to plead in such a way as to protect the incumbent, see *Boulement* v. *Archbishop of York,* Y.B., M. 22 H. 6, 28, F.G.A., "Quare Impedit," no. 83-84 (1443); cf. note 109, *supra.* On the defenses available to the bishop in *quare non admisit,* see *R.* v. *Bishop of Norwich,* R.S., 16 Edw. 3, i, 162 (1342); *Despenser* v. *Bishop of Norwich,* R.S., 20 Edw. 3, i, 26 (1346); *R.* v. *Bishop of Exeter,* Y.B., M. 23 E. 3, 22, F.G.A., "Quare non Admisit," no. 11 (1349). The last of these involved a notorious and successful fraud, which contributed to the enactment of the 1350 statute. *Rot. Parl.,* ii, 245b (1351-52). The Baron of Stafford, having lost a presentment by allowing a lapse to occur, caused a fictitious *quare impedit* suit to be brought against him on the king's behalf. He then defaulted, and the king, not being bound by the lapse, had a writ to the bishop. The bishop refused the king's presentee, and, in the ensuing *quare non admisit* case, attempted to show that the king had no title. He was not allowed to do so.

118. The following discussion of spoliation is based on F.N.B., 85-87, and *Anon.,* Y.B., H. 38 H. 6, 19, F.G.A., "Consultacion," no. 1 (1459).

119. If the spoliation action went through without being prohibited, the second presentee might have some trouble. See *R.* v. *Bishop of Carlisle,* Y.B., P. 46 E. 3, 13, F.G.A., "Encumbent," no. 3 (1372), a *scire facias* action based on a *quare impedit* judgment, where the issue was whether the judgment had been executed when the king's presentee was put in the benefice, then put out again in an ecclesiastical proceeding by the former incumbent.

120. *R.* v. *Abbot of Bec,* Y.B., T. 10 E. 3, 39, F.G.A., "Encumbent," no. 5 (1336)

is a successful use of a charter confirming an incumbent's status; *R.* v. *Archbishop of York,* F.G.A., "Quare Impedit," no. 16 (1351); and *R.* v. *Archbishop of Canterbury,* id., no. 161 (1357) are unsuccessful ones. For examples of presentments revoked for lack of a showing that the king had a right, see *Cal. Pat. Rolls, 1348-50,* 33 (1348); id., *1396-99,* 340, 343, 429 (1398); id., *1446-52,* 212 (1448); *Petition of Wotton, Rot. Parl.,* ii, 181b (1347). 25 Edw. 3, St. 3, c. 3 (1350) and *Rot. Parl.,* ii, 244a (1351-52) contemplate some kind of investigation before the presentment is made, but I find no record of this being done.

121. 13 Ric, 2, St. 1, c. 1 (1389), amended, 4 Hen. 4, c. 22 (1402). *Frisby* v. *Storton,* Y.B., H. 8 H. 4, 21, F.G.A., "Quare Impedit," no. 114 (1407) is an action of *scire facias* on this statute, presumably to cancel the presentment. But see Note, Y.B., H. 2 H. 4, 17, F.G.A., id., no. 112 (1400), which says that the only remedy is a petition to the king.

122. The appropriator could claim its rights in an action of trespass, but probably not until the intruded incumbent had been put out of physical possession. *Prior of J.* v. *Strade,* Y.B., M. 39 H. 6, 20 F.G.A., "Quare Impedit," no. 96 (1460). F.N.B., 86B suggests the possibility of an assize (presumably of novel disseisin), but F.N.B. 86K and *Frost* v. *Palmer,* Ames, 12 Ric. 2, 79 (1388) indicate that tenure of a benefice under color of ecclesiastical law cannot be treated as a nullity in the lay courts even if it is canonically invalid. On spoliation, see *Anon.,* Y.B., H. 38 H. 6, 19, F.G.A., "Consultacion," no. 1 (1459). But see *Cal. Close Rolls, 1396-99,* 273 (1398), where the king allowed such a suit to go forward notwithstanding a prohibition. On the writ of right of advowson, see *Anon.,* F.G.A., "Quare Impedit," no. 197 (1360).

123. *Newers* v. *Prior of F.*, F.G.A., "Darrain Presentment", no. 8 (1361); *Earl of Salisbury* v. *Prior of Montague,* Y.B., H. 29 E. 3, 2, 9, F.G.A., "Quare Impedit," no. 191 (1355); I suspect that *Misterton* v. *Archbishop of York,* S.S., xix, 165 (1308-10) (defendant may deny plaintiff's presentment without claiming anything for himself) was also an appropriation case, in view of the long time since the last presentment. The church in question was appropriated to the Dean and Chapter of York. "Misterton" in Lewis, *Topographical Dictionary of England* (1844). *Adam* v. *Abbot of Newham,* Y.B., T. 2 E. 3, 23, F.G.A., "Quare Impedit," no. 41 (1328). *Abbot of Newenham* v. *Dean and Chapter of York,* Y.B., H. 7 E. 3, 4, F.G.A., "Quare Impedit," no. 19 (1333), *Rot. Parl.,* ii, 94b (1335).

124. *R.* v. *Archbishop of York,* R.S., 17 Edw. 3, 524 (1343) (right to elect is not advowson). On election as a condition precedent, compare *Earl of Lancaster* v. *Subprior and Convent of Tabyn,* F.G.A., "Quare Impedit," no. 157 (1337) with *Roys* v. *Bishop of London,* Y.B., M. 30 E. 3, 21, F.G.A., id., no. 4 (1356).

125. *R.* v. *Anon.,* Y.B., T. 47 E. 3, 4, F.G.A., "Quare Impedit," no. 140 (1373).

126. *Cal. Pat., Rolls 1348-50,* 137 (1348), *Reg. Trillek,* 305 (1347). Cf. *Fressingfeld* v. *Parson of Cookley,* S.S., xx, 12 (1308).

127. 7 Edw. 1, St. 2 (1279); 52 Hen. 3, c. 18 (1267); cf. Magna Carta, 9 Hen. 3, c. 36 (1224). Lay corporations were covered by 15 Ric. 2, c. 5 (1391). See *Cal. Pat. Rolls, 1446-52,* 164 (1448) for a mortmain license to the Haberdashers Guild. As to trusts, see *Anon.,* F.G.A., "Mortmayn" no. 10 (1358); *Anon.,* 43 Lib. Ass., 33, F.G.A., id., no. 20 (1369); *Anon.,* 43 Lib. Ass., 34, F.G.A., id., no. 21 (1369); *Anon.,* 40 Lib. Ass., 26, F.G.A., id., no. 22 (1366). These were finally brought under the mortmain laws by 23 Hen. 8, c. 10 (1531), then taken out again by a restrictive interpretation in the 1590s. See c. IV, note 114, *infra.*

128. *Rot. Parl.,* ii, 356a (1376). *Reg. Pontissara,* 774.

129. On advowsons see *Dacre* v. *Dean and Chapter of Lincoln,* R.S., 16 Edw. 3, 208 (1342). There was considerable debate over whether an appropriation caused the

advowson to be forefeited under the mortmain laws; the courts seem finally to have decided it did not. *Montague* v. *Abbot of Welbeck,* Y.B., H. 21 E. 3, 5, F.G.A., "Mortmayn," no. 11 (1347); Notes, F.G.A., id., no. 13 (1340), 16 (1348). Some of the colloquy in *Montague* suggests that the mortmain laws had something to do with the king's claim that appropriations required his license. See the language of the license in *Cal. Pat. Rolls, 1396-99,* 477 (1398). But see *R.* v. *Prior of Worcester,* S.S., lviii, 125 (1304). As to other covered interests, see *Anon* v. *Abbess of G.,* Y.B., T. 21 E. 3, 18, F.G.A., "Mortmayn," no. 12 (1347) (rentcharge); *Abbot of St. Albans* v. *Anon.,* Y.B., P. 6 E. 3, 21, F.G.A., id., no. 4 (1332) (duty to grind corn); *Prior of Trinity, London* v. *Abbot of Colchester,* Y.B., H. 17 E. 3, 5, F.G.A., "Collusion," no. 22 (1343) (relief on each voidance); *Abbot of Westminster* v. *P.,* Y.B., M. 50 E. 3, 22, F.G.A., id., no. 27 (1376) (seignory). As to pensions, see note, Y.B., M. 20 H. 6, 7, F.G.A., id., no. 23 (1441); *Prior of Merton* v. *Gogan,* S.S., xlvii, 48 (1471). It seems that a term of years was not covered either, unless it was long enough to be tantamount to a life estate. *Anon.,* R.S., 33-35 Edw. 1, 148 (1306); *C.* v. *Abbot of Boxeley,* Y.B., H. 4 H. 6, 9 F.G.A., "Mortmayn" no. 1 (1425).

130. Note, F.G.A., "Mortmayn," no. 8 (1345) (exchange); *Cal. Pat. Rolls, 1292-1301,* 341 (1298) (bishop to chapter); *Dean and Chapter of Warr'* v. *Prebendary of S.,* F.G.A., "Collusion" no. 28 (1339) (chapter to prebendary); *Cal. Pat. Rolls, 1348-50,* 58 (1348) (archbishop to parson); *Warden of the House of Holy Trinity of Werland* v. *de Mouhaut,* S.S., lv, 161 (K.B. 1286). (bishop to religious house); *Cal. Pat. Rolls 1396-9,* 377 (1398) (chapter to chaplain); *Cal. Close Rolls, 1447-54* 78-80 (1448) (parson to chantry in his church). The only case I have found in which it was argued that the act should not apply to a transfer from one form of mortmain to another is *R.* v. *Dean of Wolverhampton,* S.S., xlv, 43 (1315), where no decision is recorded.

131. *Anon.,* 43 Lib. Ass. 34, F.G.A., "Mortmayn," no. 21 (1369) (heir violates will); *R.* v. *Dant',* Y.B., M. 47 E. 3, 10, F.G.A., "Quare Impedit," no. 141 (1373) (bishop usurps advowson).

132. *Bishop of Carlisle* v. *Abbot of Dorchester,* R.S., 13-4 Edw. 3, 12 (1340); *Bishop of Exeter* v. *Anon.,* Y.B., M. 41 E. 3, 21, F.G.A., "Mortmayn," no. 5 (1367); Note, F.G.A., id., no. 2 (1440); F.N.B., 513B. The Commons were worried about churchmen taking over lands purchased by their villeins. *Rot. Parl.,* iii, 294a (1391). They also suspected churchmen of marrying off their villeins to free women in order to take the latter's lands in the next generation. *Id.,* 319a (1393-94).

133. *Bishop of Carlisle* v. *Abbot of Dorchester, supra,* note 132.

134. *C.* v. *Abbot of Boxeley, supra,* note 129 (conveyance); *Isabel* v. *de Hereford,* R.S., 20-21 Edw. 1, 262 (1292) (heir); *Anon.* v. *Abbot of Waltham,* Y.B., T. 41 E. 3, 16, F.G.A., "Mortmayn," no. 4 (1367) (villein). I have not found any medieval precedent for *Anon.,* 2 Dyer 1886, 73 Eng. Rep. 415 (1560) (without special writ, judges will not register fine in favor of Oxford college).

135. 13 Edw. 1, St. 1, c. 32 (1285). The 1283 case described in text is *Prior of Breedon* v. *Furnace,* S.S., lv, 118 (1283). Cases extending the statute to other interests in land include: *Prior of Trinity, London* v. *Abbot of Colchester,* Y.B., H. 17 E. 3, 5, F.G.A., "Collusion," no. 22 (1343) (feudal tenancy); *Abbot of Westminster* v. *P.,* Y.B., M. 50 E. 3, 22, F.G.A., id., no. 27 (1376) (same); *A.* v. *William and John,* R.S., 20-21 Edw. 1, 222 (1292) (warranty); *Anon.,* Y.B., T. 45 E. 3, 18, F.G.A., "Mortmain," no. 6 (1371) (same). The statute also applied to an action for waste, since the plaintiff was entitled to recover possession of the wasted tenements. Note, R.S., 16 Edw. 3, ii, 537 (1342); *Anon.,* Y.B., M. 3, E. 4, 12, F.G.A., "Collusion," no. 38 (1463); and to an action of trespass where the defendant made good a claim of title that he could use to support a possessory action another time, *Anon.* v. *Abbot of F.,* Y.B., P.

29 E. 3, 35, F.G.A., "Collusion," nos. 13, 45 (1355); but cf. *John* v. *Abbot of Westminster*, Y.B., M. 5 E. 3, 67, F.G.A., id., no. 3 (1331) (no inquest where plaintiff in replevin admits avowant's claim to seignory). Cases where the merits were not fully litigated include: *Abbot of Westminster* v. *P. supra* (admission); *Anon.* v. *Abbot of F.*, *supra*, (same); *Dean of Wells* v. *Anon.*, R.S., 16 Edw. 3 ii, 9 (1342) (issue not covering full right). Where a plaintiff took a nonsuit in favor of an ecclesiastical defendant, the statute did not generally apply, because the judgment could not affect either possession or title. Note, Y.B., P. 6 E. 3, 25, F.G.A., "Collusion," no. 6 (1332), (possession). But if a plaintiff was nonsuited in *quare impedit*, the statute would apply unless the defendant waived his right to have a writ to the bishop. *Ockingham* v. *Prior of Pount*, Y.B., P. 6 E. 3, 23, F.G.A., id., no. 5 (1332). The defendant had his writ without an inquest in *Abbot of Our Lady of York* v. *Richmond*, R.S., 20 Edw. 3, ii, 52 (1346), but the reporter queried the result.

136. 15 Ric. 2, c. 5 (1391); cf. 13 Edw. 1, St. 1, c. 33 (1285). For complaints of the devices referred to in text, see *Rot. Parl.*, iii, 291b (1391) (boundary change); id., ii, 368a (1376-77) (strawman); iii, 19a (1377) (same).

137. E.g., *Cal. Pat. Rolls, 1396-99*, 452 (1398) (25 marks for license to amortize lands worth 100 s. a year); id., 484 (1398) (£ 50 for license to appropriate rectory of Quinton, Gloucs., valued at £ 14 in *Taxatio* of 1291); *Cal. Pat. Rolls, 1446-52*, 158 (1448) (£ 6 for license to set up chantry and endow with lands worth £ 6 a year); id., 204 (1448) (20 marks for license to amortize lands worth £ 10 a year). On the other hand, the ratification in id., 173 (1448) appears to have been free. For more material on mortmain licenses, see Wood-Legh, 80-88. On the rights of the mesne lord, see 34 Edw. 1, St. 3 (1306); *Cal. Close Rolls, 1346-49*, 595 (1348) (license confirmed by mesne lord); *Montague* v. *Abbot of Welbeck*, Y.B., H. 21 E. 3, 5, F.G.A., "Mortmayn," no. 11 (1347); Cf. *Rot. Parl.*, iii, *117b (1381)*.

138. F.N.B., 509-18; *Rot. Parl.*, i, 198b (1306).

139. See the deed in *Cal. Close Rolls, 1447-54*, 50 (1448), referring to the license and to the results of the inquest. The complaint referred to in text appears in *Rot. Parl.*, iii, 213a (1385). It is not clear how the medieval administrative process would have coped with the problem of a person who took out, say, a £ 50 license and used it to buy three separate pieces of land worth £ 25 each. Perhaps each purchase could have been physically endorsed on the license, but I doubt if it was. Cf. 18 Edw. 3, St. 3, c. 3 (1344).

140. *Rot. Parl.*, i, 63b (1290); *Id.*, 78b (1292); *Stat. at Large* i, 400 (1292).

141. On incumbents living abroad, see *Cal. Close Rolls, 1296-1302*, 158 (1298); *Rot. Parl.*, ii, 312b (1372), iii, 163b (1383). The subjects of the king's dominions on the continent were not considered aliens, *Reg. Trillek*, 337 (1352), a point which the Commons evidently found hard to understand. *Rot. Parl.*, ii, 162a-163b (1346) (petition against the papal legate Pelegrini). On the 1298 chapter at Citeaux, see *Cal. Close Rolls, 1296-1302*, 215-18. It appears that some abbots got to Citeaux despite the king's strictures, and his order to the Warden of the Cinque Ports to stop them. In 1300, he let them go as long as they did not take any money. Id., 348-49. As to foreign superiors and motherhouses generally, see 35 Edw. 1, St. 1 (1307); Knowles, R.O., ii, 141-42; W. E. Lunt, *Financial Relations of the Papacy with England 1327-1534* (Cambridge, Mass., 1962), 203; *Abbot and Convent of Cormailles* v. *Prior and Convent of Santa Barbara, Rot. Parl.*, i, 274b (1308-09) (defendant is plaintiff's farmer, and not a daughterhouse; *mandamus* to issue to compel defendant to pay farm to plaintiff). It seems to be land rather than daughterhouses that is envisaged in the entry in *Cal. Papal Reg.*, iii, 276 (1349), commissioning a bishop to check on a proposal by a French abbey to exchange English for French lands, as they received no profit from the English, and

in the entry in *Cal. Pat. Rolls, 1396-99,* (1398), granting the abbey of Fécamp half their former farm from their English possessions. The problem of suits in the papal court appears in *Rot. Parl.,* ii, 333a (1373). For more material on alien priories see pp. 8-11 *supra.*

142. Export of gold and silver was forbidden by 9 Edw. 3, St. 2 (1335) and 5 Ric. 2, St. 1, c. 2 (1381). The requirement that anyone selling letters of exchange buy English merchandise with the proceeds was imposed by 14 Ric. 2, c. 2 (1390). In a typical transaction, an English traveler would buy from an Italian merchant in London a letter of exchange that he could cash in Italy. The merchant would then buy English wool and ship it to Flanders, and the Flemish consignee of the wool would ship gold or silver to Italy to cover the letter of exchange. Lunt, *supra,* note 141, at 204. Twenty years after the statute of 1390, it was found necessary to tighten up the enforcement. *Rot. Parl.,* iii, 626b (1409-10).

143. *Rot. Parl.* ii, 162a-163b (1346); id., ii, 22a (1377); 3 Ric. 2, c. 3 (1379); 7 Ric. 2, c. 12 (1383); *Rot. Parl.,* iii, 529a (1403-4); cf. id., iv, 13a (1413). It was possible to be exempted from all these measures by a royal license. *Cal. Pat. Rolls, 1446-52,* 125 (1448) (license for Cardinal of Venice to take benefices worth up to £ 100 a year). It was also possible to escape the effects of being an alien by obtaining a royal charter of denization. *Rot. Parl.,* iv, 11a (1413). It should be noted, incidentally, that as early as Edward I's time an invasion scare had led to the temporary removal of foreign clergy from the vicinity of the coast. *Reg. Pontissara,* xlvii-xlviii.

144. E.g., *Reg. Trillek,* 260 284, 337.

145. *Rot Parl.,* iii, 213a (1385); cf. *Cal. Pat. Rolls, 1348-50,* 180 (1348) (protection for man appointed by pope to collect alms for hospital in Rome).

146. Sumptuary rules: 37 Edw. 3, c. 13 (1363); 13 Ric. 2, c. 13 (1389); cf. Rot. Parl., iii, 593a (1406). On the canonical standards, see Vol. I, 39-42. Wills: *Reg. Pontissara, 775; Rot Parl.,* ii, 149b, 150a (1341); *Thyke* v. *Fraunceys,* S.S., lxiii, 240 (1311). But the wills of villeins were evidently recognized in some manor courts. Pollock and Maitland, i, 416. Stipendiary priests: 23 Edw. 3, St. 1, c. 8 (1349); 36 Edw. 3, St. 1, c. 8 (1362); *Reg. Trillek,* 321 (1349); Putnam, "Minimum Wage Laws for Priests after the Black Death," *Am. Hist. Rev.,* xxi, 12 (1915). Children in religious orders: 4 Hen. 4, c. 17 (1402). The Commons were ambivalent on this point. In 1402, they wanted a twenty-one year age limit instead of the fourteen-year provision that was adopted. *Rot. Parl.,* iii, 502a (1402). But in 1376-77 they wanted anyone who wore the habit without complaint beyond the age of fifteen to be barred from any inheritance if he left the religious life. Id., ii, 370b. Villeins in clergy: The canons forbade the ordination of villeins, but a villein once ordained was free. Pollock and Maitland, i, 429; Vol. I, 43. Since the procedures for checking on the background of a person who presented himself for ordination were inadequate, the best way to keep your villein from being ordained was to see that he did not come by the necessary book learning. See *Wakefield Rolls,* iii, 166 (1286), where a man was reported for putting his sons to book learning; *Rot. Parl.,* iii, 294a (1391), where the Commons requested a law against villeins sending their children to schools — the king turned them down.

147. Guardians' rights: 20 Hen. 3 c. 6-9 (1235); 3 Edw. 1 c. 22 (1275); Pollock and Maitland, i, 318-29, F.N.B., 330D-332K. 52 Hen. 3, c. 17 (1267) forbids a guardian to sell a marriage except for the ward's profit. I have not been able to discover how this affected the "value of the marriage" which the guardian was still entitled to collect if the ward defied him. Dower: F.N.B., 351L; cf. *Batecoke* v. *Coulynge,* S.S., xx, 189 (1310). Illegitimacy of issue after annulment: *Anon.,* F.G.A., "Bastardy," no. 21 (1301) (consanguinity); *Bliont* v. *Anon.,* S.S., lxi, 262 (1317) (betrothal). It appears that a child could be validly betrothed at the age of seven. Pollock and Maitland, ii, 390-92.

Women carried off: 6 Ric. 2, c. 6 (1389).

148. Barlow, *Cases of Conscience,* (London 1692), c. vi, argues that the medieval canon law did not admit of dissolving a marriage on grounds of parental coercion. As a guide to medieval English practice in matters of this kind, seventeenth-century Anglican scholarship is not to be taken lightly. On the state of the canonical authorities on the question, see Noonan, *Power to Dissolve* (Cambridge, Mass., 1972), 27-47.

149. For the general rule, see *Anon.,* R.S., 33-35 Edw. 1, 566 (1307) (monk); *Campo Arnulphi* v. *Abbot of Tavistock,* Y.B., T. 7 E. 3, 35, F.G.A., "Abbe" no. 16 (1333) (prior). On the abbot's personal liability, see *Anon.* v. *Abbot of St. Augustine's,* Y.B., P. 5 H. 7 24, F.G.A., "Abbe" no. 6 (1489) (abbot sued on debt he incurred while prior of another house). Of course, the distinction between the abbot and the house was not as clear to medieval lawyers as it is us. Pollock and Maitland, i, 504-8; cf. note 8 *supra.* For the early rule on sealed instruments, see Pollock and Maitland i, 508, and for the developed rule, e.g., *Anon.,* F.G.A., "Abbe," no. 12 (1338). There was an exception where the abbot acknowledged the transaction in open court. *Prior of Wartre* v. *Abbot of Fountains,* R.S., 16 Edw. 3, i, 183, ii, 522, 19 Edw. 3, 422 (K.B. 1342-5); *Anon.,* F.G.A. "Abbe," no. 7 (1383). The requirement of community consent is attributed to the Statute of Carlisle in *Anon.,* F.G.A., "Abbe," no. 14 (1345). The statute is 35 Edw. 1, St. 1, c. 4 (1307). Cf. *Anon.,* R.S., 33-35 Edw. 1, 144 (1306). Pollock and Maitland, i, 509 suggest that nothing came of the statute. *Master of the Hospital* v. *C.,* Y.B., M. 15 E. 2, 452 (1321) indicates that failure to have a common seal does not affect either the necessity or the sufficiency of a showing that the community did not consent to a transaction. See also *Anon.,* Y.B., M. 8 H. 5, 10, F.G.A., "Abbe," no. 28 (1420), where an obligation sealed by a prior with the common seal was held not to bind his successors on the ground that the community could not have consented because they had all died off in the plague.

150. F.N.B., 450-51. The parson under the same circumstances used *utrum.* F.N.B., 113-116. By 14 Edw. 3, St. 1, c. 17 (1340), the heads of hospitals and the like could use either *utrum* or *sine assensu capituli* as they chose. *Askham* v. *Warde,* R.S., 14-15 Edw. 3, 43 (1341). The principle that the house is barred during the tenure of the abbot who made the grants is implicit in many places, including the material cited here and Pollock and Maitland, i, 504-5, although I have found no explicit statement of it in the medieval cases. As to the successor abbot who accepts rent or fealty, see *Bishop of Winchester* v. *Hale,* S.S., lxiii, 40 (1311) (not barred); *Anon.* v. *Prior of the Hospital of Ely,* Y.B., M. 37 H. 6, 3, F.G.A., "Abbe," no. 2 (1458) (barred); *Parson of F.* v. *Anon.,* F.G.A., "Juris Utrum," no. 3 (1337) (barred).

151. 3 Edw. 1, c. 1 (1275), referred to in Art. Cler., 9 Edw. 2, St. 1, c. 11 (1315).

152. *Leyerton's Petition, Rot. Parl.,* i, 13a (1278); *Prior of Lewisham and Greenwich* v. *Abbot of Gaunt,* id., ii, 49a (1330); *Commons of Latchford* v. *Abbot of Thame,* id., ii, 184a (1347). In 1425 a petition in Commons was answered with a statement that there was a sufficient remedy in either spiritual or temporal law for the failure to keep up services in chapels of ease. Id., iv, 290a. *Petition of Prior of Plympton,* id., i, 461a (1302-07) indicates that such matters can be inquired of in the eyre. *Broks* v. *Abbot of Woburn,* Y.B., H. 22 H. 6, 46, F.G.A.,"Accion sur le Case," no. 12 (1443) supports an action on the case.

153. 13 Edw. 1, St. 1, c. 41 (1285). The remedy on alienation was not available where thesuccessor could recover the lands in *sine assensu capituli.* F.N.B., 485D. To recover an advowson, the grantor had to use *quare impedit,* rather than *contra formam collacionis* (F.N.B., 485F) or *cessavit (Anon.,* F.G.A., "Cessavit," no. 24 (1358). For the two-pronged process in *contra formam collacionis,* see F.N.B., 484A-B. The reversion of the land to the grantor in *cessavit* was the subject of a draft

grievance in *Reg. Pontissara, 777. Cessavit* for secular services was created by 6 Edw. 1, St. 1, c. 4 (1278), expanded in coverage by 13 Edw. 1, St. 1, c. 21 (1285). On arrears of spiritual services, see *Anon.,* R.S., 33-35 Edw. 1, 262 (1306). In *Anon.* v. *Prior of Salisbury,* id., 489 (1307), it was unsuccessfully contended that the spiritual services should be more definitely stated so that the arrears might be a thing certain. In any event, the services had to be in some way specific for *cessavit* to lie. F.N.B., 484E.

154. The most interesting case of this kind is *Abbot of Hartland* v. *Beaupel,* S.S., xx, 164 (1310), lxiii, 281 (1311), xlv, 105 (1316). This was a writ of mesne brought by the abbot against the defendant as his intermediate feudal lord, for exoneration from services demanded by the overlord. The defendant denied the feudal relationship. It developed that he had purchased the rights of one Diana, of whom the abbot had held by spiritual services, and that the abbot had attorned to him. The question was whether it was possible to attorn for spiritual services — if the analogy were perfect, the monks would have to stop praying for Diana and start praying for the defendant. No decision on the precise point is recorded. The abbot eventually won on the basis of a deed executed by the defendant.

155. F.N.B., 483C *(cessavit);* 486 *(contra formam collacionis).* As to alternative remedies, see F.N.B., 483 (covenant); *Anon.,* R.S., 33-35 Edw. 1, 252 (1306) (distress); *Prior of Warter* v. *Bentley,* S.S., lviii, 40 (K.B., 1295) (same); *Anon.,* R.S., 33-35 Edw. 1, 552 (1307) (right of entry).

156. This section, where not otherwise documented, is based on Wood-Legh, 1-59. For examples of the king's intervention in internal affairs, see *Cal. Close Rolls, 1396-99,* 250, 363 (1398); *Abbot of Abingdon's Case, Rot. Parl.,* i, 355b (1320). It is 13 Edw. 1, St.1, c. 41 (1285) that provides for taking lands into the king's hand on account of alienation. For an application, see *Cal. Close Rolls, 1296-1302,* 182 (1298), where the seizure is until further order. In other cases where the law provided for seizing lands improperly alienated, the seizure was released on payment of a fine. 1 Edw. 3, c. 12 (1327); F.N.B., 404. On seizing lands for abuse, see *Foedera* iii, ed. Rymer (London, 1704-17), vi, 677 (1371), where the king states that he is entitled to take back all the endowments of St. Paul's on account of abuses there, but, out of piety, will content himself with having the abuses reformed. As to receiverships, the complaint in *Rot Parl.,* iv, 469b (1400-1401) indicates that they were generally asked for by the house involved. But the custody of Dunbrothy abbey initiated in *Cal. Pat. Rolls, 1348-50,* 17 (1348) was involuntary, and was revoked, id., 134, on the abbot's showing that reports of his mismanagement were untrue. Protections were included in the 1400-1401 complaint and in a petition of a group of corrody holders in *Rot. Parl.,* iv, 520a (1402).

157. *Shiraks* v. *Archbishop of York,* Y.B., M. 8 E. 3, 69, F.G.A., "Excommengement," no. 2 (1334). In 2 Hen. 5, St. 1, c. 1 (1414), the king orders the ordinaries to correct hospitals of royal foundation as his delegates, and to correct those of private foundation in accordance with ecclesiastical law.

158. On dismissing the head of a religious house, see Vol. I, 250-51. Whether the ordinary could dismiss the head of a hospital was debated in the *Shiraks* case, *supra,* note 157, with no clear result.

159. *Petition of Archbishop of Canterbury, Rot. Parl.,* iii, 224a (1393-94) complains of lay process interfering with ecclesiastical proceedings against unlicensed masters. No answer is recorded, but the petition referred to in text, *Rot. Parl.,* v, 137a (1447), indicates that the churchmen must have had their way.

160. On the friars, see *Petition of Mendicants, Rot. Parl.,* iii, 341b (1397); Knowles, R.O., ii 156. *Cal Close Rolls, 1396-99, 317 (1398) refers to a statute of 20*

Ric. 2 (1396) on the point, but I have not been able to find such a statute. On the rights of the archbishop of York see *Archbishop of York's Petition, Rot Parl.*, iii, 69a (1379); *V.C.H. Oxford*, iii, 133. On the archbishop of Canterbury as visitor of the University of Oxford, see *Rot. Parl.*, iii, 651a (1411), from which the quote is taken.

161. Trees in the churchyard: 35 Edw., 1 St. 2 (1307). Compensation for lost tithes: *Cal. Close Rolls, 1396-99*, 260 (1398); *Petition of Parson of Devises, Rot. Parl.*, i, 319a (1314-15). The principle that the titheholder cannot complain of a change in land use is reiterated in *R.* v. *Commissioners of Nene Outfall*, 9 B. & C. 874, 109 Eng. Rep. 325 (1829). Alienations and pensions: *Prior of Bermondsey* v. *Parson of Fyfield*, R.S., 16 Edw. 3, ii, 550 (1342); *Prebendary of T.* v. *Prior of Huntingdon*, F.G.A., "Annuitie," no. 53 (1384); F.N.B., 113D, 114I. Bulls of exemption from tithe: 2 Hen. 4, c. 4 (1400); 7 Hen. 4, c. 6 (1405); *Rot. Parl.*, iii, 457b, 464b (1400-1401), 594a (1406).

162. Wood-Legh, 127-53; *R.* v. *Prior of Worcester*, S.S. lviii, 125 (K.B. 1304). For the statutory conditions, see 15 Ric. 2, c. 6 (1391); *Rot. Parl.*, iii, 293b (1391). Examples of licenses requiring the conditions include: *Cal. Pat. Rolls, 1396-9*, 289, 322, 406 (1398); id., *1446-52*, 124, 184 (1448). An example of a license waiving them is id., *1396-99*, 325 (1398). The agreement to stop waiving them is found in 4 Hen. 4, c. 12 (1402); *Rot. Parl.*, iii, 499a (1402), 542a (1403-4). But the king refused to do away with further appropriations entirely. Id., 468a (1400-1). In *Cal. Papal Ltrs.*, iv-v, I found thirteen licenses for 1398 alone allowing vicarages to be appropriated or not set up.

163. *Rot. Parl.*, iii, 468a (1400-1401), 501b (1402), 594b (1406), 645a (1409-10), iv, 305b (1425).

164. *Cal. Pat. Rolls, 1348-50*, 101, 106, 108, 180 (1348).

165. The statutes mentioned in text are 5 Ric. 2, St. 2 c.5 (1382); 2 Hen. 4 c. 15 (1400); 2 Hen. 5, St. 1, c. 7 (1414). The 1382 act was repealed in the same year when the Commons protested that they had not agreed to it, and had no intention of being more subject to the jurisdiction of the prelates than their ancestors had been. *Rot. Parl.*, iii, 141 (1382). For the elaborate proceedings by which William Sawtrey was burned as a heretic, see *D.N.B.*, Sawtrey; Wilkins, iii, 259; *Rot. Parl.*, iii, 459a (1400-1401). On the burning of heretics at common law, see Pollock and Maitland, ii, 544-52.

166. F.W. Maitland, *Roman Canon Law in the Church of England* (1898), especially chapters 5 and 6; *Rot. Parl.*, i, 83b (1292); *Cal. Pat. Rolls, 1348-50*, 105 (1348) is an apostate religious case where the form writ in F.N.B., 533 would have done just as well. *Cal. Pat. Rolls, 1348-50*, 151 (1348) is more general, and id., *1396-99*, 362 (1398) may require more force than the sheriff can muster. A case that required a combination of routine and special processes is *Friars Preachers of London* v. *Abbot and Convent of Hyde, Rot. Parl.*, ii, 186b (1347), a dispute over which community a certain man belonged to.

167. Purveyances: 3 Edw. 1, c. 1 (1275); 14 Edw. 3, St. 3, c. 1 (1340); 1 Ric. 2, c. 3 (1377). Spurious crimes: 1 Ric. 2, c. 13 (1377). Commissions of oyer and terminer: *Hereford* v. *Appleby, Rot. Parl.*, ii, 32a (1330); *Cal. Pat. Rolls, 1348-50*, 164, 169, 245 (1348).

168. Case on renewing suit after absolution: *Anon.*, Ames, 11 Ric. 2, 229 (1387). Cases where bishop is party: *Prior of Carlisle* v. *Bishop of Carlisle*, Y.B., H. 5 E. 3, 8, F.G.A., "Excommengement," no. 1 (1331); *Haselshawe* v. *Bishop of Bath and Wells*, R.S., 16 Edw. 3, ii, 159 (1342). Cases on whose certificate will not be received: *Seton* v. *Luce C.*, 30 Lib. Ass. 19, F.G.A., "Excommengement," no. 10 (1356) (pope); *Anon.*, Y.B., M. 20 H. 6, 1, F.G.A., id., no. 11 (1441) (bishop's commissary); *Anon.*, Y.B., M. 12 E. 4, 15, F.G.A., id., no. 17 (1472) (exempt jurisdiction); *Anon.*, F.G.A.,

id., no. 24 (1346) (same); *Anon.*, F.G.A., id., no. 29 (1359) (English bishop relying on certificate of Irish bishop). The refusal to accept excommunication by foreign bishops was attributed partly to the problem of authenticating the seals, partly to the fact that the king had no control over such bishops. Case where defendant brought about excommunication: *Anon.*, Y.B., M. 3 H. 4, 3, F.G.A., id., no. 19 (1401). The result would be the same if the excommunication was in violation of a prohibition. *Freiselle* v. *Sudbury*, R.S., 20 Edw. 3, i, 214 (1346).

169. Pollock and Maitland, i, 478-80; F.N.B., 144-52; Logan, *Excommunication and the Secular Arm in Medieval England* (Toronto, 1968). The practice on the writ *de cautione admittenda* was included among the draft clerical grievances in *Reg. Pontissara*, 771. The Commons, for their part, proposed in 1350-51 that no writ *de excommunicato capiendo* be issued until it had been established in an adversary proceeding that the excommunication was in a case the church courts were entitled to hear, but the king refused. *Rot. Parl.*, ii, 230a.

170. *Abbot of Newenham* v. *Courtenay*, *Rot. Parl.*, iii, 482b (1402); but cf. *Abbot of Nutley's Petition*, id., 180b (1383-84), where a similar complaint is answered "Ce n'est pas Bille de Parlement;" *R.* ex rel. *St. John* v. *Bishop of Lincoln*, S.S., lviii, 11 (K.B. 1294).

171. F.N.B., 124-25. The further discussion of this writ is based on this source. The Close Roll entries referred to in text are *Cal. Close Rolls, 1247-51*, 71-2, 105 (1248). Later examples present special circumstances indicating why the form writ was not used. id., *1296-1302*, 203 (1298) indicates that the sheriff has had a form writ, but was overzealous in executing it and needs more explicit instructions. *Cal. Pat. Rolls, 1348-50*, 168 (1348) seems to involve a complicated case which the sheriff could not handle.

172. *Rot. Parl.*, iii, 288b (1391) (excommunication of housebreaker); *Cal. Pat. Rolls, 1446-52*, 154, 260 (1448), 279 (1449) (exemptions from motherhouses); *Succession of William of Monte Canis, Rot. Parl.*, i, 16b, 38b, 84a (1290) (bull appointing judges delegate in bastardy case, permission to use denied); *Ripon* v. *Franks*, id., iv, 27b (1414) (bull confirming election of abbot, execution permitted after experts decided it was not a provision).

173. *Rot. Parl.*, i, 207a, 219a-223b (1306); ii, 337a-340a (1376); Vol I, 197-200 W.A. Pantin, *The English Church in the Fourteenth Century* (Cambridge, 1955), 81-98.

174. Vol. I, 180-84; Deeley, "Papal Provision and Royal Rights of Patronage in the early Fourteenth Century," *Eng. Hist. Rev.*, xliii, 497 (1928). This is to prescind from problems concerning the appointment of bishops, as to which, see Vol. I, 174-77. Early cases on provisions include that of John Colonna, provided to a prebend of York. *Cal. Close Rolls, 1296-1302*, 223, 292, 300, 301, 309 (1298-99) (*R.* v. *Archbishop of York*, S.S., lviii, 136 (1304) may be a later stage of the same case) and *Anon.*, R.S., 13-4 Edw. 3, 4 (1340). The first ordinance against provisors is *Rot. Parl.*, i, 219a (1306); see note 4 *supra*. Fourteenth-century parliamentary complaints appear in *Rot. Parl.*, ii, 7-11 (1326-27), 141b 144b (1343), 153a-154a (1344), 228a (1350-51), 336b-340a (1376); iii, 18b-19a (1377), 82b (1379-80), 222a (1386). As to the incidence of foreigners in English benefices at the time, see Pantin, *supra*, note 173, at 58-63. The actual Statute of Provisors is 25 Edw. 3 st. 6 (1350), reenacted 13 Ric. 2, St. 2, c. 2-3 (1389), and 9 Hen. 4, c. 8-10 (1407). On its enforcement, see *R.* v. *Bishops of Sarum and St. David's* Y.B., M. 11 H. 4, 37, 59, 76, F.G.A., "Quare Impedit," no. 120 (1409). On the negotiations between king and pope in the late fourteenth century, see Pantin, 89-93 *Rot. Parl.*, ii, 339b (1376). On licenses, see id., iii, 163b (1383); 285a (1391), 301a-b (1392-93), 340b (1397); 419b (1399); 428b (1399), 458b (1400-1401); 490b (1402); 621a (1407).

175. *Rot. Parl.*, iii, 596a, 599b (1406); 3 Hen. 5, St. 2, c. 4 (1415).

176. Procurations for nuncio: *Reg. Trillek*, 63, 86, 299-300, 318 (1346-48). Presentee vs. provisor: *Cal. Papal Reg.*, v. 98 (1398); *Rot. Parl.*, ii, 178a-b (1347). Stopping people and process at ports: *Cal. Pat. Rolls, 1348-50,* 313 (1350); *Rot. Parl.*, iii, 258b (1389); *Cal. Close Rolls, 1396-99,* 278, 359 (1398). Imprisonment: *Cal. Pat. Rolls, 1348-50,* 152 (1348); 13 Ric. 2, St. 2, c. 3 (1389), *Rot. Parl.*, iii, 288b (1391).

177. Plenarty: *R. v. Anon.*, F.G.A., "Trial," no. 54 (1381); *R. v. Northumbergham,* Y.B., M. 29 E. 3, 44, F.G.A., "Quare Impedit," no. 192 (1355). Presentment: *Anon.,* F.G.A., id., no. 169 (1319) — before the statute, to be sure, but after the 1307 ordinance. Cf. *R. v. Anon.*, Y.B., H. 44 E. 3, 3, F.G.A., id., no. 136 (1370), where a papal provision would evidently have been accepted as a filling of a benefice by the bishop in whose gift it was, had the provisor gotten corporal possession before the bishop died.

178. *Rot. Parl.*, ii, 333a (1376).

179. This account, where not otherwise documented, is based on the following cases: *Henry de Harewedon, Cal. Pat. Rolls 1345-48,* 229 (1346); id., *1348-50*, 183, 208, 242 (1348); *Cal. Close Rolls, 1346-49,* 482 (1348); *Cal. Papal Reg.*, ii, 404 (1334), iii, 140 (1343), 171 (1344), 457 (1349); Emden, "Harowden;" in *A Biographical Register of the University of Oxford to 1500* (Oxford, 1969), *William de Hendrea* and *John de Bisshopestow, Cal. Pat. Rolls, 1348-50,* 204 (1348); id., *1350-54,* 2 (1350), 395 (1352); *Cal. Papal Reg.*, iii, 149 (1344); *Robert de Barton* and *David Wollore, Rot. Parl.*, ii, 196a (1347); *Cal. Close Rolls, 1346-49,* 485, 489 (1348); *Cal. Papal Reg.*, iii, 241 (1347), 279 (1348); *Cal. Papal Reg.*, iii, 241 (1347), 279 (1348); *Philip de Weston, Cal. Papal Reg.*, iii, 253, 255, 302, 337, 434, (1348); J. Le Neve, *Fasti Ecclesiae Anglicanae*, ed. Hardy (Oxford, 1854), iii, 123; *Nicholas Hethe, supra,* note 82; *Thomas de Everdon, Cal. Papal Reg.*, v, 98 (1398); *Nicholas Slake, Cal. Pat. Rolls, 1396-9,* 322 (1398); *Nicholas Bubwith, Henry Chichele,* and *Walter Medford, Reg. Chichele,* xxi-ii; *Cal. Pat. Rolls, 1396-99,* 188, 376 (1398); *Cal. Papal Reg.*, v, 82, 205-6 (1398); *Cal. Close Rolls, 1396-99,* 359 (1398).

180. It is not altogether clear to me what the relation was between the ordinary and the executors named in a bull of provision. My impression is that the ordinary was expected to confer the benefice on the provisor. Churchill, i, 46, 115 (London, 1933). Presumably the executors were there to take a hand if the ordinary failed to do so. The case of the king writing the pope, *Rot. Parl.*, ii, 393b (uncertain date *temp.* Edw. 3), is on behalf of an executor. Cases indicating that the bishop will be let off in *quare impedit* if he pleads that he claims only as ordinary are *Despenser* v. *Bishop of Norwich*, R.S., 20 Edw. 3, i, 26 (1346); *Anon.*, Y.B., P. 5 H. 7, 19 F.G.A., "Quare Impedit," no. 106 (1489). Cases indicating that he should put the king's presentee in on top of the provisor are *R. v. Bishop of Lincoln*, R.S., 19 Edw. 3, 164 (1345); *R. v. Bishop of Exeter*, id., 214 (1345).

181. Note, F.G.A., "Premunire Facias," no. 1 (1424); cf. *R. v. Prior of W.*, Y.B., M. 30 E. 3, 11, F.G.A., "Judgement," no. 145 (1356) (penalties of Statute of Praemunire cannot be applied in an attachment on a prohibition). On the possibility of using *praemunire* in anticipation of litigation in Rome, see *Anon.*, F.G.A., "Premunire Facias," no. 12 (1385), where the defendants seem to be required to give surety against going.

182. 25 Edw. 3, St. 6 (1350).

183. On suspending the disabilities of an excommunicate, see note 168 supra. On deprivation, *R. v. Anon.*, F.G.A., "Trial" No. 54 (1382). On reversal of deprivation, *Despenser* v. *Bishop of Norwich*, R.S., 20 Edw. 3, i, 26 (1346); *Latimer* v. *Latimer,*

S.S., xxii, 170 (1310). On dispensations, *R.* v. *Bishops of Sarum and St. David's* Y.B., M. 11 H. 4, 37, 59, 76, F.G.A., "Quare Impedit," no. 120 (1409). Dispensations from religious obedience or from payment of tithe were forbidden by statute at the beginning of the fifteenth century. 2 Hen. 4, c. 3-4 (1400); 7 Hen. 4, c. 6 (1405).

184. *Anon.,* F.G.A., "Excommengement," no. 4 (1342); *Anon.,* id., no. 6 (1357); *Seton* v. *C.,* 30 Lib. Ass. 19, F.G.A., id., no. 10 (1356).

2. Uitlity and Reform

Note: References to medieval parliamentary material not documented here will be found in the previous chapter. Many of the more general statements about the forces at work in the Reformation are based on P. Hughes, *The Reformation in England* (3 vols., London, 1954-56) (Hughes); A.G. Dickens, *The English Reformation* (revised ed., 1957); L.B. Smith, *Tudor Prelates and Politics, 1536-1558* (Princeton, 1953); W.P. Haugaard, *Elizabeth and the English Reformation* (Cambridge 1968); T.A. Lacy, *The Reformation and the People* (London, 1929) and J.E. Neale, *Elizabeth I and her Parliaments* (London, 1953).

1. *Doctor and Student,* d. I, c. 24.
2. id., d. II, c. 16.
3. id., d. II, c. 54.
4. id., d. II, c. 25.
5. id., d. I, c. 6; d. II, c. 25.
6. id., Add c. 1.
7. ibid.
8. *Doctor and Student,* Add. c. 10.
9. id., Add. c. 8.
10. After the *Treatise,* the pamphlets are More, *The Apologye of Syr Thomas More Knight* (no date); St. Germain, *Salem & Bizance* (1533); More, *The Debellacyon of Salem and Bizance* (no date); St. Germain, *The Addicions of Salem and Bizance* (1534).
11. *Doctor and Student,* Add. c. 1.
12. id., Add. c. 10.
13. id., d. II, c. 31.
14. id., Add. c. 10.
15. id., d. II, c. 26.
16. 21 Hen. 8, c. 13 (1529).
17. 28 Hen. 8, c. 13 (1536).
18. "Privileges and Restraints of the Clergy," Burn, ii, 224, 237 says that the necessity of maintaining the household was accepted in every case.
19. *Rot. Parl.,* iv, 645a (1410).
20. 31 Hen. 8, c. 14 (1539) (Six Articles Act); 37 Hen. 8, c. 21 (1545) (union of benefices — on the power of the ordinary to act without using it, see *Austin* v. *Twyne,* Cro. Eliz. 500, 78 Eng. Rep. 750 (1595),; 31 Hen. 8, c. 9 (1539) (new bishoprics); 26 Hen. 8, c. 14 (1534) (suffragans).
21. 27 Hen. 8, c. 28 (1536); 31 Hen. 8, c. 13 (1539); 37 Hen. 8, c. 4 (1545); cf. 1 Edw. 6, c. 14 (1547).
22. Knowles, R.O., iii, 327-9; Dickens, "Secular and Religious Motivation in the Pilgramage of Grace", *Studies in Church History,* iv. ed. Cuming (Leiden, 1967), 39.

The quotation from Aske is given by Knowles.

23. *Halsbury's Laws of England,* (4th ed.), xiv (1975), 570-71 "Church", Burn, i, 231, 236-37 gives a case of a monastic chapel restored to divine service after a long period as a barn; a reconciliation, rather than a new consecration, sufficed.

24. *Rot. Parl.*, vi, 143a (1475).

25. "Monasteries", Burn, ii, 49, 62-4 has a list of medieval precedents. See also Knowles, R.O., iii, 161-63, 387 on Wolsey's suppression of monasteries to endow projects of his.

26. 21 Hen. 8, c. 6 (1529).

27. Though Henry settled the long controversy over tithes in London. 27 Hen. 8, c. 21 (1535); 37 Hen. 8, c. 12 (1545); "Tithes", Burn, ii, 373, 459-65.

28. 2 Co. Inst. *644-45.

29. 32 Hen. 8, c. 7 (1540). The quoted passage is from §7.

30. 27 Hen. 8, c. 20 (1535) made the sentence of the ecclesiastical court in a tithe case enforceable by the justices of the peace. This provision evidently continued in force, although it was little used. *R.* v. *Sanchee,* 1 Ld. Raym. 323, 91 Eng. Rep. 1111 (1697).

31. 26 Hen. 8, c. 3 (1534).

32. "First Fruits and Tenths", Burn, i, 567. Coke is more cautious, at least as to tenths. 4 Co. Inst. *121; *Case of First Fruits and Tenths,* 12 Co. Rep. 45, 77 Eng. Rep. 1325 (1608). See W. E. Lunt, *Financial Relations of the Papacy with England, 1327-1534* (Cambridge, Mass., 1962)

33. *Rot. Parl.*, ii, 153a-154a.

34. 21 Hen. 8, c. 5 (1529).

35. 23 Hen. 8, c. 9 (1532). The fee for issuing a citation at the behest of a litigant was limited to 3d by the same statute.

36. 25 Hen. 8, c. 19 (1534). The preliminary documents are in H. Gee and W.J. Hardy, *Documents Illustrative of English Church History* (1896), 145-78. The 1376 petition referred to in text is *Rot. Parl.*, ii, 368b. For other medieval precedent, see Coke in *Case of Convocations,* 12 Co. Rep. 71, 77 Eng. Rep. 1350 (1611).

37. *Middleton* v. *Crofts,* 2 Atk. 650, 26 Eng. Rep. 788 (1736). Coke, however, adumbrates the same position in *Case of Convocations, supra,* note 36.

38. 25 Hen. 8, c. 19, 21 (1534).

39. 25 Hen. 8, c. 20 (1534). The election procedure was replaced by direct royal appointment in 1 Edw. 6, c. 2 (1547), but Henry's procedure, rather than Edward's, was revived by 1 Eliz 1, c. 1 (1558).

40. The statutes on sanctuary are 22 Hen. 8, c. 14 (1531); 27 Hen. 8, c. 19 (1536); 32 Hen. 8, c. 12 (1540). Those on benefit of clergy are 4 Hen. 7, c. 13 (1487); 23 Hen. 8, c. 1 (1532); 25 Hen. 8, c. 6 (1534); 27 Hen. 8, c. 17 (1536); 28 Hen. 8, c. 1 (1536); 32 Hen. 8, c. 3 (1540); 37 Hen. 8, c. 8 (1545). An earlier restrictive act, 4 Hen. 8, c. 2 (1512), was temporary and failed of renewal in 1515 as a consequence of the Hunne affair, Hughes, i. 149-54.

41. Cox, *The Sancuaries and Sanctuary Seekers of Medieval England* (London, 1911), 23.

42. Theoretically, you had to be literate to have benefit of clergy, but it seems that the same text (the "neck verse") was always used to test literacy, so that anyone who memorized it could escape hanging. See *Anon.,* 2 Dyer 205b, 73 Eng. Rep. 453 (1562), where a man learned to read between two terms of court. Cf. c. 1, note 94, *supra.*

43. Usury: 37 Hen. 8, c. 9 (1545). The 1494 act is 11 Hen. 7, c. 8. Poor relief: 27 Hen. 8, c. 25 (1536).

44. 23 Hen. 8, c. 20 (1532).
45. It is interesting that the act also made provision for preventing the enforcement of a papal interdict — a measure that had not been taken by Rome since Innocent III's confrontation with King John.
46. 24 Hen. 8, c. 12 (1533).
47. 25 Edw. 3, st. 6 (1350), quoted, *supra,* p. 2.
48. Compare *Rot. Parl.*, ii, 373b (1376-77): Le Roy ne poet mye departir de son droit qil ne face la Loie a touz ses Subjez en lour Petition.; id., iii, 343b (1397):.. nr̄e Sr̄ le Roy, come entier Emperour de son Roialme d'Engleterre . . .''
49. Cf. Koebner, ''The Imperial Crown of this Realm . . .'', *Bulletin of the Inst., of Hist. Research,* xxvi (1953), 29.
50. 25 Hen. 8, c. 21 (1534).
51. 26 Hen. 8, c. 1 (1534).
52. 37 Hen. 8, c. 18 (1545); Art. 37.
53. Pickthorn, *Early Tudor Government – Henry 8* (Cambridge, 1951), 207-08 quotes a highly unctuous exchange between Henry and Cranmer establishing the latter's authority to annul the marriage with Catherine of Aragon.
54. 31 Hen. 8, c. 14 (1539).
55. The relevant statutes are as follows: on chantries, 1 Edw. 6, c. 14 (1547); on uniformity, 2-3 Edw. 6, c. 1 (1548) and 5-6 Edw. 6, c. 1 (1551); on clerical marriage, 2-3 Edw. 6, c. 21 (1548) and 5-6 Edw. 6, c. 12 (1551); on images, 3-4 Edw. 6, c. 10 (1549); on the calendar, 2-3 Edw. 6, c. 19 (1548) and 5-6 Edw. 6, c. 3 (1551); repealing doctrinal tests: 1 Edw. 6, c. 12 (1547); on reviling the Sacrament, 1 Edw. 6, c. 1 (1547); on brawling in church, 5-6 Edw. 6, c. 4 (1551); on tithe, 2-3 Edw. 6, c. 13 (1548); on benefit of clergy and sanctuary, 1 Edw. 6 c., 12 (1547). The Marian restoration is embodied in 1-2 Ph. & M., c. 8 (1554). See also 1-2 Ph. & M., c. 6 (1554), which revived the medieval but not the Henrician heresy legislation. On Mary's earlier parliaments, see Hughes, ii, 201-02.
56. On the effect of the Chantries Act, see A.G. Dickens, *The English Reformation* (revised ed., 1967), 284-301.
57. L. B. Smith, *Tudor Prelates and Politics, 1536-1558* (Princeton, 1953), 258-59 and passim.
58. 21 Jac. 1, c. 28 (1624).
59. 1 Eliz. 1, c. 1, 2, 4, 19 (1559).
60. *Case of Heresy,* 12 Co. Rep. 56, 77 Eng. Rep. 1335 (1602); 29 Car. 2, c. 9 (1676). See Hughes, iii, 411-13 for a writ *de haeretico comburendo* of 1576. The statutory limitation on what could be called heresy applied in terms only to the High Commission, but Coke, *supra* said the bishops would do well to follow it.
61. 13 Eliz. 1, c. 12 (1571).
62. Hughes, ii, 183.
63. Carleton, *The Life of Mr. Bernard Gilpin* (London, 1629)
64. K., cxvi.
65. *York Civic Records,* (Y.A.A., xcviii, ciii, cvi, cviii, cx, cxii, cxv, cxix), iii, 176, v, 87, 100, 120, vi, 8, 15, 17, 35, 124, 128, 133-34, 144, vii, p. vi, 47, vii, p. v.
66. On bells, see Purvis, 174-75. The priest who said *de profundis* is in *Reg. Cooper,* 136. The woman who referred to priest calves is in Foster, lxvii.
67. For a typical Protestant critique of the settlement and statement of how a church ought to be run, see Anon., *A Learned Discourse of Ecclesiasticall Government* (London, 1584) Bodl. Gold. 8° C 24 Th.
68. See Sykes, *Old Priest and New Presbyter* (Cambridge, 1957)
69. Jewel, *An Apology of the Church of England* (Works, iii, Parker Soc. xxv,

Cambridge, 1848), 65.

70. *State Trials* (Howell ed.), iv, 315, 526.

71. *Austin* v. *Twyne*, Cro. Eliz. 500, 78 Eng. Rep. 750 (1595); *Dean and Chapter of Norwich*, 3 Co. Rep. 73a, 76 Eng. Rep. 793 (Ch. 1598). For a later case along the same lines, see *Commendam Case*, Hobart 140, 80 Eng. Rep. 290 (1613).

72. 5 Co. Rep. 1, 77 Eng. Rep. 1 (1591).

73. See Rogers, *The Protestant Church Existent* (London, 1638) Bodl. Pamph. D 36 (12), a refutation of the attacks of the Jesuit, Fisher. Rogers is extremely effective in supporting his own claims by establishing the relatively late origin of many Roman Catholic doctrines and practices — an argument for which Catholics had no satisfactory reply until Newman's *Essay on the Development of Christian Doctrine* (London, 1845).

74. 2 Co. Inst. *599-618.

75. Cf. *Dr. James's Case*, Hobart, 18, 80 Eng. Rep. 168 (1622), where a prohibition was awarded against one ecclesiastical court hearing a case that belonged to another.

76. See, respectively, *Case de Modo Decimandi*, 13 Co. Rep. 37, 77 Eng. Rep. 1448 (1610); *Premunire*, 12 Co. Rep. 37, 77 Eng. Rep. 1319 (1608); *Lady Throgmorton's Case*, 12 Co. Rep. 69, 77 Eng. Rep. 1347 (1611) and *Sir Anthony Roper's Case*, 12 Co. Rep. 45, 77 Eng. Rep. 1326 (1608); *Porter and Rochester's Case*, 13 Co. Rep. 4, 77 Eng. Rep. 1416 (1608).

77. See Charles I, 1627, Cardwell, *Doc. Ann.*, ii, 221.

78. After the Restoration, there is Davis, *De Jure Uniformitatis Ecclesiasticae* (London, 1669).

3. By Law Established

Note: The main primary sources for this chapter are so accessible, and in such short compass, that it seems both cumbersome and superfluous to document every point with specific page references. The articles of inquiry used by the Elizabethan bishops in connection with their visitations, and the ensuing injunctions, are collected for the years 1559-1575 in *Visitation Articles and Injunctions*, ed. Frere (London, 1910), iii (F.) and *Elizabethan Episcopal Administration*, ed. Kennedy, (London, 1924) (K.), ii, iii. The first volumes of the respective sets are devoted to extensive introductions, which give access to the material dealing with particular subjects. The only other visitation articles I have used are those from Bancroft's 1604 visitation of the London diocese, which are found in Cardwell, *Doc. Ann.*, ii, 101.

The presentments, returns, and other disciplinary materials I have used are mainly taken from three works: *Tudor Parish Documents of the Diocese of York* ed. Purvis (Cambridge, 1948) (Purvis), *Acts of the Archdeacon's Court of Oxford, 1584*, ed. Brinkworth (Oxfordshire Record Soc., xxiii, xxiv, (1942-46) (Brinkworth), and *Bishop Redman's Visitation, 1597*, ed. Williams (Norfolk Record Soc., xviii, 1947) *(Redman's Visitation)*. The first of these is arranged by subject-matter; the others have extensive introductions.

So it has not seemed necessary to refer the reader to specific pages to enable him to determine how well the material collected in these works supports the general statements in text. Accordingly, I have cited to this material only where I have quoted it, referred to a specific case, or made an especially obscure point.

In the way of secondary materials, I have drawn extensively on Hughes, iii, 133-236, Hill, Marchant, and Hart, *Country Clergy*, and less extensively on Hart, *The Man in the*

Pew, W.P. Haugaard, *Elizabeth and the English Reformation* (Cambridge, 1968), and T.A. Lacey, *The Reformation and the People* (London, 1929). Here again in most cases it has not seemed necessary to give specific references in the notes.

The material which I have tried to cite specifically includes the different canons and other documents of more or less canonical force, and some other primary sources, such as Parker's and Cooper's Registers, where the particular matters to which I want to draw attention are a little more difficult to extract from the mass.

1. *Reg. Cooper*- 135, 136. See also Purvis, 139-40, 167-68, 203-9.

2. Note that a good deal of the work of renovating the old material was initiated at Cardinal Pole's 1557 synod under Mary. Cardwell, *Synodalia,* ii, 448-89.

3. Hughes, iii, 138-40 gives statistics. On lay readers see Foster, xxii-xxiii; Bishops, 1560-61, F., 67; Anon., 1560, #21, F., 89; 1571, p. 115; Parker, 1575, #2, F., 374. See also, Bishops, 1560-61, #9, F., 61, providing that deprived incumbents can be made to serve as curates on account of the shortage of ministers.

4. Strype, ii, pt. ii, 521-24. For the assessment of Parkhurst, see *D.N.B.,* Parkhurst.

5. The canons and other rulings on this subject are Bishops, 1560-61, #24-5, F., 63; Parker, Advts., 1566, #22, F., 177; 1571, p. 113-14; 1575, c. 1, 2, 6; Whitgift, 1584, art. 7, 8; 1585, p. 139-42; 1597, p. 157-59; 1604, c. 33-6. Some of the provisions brought into the canons in 1575 track those adopted by Parliament in 13 Eliz. 1, c. 12, § 5 (1571). The Commons wanted stricter standards. See #5-9 of their 1584 articles, Cardwell, *Doc. Ann.,* ii, 8-9. On York legislation, see K., 195 (1585).

6. 1604, c. 35. This provision was anticipated in part by a regulation adopted for York province in 1585, K., 196. 1575, c. 1 requires the ordinand to be able to give an account of his faith in Latin to the bishop, but does not expressly require the bishop to examine him in any particular manner.

7. Overton, 1585, #25, K., 170, may be an attempt to deal with this problem.

8. The Canons of 1585, p. 142, required every bishop to send the archbishop twice a year a list of the names, degrees, and qualities of every man he had ordained or put into a benefice. This seems a useful device, but it was not continued in later canons. A companion provision required the metropolitan to suspend from ordaining for two years any bishop who ordained unsuitable men or men without title. This device was an old one in the canon law (see the source notes to *Codex Juris Canonici* (1918), c. 2372), but I do not find it in pre-Reformation English material. It was carred over and extended in 1604, c. 35.

9. The 1575 canons, c. 6, provided also for the traditional patrimonial title, but the provision was not continued. An exception for members of cathedral or collegiate churches or colleges appeared in 1575. It was limited in 1604, c. 33 to persons with religious functions in their churches, chaplains or fellows of colleges, or masters of arts of five years standing who were living in Oxford or Cambridge at their own expense.

10. *Reg. Pilkington,* 151-2 is an example.

11. 1575, c. 6; Whitgift, 1584, art. 9; 1585, p. 142. 1604, c. 39 is less explicit, requiring only that he be found "worthy of his ministry." The reference to the *duplex querela* proceeding is found in 1584 and 1585, but not in 1604 (c. 95 is much narrower). For examples of the bishops at work under these canons, see *Reg. Cooper,* 138, 143; Purvis, 98-103. Overton, 1584, #22, K., 167-8, has an especially elaborate provision for examining presentees. He includes a provision for having the presentee preach before his new parishioners before coming to the bishop for institution.

12. *Bell* v. *Bishop of Norwich*, 3 Dyer 254b, 73 Eng. Rep. 564 (1568). Cf. *Specot's Case*, 5 Co. Rep. 57a, 77 Eng. Rep. 141, 3 Leonard 198, 75 Eng. Rep. 630 (1591),

holding that a bishop's statement that a presentee was a *"schismaticus inveteratus"* was not a sufficient excuse. In this case, the point was not that a bishop should put an inveterate schismatic into a benefice, but that the lay court should be told enough to make its own decision as to whether he was a schismatic or not.

13. Canons and other rulings on this subject are Q. Inj. #44; Bishops, 1560-61, #25-26, F., 63; Bishops, 1561, #5, F., 95; Parker, Advts, 1566, #24, F., 177; 1571, p. 120, 125; 1575, c. 3; 1604, c. 48, 76. For examples of various forms of implementation at the diocesan level, see Sandys, 1569, #17, F., 225; Parker, 1575, #4, F., 375; Cooper, 1577, #1-2, K., 41; Purvis, 102; *Reg. Pilkington*, 147 (example of letters of orders); *Reg. Cooper*, 134, 143 (examples of licenses).

14. Canonical material on preaching licenses is Q. Inj. #4, 8; Bishops, 1560-61, #1, 2, F. 59-60; Parker, Advts., 1566, #1-6, F., 172-74, 1571, p. 122, 125-27; 1575, c. 3, 8; Whitgift, 1584, art. 3, 5; 1604, c. 49-52, 66-67. For examples of licenses, showing various restrictions as to locality, see *Reg. Parker*, 333; *Reg. Cooper*, 109-10, 116, 140, 141, 143. Piers, 1590, #7, K., 259 indicates that in York Province a man could still preach in his own cure without a license. Some bishops required a non-preacher to contribute to the support of preachers. *Reg. Cooper*, 144-45; Bentham, 1565, #12, F., 167.

15. Anon., *A Learned Discourse of Ecclesiasticall Government*, Bodl. Gold. 8° C 24 Th (London, 1584). 1575, c. 9 forbids giving a preaching license to anyone not a priest or deacon; 1604, c. 57 condemns at considerable length anyone who refuses to receive the sacraments from a non-preacher.

16. Q. Inj. #49, Elizabeth I, 1561, Cardwell, *Doc. Ann.*, i, 307; Commons, 1584, #1, 4, Cardwell, *Doc. Ann.*, ii, 1, 5; 1597, p. 150-2; 1604, c. 42-4; Hill, 48-9, 224-41.

17. 13 Eliz. 1, c 12, §§ 5-6 (1571) (this statute, unlike the canons, provided for exempting a preacher from the requirement that he know Latin); 1575, c. 7 (cf. Parliamentary petitions, 1584, #10, Cardwell, *Doc. Ann.*, ii, 9, where the prelates seem to have agreed to lowering the limit to £ 20); 1585, p. 145; Convocation, 1586, #5, Cardwell, *Synodalia*, ii, 563-64; 1604, c. 41.

18. *Bland* v. *Maddox*, Cro. Eliz. 79, 78 Eng. Rep. 339 (1588) held that even a layman can be presented to a cathedral prebend, because it is without cure. The prelates, in their answer to Parliamentary Petitions, 1584, #4, Cardwell, *Doc. Ann.*, ii, 5-7, insisted that the prebendary be in orders. But the requirement of a degree or a preaching license to hold a benefice worth £ 30 applied only to benefices with cure. Of the more general requirements for admission to a benefice, cited *supra*, note 11, 1575, c. 6 applied only to benefices with cure, the later ones to all benefices.

19. Grindal, 1576, #1, K., 21, expressly requires preaching in person. Scambler, 1576, #2, K., 40 and Coldwell, 1593, #4, K., 273, by making no provision for a deputy, presumably have the same effect. Piers, 1576, #1, K., 33; Whitgift, 1577, #1, 3, K., 66-67, and Young, 1578, #1, K., 102 expressly allow for a deputy. 1597, p. 151-52 and 1604, c. 43 both expressly require preaching in person.

20. On prophesyings, see Cardwell, *Doc. Ann.*, i, 389-91, 422-24, 428-35, 441-46; Parker, 1575, #43, F., 382-83; Strype, ii, pt. ii, 612-13, 695-701 (an ingenious proposal to combine the prophesying with the traditional office of the rural dean); *Reg. Cooper*, 118. On assignments and examinations, see K. xcvii-ciii; Q. Inj. #16; Bishops, 1560-61, #3, F., 60; Parker, Advts, 1566, #26, F., 178; 1571, p. 117; 1575, c. 11; Cooper, 1577, #16-17, K., 45-46; Barnes, 1577, #12, K., 75-76; Cardwell, *Doc. Ann.*, ii, 21 (1585); Cardwell, *Synodalia*, ii, 562-64 (1586); See also *Reg. Cooper*, 113, 138, imposing similar requirements in individual cases.

21. Hughes, iii, 138-42. The returns given in Purvis, 109-25, evidently from a systematic examination of all the clergy of the York diocese in 1575, seem rather more

encouraging. An entry on p. 117, incidently, suggests some caution in accepting the prevailing view of the low quality of the pre-Reformation clergy: *"Latinum sermonem bene intellegit ac loquitur (ut solent senes)."*

22. K., cii.

23. On licensing, letters dimissory, and not serving two cures at once: Bishops, 1560-61, #25-26, F., 72; 1571, p. 114; 1604, c. 48; On tenure: c. 24, Canterbury, 1213-14, Powicke and Cheney, 30; Cardwell, *Doc. Ann.,* ii, 36 (1588); id., 233 (1633). On stipends: 1571, p. 130; *Reg. Cooper,* 111 (1574) (£ 20); Parliamentary Petitions, 1584 #12, Cardwell, *Doc. Ann.,* ii, 19. Cf. 1604, c. 78, giving the local curate first chance to teach the local school. On the condition of curates generally, see Owen, "Parochial Curates in Elizabethan London," *J. of Eccles. Hist.,* x (1959), 66.

24. Concerning the puritan attack on pluralism and nonresidence, see Parliamentary Petitions, 1584 #12, Cardwell, *Doc. Ann.,* ii, 19; Parliamentary Petitions, 1584 #8, Strype, iii, pt. ii, 281; Clergy, 1584, Cardwell, *Synodalia,* ii, 556; *Commons Journal,* 1610, p. 393; *Lords Journal,* 1610, p. 658-9; Bancroft, 1610, Cardwell, *Doc. Ann.,* ii, 154. On dispensations in the traditional form, see *Reg. Parker,* xxviii. Foster, 459, has some statistics on pluralism. For canonical material on pluralism, nonresidence, and service of nonresidents' cures, see Q. Inj. #11; Bishops, 1560-61, #30, F., 63; 1571, p. 127-28; 1585, p. 145; Convocation, 1586 #6, Cardwell, *Synodalia.* ii, 564; 1597, p. 150-51; 1604, c. 41-44, 47.

25. The quoted inquiries are Sandys, 1578, #6, K., 92, and Piers, 1590, #5, K., 259.

26. *Reg. Cooper,* 111, 113, 125, 139, 140. See also *Reg. Pilkington,* 141-42, 144. The requirement in Q. Inj. #11 that a nonresident with a living worth £ 20 or more (evidently in actuality, rather than in the queen's books) distribute one-fortieth to the local poor was enforced on occasion by the justices of the peace as part of their duty to administer poor relief. *West Riding Sessions,* 3, (1611).

27. Note that King James used cathedral prebends to support his Bible translators. Cardwell, *Doc. Ann.,* ii, 84 (1604) Examining chaplains often had cathedral preferment, as did ecclesiastical judges if they were clergy. Early in the reign, even a few laymen were included.

28. On incontinence, drinking, rowdiness and the like, the canonical documents are Q. Inj. #7; 1571, p. 119; 1604, c. 74.

29. Q. Inj. #29. For examples of licenses, see *Reg. Parker,* 705; *Reg. Cooper,* 111; cf. Tate, 79, a letter from local justices of the peace to the bishop concerning the suitability of the intended bride. On Elizabeth's feelings about clerical marriage, see Cardwell, *Doc. Ann.,* i, 307. All restrictions on clerical marriage were finally done away with by 2 Jac. 1, c. 25 §§ 49-50 (1604).

30. E.g., *Reg. Cooper,* 137; *Winchester Cons. Ct.,* 4, Brinkworth, xi; Redman's Visitation, 20.

31. For proceedings against hunting clerics, see Purvis, 196.

32. In addition to Kennedy's material, see Purvis, 195-96. The practice was forbidden by 21 Hen. 8, c. 13 § 32 (1529).

33. Parker, 1575, #5, F., 375. There are some proceedings in *Redman's Visitation,* 20-21. The promises to be exacted of ministers, set forth at the end of Parker, Advts. 1566, F., 180 included an undertaking by anyone with ecclesiastical income of 20 nobles (£6 13s. 4d.) not to "intermeddle with any artificer's occupations as covetously to seek gain thereby." Cooper evidently enforced these promises. *Reg. Cooper,* 107-8. The restriction is related to that against ministers living as laymen. 1571, p. 120; 1604, c. 76.

34. Canonical materials on clerical dress include Q. Inj. #30; Bishops, 1560-61,

#8, F., 60-61; Parker, Advts., 1566, #30-38, F., 178-79; 1571, p. 119; 1604, c. 74. The quotations are from Barnes, 1577, #7, K., 72, and Bickley, 1586, #47, K., 216.

35. Bishops, 1560-61, #25, F., 63; *Reg. Cooper,* 120; P.A. Welsby, *George Abbot, the Unwanted Archbishop* (London, 1962), 91-104. I cannot find what became of the companion rule that excluded twice-married men from the ministry. It has a firm basis in scripture, but it makes no appearance in this period beyond adding fuel to Elizabeth's annoyance with a couple of her bishops. Hughes, iii, 191, 193.

36. Canonical materials include Parker, Advts. 1566, #5, F., 173; 1604, c. 53; James I, 1622 #v, Cardwell, *Doc. Ann.,* ii, 198, 202. The quotation is taken from Bickley, 1586, #45, K., 216. For proceedings in particular cases, see *Winchester Cons. Ct.,* 42; *Redman's Visitation,* 18; Purvis, 135-6, 209-25.

37. Q. Inj. #48; 1571, p. 120-21, 125; 1604, c. 13-15, 21, 68-69. See Anon., 1560, #14, F., 88 for the rule that a minister must say morning and evening prayer from the Prayer Book at least privately every day. For examples of haste due to pluralism, see Purvis, 21, 25, 62. For a case of a curate inhibited from the diocese for mumbling see id., 127.

38. K., civ, cxv-cxvi; Parker, Advts., 1566, #15, F., 175; Grindal, 1571, #7, F., 255; Grindal, 1571, #4, F. 275; Middleton, 1583, #1, 4, K., 146-47; Bancroft, 1601, #16, K., 339, Purvis, 66 (wafer bread with printing), 153-55.

39. Parker Advts. 1566, #11, 13, F., 175; Foster, lxvi.

40. Bishops, 1560-61, #21, F., 62; 1571, p. 124; 1604, c. 67; cf. W.P. Haugaard, *Elizabeth and the English Reformation* (Cambridge, 1968), 114-16 on the queen's Latin Prayer Book of 1560.

41. Elizabeth 1, 1561 #5, 7, F. 109-10; Parker, Advts., 1566, #16, F. 176; 1571, p. 123; 1604, c. 29-30, 68-69, 81.

42. Q. Inj. #18-20; Bishops, 1560-61, #4, F., 60; Parker Advts., 1566, #21, F., 177; 1604 c. 64, 88; Cf. Barnes, 1577, #16, K., 77 (no marriages in Lent).

43. Q. Inj. #3, 4, 8; Bishops, 1560-61, #1, F., 59-60; Parker, Advts , 1566, F., 173-74; 1571, p. 127; Convocation, 1586 #6, 7, Cardwell, *Synodalia,* ii, 564; 1604, c. 45-7; James I, 1622, Cardwell, *Doc. Ann.,* ii, 198. Some bishops imposed a tax on nonpreaching incumbents for the support of preachers. Bentham, 1565, #12, F., 167 (8d. in £). *Reg. Cooper,* 144-45.

44. Q. Inj., #4, 5, 14, 27; 1575, c. 10; Cf. Cooper, 1577, #19, K., 47 (duty to read off bishop's injunctions after visitation).

45. Q. Inj. #1, 2, 25; Parker, Advts., 1566, #2, 3, 5, F., 172-73; 1571, p. 122; 1575, c. 9; 1604, c. 1, 53. The quotation in text is from a set of articles that Cooper required preachers to subscribe. *Reg. Cooper,* 107-8.

46. Q. Inj. #44; Bishops, 1560-61, #6, F., 60; Parker, Advts., 1566, #23, F., 177; 1571, p. 120-22; 1575, c. 10; 1604, c. 49, 61.

47. Q. Inj. #19; 1604, c. 67, 71, 113. On reservation of the Sacrament, see W. P. M. Kennedy, *Law and Custom on Reservation* (Cambridge, 1929).

48. 1 Eliz. I, c. §§ *14-18 (1558);* Q. Inj. #33, 46; Bishops, 1560-61, #13, F., 61; 1571, p. 123-24, 125; 1604, c. 28; 90. On the relation between lay and ecclesiastical authority to punish violators, see *Anon.,* Marsh, N.R. 92, 82 Eng. Rep. 426 (1640).

49. Q. Inj. #38. The same language is included in 1604, c. 18. For another formulation, see 1571, p. 21.

50. Purvis, 214-15.

51. Q. Inj. #36; Parker, Advts., 1566, #5, F., 173; Q., 1559 #25-26, 32, F., 4-5; Bancroft, 1605, #13, Cardwell, *Doc. Ann.,* ii, 104; Purvis, 85-86, 137.

52. Bancroft, 1601, #27, K., 341; Purvis, 87-91; Brinkworth, 170-71. The 1287

canon referred to in text is c. 12, Exeter 1287, Wilkins, ii, 139, 140, Powicke and Cheney, 1005, 1007. On the applicable law, see Chapter IV, note 122 and accompanying text, *infra*.

53. Q. Inj. #20, 34; Bishops, 1560-61, #5, F., 69; Parker, Advts., 1566, #20, F., 176; 1571, p. 123-24; 1604, c. 13. The cases referred to in text are from Purvis, 82, 137, and 94-95.

54. 31 Hen. 8, c. 14 (1539). The Declaration of Sports appears in Wilkins, iv, 483. For the history of secular legislation on Sunday observance (abortive attempts in Elizabeth's reign; a statute finally passed in Charles's), see "Lord's Day", Burn, i, 671. Hart, *Country Clergy*, 71-74 suggests that the main opponents of Sunday sports were the justices of the peace, who worried about disorder.

55. Q. Inj. #6, 23-5, 47; Parker, Advts., 1566, #14, F., 175; 1571, p. 123; 1604, c. 80-4. On the parish chest, see also Tate, 34-42. On preserving the traditional baptismal font, see note 41, *supra*.

56. Q. Inj. #13 (one-fifth income of benefice to be used for repair of chancel and parsonage); 1571 p. 123; 1604 c. 85-86. On the queen's failure to discharge her responsibilities as a rector, see 1571 p. 129; Purvis 182. On remedies, see 13 Eliz. 1, c. 10 (1571); *Bishop of Salisbury's Case*, Godbolt 259, 78 Eng. Rep. 151 (1614).

57. *Visitations in the Diocese of Lincoln, 1517-31*, ed. Thompson, i (L.R.S. xxxiii, 1940), 119-40.

58. 1604, c. 85.

59. 1571, p. 124; 1604, c. 88; *Reg. Cooper*, 138; *C.S.P.D.*, *1637-38*, 63 (mock marriage service for Lord of Misrule and Christmas Wife). The case of the puppet plays is *Reg. Cooper*, 137, 138; that of the bowlers who beat up the curate Purvis, 92. For the medieval situation, see J.R.H. Moorman, *Church Life in England in the Thirteenth Century*, (Cambridge, 1946), 147.

60. Stubbs, *Anatomy of Abuses*, ed. Furnival (1877), 98. Cf. Parliamentary Petitions, 1584, #27-8, Strype, iii, pt. ii, 295.

61. Brinkworth, i, 101, 110 has a case of two men cited in for a quarrel of unspecified nature, and dismissed upon their assurances that they had become reconciled.

62. Art. 43, Mansi, xxiii, 329.

63. Elizabeth 1, 1559, #35, F., 5.

64. 1571, p. 124; 1604, c. 26, 109, 113.

65. Oath of Churchwardens and Sidesmen, appended to Bickley, 1586, K., 221.

66. Squire, 1582, #37, K., 132-33. 1604, c. 26 provides that a churchwarden who fails to make presentments is to be repelled from communion as a perjurer. Cases of churchwardens being corrected for failure to report offenders are referrred to in Hart, *The Man in the Pew*, 62, and Purvis, 185.

67. Bancroft, 1605, #70, Cardwell, *Doc. Ann.*, ii, 115. The language about bawds, etc. is from Chaderton, 1581, #46, K., 122.

68. Cf. Brinkworth i, 52. Bishops, 1560-61, #31-32, F., 64; 1571, p. 122, 130; 1585, p. 143; 1597, p. 153-55; 1604, c. 62-63, 99-104, 107.

69. Q. Inj., #21. For the historical basis of the principle, see Iung, "Communion", *Dictionnaire de Droit Canonique*, iii (Paris, 1942), 1098, 1115-16.

70. Bickley, 1586, #38, K., 215.

71. Under 1604, c. 113 ministers also had power to make presentments if the churchwardens were remiss, but I find no evidence that they made a practice of doing so. The presentment cost money to process, whereas the use of the rubric to repel sinners from communion cost nothing.

72. Cooper, 1577, #13, K., 44-45.

73. Q. Inj. #28. The pieces of invective quoted in text are from, respectively, Purvis, 137, id., 140, and Foster, lxvii. For another interesting case, see *Reg. Cooper*, 115.

74. *Love* v. *Prin*, Cro. Eliz. 754, 78 Eng. Rep. 985 (Q.B., 1599).

75. *Gaudye's Case*, 2 B. & G. 38, 123 Eng. Rep. 802 (1610); *The Parish Clerk*, 13 Co. Rep. 70, 77 Eng. Rep. 1479 (1611).

76. On the chest for the poor, see Q. Inj., #25; 1604, c. 85. On churchwardens' accounts, 1571, p. 122; 1604, c. 89.

77. 1571, p. 130; 1604, c. 87. "Terrier", Burn, ii, 367 has a copy of Burn's own terrier, showing the different kinds of rights that may be included. For a couple of examples of depredations turned up by the compilers of terriers, see Hill, 213.

78. For an almost contemporary treatment of the principles of accountancy, see Richard Dafforne, *The Merchants Mirrour*, (London, 1635).

79. The writ is in *The Correspondence of Dr. Matthew Hutton*, ed. Raine (Surtees Soc., xvii, 1843), 76. See also Strype, iii, pt. i, 686. Cecil's argument is in a letter from him and Sir John Wolley to Matthew Hutton, who was worried about simony in making promises to the queen on his appointment to the see of York. *The Correspondence of Dr. Matthew Hutton, supra*, 93-94.

80. 1 Eliz. 1, c. 19 (1559). On Crediton, see D.N.B., Babington.

81. 1. Eliz. 1, c. 19 (1559); 13 Eliz. 1, c. 10 (1571); 18 Eliz. 1, c. 11 (1576); 2 Jac. 1, c. 3 (1604). These statutes are taken up more fully in Chapter IV.

82. *C.S.P.D., 1629-31*, 122. 5-6 Vic., c. 108 (1842) abolished entry fines in connection with a general reform of ecclesiastical leases.

83. 1571, p. 114-15. Most of the leases mentioned in Hill, 115-17 were adopted before 1571.

84. 13 Eliz. 1, c. 20 (1571) (a temporary act, kept in force by periodic continuations, and made perpetual by 3 Car. 1, c. 4 (1627). On death as nonresidence, see *Mott* v. *Hales*, Cro. Eliz. 123, 78 Eng. Rep. 380 (1588), overruled, *Baily and Mum and Silby*, 3 Keble 106, 84 Eng. Rep. 620 (1673).

85. Parkhurst, 1569, #5, F., 208. The quote is from Barnes, 1577, #9, K., 73-4. The sequestration for nonresidence in *Reg. Pilkington*, 141-3 refers to farming the benefice.

86. Bickley, 1586, #78, K., 221. More often, the inquiry was simply whether the church was vacant and, if so, who was taking the revenues. E.g., Grindal, 1571, #35, F., 263. On patrons making themselves impropriators, and impropriators moving into vicarages, see Westfaling, 1586, #69-70, K., 234.

87. Most of these schemes are inquired after in Grindal, 1571, #34, F., 263. On marrying the patron's daughter, see Hill, 68. See also Harison, 160-62, where the presentee appointed his patron to be parish clerk. It appears that leasing the tithes to the patron would not be evidence of a simoniacal agreement if the rental was reasonable. *C.S.P.D., 1634-35*, 336.

88. Johnson, 447-52 (1392); Reg. Cooper, 110; 1604, c. 40; Bishops, 1561, #4, F., 95-96. The canonical basis for the actual prohibition and punishment of simony was 1571, p. 129, plus the pre-Reformation canons.

89. 31 Eliz. 1, c. 6 (1589). Cases include *Booth* v. *Potter*, Cro. Jac. 533, 79 Eng. Rep. 457 (1619) (invalidity of lease); *Winchcombe* v. *Bishop of Winchester*, Hobart 166, 80 Eng. Rep. 313 (1616) (right of king to present). I read *Riesby* v. *Wentworth*, Cro. Eliz. 642, 78 Eng. Rep. 881 (1598) as recognizing that the statute is a defense in a tithe suit: it denies prohibition because that defense should be tried in a church court.

90. 1571, p. 114-15. On the Lincoln registers, see *Reg. Cooper*, 241ff.

91. Cardwell, *Doc. Ann.*, ii, 53.

92. 11 Hen 7, c. 8 (1494); 37 Hen. 8, c. 9 (1545); 5-6 Edw. 6, c. 20 (1552); 13 Eliz. 1, c. 8 (1571) (temporary act kept in force by periodic continuations until made perpetual by 39 Eliz. 1, c. 18, § 12 (1597).

93. Cardwell, *Synodalia,* ii, 436 (1554).

94. 1571, p. 124; 1604, c. 109. 1597, p. 155 refers to excommunicating usurers. The cases referred to in text are from Purvis, 200-201.

95. 21 Jac. 1, c. 17 (1624).

96. 27 Hen. 8, c. 25 (1536).

97. Q. Inj., #25; Edw. 6 Inj., #29, Cardwell, *Doc. Ann.,* i, 17-18; Charles Drew, *Early Parochial Organisation in England: The Origins of the Office of Churchwarden* (St. Anthony's Hall Pub. No. 7, York, 1954), 15-18. The device of multiple locks provided for in these Injunctions goes back to Archbishop Winchelsea in 1296. Ibid. The incumbent's fortieth is provided for in Q. Inj., #11, the 12d fines in 1 Eliz. 1, c. 2, § 14 (1559). *West Riding Sessions Records 1611-42,* ed. Lister (Y.A.A., iv, 1915), 3 (1611) indicates that the justices of the peace could require the churchwardens to levy the fortieth.

98. 5-6 Edw. 6, c. 2 (1552). The Elizabethan statutes are 5 Eliz. 1, c. 3 (1563) and 14 Eliz. 1, c. 5 (1572).

99. Bickley, 1586, #76, K., 220.

100. 39 Eliz. 1, c. 6 (1597-8). This was repealed in 1601 and replaced by 43 Eliz. 1, c. 4 (1601), to approximately the same effect. On the operation of this legislation, see c. IV, notes 115-20 and accompanying text, *infra.* The 1414 act is 2 Hen. 5, St. 1, c. 1. It expired in a year and was not renewed.

101. Tate, 119-24; *Reg. Parker,* 444-45.

102. 1571, p. 127-28. See also 1597, p. 150-51, 1604, c. 42. Hospitalities are mentioned in the 1307 language on provisors (quoted *supra,* p. 2) as among the purposes for which the church was founded.

103. Foster, 461. On Gilpin's feeding his parishioners, see Hart, *Country Clergy,* 137.

104. Q. Inj., #39-42; 1571, p. 128-29 (subject to an exception for the "primary nobility"); 1604, c. 77-79 (no exception). For wholesale examination of incumbent schoolmasters, seé Purvis, 103-9, involving the issuance of new licenses, and Overton, 1584, #24, K., 169-170, involving the taking up of old ones. The case of the man left in his place for lack of a replacement is Purvis, 109. Overton proposes to abolish general licenses for the diocese, and license only for specific places. Purvis has examples of both kinds. 1604, c. 78, with its provision for giving the parish curate first chance, evidently envisages only local licenses. For examples of licenses, see *Reg. Parker,* 383; *Reg. Cooper,* 110.

105. Hart, *The Man in the Pew,* 110-7; Barnes, 1577 #11, K. 74-75; 1604 c. 78.

106. 3 Hen. 8, c. 11 (1511). 14-15 Hen. 8, c. 5 (1522) turned over the examining function as regards physicians (but not surgeons) to an incorporated body of London physicians. Burn ("Physicians", in ii, 150) seems to think that this statute excluded the bishops from the licensing function as well. But Middleton 1583, #42, K., 144 still contemplates licensing by the ordinary. In any event, unlicensed practitioners continued to be inquired after on visitations. *Redman's Visitation,* 27.

107. What was expected of a midwife can be seen in the oath administered after examination in *Reg. Parker,* 470-72, and in the visitation inquiries Parker, 1575, #45, F., 383; Bickley, 1586, #58, K., 218. Note that on baptism by midwives, Parker takes a different position in his visitation article from the one he takes in the oath. There was considerable ambivalence on this point: allowing laypeople, especially women, to baptize in emergencies seemed to presuppose that the sacrament had a supernatural

effect, and was not a mere initiation into the Christian community.

108. On subscription, see 1571, p. 118, 120, 127; 1575, c. 1; 13 Eliz. 1, c. 12 (1571). As to examination for beliefs, see Purvis, 103; *Reg. Cooper,* 151-52. The authorities also required an imprimatur for books. Q. Inj., #51.

109. E.g., Bancroft, 1601, #47, K., 346: ''. . . which it is to be conjectured they do keep for a day, as they call it.''

110. Q., 1559, #51., F. 7.

111. 1571, p. 120; Whitgift, 1584, art. 2, 1604, c. 71. On domestic chapels, see also 23 Eliz. 1, c. 1 § 12 (1581).

112. 1575 c. 9; Whitgift, 1584, art. 5 is to the same effect. On the need for episcopal ordination, see Sykes, *Old Priest and New Presbyter* (Cambridge, 1956). The civil courts held that a non-ordained person validly occupied his ecclesiastical position until canonically deprived *Bedinfield* v. *Archbishop of Canterbury,* 3 Dyer 293a, 73 Eng. Rep. 657 (1570); *Costard* v. *Winder,* Cro. Eliz. 775, 78 Eng. Rep. 1005 (1599).

113. Cooper, 1577, #3-4; K., 42 Whitgift, 1584 art. 3; 1604 c. 56. See Grindal, *Remains,* 413-14. On nonconformists with conforming curates, see Purvis, 214.

114. 1 Eliz. 1, c. 2, § 14 (1559); Q. Inj., #33; Q., 1559, #39, F., 5; Marchant, 131; Bancroft, 1601, #48-51, K., 346-7, #69, K., 351. See also #65, K., 350, on people who come to sermons but do not attend liturgical services at all.

115. *Dedham Classis.*

116. Aylmer, 1577, #55, K., 49; Aylmer, 1586, #25, K., 202.

117. Bancroft, 1601, #56, 60, K., 348-9.

118. *Queen Elizabeth's Defence. . .,* ed. Collins (1849).

119. On the king's legislative powers, see *Memorandum,* Cro. Jac. 37, 79 Eng. Rep. 30 (1604). On dispensation, see *Walrond* v. *Pollard,* 3 Dyer 294a, 73 Eng. Rep. 659 (1570); *Dean and Chapter of Norwich's Case,* 3 Co. Rep. 73a, 76 Eng. Rep. 793 (Ch. 1598); *Commendam Case,* Hobart 140, 80 Eng. Rep. 290 (1613); *Britton* v. *Wade,* Cro. Jac. 515, 79 Eng. Rep. 440, 1619); *Evans and Kiffins* v. *Askwith,* Jones, W. 158, 82 Eng. Rep. 84 (1625). On pardon: *Hall's Case,* 5 Co. Rep. 51a, 77 Eng. Rep. 132 (1604); *Conway's Case,* 2 Brown and Golds. 37, 123 Eng. Rep. 801 (1610).

120. R.G. Usher, *The Rise and Fall of the High Commission* (Oxford, 1913) seems to be regarded with misgivings by the present generation of seventeenth-century historians. Nevertheless, it remains the only available book-length treatment of the subject, and I have had perforce to rely on it for some points.

121. See Usher, *supra,* note 120, at 191-201, 308-11; Marchant, 63, 66-69, 131-2 (all Laudian). Barnes, 1577 #3, K., 71 contemplates clergy presenting offenders to the bishop or to the diocesan High Commission as they choose. 1604, c. 86 contemplates presentments to the High Commission only, but Marchant says it was not enforced in this way. On the available records (all Laudian) from the London High Commission, see Usher, 367-68. There is an almost complete set from York (see Purvis, xiv-xv); I have not had the opportunity to examine the still unpublished work of Dr. Philip Tyler on this material. The lay cases restricting the jurisdiction of the High Commission include *Sir Anthony Roper's Case,* 12 Co. Rep. 45, 77 Eng. Rep. 1326 (1608), *Sir William Chancey's Case,* 12 Co. Rep. 82, 77 Eng. Rep. 1360 (1611), *Langdale's Case,* 12 Co. Rep. 50, 58, 77 Eng. Rep. 1330, 1338 (1608). See also *Lady Throgmorton's Case,* 12 Co. Rep. 69, 77 Eng. Rep. 1347 (1611), holding that the Commission was not a court of record, and therefore could not punish for contempt. *Langdale* was a prohibition case; the others were habeas corpus. Coke's line in these cases resulted in another inconclusive confrontation between him and the king. *High Commission,* 12 Co. Rep.

84, 77 Eng. Rep. 1361 (1611). Of course the Commission was never effectively kept within the limits Coke assigned it.

122. E.g., *Reg. Cooper*, 113, 137, 139.

123. On the contrast between medieval and Elizabethan archdeacons, see B.L. Woodcock, 68-69. On the functions of the latter, see 1571, p. 117-8; 1575, c. 11-13; Cooper, 1577, #1, K., 41 (licensing curates); Peters. The presbyterian proposal is in *Dedham Classis*, 85.

124. Marchant, 127-8; Purvis, 34, 202; 1571, p. 117. Grindal, 1571, #64, F., 272 lumps rural deans and apparitors. On reviving the office, see Cardwell, *Synodalia*, ii, 505n; Strype, ii, pt, ii, 695-701. The quote from Burn is in "Deans and Chapters", i, 440, 476.

125. Marchant, 35-6, 82-4. Harison is the record of the man who was legal secretary to the bishop of Norwich from 1602 to 1617.

126. Purvis, 100, 109-25.

127. Wilkins, iv, 222 (Parker, 1560); 329 (Whitgift, 1587); 1604, c. 93-94; *Reg. Cooper*, 124.

128. *Reg. Parker*, xxviii; Grindal, *Remains*, 448-50.

129. Cardwell, *Doc. Ann.*, i, 466-67n.

130. On the history of the churchwardens' office, see Charles Drew, *Early Parochial Organisation in England; The Origins of the Office of Churchwarden* (St. Anthony's Hall Pub. No. 7, York, 1954); Tate, 83-118. On secular functions, see also Lambarde, *The Duties of Constables,* (London, 1587), 45-54; *West Riding Sessions*, xxxii, 11, 3, 278. On status as a lay office, see *Bishopp's Case*, 2 Rolle 71, 81 Eng. Rep. 666 (1618) (churchwardens need not render accounts before ecclesiastical court); but cf. *Brown* v. *Lowther*, Goldsboro 113, 75 Eng. Rep. 1031 (1597) (defamation action based on accusation of false account may be tried in church court, as it is spiritual matter). On election, see 1571, p. 122; 1604, c. 89. It appears that at one time the function of responding to the bishop or archdeacon belonged not to the churchwardens but to men called questmen (= inquestmen) or sidesmen (= synodsmen). These functions were taken over by the churchwardens as early as the fourteenth century, but the names of the old offices continued in various forms. The Canons of 1604 (89-90) use "questman" as a synonym for churchwarden, and "sidesman" to refer to one of the assistants delegated under Q. Inj., #46 to help keep order and enforce attendance.

131. However, Lambarde, *supra*, note 130 says that the churchwardens are not to hold land for the parish.

132. 1571, p. 125-26; 1604, c. 50, 52; Cooper, 1577, #1, 2, 4, 10, K., 41-44. Cf. Q. Inj., #10, on the register of births, marriages, and deaths.

133. *Churchwardens of Northwould* v. *Scot; Choyce* Cases 155, 21 Eng. Rep. 91 (Ch. 1581-82) (duty of parson to contribute to poor); *Churchwardens of Fetherstones Case*, 1 Leonard 177, 74 Eng. Rep. 163 (1588) (trespass); *C.S.P.D.* 1634-35, 422 (augmentation of vicarage).

134. *Bishopp's Case, supra* note 130, holds that a churchwarden who has once accounted before minister, parishioners, and successor churchwardens need not account before an ecclesiastical judge. If he has not accounted before minister, parishioners and successors, the case leaves room for an ecclesiastical judge to make him do so.

135. 1604, c. 26. For examples of oaths, see Grindal, 1571, F., 272-73; Barnes, 1577, K., 173. *Winchester Cons. Ct.*, 51 has a case of a churchwarden evidently moved by strictures of this kind to report an offense he had previously passed over.

136. K., cxxxi.

137. The issue of whether the Canons bind the laity *proprio vigore* was not finally settled in the lay courts until *Middleton* v. *Crofts*, 2 Atk. 650, 26 Eng. Rep. 788 (1736).

On the situation before that, compare the appendices of Frere (p. 265) and Dibdin (p. 279) to the *Report of the Archbishops' Committee on Church and State* (London, 1918). For my own part, I agree with Dibdin's conclusion: "It would be extremely hazardous to assume that at any time between 1603 and 1736. . .there was any general acceptance (outside ecclesiastical circles) of the Canons as binding on laymen." There are three Jacobean cases that bear on the question: *Bird* v. *Smith*, Moore K.B. 781, 72 Eng. Rep. 902 (1606); *Of Convocations*, 12 Co. Rep. 72, 77 Eng. Rep. 1350 (1610); *Shipden* v. *Chancellor of Norwich*, Palmer 296, 81 Eng. Rep. 1090 (1622).

138. Most of the canonical material is supplied with notes in Cardwell, *Synodalia* or *Doc. Ann.* See also W.P. Haugaard, *Elizabeth and the English Reformation* (Cambridge, 1968), 225-26 on the origin of Parker's Advertisements; Aylmer, 1586, #39, K., 204 on the royal assent to the articles adopted in the Convocation of 1586, and Marchant 129-30 on the adoption of the Canons of 1604 in York.

139. *Reg. Trillek*, 157-9.

140. Cardwell, *Doc. Ann.*, ii, 20.

141. Grindal, 1571, #14, F. 279; Cooper, 1577, #19, K., 47; Q. Inj., #14. On reading the Canons of 1604, see Cardwell, *Synodalia*, i, 329; Bancroft, 1605, #1, Cardwell, *Doc. Ann.*, ii, 101.

142. Whitgift, 1584, art. 3; 1604, c. 54, 56. Cf. Parker, Advts., 1566, #25, F., 177, providing for checking on the progress of anyone dispensed from residence for purposes of study.

143. *Reg. Parker*, 470-72.

144. 1571, p. 112, 118, 119; 13 Eliz. 1, c. 12 (1571); Whitgift, 1584, art. 6; 1604, c. 36. Cf. 1604, c. 98, requiring subscription to Whitgift's three articles before anyone accused of a liturgical violation could appeal. The 1571 statute required subscribing to "all the articles of religion which only concern the confession of the true Christian faith and doctrine of the sacraments. . ." thus leaving room to exclude those articles that concern ecclesiastical polity. The stricter canonical requirement was imposed in spite of the statute.

145. Cooper, 1577, #3, K., 42; Whitgift, 1584, art. 3; 1604, c. 56.

146. Parker, Advts., 1566, Appendix, F., 179-80; Bishops, 1561, Appendix, F., 67-68; *Reg. Parker*, 141-42.

147. Whitgift, 1584 art. 11; 1585, p. 143; 1597, p. 154; 1604, c. 41, 101-2, 107; *Reg. Cooper*, 135; *Mrs. Paschall's Case*, 2 Leonard 179, 74 Eng. Rep. 459 (Exch. 1588).

148. On registers of births, marriages, and deaths, see Tate, 43-46; Injunctions of Henry VIII (i.e., Cromwell), #12, F., ii, 39-40 (1538); Q. Inj., #10; 1597, p. 160-1; 1604, c. 70. On terriers: 1571, p. 130; 1604, c. 87. On lists of preachers: 1571, p. 125-6; 1604, c. 52. On ordination lists: 1597, p. 142 (not carried over in 1604). See also 1604, c. 126, providing for keeping copies of wills in the bishop's register.

149. Marchant, 154-5; *Reg. Cooper*, 134.

150. In addition to the material cited at the head of this chapter, I have drawn on accounts of visitations in Foster; *Ecclesiastical Proceedings of Bishop Barnes* (Surtees Soc., xxii, 1850); *The Primary Visitation of the Diocese of Lincoln by Bishop Neile A.D. 1614*, ed. Venables (Assoc. Arch. Soc. Rep. xvi, 1881); "Visitation of the Dean of York's Peculiar", *Yorks. Archaeol. Journal*, xviii, 197, 313 (ed. Fallow, 1904-5); "Visitation of Warrington Deanery 1592", *Hist. Soc. of Ches. and Lancs.* (n.s.), x, 183 (ed. Irvine, 1895); "Visitations of the Archdeacon of Canterbury" *Archaeologia Cantiana*, xxv, 11, xxvi, 17, xxvii, 123 (ed. Hussey, 1903-5); Peters, 37-48.

151. Cardwell, *Doc. Ann.*, i, 309. See response in *Reg. Cooper*, 151-2; cf. 1585, p. 146; 1604, c. 86. Elizabeth's 1561 inquiry appears at Cardwell, *Doc. Ann.* i, 307. For

the 1346 request for a list of aliens, see *Reg. Trillek,* 260, 284.

152. F., 374.

153. Strype, ii., pt. ii, 524-28.

154. 1571, p. 117; cf. 1604, c. 128.

155. See *Reg. Cooper,* 137 for a case of clerical incontinence turned up by presentment on an archdeacon's visitation, and heard by the bishop in his parlor. Marchant refers to "correction courts", but it does not seem to me that these were anything but the regular courts showing some flexibility as to where they sat.

156. 1597, p. 159; 1604, c. 120, 138. The quote is from Sandys, 1578, #38, K., 100. 1604, c. 109-21 contain further regulations of the presenting process. See Harison, 30-1, 43-5 for one bishop's efforts to control the apparitors in his diocese.

157. Strype, *Whitgift,* iv 374-8; Wilkins, iv, 364.

158. This discussion is mainly based on Marchant, and on the following Canons: 1571 p. 118-19; 1585 p. 144-45; 1597 p. 159-61; 1604 c. 92-94, 96-97, 121, 127-38. See also Harison, 26-33. On the eligibility of laymen for cathedral benefices, mentioned below, see *Bland* v. *Maddox,* Cro. Eliz. 79, 78 Eng. Rep. 339 (1588).

159. Marchant, 180; Peters, 59.

160. Peters, 35-36; Harison, 30-31, 43-5. The Canons limiting the number of apparitors are 1597, p. 159 and 1604, c. 138.

161. *Reg. Parker,* 254, 513-19; 18 Eliz. 1, c. 7 (1576). The statute was interpreted as taking away the bishop's power to deprive a minister for conduct amounting to a clergyable felony. *Searle* v. *Williams,* Hobart 288, 80 Eng. Rep. 433 (1618). For proceedings on a matrimonial case referred by a lay court, see *Reg. Cooper,* 126-34 (1576).

162. Collusive annulments continued to be a problem. 1597, p. 154-55; 1604, c. 105-8.

163. 1597, p. 159; 1604, c. 138; Cardwell, *Synodalia,* ii, 580-3 (1601); Sandys, 1578, #39, K., 100; Bancroft, 1605, #72, Cardwell, *Doc. Ann.,* ii, 115.

164. Harison, 33.

165. Marchant, 229; cf. c. 17 of the Canons of 1640, Cardwell, *Synodalia,* i, 413.

166. The cases mentioned in this and the following paragraphs are: the mumbling curate, Purvis, 127; letter from justices, *Reg. Cooper,* 116; parishoners complaining, id. 136, 139, Harison, 160-62; lack of letters, *Reg. Cooper,* 134, 143; vicar seducing woman, id., 137, 139; supplying drink for perambulations, Purvis, 63; Cooper calling in official, *Reg. Cooper,* 125-26. For examples of cases heard on articles, see Purvis, 203-31.

167. In addition to the material cited at the head of this chapter, this account draws heavily on cases from *Reg. Cooper.*

168. 1604, c. 56-59, 62-63, 68-69, 71-72.

169. Foster, lxvi-lxxv; Marchant, 132-33. For a case involving especial patience, see *C.S.P.D.,* 1633-34, 317, 321, 326.

170. "Some Elizabethan Penances in the Diocese of Ely", *Trans of the Royal Hist. Soc.* 3d Ser., i. 263 (ed. Hall, 1907).

171. 1571, p. 118-19; 1575 c., 12; Whitgift, 1584, art. 11; 1585, p. 142-43; Harison, 24-33; Bancroft, 1605 #68, Cardwell, *Doc. Ann.,* ii. 114.

172. 1585, p. 145-46; 1604, c. 135-36. Most of this discussion of costs and contumacy is based on Marchant.

173. Strype, *Whitgift,* iv. 374-78.

174. Anon., *A Learned Discourse of Ecclesiasticall Government* (Bodl. Gold. 8° C. 24 Th.) (London, 1584), 133-34.

174. Anon., *The Proctor and Parator their Mourning* (Bodl. Pamph. D. 40

(34) (1641).

175. F.D. Price, "An Elizabethan Church Official — Thomas Powell, Chancellor of the Diocese of Gloucester":, *Church Qtrly Rev.,* cxxviii, (1939); "Elizabethan Apparitors in the Diocese of Gloucester", id., cxxxiii (1942). I have also had the benefit of several conversations with Mr. Price concerning the situation in Gloucester.

176. *Loc. cit. supra,* note 174.

177. *Of Oaths Before an Ecclesiastical Judge ex Officio,* 12 Co. Rep. 26, 77 Eng. Rep. 1308 (1607); *C.S.P.D., 1637-8,* 229-30; Maguire, "The Attack of the Common Lawyers on the Oath ex Officio", *Essays in Honor of C. H. McIlwain,* (Cambridge, Mass. 1936), 199.

178. Marchant. 245.

179. I place in the first category Canons 19, 33, 35, 41-47, 50, 52-53, 59, 62-63, 70, 77-78, 84, 86-87, 90, 92-97, 100-8, 116-38; and in the second Canons 13, 20, 26, 31-32, 39-40, 60-61, 64-65, 68-69, 71-72, 75-76, 81, 85, 88, 91, 109, 111-14. Canons 83 and 89 belong in one category or the other, but I am not sure which.

4. Coke and the Common Law

1. Holdsworth, iv, 1-293, passim.

2. The examples in text are, respectively, *Dolman* v. *Levesque de Sarum,* Moore (K.B.) 119, 72 Eng. Rep. 479 (1583) (actually, the dispensation was held to have been beyond the powers of the pope); *Chrimes* v. *Smith,* 12 Co. Rep. 4, 77 Eng. Rep. 1287 (Exch. Ch. 1586); *Dean and Chapter of Norwich's Case,* 3 Co. Rep. 73a, 76 Eng. Rep. 793 Ch. 1598. See also *Priddle and Napper's Case,* 11 Co. Rep. 8b, 77 Eng. Rep. 1155 (1613); *Bishop of Winchester's Case,* 2 Co. Rep. 38a, 76 Eng. Rep. 501 (Q.B. 1596); *Stathome's Case,* 3 Dyer 277b, 73 Eng. Rep. 621 (1568) on discharge from tithes; *Britton* v. *Wade,* Cro. Jac. 515, 79 Eng. Rep. 440 (1619) on dissolution of a vicarage.

3. *Evans and Kiffens* v. *Askwith,* Jones W. 158, 82 Eng. Rep. 84 (1625); *Commendam Case,* Hobart 140, 80 Eng. Rep. 290 (1613); *Austin* v. *Twyne,* Cro. Eliz. 500, 78 Eng. Rep. 750 (Q.B. 1595); *Grendon* v. *Bishop of Lincoln,* 2 Plowden 493, 75 Eng. Rep. 734 (1573) are all cases in which the scope of royal power is determined by examining the former scope of papal power. The theoretical basis for this situation was elaborated by Coke in *Caudrey's Case,* 5 Co. Rep. 1a, 77 Eng. Rep. 1 (1595). See also 2 Co. Inst. *604. There is a certain inconsistency in Coke's reasoning here: he uses the same material to establish that the king exercised ecclesiastical jurisdiction before the Reformation and to show that he set limits to its exercise. Maitland in *Roman Canon Law in the Church of England,* c. 3 (1898) found similar inconsistencies in some of the Anglican thinking of his own time.

The prerogative, established in *Wentworth* v. *Wright,* Cro. Eliz. 526, 78 Eng. Rep. 774 (1596), of appointing to a benefice whose incumbent is made a bishop is similar to a power claimed by the pope, but was not treated as derived from that power. *Armiger* v. *Holland,* Cro. Eliz. 542, 78 Eng. Rep. 789 (1597). See the arguments in *R.* v. *Eton Coll.,* 8 El. & Bl. 610, 120 Eng. Rep. 228 (1857).

4. *Oldbury* v. *Gregory,* Moore K.B. 564, 72 Eng. Rep. 761 (1598) (bond enforceable in lay court despite simoniacal consideration); *Holland's Case,* 4 Co. Rep. 75a, 76 Eng. Rep. 1047 (1597) (relation between statutes and canons on pluralism);

Caudrey's Case, 5 Co. Rep. 1a, 77 Eng. Rep. 1 (1595) (relation between canonical and statutory remedies for preaching against the Book of Common Prayer). Cf. *Prohibition,* 12 Co. Rep. 76, 77 Eng. Rep. 1354 (1611) (prohibition will not stop execution of writ *de excommunicato capiendo,* as that is royal, not ecclesiastical, process).

5. *Of Convocations,* 12 Co. Rep. 71, 77 Eng. Rep. 1350 (1611); *Warner's Case,* Cro. Jac. 532, 79 Eng. Rep. 456 (1620); *Orme* v. *Pemberton,* Cro. Car. 589, 79 Eng. Rep. 1106 (1641); *Case de Modo Decimandi,* 13 Co. Rep. 36, 77 Eng. Rep. 1448 (1610); *Premunire,* 12 Co. Rep. 37, 77 Eng. Rep. 1319. For Coke's confrontation with Bancroft, see 2 Co. Inst. *599-618. See pp. 108-10 *supra.*

6. For the power of the common law courts to try questions of statute and custom, see, respectively, *Porter and Rochester's Case,* 13 Co. Rep. 4, 77 Eng. Rep. 1416 (1609) and *Case de Modo Decimandi, supra.* For the economic background of the latter case, see Hill, 93-99.

7. The cases referred to in text are *Bennet* v. *Easedale,* Cro. Car. 55, 79 Eng. Rep. 651 (1627) and *Searle* v. *Williams,* Hobart 288, 80 Eng. Rep. 433 (1618). See also *Cases of Pardons,* 6 Co. Rep. 13a, 77 Eng. Rep. 272 (1587).

8. *Supra,* note 6. *Anon.,* Y.B., M. 8 E. 4, 13, F.G.A., ''Prohibicion'' no. 9 (1469) seems to support the lay courts here, though no judgment is given.

9. 4 Co. Inst. *332-35; *Q. if High Commissioners have Power to Imprison,* 12 Co. Rep. 19, 77 Eng. Rep. 1301 (1607); *High Commission,* 12 Co. Rep. 49, 77 Eng. Rep. 1329 (1609); note 53, *infra;* vol. I, 94, 139. The 1485 statute referred to in text is 1 Hen. 7, c. 4.

10. 2 Hen. 4 c. 15 (1400). See *Case of Heresy,* 12 Co. Rep. 56, 77 Eng. Rep. 1335 (1601). Maitland's case is in *Roman Canon Law in the Church of England,* c. 6 (1898); Pollock and Maitland, ii, 547-52.

11. With one exception perhaps. *Priddle and Napper's Case,* 11 Co. Rep. 8b, 77 Eng. Rep. 1155 (1613); *Botham and the Lady Gresham's Case,* 3 Leonard 203, 74 Eng. Rep. 634 (1588); *Grendon* v. *Bishop of Lincoln,* 2 Plowden 493, 75 Eng. Rep. 734 (1573) suggest a more sympathetic attitude toward appropriators: this change may respond to the fact that most appropriations were now in the hands of laymen.

12. See Holdsworth, ix, 246-47.

13. This description of the two-step process in prohibition is based mainly on the following cases: *Hinde* v. *Bishop of Chester,* Cro. Car. 238, 79 Eng. Rep. 808 (1632); *Priddle and Napper's Case,* 11 Co. Rep. 8b, 77 Eng. Rep. 1155 (1613); *Bishop of Winchester's Case,* 2 Co. Rep. 38a, 76 Eng. Rep. 501 (Q.B. 1596); *Jeffrey's Case,* 5 Co. Rep. 64b, 66b, 77 Eng. Rep. 153, 155 (C.P. and Q.B., 1589-90); *Slugge and the Bishop of Llandaff's Case,* 1 Leonard 181, 74 Eng. Rep. 167 (Q.B. 1589); *Wiggin and Arscot's Case,* 2 Leonard 212, 74 Eng. Rep. 487 (Q.B. 1588); *Stafford's Case,* 1 Leonard 111, 74 Eng. Rep. 103 (1588); *Sutton and Dowses Case,* 1 Leonard 11, 74 Eng. Rep. 10 (1583); *Hilliar* v. *Kendall,* Cary 98, 21 Eng. Rep. 52 (1579-80), *Mayhoe* v. *Vicar of Lostwithal,* Choyce Cases 137, 21 Eng. Rep. 82 (1579). It appears that in later years the writ out of Chancery was replaced by a writ out of the court itself, and the informal consultation proceeding by a proceeding on an order to show cause why a prohibition should not issue. See the 1826 note to *Bishop of Winchester's Case,* beginning on p. 501 of 76 Eng. Rep. The plenary proceeding on a fictitious attachment evidently remained the same. It is referred to in the reports by statements that the plaintiff was ordered or permitted ''to declare.'' The power of the Common Pleas court to issue its own writs of prohibition was established in *Langdale's Case,* 12 Co. Rep. 58, 77 Eng. Rep. 1338 (1609).

14. 2-3 Edw. 6, c. 13, § 14 (1548). For cases applying or limiting this provision, see *Wiggin and Arscot's Case,* 2 Leonard 212, 74 Eng. Rep. 487 (Q.B. 1588); *Bloure's*

Case, 3 Dyer 371b, 73 Eng. Rep. 832 (1580); *Wolfe* v. *Clums,* Cary 79, 21 Eng. Rep. 42 (1579); 2 Co. Inst. *661-62.

15. Cases prohibited at the outset include *Love* v. *Prin,* Cro. Eliz. 754, 78 Eng. Rep. 985 (Q.B. 1600) (suit for assault — as distinguished from battery — on cleric); *Porter and Rochester's Case,* 13 Co. Rep. 4, 77 Eng. Rep. 1416 (1609) (citation outside diocese); *Barnaby* v. *Dickenson,* March N.R. 90, 82 Eng. Rep. 425 (1642) (defamation proceeding, words not actionable).

16. *Perry* v. *Soam,* Cro. Eliz. 139, 78 Eng. Rep. 395 (Q.B. 1588). For other tithe cases, see note 23, *infra.* See also *Kelly* v. *Walker,* Cro. Eliz. 655, 78 Eng. Rep. 894 (Q.B. 1599), involving a claim of self-defense in a case of laying violent hands on a cleric. The difference between traversable and non-traversable allegations concerning the refusal to hear a defense is discussed by Coke in *Bishop of Winchester's Case,* 2 Co. Rep. 38a, 76 Eng. Rep. 501 (Q.B. 1596).

17. E.g., *Botham and the Lady Gresham's Case,* 3 Leonard 203, 74 Eng. Rep. 634 (1588); *Roberts' Case,* 12 Co. Rep. 65, 77 Eng. Rep. 1344 (1611); cf. *Bagnall* v. *Stokes,* Cro. Eliz. 89, 78 Eng. Rep. 347 (1588) (defendant in church court has release, but only one witness to it). See also the general statement in *Somerset* v. *Markham,* Cro. Eliz. 595, 78 Eng. Rep. 838 (1597). *Juxon* v. *Lord Byron,* 2 Lev. 64, 83 Eng. Rep. 451 (1673) may go farther in sustaining the church than the Elizabethan or Jacobean judges would have gone.

18. *Fuller's Case,* 12 Co. Rep. 41, 77 Eng. Rep. 1322 (1607) points out that a consultation can be issued as to some but not all of the issues in a case.

19. *Porter and Rochester's Case,* 13 Co. Rep. 4, 77 Eng. Rep. 1416 (1609). The case on excuses for not going to church is *Anon.,* March N.R. 92, no. 162, 82 Eng. Rep. 426 (1641); that on mortuaries in Chester is *Hinde* v. *Bishop of Chester,* Cro. Car. 238, 79 Eng. Rep. 808 (1632). See also *Riesby* v. *Wentworth,* Cro. Eliz. 642, 78 Eng. Rep. 881 (1599), which gives the church courts power to apply 31 Eliz., 1 c. 6 (1589) on simony.

20. *Jeffrey's Case,* 5 Co. Rep. 64b, 66b, 77 Eng. Rep. 153, 155 (C.P. and Q.B. 1589-90).

21. Marchant, 112-13, Holdsworth, v, 319-20. Trespass on the case: *Salkard* v. *Beckwith,* 1 Lutw. 116, 125 Eng. Rep. 61 (1618) (dilapidation); *Bishop of Salisbury's Case,* Godbolt 259, 78 Eng. Rep. 151 (1615) (same). Trespass: *Green's Case,* 6 Co. Rep. 28b, 77 Eng. Rep. 295 (Q.B. 1602) (incumbency); *Churchwardens of Fetherstones Case,* 1 Leonard 177, 74 Eng. Rep. 163 (1589) (carrying off of church bell). *Prior of J.* v. *Strade,* Y.B., M. 39 H. 6, 20 F.G.A., "Quare Impedit," no. 96 (1460) is a medieval precedent for the incumbency case. Chancery intervention in probate matters: *Savil* v. *Savil,* 1 Chan. Rep. 78, 21 Eng. Rep. 512 (1634-35); *Parr* v. *Tipladie,* Choyce Cases 137, 21 Eng. Rep. 82 (1579); *Banvill* v. *Banvill,* Cary 64, 21 Eng. Rep. 34 (1576-77). In tithe matters: *Brown* v. *Thetford,* 1 Chan. Rep. 26, 21 Eng. Rep. 497 (1628-29); *Pleadall* v. *Goddard,* Choyce Cases 157, 21 Eng. Rep. 92 (1581-82).

22. Hill, 79-131.

23. *Modus* cases include *Perry* v. *Soam,* Cro. Eliz. 139, 78 Eng. Rep. 395 (1596); *Dullingham* v. *Kiefeley,* Cro. Eliz. 251, 78 Eng. Rep. 506 (Q.B. 1596); *Scot* v. *Wall,* Hobart 248, 80 Eng. Rep. 393. The statutes mentioned in text are 31 Hen. 8, c. 13 § 21 (1539) and 2-3 Edw. 6, c. 13, § 5 (1548). Henry's statute is involved in *Nash and Mollins Case,* 1 Leonard 240, 74 Eng. Rep. 220 (Q.B. 1590) and *Parson of Peykirke's Case,* 3 Dyer 349b, 73 Eng. Rep. 784 (1574), Edward's in *Banister* v. *Wright,* Style 137, 82 Eng. Rep. 591 (1649) (late, to be sure, but evidently not affected by the Civil War or the impending Interregnum) and *Pelles* v. *Sanderson,* 2 Dyer 170b,

73 Eng. Rep. 374 (1559). Coke's treatment of 18 Edw. 3, c. 7 (1344) and 2-3 Edw. 6, c. 13 (1548) in 2 Co. Inst. *639-64 deals with many of these questions. "Tithe" in Burn, ii, 373 also contains considerable material from the period under consideration. *Select Tithe Causes,* ed. Purvis (Y.A.A., cxiv, 1949) indicates that the church courts in the period were doing a good deal of tithe business that the lay courts would have prohibited if asked.

24. *Parson of Facknams Case,* 1 Leonard 58, 74 Eng. Rep. 54 (1587) (jurisdiction declined); *Doctor Leyfield's Case,* 10 Co. Rep. 88a, 77 Eng. Rep. 1057 (K.B. 1611) (right to tithe not in issue); *Stransham* v. *Cullington,* Cro. Eliz. 228, 78 Eng. Rep. 484, 3 Leonard 129, 74 Eng. Rep. 585 (Q.B. 1591) (parish boundary exception).

25. 32 Hen. 8, c. 7, § 7 (1540).

26. *Robinson* v. *Bedel,* Cro. Eliz. 873, 78 Eng. Rep. 1098 (1602).

27. *Withy and Saunders Case,* 1 Leonard 23, 74 Eng. Rep. 22 (Q.B. 1584).

28. E.g., *Green* v. *Penilden,* Cro. Eliz. 228, 78 Eng. Rep. 484 (Q.B. 1591); *Dullingham* v. *Kyfeley,* Cro. Eliz. 251, 78 Eng. Rep. 506 (Q.B. 1596).

29. The cases referred to in text are *Wiggen and Arscot's Case,* 2 Leonard 212, 7 Eng. Rep. 487 (Q.B. 1588) (Articles); *Riesby* v. *Wentworth,* Cro. Eliz. 642, 78 Eng. Rep. 881 (1598) (simony); *Woodward and Bugg's Case,* 2 Leonard 29, 74 Eng. Rep. 331 (Q.B. 1588) (composition); *Tomson's Case,* Littleton 59, 124 Eng. Rep. 136 (1628) (improper presentment.).

30. A composition is a contractual undertaking by a parson to forego his tithes in exchange for some other consideration. A *modus* is a "way of tithing," a replacement of the mathematical tenth by something equivalent but easier to compute. A *modus* could arise by custom, whereas a composition required an express contract, and a *modus* could be reviewed to see if it was a fair equivalent for the tenth (i.e., a fair equivalent at the time it arose: if you agreed to take your tithes in cash instead of in kind, the burden of inflation was on you), whereas a composition was binding in the same way as any other contract. A composition could be either personal, binding only the parson who made it, or real, binding his successors as well. But a composition real was subject to all the common law and statutory restraints on the alienation of church lands.

31. *Roberts' Case,* 12 Co. Rep. 65, 77 Eng. Rep. 1344 (1611); compare the Restoration case of *Juxon* v. *Lord Byron,* 2 Lev. 64, 83 Eng. Rep. 451 (1673).

32. *Gatefould and Penns Case,* 1 Leonard 128, 74 Eng. Rep. 119 (Q.B. 1588); *Green* v. *Penilden,* Cro. El. 228, 78 Eng. Rep. 484 (Q.B. 1591); (church court refused to hear contention); *Transam's Case,* Cro. Eliz. 178, 78 Eng. Rep. 434 (Q.B. 1590) (parish boundaries — another phase of *Stransham* v. *Cullington, supra,* note 24); see note 24, *supra,* on the trespass cases.

33. *Botham and the Lady Gresham's Case,* 3 Leonard 203, 74 Eng. Rep. 634 (1588).

34. 2-3 Edw. 6, c. 13, §§ 1-2 (1548); *Bedell and Sherman's Case,* 13 Co. Rep. 47, 77 Eng. Rep. 1457 (1597); *Sprat and Heal's Case,* 13 Co. Rep. 23, 77 Eng. Rep. 1434 (Q.B. 1602); 2 Co. Inst. *648-51.

35. I find no trace of anyone invoking the provision of 27 Hen. 8, c. 20 (1536) for having the justices of the peace enforce the tithe judgments of the church courts, although it was held in later years to have continued in force. *R.* v. *Sanchee,* 1 Ld. Raym. 323, 91 Eng. Rep. 1111 (1697).

36. *Palmer* v. *Thorpe,* 4 Co. Rep. 20a, 76 Eng. Rep. 909 (Q.B. 1583). The specific cases referred to in text are *Davis* v. *Gardiner,* 4 Co. Rep. 16b, 76 Eng. Rep. 897 (1593) (loss of marriage, with Coke's treatment of other cases on slander of chastity and bastardy); *Edward's Case,* 13 Co. Rep. 9, 77 Eng. Rep. 1421 (physician); *Ralph Morris's Case,* 2 Leonard 53, 74 Eng. Rep. 352 (Q.B. 1587) (witch); *Barnaby* v.

Dickenson, March N.R. 90, 82 Eng. Rep. 425 (1642) (copper-nose quean); *Brown* v. *Lother,* Goldsborough 113, 75 Eng. Rep. 1031 (1597) (perjury); *Gobbet's Case,* Cro. Car. 340, 79 Eng. Rep. 897 (1634) (cuckold). Cf. *Webb* v. *Cook,* Cro. Jac. 535, 625, 79 Eng. Rep. 459, 538 (1620, 1622) (putative father convicted before justices of the peace cannot reopen the question of his paternity in a defamation action). Note that the lay remedies for defamation were supplemented by remedies for libel (*Case de Libellis Famosis,* 5 Co. Rep. 125, 77 Eng. Rep. 250 (1606)) and *scandalum magnatum* (2 Ric. 2, c. 5 (1378); *Lord Cromwell's Case,* 4 Co. Rep. 12b, 76 Eng. Rep. 877 (1578)), which had always been lay.

37. Y.B., M. 22 E. 4, 20, 29 (1482).

38. See the description in Marchant, 72-75. Marchant shows that abusive language was often dealt with on the same terms as defamatory, whereas the lay courts would prohibit any suit that did not complain of a specific false accusation. *Parlor* v. *Butler,* Moore K.B. 460, 72 Eng. Rep. 694 (1586); *Barnaby* v. *Dickenson, supra,* note 36; *Pew and Wife* v. *Jeffreyes,* Cro. Car. 456, 79 Eng. Rep. 996 (1637); ("jade" held defamatory as meaning whore, as against the contention "they are only words of heat and no slander").

39. Purvis, 94, 110.

40. 5-6 Edw. 6, c. 4 (1551); *Large* v. *Alton,* Cro. Jac. 462, 79 Eng. Rep. 395 (1618).

41. The cases referred to in text are *Love* v. *Prin,* Cro. Eliz. 754, 78 Eng. Rep. 985 (Q.B. 1600) and *Kelly* v. *Walker,* Cro. Eliz. 655, 78 Eng. Rep. 894 (Q.B. 1599).

42. Marriage: *Mattingley* v. *Martyn,* Jones W. 257, 82 Eng. Rep. 134 (1632); *Hyet's Case,* Cro. Jac. 364, 79 Eng. Rep. 312 (1615), but cf. *Man's Case,* Cro. Eliz. 228, 78 Eng. Rep. 484, 4 Leonard 16, 74 Eng. Rep. 697 (Q.B. 1591). Church attendance: *Anon.,* March N.R. 92, no. 162, 82 Eng. Rep. 426 (1641) (to be received with caution of course because of the late date, but the fact that no one seems to have raised the contention earlier may be indicative of its lack of merit). Clerical discipline: *Caudrey's Case,* 5 Co. Rep. 1, 77 Eng. Rep. 1 (1595).

43. *Bennet* v. *Easedale,* Cro. Car. 55, 79 Eng. Rep. 651 (1627); *Cases of Pardons,* 6 Co. Rep. 13a, 77 Eng. Rep. 272 (1587); *Searle* v. *Williams,* Hobart 288, 80 Eng. Rep. 433 (1618).

44. Cf. *Butler and Goodale's Case,* 6 Co. Rep. 21b, 77 Eng. Rep. 285 (Q.B. 1598), where Coke says imprisonment is a good excuse for a cleric's not residing on his benefice since the law does not require the impossible. Hill, 52 suggests that the attitude toward a benefice as a property right hindered the removal of scandalous ministers. The 1828 case that sorted out the problems was *Free* v. *Burgoyne,* 2 Bligh N.S. 65, 4 Eng. Rep. 1055 (H.L.1828), affirming 5 B. & C. 399, 108 Eng. Rep. 149 (K.B. 1826), awarding consultation on 2 Add. 414, 162 Eng. Rep. 347 (Arches 1825). It was foreshadowed by one or two earlier cases, notably *Slader* v. *Smalbrooke,* 1 Lev. 138, 83 Eng. Rep. 337 (1664). The imprisonment case finally came up, and was decided against the imprisoned cleric, in *Ex parte Bartlett,* 12 Q.B. 488, 116 Eng. Rep. 950 (1848). The court took the view that the cleric could not use impossibility as an excuse when it was attributable to his own misconduct.

45. Habeas corpus: *Sir Anthony Roper's Case,* 12 Co. Rep. 47, 77 Eng. Rep. 1326 (1608); *Lady Throgmorton's Case,* 12 Co. Rep. 69, 77 Eng. Rep. 1347 (1611); *Sir William Chancey's Case,* 12 Co. Rep. 82, 77 Eng. Rep., 1360 (1612); *Dighton and Holt's Case,* Cro. Jac. 388, 79 Eng. Rep. 332 (1616). Collateral attack: *Bunting's Case,* Moore K.B. 169, 72 Eng. Rep. 510 (1582); *Morris* v. *Webber,* Moore K.B. 225, 72 Eng. Rep. 545 (1588); but cf. *Frankwell's Case,* 2 Leonard 176, 74 Eng. Rep. 455

(Q.B. 1588). On the justices of the peace, see Lambarde 337-38, quoted in Holdsworth, iv, 551-53.

46. St. Germain, *A Treatise Concernynge the Division Betwene the Spiritualtie and Temporaltie* (London 1532).

47. *Case of Heresy,* 12 Co. Rep. 56, 77 Eng. Rep. 1335 (1601). The statutory restriction on the commission is 1 Eliz. 1, c. 1, § 36 (1558).

48. Harison, 33.

49. Maguire, "The Attack of the Common Lawyers on the Oath ex Officio" in *Essays in Honor of C.H. McIlwain* (Cambridge, Mass. 1936), 199; *Dighton and Holt's Case,* Cro. Jac, 388, 79 Eng. Rep. 332 (1616). The Coke-Popham response is *Of Oaths Before an Ecclesiastical Judge ex Officio,* 12 Co. Rep. 26, 77 Eng. Rep. 1308 (1607); the case of the man who drew the horn is *Edward's Case,* 13 Co. Rep. 9, 77 Eng. Rep. 1421 (1609).

50. See *C.S.P.D., 1637-38,* 229-30, where Finch, C.J., writes to Laud apologizing for issuing a prohibition in a case where a man is being sued for a benefice in the High Commission and has been given no articles. Finch explains that he hates to interfere, but the precedents give him no alternative.

51. The Statute of Citations is 23 Hen. 8, c. 9 (1531). Cases applying it include *Porter and Rochester's Case,* 13 Co. Rep. 4, 77 Eng. Rep. 1416 (1609); *Gobbet's Case,* Cro. Car. 340, 79 Eng. Rep. 897 (1634); *Pit* v. *Webley,* Cro. Jac. 321, 79 Eng. Rep. 275 (1614); *Smith* v. *Poyndreill's Executors,* Cro. Car. 97, 79 Eng. Rep. 686 (1628); *Kadwalader* v. *Bryan,* Cro. Car. 162, 79 Eng. Rep. 741 (1630); *Jones* v. *Boyer,* 2 Brownl. & Gold. 27, 123 Eng. Rep. 795 (1610). The other venue cases referred to in the following paragraph are *Dr. James's Case,* Hobart 18, 80 Eng. Rep. 168 (1622), and *Dunne's Case,* 2 Leonard 155, 74 Eng. Rep. 438 (Q.B. 1578).

52. Coke's discussion is in *Sir Anthony Roper's Case,* 12 Co. Rep. 45, 77 Eng. Rep. 1326 (1608), and in 4 Co. Inst. *324-35. The quotation is from *326. Other cases include *Edwards's Case, supra,* note 49; *Parker's Case,* 2 Brownl. & Gold. 37, 123 Eng. Rep. 801 (1609); *Dame Sherley's Case,* Hetly 95, 124 Eng. Rep. 370 (1628-32); *Sir William Chancey's Case,* 12 Co. Rep. 82, 77 Eng. Rep. 1360 (1612); *Drake's Case,* Cro. Car. 220, 79 Eng. Rep. 792 (K.B. 1632). *Mortimer* v. *Freeman,* 1 Brownl. & Gold. 70, 123 Eng. Rep. 671 (1610) seems to give the commissioners more scope. On how the ecclesiastics perceived these limits, see Marchant, 66.

53. *Lady Throgmorton's Case,* 12 Co. Rep. 69, 77 Eng. Rep. 1347 (1611) (High Commission can imprison for heresy, but not for offense against marriage); *Sir William Chancey's Case, supra,* note 53 (cannot imprison for adultery); *High Commission,* 12 Co Rep. 49, 77 Eng. Rep. 1329 (1609) (the case of the man killing the pursuivant). On the kinds of cases the High Commission was hearing in the 1630s see *C.S.P.D., 1634-35,* 314-37.

54. *Rot Parl.,* iii, 141a-b (1382).

55. *Cave* v. *Roe, C.S.P.D., 1634-35,* 325 is an adultery case involving both a £ 500 fine and the posting of bond. On the posting of bond, see also *Mrs. Paschall's Case,* 2 Leonard 179, 74 Eng. Rep. 459 (Exch. 1589).

56. Bribery: *Dr. Trevor's Case,* 12 Co. Rep. 78, 77 Eng. Rep. 1356 (1611). Contempt: *Lady Throgmorton's Case, supra,* note 54; *Fuller's Case,* 12 Co. Rep. 41, 77 Eng. Rep. 1322. Alteration of records: *Kenton* v. *Wallinger,* Cro. Eliz. 838, 78 Eng. Rep. 1064 (Q.B. 1601). Costs: *Transam's Case,* Cro. Eliz. 178, 78 Eng. Rep. 434, s.c., *Stransham and Medcalfes Case,* 1 Leonard 131, 74 Eng. Rep. 121 (Q.B. 1591 or 1588); *Eaton* v. *Ayliffe,* Hetly 95, 124 Eng. Rep. 370 (1628-32).

57. *Prohibition,* 12 Co. Rep. 76, 77 Eng. Rep. 1354 (1611) contains Coke's general treatment of these matters. The simony case referred to in text is *Baker* v. *Rogers,* Cro.

El. 788, 78 Eng. Rep. 1018 (1601). See also *Smith* v. *Poyndreill's Executors,* Cro. Car. 97, 79 Eng. Rep. 686 (1628) (objection to citation outside diocese comes too late when church court has already pronounced judgment).

58. In the order mentioned in text: *Walrond* v. *Pollard,* 3 Dyer 273a, 73 Eng. Rep. 610 (Q.B. 1568); *Allen* v. *Nash,* Jones W. 393, 82 Eng. Rep. 206 (1638); *Frankwell's Case,* 2 Leonard 176, 74 Eng. Rep., 455 (Q.B. 1588); *Parker's Case,* 2 Brownl. & Gold. 37, 123 Eng. Rep. 801 (1609); *Mortimer* v. *Freeman,* 1 Brownl. & Gold. 70, 123 Eng. Rep. 671 (1610).

59. Forged will: *Hersey's Case,* 12 Co. Rep. 103, 77 Eng. Rep. 1378 (Star Chamber). Other probate cases: *Dunne's Case,* 2 Leonard 155, 74 Eng. Rep. 459 (1589). Certificate on question: *Anon.,* 3 Dyer 305b, 73 Eng. Rep. 689 (1571), 3 Dyer 368b, 73 Eng. Rep. 826 (1580) (bishop returns special statement of facts on question of marriage: bishop is fined £ 40 for not answering question, but dower is awarded on basis of his certificate); cf. *R.* v. *Blaucher,* Cro. Eliz. 81, 78 Eng. Rep. 340 (Exch. 1587). Annulment: Bunting's Case, Moore K.B. 169, 72 Eng. Rep. 510 (1582); *Morris* v. *Webber,* Moore K.B. 225, 72 Eng. Rep. 545, 2 Leonard 169, 74 Eng. Rep. 449 (1587), S.C., *Bury's Case,* 5 Co. Rep. 98b, 77 Eng. Rep. 207 (1597).

60. *Trollop's Case,* 8 Co. Rep. 68a, 77 Eng. Rep. 577 (1609); *Bloure's Case,* 3 Dyer 371b, 73 Eng. Rep. 832 (1580) *Hobbes* v. *Hobbes and Churchill,* Choyce Cases 141, 21 Eng. Rep. 84 (1579-80).

61. *Boult* v. *Blunt,* Cary 51, 21 Eng. Rep. 27 (1576-77); *Bird* v. *Smith,* Moore K.B. 781, 72 Eng. Rep. 902 (1607).

62. *Bird* v. *Smith, supra,* note 61. It appears that the justices of the peace also concerned themselves on occasion with the possession of church premises, by invoking the statutes against brawling, *West Riding Sessions,* 364-65, or against disrupting services, *Creswick* v. *Rooksby,* 2 Bulstr. 47, 80 Eng. Rep. 948 (1613). In the latter case, they had arrested the churchwardens for interfering with a preacher.

63. 5 Eliz. 1 c. 23 (1563); *Hughes's Case,* Cro Car. 197, 79 Eng. Rep. 773 (1631); *Smith* v. *Ferry,* Choyce Cases 152, 21 Eng. Rep. 90 (1581-82).

64. 2 Co. Inst. *623. Compare *R.* v. *Fowler,* 1 Ld. Raym. 618, 91 Eng. Rep. 1313, 1 Salk. 350, 91 Eng. Rep. 306 (1700).

65. On the application of the mortmain laws, see *Porter's Case,* 1 Co. Rep. 16b, 76 Eng. Rep. 36 (1592); Hill, 273-74.

66. It appears, for instance, that the action of *quare impedit* absorbed the work of *quare non admisit. Bell* v. *Bishop of Norwich,* 3 Dyer 254b, 73 Eng. Rep. 564 (Q.B. 1566).

67. Compare Coke's metaphor of a river that overflows its banks, 2 Co. Inst. *4.

68. *Anon.,* 3 Leonard 46, 74 Eng. Rep. 531 (1573).

69. *Bedinfield* v. *Archbishop of Canterbury,* 3 Dyer 293a, 73 Eng. Rep. 657 (1570). The court reasons that there has been a de facto incumbency, and a new vacancy when the ipso facto voidance was established in court. Cf. *Windsor's Case,* 5 Co. Rep. 102a, 77 Eng. Rep. 213 (1599).

70. First fruits and tenths: 26 Hen. 8, c. 3, § 17 (1534), revived by 1 Eliz. 1, c. 4 (1559); *Anon.,* 2 Dyer 237a, 73 Eng. Rep. 524 (1565). Pluralism: 21 Hen. 8, c. 13, §§ 9-10 (1529); *Holland's Case,* 4 Co. Rep. 75a, 76 Eng. Rep. 1047 (1597); *Weston's Case,* 3 Dyer 347b, 73 Eng. Rep. 780 (1576); *R.* v. *Archbishop of Canterbury and Pryst,* Cro Car. 354, 79 Eng. Rep. 910 K.B. (1629).

71. 13 Eliz. 1, c. 12, § 8 (1571); *Bacon* v. *Bishop of Carlisle,* 3 Dyer 346a, 73 Eng. Rep. 778 (1576); *Anon.,* 3 Dyer 377b, 73 Eng. Rep. 828 (1580); *Green's Case,* 6 Co. Rep. 28b, 77 Eng. Rep. 295 (Q.B. 1602).

72. 3l Eliz. 1, c. 6, §§ 5-6 (1589); *R.* v. *Bishop of Norwich,* Cro. Jac. 385, 79 Eng.

Rep. 329 (1616); *Winchcombe* v. *Bishop of Winchester,* Hobart 166, 80 Eng. Rep. 313 (1617); 3 Co. Inst. *153-56. As to the innocence of the patron, see *R.* v. *Bishop of Norwich, supra.* As to that of the presentee, see *Doctor Hutchinson's Case,* 12 Co. Rep. 101, 77 Eng. Rep. 1376 (1611). Coke, relying on that case and on the text of the statute, holds that an innocent presentee can have the same benefice later on a new and untainted presentment. But *Booth* v. *Potter,* Cro. Jac. 533, 79 Eng. Rep. 457 (1620) seems to hold the opposite.

73. *Elvis* v. *Archbishop of York,* Hobart 316, 80 Eng. Rep. 458 (1620); *Commendam Case,* Hobart 140, 80 Eng. Rep. 290 (1613); *Hall and the Bishop of Bath's Case,* 2 Leonard 58, 74 Eng. Rep. 356 (1590); *Anon.,* 3 Dyer 364a, 73 Eng. Rep. 816 (1580); *Green's Case,* 6 Co. Rep. 28b, 77 Eng. Rep. 295 (Q.B. 1602); *Boswel's Case,* 6 Co. Rep. 48b, 77 Eng. Rep. 326 (K.B. 1606). See also *Arundel and the Bishop of Gloucesters and Chaffins Case,* 1 Leonard 194, 74 Eng. Rep. 179 (1589), where the incumbent fell into a neat pleading trap. On the medieval material, see pages 40-42, *supra.*

74. *Green's Case, supra,* note 73.

75. *Elvis* v. *Archbishop of York,* Hobart 316, 319-20, 80 Eng. Rep. 458, 462 (1620).

76. On grounds for objection: *Bell* v. *Bishop of Norwich,* 3 Dyer 254b, 73 Eng. Rep. 564 (Q.B. 1566) (haunter of taverns); *Albany and the Bishop of St. Asaphs Case,* 1 Leonard 31, 74 Eng. Rep. 29 (1585) (speaking no Welsh); *Specot's Case,* 5 Co. Rep. 57a, 77 Eng. Rep. 141 (1590) (inveterate schismatic). On examining the presentee: *Palmes and the Bishop of Peterboroughs Case,* 1 Leonard 230, 74 Eng. Rep. 211 (1591); *Anon.,* 3 Leonard 46, 74 Eng. Rep. 531 (1573); compare the medieval treatment in *R.* v. *Anon.,* Y.B., P. 15 H. 7, 6, F.G.A., "Encumbent," no. 14 (1498). On notice: *Archbishop of York and Willock's Case,* 3 Dyer 327b, 73 Eng. Rep. 740 (1573); *Albany and the Bishop of St. Asaphs Case, supra.*

77. *Specot's Case,* 5 Co. Rep. 57a, 57b, 77 Eng. Rep. 141, 142 (1590).

78. Hill, 77-131. On the tithes of minerals, see id., 84-85. Coke's view is set forth in 2 Co. Inst. *651-52. He cites as medieval authority F.N.B., 53G, which supports him, and *Rot. Parl.,* ii, 370a (1376), the parliamentary complaint referred to in text. See also *Rot. Parl.,* iii, 540b (1403-4) and 591b (1406), involving rocks and slates. *Daw's and Molline's Case,* 2 Leonard 79, 74 Eng. Rep. 374 (Q.B. 1584) is a classic case on tithes of wood — just like the medieval ones.

79. The cases referred to in this paragraph are *Savel and Woods Case,* 1 Leonard 94, 74 Eng. Rep. 87 (Q.B. 1588); *Stebbs and Goodlacks Case,* 1 Leonard 99, 74 Eng. Rep. 92 (Q.B. 1588). See also *Gatefould and Penns Case,* 1 Leonard 128, 74 Eng. Rep. 119 (Q.B. 1588); *Botham and the Lady Gresham's Case,* 3 Leonard 203, 74 Eng. Rep. 634 (1588).

80. *Bishop of Lincoln and Cowpers Case,* 1 Leonard 248, 74 Eng. Rep. 226 (Q.B. 1591); *Woodward and Bugg's Case,* 2 Leonard 29, 74 Eng. Rep. 331 (Q.B. 1588); *Anon.,* 1 Dyer 43a, 73 Eng. Rep. 93 (1539); *Harris* v. *Cotton,* 1 Brownl. & Gold. 69, 123 Eng. Rep. 671 (1610) (lessee of glebe pays tithe); *Stile and Millers Case,* 1 Leonard 300, 74 Eng. Rep. 273 (Q.B. 1589) (lease "free of exactions").

81. The statute is 31 Hen. 8, c. 13, § 21 (1539). On lands of greater versus lesser monasteries, see *Gerrard* v. *Wright,* Cro. Jac. 607, 79 Eng. Rep. 518 (1618); cf. *Archbishop of Canterbury's Case,* 2 Co. Rep. 46a, 76 Eng. Rep. 519 (Q.B. 1596) (greater monasteries versus colleges). On discharges by papal authority, *Strathome's Case,* 3 Dyer 277b, 73 Eng. Rep. 621 (1568); *The Countess of Linnox Case,* 2 Leonard 71, 74 Eng. Rep. 366 (Exch. 1587). On questions of unity of possession, *Priddle and Napper's Case,* 11 Co. Rep. 8b, 77 Eng. Rep. 1155 (1613); *Anon.,* Moore K.B. 46, 72

Eng. Rep. 431 (1562); *Anon.*, Moore K.B. 50, 72 Eng. Rep. 434 (1563); *Knightly and Spencers Case*, 1 Leonard 331, 74 Eng. Rep. 301 (Q.B. 1591); *Gerrard* v. *Wright, supra.* On other discharge problems, *Blinco* v. *Barksdale,* Cro. Eliz. 577, 78 Eng. Rep. 821 (Q.B. 1597) (lay impropriator need not pay tithe to vicar for glebe); *Parson of Peykirke's Case,* 3 Dyer 349b, 73 Eng. Rep. 784 (1576); *Nash and Mollins Case,* 1 Leonard 240, 74 Eng. Rep. 220 (Q.B. 1590). See Coke's discussion in 2 Co. Inst. *651-55.

82. 2-3 Edw. 6, c. 13, § 5 (1548); *Pelles* v. *Saunderson,* 2 Dyer 170b, 73 Eng. Rep. 374 (1559); 2 Co. Inst. *655-56.

83. As to London: 37 Hen. 8, c. 12 (1545); *Case of Tithes in London,* Calthrop, 80 Eng. Rep. 672 (1618). It seems that the 1545 statute superseded the discharge of property formerly monastic. *Green* v. *Piper,* Cro. Eliz. 276, 78 Eng. Rep. 531 (1592). For later developments, see Burn, ii, 459-70. As to urban parishes not covered by the London agreement and statute, see *Dr. Graunt's Case,* 11 Co. Rep. 15b, 77 Eng. Rep. 1165 (1614).

84. *Supra,* note 83. The quotation is at 11 Co. Rep. 16b, 77 Eng. Rep. 1166.

85. Pension: *Sir Anthony Roper's Case,* 12 Co. Rep. 45, 77 Eng. Rep. 1326. Repairs: Hill, 144. Some bishops attempted to enforce repairs by sequestering lay rectories. Marchant, 125n. The lay courts finally established in 1678 that this practice was inconsistent with the lay status of the rectories. *Walwyn* v. *Awberry,* 1 Mod. 258, 2 Mod. 254, 86 Eng. Rep. 866, 1057 (1678); "Church" in Burn, i, 248. But if the lay courts ever stopped a church proceeding to compel a lay rector to repair a chancel on pain of excommunication followed by lay process to imprison him, the case has not turned up in my examination of the reports.

86. There are a number of reports of this case. The arguments are most accessible in Cro. Jac. 515, 79 Eng. Rep. 440, the decision in 2 Rolle 127, 81 Eng. Rep. 703.

87. 2 Rolle Abr. 337, Hill, 321-31.

88. 32 Hen. 8, c. 7 (1540); cf. *Withy and Saunders Case,* 1 Leonard 23, 74 Eng. Rep. 22 (Q.B. 1584) on other problems concerning the effect of this statute.

89. Lambarde, *The Duties of Constables . . .* (London 1587), 45-54; *Gore* v. *Stark,* Noy 130, 74 Eng. Rep. 1093 (1610); *Churchwardens of Fetherstones Case,* 1 Leonard 177, 74 Eng. Rep. 163 (1589).

90. *Evelin's Case,* Cro. Car. 551, 79 Eng. Rep. 1074 (1640); *Le Parish de S. Balaunce in Kent,* Palmer 51, 81 Eng. Rep. 973 (1620). I say "men" although Hart, *The Man in the Pew,* 60 reports some instances of women serving as churchwardens.

91. *Bishopps Case,* 2 Rolle 73, 81 Eng. Rep. 666 (1619); *Bishop and Turner's Case,* Godbolt 279, 78 Eng. Rep. 163 (1619) (s.c.?). But cf. *Brown* v. *Lother,* Goldsborough 113, 75 Eng. Rep. 1031 (1597). Lambarde, *supra,* note 89, says that the parishioners may bring an action of account in a lay court against the parish churchwardens.

92. Hart, *The Man in the Pew,* 89-103; Hill, 172-74; "Parish Clerk", Burn, ii, 135. The medieval canon on this office is c. 29, Exeter 1287, Powicke and Cheney, 1026, Johnson, 209. The 1604 one is c. 91.

93. Election: *Parish Clerk,* 13 Co. Rep. 70, 77 Eng. Rep. 1479 (1611); *Walpoole's Case,* 2 Rolle Abr. 234 (1624); *Orme* v. *Pemberton,* Cro. Car. 589, 79 Eng. Rep. 1106 (1641). Deprivation: *Candict and Plomer's Case,* Godbolt 163, 78 Eng. Rep. 99 (1611); *Gaudyes Case,* 2 Brownl. & Gold. 38, 123 Eng. Rep. 802 (1609). Suing for wages: *Marsh* v. *Brook,* 2 Rolle Abr. 286 (1632). Since the clerk had no wages except

those assigned him by custom, the rule reserving determination of custom for the lay courts would presumably be ground for not letting him sue in the church court for them.

94. *Bishop of Salisbury's Case,* 10 Co. Rep. 58b, 61a, 77 Eng. Rep. 1013, 1019 (1614).

95. *Shiraks* v. *Archbishop of York,* Y.B., M. 8 E. 3, 69, F.G.A., "Excommengement," no. 2 (1334); *Hunt* v. *Ellisdon,* 2 Dyer 152b, 73 Eng. Rep. 332 (1558); cf. *Robotham* v. *Trevor,* 2 Brownl. & Gold. 12, 123 Eng. Rep. 786 (1610) (chancellorship of diocese); *Coveney's Case,* 2 Dyer 209a, 73 Eng. Rep. 461 (1561) (mastership of college). As early as 1230, the bishop of Lincoln found it necessary to buy off a man who claimed the right to various offices in his household. *Reg. Antiq.* no. 342.

96. *Sutton's Case,* Godbolt 390, 78 Eng. Rep. 230 (1628); *Bennet* v. *Easedale,* Cro. Car. 55, 79 Eng. Rep. 651 (1627); *Young* v. *Fowler,* Cro. Car. 48, 79 Eng. Rep. 1078 (1640); *Bishop of Rochester's Case,* Jenk. 121, 145 Eng. Rep. 85 (1608); *Howse* v. *L'Evesque de Eley,* Moore K.B. 88, 72 Eng. Rep. 459 (1568).

97. *Bishop of Salisbury's Case,* 10 Co. Rep. 58b, 77 Eng. Rep. 1013 (1614); *Walker* v. *Lamb,* Cro. Car. 258, 79 Eng. Rep. 825 (1632). The requirement that the office be "necessary" was overruled by Lord Mansfield in *Trelawny* v. *Bishop of Winchester,* 1 Burr. 218, 97 Eng. Rep. 281 (1757). The statutes referred to in this paragraph are those discussed in the next section of this chapter.

98. 32 Hen. 8, c. 28 (1540).

99. *Jewel's Case,* 5 Co. Rep. 3a, 77 Eng. Rep. 51 (Q.B. 1588). The distinction rests on whether there is anything on the property that can be distrained for the rent.

100. 1 Eliz. 1, c. 19 (1559), extended to the crown by 1 Jac. 1, c. 3 (1603); 13 Eliz. 1, c. 10 (1571). On the applicability of the 1571 act to the crown, see *Case of Ecclesiastical Persons,* 5 Co. Rep. 14a, 77 Eng. Rep. 69 (1602).

101. 18 Eliz. 1, c. 11 (1576). Another evasion forbidden by this act was the making of a covenant to renew a lease. § 3. Cf. 14 Eliz. 1, c. 11, § 15 (1572).

102. *Bishop of Salisbury's Case,* 10 Co. Rep. 58b, 77 Eng. Rep. 1013 (1614). On the successor's being bound by accepting rent, see "Leases," Burn, i, 634, 648. The rule about binding the signer for his own time does not apply to a corporation aggregate. *Magdalen College Case,* 11 Co. Rep. 66b, 77 Eng. Rep. 1235 (1616); 77 Eng. Rep. 1018n; "Leases," Burn, i, 634, 652.

103. See note 99, *supra.* This restriction was lifted by 5 Geo. 3, c. 17 (1765). Note that no statute prevented grants of copyhold land, because the grantee, once admitted, held by the custom of the manor and not by the grant. *Clarke* v. *Pennifather,* 4 Co. Rep. 23b, 76 Eng. Rep. 923, 925-26 (1584).

104. *Fox* v. *Collier,* Moore K.B. 107, 72 Eng. Rep. 472 (1579); *Elmer's Case,* 5 Co. Rep. 2a, 77 Eng. Rep. 49, Moore K.B. 253, 72 Eng. Rep. 563 (Q.B. 1588).

105. 13 Eliz. 1, c. 20 (1571). Absence such as to avoid a lease under this statute was construed more leniently than was nonresidence for other purposes. *Shepherd* v. *Twoulsie,* 1 Bulstr. 111, 80 Eng. Rep. 808 (1610) (lease good where incumbent resides in next parish and holds services in this one). On the lease of a dead incumbent, see *Mott* v. *Hales,* Cro. Eliz. 123, 78 Eng. Rep. 380 (1588). Moore's report, *Mote* v. *Hales,* Moore K.B. 270, 72 Eng. Rep. 574 (1588), has it that the judges split evenly on this point, rather than holding the lease void, as Croke has them doing. In *Bayly* v. *Munday,* 2 Lev. 61, 83 Eng. Rep. 450 (1673), it was argued that Croke's report must be inaccurate, since Coke, who served as counsel, would surely have taken note of so important a holding in his own writings. But Hale, overruling the case as "a hard opinion" says unhesitatingly that the vote was 3-1 for holding the lease void. A lessee would sometimes try to protect his lease by putting the lessor under bond not to forfeit

the incumbency. Such a bond was valid, but it was strictly construed. *Saint-John and Petits Case,* 1 Leonard 100, 74 Eng. Rep. 93 (Q.B. 1588); *Anon.*, 4 Leonard 38, 74 Eng. Rep. 714 (1577) (where incumbent is deprived for not signing Articles, he has not violated a covenant that nothing he did would result in his lessee being ousted: an omission is not an act).

106. *Anon.* Cary 31, 21 Eng. Rep. 17 (1603).

107. *Anon.*, Cary 28, 21 Eng. Rep. 15 (1603). For other cases on the confiscation of lands devoted to "superstitious" uses, see *Le Case de les Skinners de London,* Moore K.B. 129, 72 Eng. Rep. 485 (1583), *Dean of St. Paul's Case,* 3 Dyer 368a, 73 Eng. Rep. 825 (1580), Coke's compendious *Adams and Lambert's Case,* 4 Co. Rep. 96a, 104b, 76 Eng. Rep. 1079, 1091 (Q.B. 1598), and Duke, 107-8.

108. See *Cal. Pat. Rolls, 1396-9,* 452; id., *1446-52,* 120, 167, 170, 173 for examples of mortmain licenses conferring perpetual succession either on a chaplain and his successors or on a guild.

109. 39 Eliz. 1, c. 5 (1597), made perpetual by 21 Jac. 1, c. 1 (1624), discussed in 2 Co. Inst. *720-27. This statute can be regarded as the first general incorporation law in our legal system. It provided that a hospital founded in accordance with its terms would have corporate status without any individual grant from the crown.

110. Tate, 108-18. See Chapter III, notes 130-31 and accompanying text, *supra.* For a case of churchwardens suing a parson in Chancery to enforce a charity, see *Churchwardens of Northwould* v. *Scot,* Choyce Cases 155, 21 Eng. Rep. 91 (1581-82). On the corporate status of the churchwardens, see note 89, *supra.*

111. Holdsworth, iii, 592.

112. *Porter's Case,* 1 Co. Rep. 16b, 76 Eng. Rep. 36 (1592) involved a forfeiture to the heir, *Parrot* v. *Pawlet,* Cary 103, 21 Eng. Rep. 55 (1578-79) a suit in Chancery. It is worth noting that in *Porter's Case,* the heir was not planning to keep the land for himself: he had conveyed his interest to the queen so that she might re-establish the charity.

113. *Case of Thetford School,* 8 Co. Rep. 130b, 77 Eng. Rep. 671 (1609).

114. 23 Hen 8, c. 10 (1532); *Porter's Case, supra,* note 112; *Martindale* v. *Martin,* Cro. Eliz. 288, 78 Eng. Rep. 542 (1592). For earlier material on the mortmain laws, see pages 44-47, *supra.*

115. 39 Eliz. 1, c. 6 (1597); 43 Eliz. 1, c. 4 (1601), discussed in 2 Co. Inst. *707-12. The act preserved the rights of bona fide purchasers, but empowered the commissioners to require those who sold property to such a purchaser to make restitution. *Anon.,* Cary 28, 21 Eng. Rep. 15 (1603) is a case before the chancellor under this act. It involved trustees who had received land to build a chapel. They turned it over to the crown as a concealed chantry, and were given it for themselves, presumably as a reward for turning it in. The commissioners took it away from them. The exception for a charity with outside visitors did not apply if the visitors themselves were misappropriating the funds. Duke, 68-69.

116. On appointment of trustees and giving them land, see Duke, 63-64, 81, 120. On validating gifts that would otherwise have failed, see Duke, 84 (fee tail), 110 (copyhold), 114-15 (devises to corporations). The case of the parson, churchwardens, and four honest men is *Champion* v. *Smith,* Tothill 30, 21 Eng. Rep. 114 (1605). The case of *Pennyman* v. *Jenny,* Duke, 82, seems inconsistent with the general statement that the commissioners cannot empower the churchwardens to own land. Presumably the problem could be solved by appointing a trustee to pay the income to the churchwardens for distribution.

117. The question of what purposes are charitable is dealt with generally in Duke, 108-12, 131-37. On the preaching minister, see Duke, 82. A "lecture" in the present

sense is defined by the O.E.D. as a sermon outside service time.

118. Duke, 108. But note that the statement that the 1547 act (1 Edw. 6, c. 14) provided for the confiscation of subsequent gifts is erroneous: such gifts were merely void. The whole doctrine of superstitious uses was finally abandoned in *Bourne* v. *Keane*, [1919] App. Cas. 815 (H.L.) as inconsistent with the various Roman Catholic Relief Acts. The court discussed the provenance of the doctrine at great length, but overlooked the role of the 1531 act. See note 114, *supra*. It did refer to a couple of cases in which educational trusts set up by papists were invalidated on general principles of public policy: *Croft* v. *Evetts*, Moore K.B. 784, 72 Eng. Rep. 904 (1606); *Lady Egerton's Case*, Duke 133.

119. *Coveney's Case*, 2 Dyer 209a, 73 Eng. Rep. 453 (1561). This doctrine was put forth, with somewhat ambiguous results, in an earlier period. *Shiraks* v. *Archbishop of York*, Y.B., M. 8 E. 3, 69, F.G.A., "Excommengement," no. 2 (1334).

120. See pages 150-51, *supra*. Lambarde expects the justices of the peace to deal with unlicensed or nonconforming schoolmasters. Lambarde, 317ff, quoted in Holdsworth, iv, 548.

121. The cases referred to in this paragraph are *Williams's Case* 5 Co. Rep. 72b, 77 Eng. Rep. 163 (1592) (public versus private services); *Shipden* v. *Chancellor of Norwich*, Palmer 296, 81 Eng. Rep. 1090 (1623) (veil); *Reynolds Case*, Moore K.B. 916, 72 Eng. Rep. 995 (1616) (Rogation procession); *Corven's Case*, 12 Co. Rep. 105, 77 Eng. Rep. 1380 (1612) (monument); *Frances* v. *Ley*, Cro. Jac. 367, 79 Eng. Rep. 314 (1615) (same).

122. "Church," Burn, i, 231, 242-43, 252-59; *Corven's Case, supra*, note 121; *Frances* v. *Ley*, ibid; *May* v. *Gilbert*, 2 Bulstr. 151, 80 Eng. Rep. 1025 (1617) (from which the quotation is taken); 3 Co. Inst. *202; cf. *Brabin and Tradum's Case*, Popham 140, 79 Eng. Rep. 1241 (1619) (prohibition where ordinary granted seat perpetually in gross, and excommunicated anyone else who sat there: seat cannot be granted in gross, and excommunication is too harsh); *Davis* v. *Witts*, Forrest 14, 145 Eng. Rep. 1098 (1800) (aisle seat can be annexed to house outside parish, nave seat probably only to house in parish).

123. *Sutton and Dowses Case*, 1 Leonard 11, 74 Eng. Rep. 10 (1583); cf. *Doctor Clea & Son Chaplain*, Littleton 18, 124 Eng. Rep. 115 (1627).

124. *Note*, 3 Dyer 312, 73 Eng. Rep. 707-8 (1572); *Coxe's Case*, 3 Dyer 352a, 73 Eng. Rep. 789 (1576); *Underhill and Savages Case*, 1 Leonard 316, 74 Eng. Rep. 287 (Q.B. 1589); *Digby's Case*, 4 Co. Rep. 78b, 76 Eng. Rep. 1054 (Q.B. 1599).

125. *Butler and Goodale's Case*, 6 Co. Rep. 21b, 77 Eng. Rep. 245 (Q.B. 1598). On imprisonment as an excuse, compare *Ex parte Bartlett*, 12 Q.B. 488, 116 Eng. Rep. 950 (1848).

126. *Digby's Case, supra*, note 124 (ejectment case — man became pluralist before becoming chaplain); *Coxe's Case, ibid. (quare impedit* case — three benefices); *Anon.*, 3 Dyer 377b, 73 Eng. Rep. 846 (1581) *(quare impedit* case — not reading Articles); *Holland's Case*, 4 Co. Rep. 75a, 76 Eng. Rep. 1047 (1597) (tithe case); *Note*, 3 Dyer 312, 73 Eng. Rep. 707-8 (excess chaplains). On pluralism and nonresidence generally see Hill, 224-41.

127. 31 Eliz. 1, c. 6 (1589). See pages 145-47, 215-16, *supra*. Section 9 of the act expressly preserves the canonical penalties. *Riesby* v. *Wentworth*, Cro. Eliz. 642, 78 Eng. Rep. 881 (1598) holds that simony may be tried in a church court despite the existence of a statute against it.

128. *Oldbury* v. *Gregory*, Moore K.B. 564, 72 Eng. Rep. 761 (1598); 3 Co. Inst. *153n.

129. *Collins* v. *Blantern*, 2 Wils. K.B. 341, 95 Eng. Rep. 847 (1767); Holdsworth,

ix, 220. The court in *Collins* said that Chancery would enjoin a suit on a sealed instrument issued for an illegal consideration, but I find no case of its doing so before *W* v. *B,* 32 Beav. 574, 55 Eng. Rep. 226 (Rolls 1863).

130. *Mackaller* v. *Todderick,* Cro. Car. 337, 353, 361, 79 Eng. Rep. 895, 910, 915 (1634).

131. *Johns* v. *Lawrence,* Cro. Jac. 248, 274, 79 Eng. Rep. 213, 235 (1611-2) ("special" resignation bond, i.e., to resign when patron's son comes of age); *Babington* v. *Wood,* Cro. Car. 180, 79 Eng. Rep. 757 (1630) ("general" resignation bond, i.e., to resign on request). In *Web* v. *Hargrave,* Moore K.B. 641, 72 Eng. Rep. 811 (1601), misuse of a resignation bond was held to be a good defense to an action to enforce it. In later times, Chancery would enjoin the enforcement of a bond if it was misused. "Simony," Burn, ii, 334, 340-41.

132. General resignation bonds were invalidated in *Bishop of London* v. *Ffytche,* 2 Brown 211, 1 Eng. Rep. 892 (H.L. 1783), special ones in *Fletcher* v. *Sondes,* 3 Bing. 499, 130 Eng. Rep. 606 (H.L. 1826). The latter were revived, with some limitations, in 7-8 Geo. 4, c. 25 (1827) and 9 Geo. 4, c. 94 (1828). For the background of these cases, see Best, *Temporal Pillars* (Cambridge 1964), 53-59. Both of these cases treated the argument stated in text as an argument that the bond was invalid because of its simoniacal consideration — an argument that it would have been idle to make in the 1600s in view of the *Oldbury* case, *supra,* note 128. Thus, in the cases cited in note 131, *supra,* the only simony talked about was in the condition itself, i.e., the undertaking to resign. This was simoniacal only if it was held over the incumbent's head to procure advantage for the patron.

133. 1 Edw. 6, c. 1 (1547); 1 Eliz. 1, c. 2 (1559); 5 Eliz. 1, c. 1 (1563); 13 Eliz. 1, c. 2 (1571); 23 Eliz. 1, c. 1 (1581); 27 Eliz. 1, c. 2 (1585); 3 Co. Inst. *100, 101.

134. Lambarde, 317ff. Lambarde's articles are appended to Holdsworth, iv, 543-68. The ecclesiastical offenses are covered on pp. 545-48. For the actual practice of the justices, I have drawn on *Calendar of Quarter Sessions Papers,* ed. Bund (Worcester Hist. Soc., 2 vols, 1899-1900) and *West Riding Sessions,* especially the former. I am not sure what to make of the case described on pages lxxxii-lxxxiii of the former work involving defendants who gave a man a pin and a girl a piece of wood, saying "Take thee this in remembrance that Parkins of Wedgebury died for thee, and be thankful." They were indicted under 1 Edw. 6, c. 1 for depraving the Sacrament, but it is hard to see them as exemplifying a pattern.

135. The penalties referred to in text were imposed by 23 Eliz. 1, c. 1 (1581) and 3 Jac. 1, c. 5 (1605). A number of other laws, notably 21 Hen. 8, c. 13 (1529) on pluralism and nonresidence, were also fortified with penalties collectible by private informers. On the abuses of informers, see 3 Co. Inst. *191-94; Holdsworth, iv, 356-7. The statutes, 18 Eliz. 1, c. 5 (1576) and 21 Jac. 1, c. 4 (1622), aimed at correcting these abuses, do not seem on their face to be seriously inhibiting to a determined informer with evidence to support his case. In fact, the 1529 act was used with devastating effect by the evangelicals in the late eighteenth century and until its repeal in 1803. D. McClatchey, *Oxfordshire Clergy* (Oxford 1960), 31-2; W.L. Mathieson, *English Church Reform, 1815-1840* (London 1923), 21 ff.

136. Sodomy: 25 Hen. 8, c. 6 (1534), revived by 5 Eliz. 1, c. 17 (1562); 3 Co. Inst. *58. Bigamy: 1 Jac. 1, c. 11 (1603); 3 Co. Inst. *88. Witchcraft: 33 Hen. 8, c. 8 (1542), revived by 5 Eliz. 1, c. 16 (1562); 1 Jac. 1, c. 12 (1603); 3 Co. Inst. *44; Holdsworth, iv, 507-11; Pollcok and Maitland, ii, 552-56. I have advisedly not included rape and the carrying off of women among moral and religious offenses. They are crimes of violence, and the state moved against them much earlier. 3 Co. Inst. *60-62.

137. The following discussion, where not otherwise documented, is based on the

material cited in note 134 *supra,* plus Marchant, 223-26 and Holdsworth, iv, 514-15.

138. Weapon in church: 5-6 Edw. 6, c. 4 (1552). Disrupting services: 1 Mary, c. 3 (1554); *Creswick* v. *Rooksby,* 2 Bulstr. 47, 80 Eng. Rep. 948 (1613). Perjury: 5 Eliz. 1, c. 9 (1563); Holdsworth, iv, 514-19; 3 Co. Inst. *162-67. Bastardy: 18 Eliz. 1, c. 3 (1576); 7 Jac. 1, c. 4, § 7 (1610). Fishdays: 2-3 Edw. 6, c. 19 (1548); 5 Eliz. 1, c. 5, §§ 14-23, 36-40 (1563); 27 Eliz. 1, c. 11 (1585). Drunkenness: 4 Jac. 1, c. 5 (1607); 21 Jac. 1, c. 7 (1624). Swearing: 21 Jac. 1, c. 20 (1624).

139. 12 Ric. 2, c. 6 (1388); 11 Hen. 4, c. 4 (1409); 17 Edw. 4, c. 3 (1477); *Rot. Parl,* vi, 188a (1477); 33 Hen. 8, c. 9 (1542) The earlier statutes made reference to Sundays and holy days — perhaps because people were too busy the rest of the week either to play games or to practice archery.

140. *Rot. Parl.,* iii, 583a (1406).

141. My conclusions in this regard should be compared with Hill, 338-52.

Index

Abbot, George, archbishop of Canterbury
    (1611-33), 107, 128, 162
Abjuration, 30
Ad good damnum, inquest, 46
Advocates and proctors, 177, 184-85
Advowsons, *See* Patronage, right of
Alien religious houses, royal seizure of
    cells of, 8-10
Aliens
    expulsion of from English benefices and
        religious houses, 47-48
    number of in English benefices, 60
    royal custody of benefices of, 8-10, 47
Almoin tenure, 3, 12, 52
    See also Spiritual services
Alms
    collection and storage of, 142, 148
    solicitation of, 56-57, 150
Annointing of the sick, 132
Apparitors or summoners, 160, 173,
        176-77, 184-86, 187
Appeals in ecclesiastical cases
    to king's delegates 85
    to Roman curia 64, 87
Appropriation, 56, 64, 219
    remedies of appropriator, 18, 42-43
    See also Lay impropriators
Archdeacons and archdeacons' courts, 104,
    123, 160, 172-74, 179
Arches, Court of, 161, 175
Articles
    in ecclesiastical proceedings, 179
    on visitations, see Visitations
Articles of Religion, *See* Thirty-Nine
    Articles
Articuli Cleri, 9 Edw. 2, St. 1 (1315)
    analogized to Bancroft's articles of
        1606, 109

on fitness of presentees to benefices
    (c.13), 218
on lodging in monasteries (c.11), 51
on money commutation of penances
    (c.3, 4), 21
on res judicata effect of ecclesiastical
    judgments (c.6), 22
on sanctuary (c.10), 30
on violence to clergy (c.3), 206
Assizes, 19, 36
Attendance at services
    fines for nonattendance, 133, 148, 163
    requirement of, 110, 132-33, 163, 168,
        207, 236
    requirement of attendance in own
        parish, 154-55
Aylmer, John, bishop of London
    (1577-94), 156

Babington, Gervase, bishop of Exeter
    (1595-97), 143
Bancroft, Richard, bishop of London
    (1597-1604), archbishop of
    Canterbury (1604-10), 109,
    154-55, 166-67, 194, 242
Baptism, 129, 130, 237
    lay administration of, 282-84
    sign of cross in, 103, 130, 154
Barnes, Richard, bishop of Carlisle
    (1570-77), and Durham
    (1577-87), 144-45, 171, 172, 174
Bastardy
    punishment of, 205, 238-39
    trial of, 18-19
Bells, 129-30
Benefices, ecclesiastical
    qualification for, 39, 118-19, 217-18

303

Table of Statutes

Note: This table includes citations of statutes referred to in text. Some more important statutes are indexed in the main index by name, and cross-referenced here.

Table of Canons of 1604

Note: These canons are also indexed by subject in the main index.

c. 11,	157	c. 67,	120
c. 12,	156-57	c. 68,	180
c. 26,	163	c. 69,	180
c. 28,	155	c. 71,	180
c. 30,	130	c. 72,	180
c. 34,	117	c. 77,	151
c. 35,	118, 119	c. 78,	151
c. 36,	168-69	c. 79,	151
c. 40,	146	c. 87,	142
c. 41,	125, 169	c. 89,	162
c. 45,	131	c. 90,	155
c. 46,	131	c. 92,	161, 175
c. 48,	120	c. 93,	161, 175
c. 49,	120	c. 98,	168-69
c. 52,	170	c. 101,	169
c. 54,	167	c. 102,	169
c. 56,	169, 180	c. 106,	174
c. 57,	155, 180	c. 107,	169, 174
c. 58,	180	c. 109,	147-48, 174
c. 59,	180	c. 113,	173, 281
c. 62,	180	c. 120,	173
c. 63,	180	c. 121,	175
c. 65,	183	c. 122,	179
c. 66,	120	c. 138,	173, 176